Mrs.
Jack

Mrs. Jack

A Biography of
Isabella Stewart Gardner by
LOUISE HALL THARP

A FAWCETT CREST BOOK
Fawcett Publications, Inc., Greenwich, Conn.

THIS BOOK CONTAINS THE COMPLETE TEXT OF THE
ORIGINAL HARDCOVER EDITION.

A Fawcett Crest Book reprinted by arrangement with
Little, Brown and Company.

Library of Congress Catalog Card Number: 65-18129

Published by Fawcett World Library
67 West 44th Street, New York, N. Y. 10036

To my editor
Ned Bradford
who put me on the trail of Mrs. Jack

Contents

BOOK THREE: Mrs. Gardner's Palace

Book One

THE NEW YORKER IN BOSTON

ONE

Mrs. Jack Gardner

THE NIGHT WAS clear and cold although snow had been forecast.[1] A line of private carriages, with here and there a hired hack, circled a tall building standing solitary in partly reclaimed marshland. It was the evening of January 1, 1903, and the brick building, referred to by the uninitiated as "a foine brewery" was in fact a palace in the Venetian style —just completed in the Fenway, Boston, Massachusetts. This was the first social occasion at "Fenway Court" and the hour, at least as stated in the engraved invitations,[2] was "nine o'clock punctually."

As each carriage stopped at the palace door, gentlemen in top hats alighted to assist the ladies, who gathered long skirts in white-gloved hands. Flickering carriage lamps shone on sealskin and sable. Diamonds flashed, half-hidden in the furs.

There were delays—ladies were kept standing in the cold at the palace door. A tall Italian major-domo, resplendent in green velvet with gold braid, admitted guests two by two. And slowly the carriages circled, each awaiting its turn until the hour was no longer "nine punctually."

Guests entered small rooms dimly lit by candles where they laid aside greatcoats and furs. A moment more and they stepped into a big room, dazzling white and brightly lighted by Holophane lamps.[3] Now the cause of the delay at the outer door became apparent. Everyone must take his place in line to climb a curving staircase, cross a landing and then climb down again!

On the landing a small, slender woman stood alone, receiving her friends. She was "gowned in sweeping black" and wore her famous pearls, one hundred forty-nine of them! A great ruby glowed at her throat, and in her hair were two immense diamonds, the "Rajah" and the "Light of India"—one over twelve carats and the other more than twenty-five. The jewels had been the sensation of Boston but they were eclipsed tonight by the building in which the guests were assembled. It was the future Isabella Stewart Gardner Museum, built for an

11

art collection unique in the United States. The lady at the top of the stairs was Mrs. Jack Gardner.

Slowly the guests mounted, here and there a dowager puffing audibly. They were greeted by their hostess and then they crossed the landing to descend an identical staircase, men shuffling their feet in an attempt to avoid stepping on trailing satin and lace. Mrs. Jack stood smiling, enjoying to the hilt the homage she was exacting.

When the last guests went down the stairs to be seated in small ballroom chairs below, Mrs. Gardner had a carved and gilded armchair brought forward on the landing. Here she sat and signaled to Wilhelm Gericke, conductor of the Boston Symphony Orchestra. Fifty of his musicians had been tuning up on a platform at the far end of the huge music room. Now the concert could begin.

Isabella Stewart Gardner was a legend, even during her lifetime. Her "infinite variety of resources and unique gyrations" kept Boston, Beverly and points east and west in "a state of social excitement" season after season.[4] A "mid-western lady" came East "to see Mrs. Jack Gardner and the Atlantic Ocean" and was disappointed in neither. Yet Mrs. Gardner was far from beautiful and she was only moderately wealthy during the era when American millionaires flourished. Her charities were private and secret, her indiscretions all too often public and publicized with little regard for the truth. She was called "Queen of Back Bay" but she had not always been a queen.

Mrs. Jack was not even born in Boston. She was born Isabella Stewart, of Number 142 Green Street, New York City.[5] This cobblestoned, tree-lined thoroughfare ran from Canal Street to Washington Square, and it was to a small, unpretentious house that her father, David Stewart, brought his bride, the former Adelia Smith, after their wedding at St. John's Church, Brooklyn, on April 30, 1839.[6] On April 14, 1840, Isabella Stewart, first of a family of four, was born.

Years later Isabella loved to celebrate her birthday with a crowd of guests. Sometimes there was entertainment in the form of a fantasy written by one of her favorite young artists, Joseph Lindon Smith. Or there might be music by members of the Boston Symphony Orchestra with a new composition to be played by Charles Martin Loeffler, violinist. Isabella loved to be given a birthday surprise by old friends like Henry Lee Higginson; but if April 14 was the day, she was never the one to disclose the year of her birth if she could help it.

David Stewart, Isabella's father, was of pure Scottish descent, and only a second-generation American. The New York City directories listed him as "importer" as early as 1837 and finally as "David Stewart, President" in 1865—with reference to the Stewart Iron Company near Uniontown, Pennsylvania.[7] Mr. Stewart was a moneyed man by this time, but a man with few interests outside his business, sufficient unto himself and caring nothing for social prestige.

Society was a woman's business with two avenues of approach—money and ancestry. Stewart money, although more than adequate, could not compare with Vanderbilt money and Isabella's mother could point to no distinguished Dutchmen among her forebears. Her father had been Selah Smith, who kept "a tavern and stable" at Old Ferry, Brooklyn.[8]

This was a thriving business, to be sure, for Selah Smith died possessed of a house on leased land, well furnished with twenty Windsor chairs to set about the tavern table, a sideboard with "1 large mirror" to put over it, "1 lot of silver" and three sets of dinner ware—among other items. For the stable there was a "coachee," seven "riding chairs," "1 lot of saddles, bridels and whips," "1 pleasure sleigh" and one "lot of manure." Of course there were horses—"1 chair horse," a pair of brown horses and "1 stud horse"—valued at a hundred dollars. Also listed among Selah Smith's effects was "1 black man" worth fifty dollars.

Isabella Stewart's mother was only four years old when her father died. Perhaps the widow continued the business, perhaps not, but in any case Adelia Smith's girlhood must have been hard-working and humble. She was twenty-five years old when she married David Stewart. Their daughter Isabella evidently asked questions about her mother's family, because she was told that her mother was descended from "Bull Smith" of Long Island—so called because he tamed and rode a bull.[9] Bull Smith's real name was Richard. The founder of Smithtown, he purchased land of the Indians, who were said to have agreed to give him all the land he could ride around in a day. He mounted his bull, took his lunch and rode from dawn to dark, the spot where he ate being known afterwards as "Bread and Cheese Hollow." This struck Isabella as a good story and she would have liked to ride a bull herself.

The Stewart side of the family was much more important to Isabella, however. She was named for her father's mother, whom she resembled in temperament if not in appearance. Madam Isabella Tod Stewart was a lady with a mind of her own and her small granddaughter was no less opinionated.

Their wills clashed time and again, for each had a fiery temper, but neither was angry for long.

The widowed Madam Stewart had flashing dark eyes, a high-bridged nose and a mouth suggesting humor with a touch of parsimony. She lived on a large farm in Jamaica, Long Island, and, after her husband's death in 1813, she managed her own affairs with success. In 1829, she was a pew-holder at Grace Episcopal Church, Jamaica—a lady of importance in the community as well as a landowner who took prizes at stock and horticultural shows.[10]

Isabella was fond of believing that her grandmother owned many slaves. Madam Stewart's field hands and house servants were doubtless former slaves but in New York State a law was passed in 1841 which "extinguished all privileges of slaveowners and all slave ownership." [11] Grandmother Stewart trained her servants well in any case. They served her handsomely and she looked after them in sickness and in health. Isabella never forgot the tall dignity of her grandmother's butler.

Isabella did not look like her father's mother and it would have pleased her if she had. Instead, she resembled her Great-grandmother Mary Brough, whose portrait looked down from a wall in Grandmother Stewart's house. Mary Brough had a round face, round eyes, a stubborn mouth and little hands too firmly crossed, one above the other. Not even a huge fluted bonnet could make her pretty, but she looked competent to deal with any fate. Belle Stewart's grandmother must have loved her all the more because she looked like this Scottish portrait and was not a pretty child.

Since it was the custom to send an older child to visit relatives when an addition to the family was expected, the two-year-old Isabella was doubtless sent to her Grandmother Stewart when her sister Adelia was born on April 6, 1842. Belle, as they always called Isabella in the family, proved extremely lively and difficult for her gentle mother to handle, and she was more and more often sent off for her Grandmother Stewart to cope with. People probably said that her grandmother spoiled her but such was not her own impression.

Belle remembered that there had been a traveling circus in Jamaica one summer and that she longed passionately to see it.[12] She was told that she could not go, so she set out alone. Her absence was too soon discovered and her grandmother's butler was sent in pursuit. Belle saw him and ran. Forgetting his dignity, the butler ran, and his legs were longer than hers. She was just crawling under the edge of the tent when she felt

14

his powerful hands. She was ignominiously pulled out and carried back to her grandmother's house, screaming with rage.

Isabella's passion for circuses may have dated from this humiliating day. Eventually, she was to ride on an elephant provided for her by a king of Cambodia. She petted lions at the Boston zoo and carried a lion cub about with her in her carriage. But it was not true that she ever kept live lions in the basement of her Venetian palace on the Fenway in Boston.

Belle's mother did her best with this high-spirited child of hers. To judge by a picture taken of Mrs. Stewart, she was mild, rather pretty, and anxious to please. She displayed an ermine stole, draped over a handsome, hoop-skirted gown but her eyes, tinted blue in the daguerreotype, looked anxious, and her smile was a trifle apologetic, as if she needed reassurance about all this fine array. Baffled by her high-spirited daughter Belle, she turned to her clergyman for advice concerning child training, and received two little books, bound in blue and gold, their contents recommended by a bishop of the Anglican Church.

Peep o' Day and *Line upon Line* contained "the earliest religious instruction the infant mind is capable of receiving," according to the introduction. Bible stories were retold, each ending with a so-called poem, the author, Mrs. Favell Lee Bevan Mortimer, being a lady of piety but not of literary genius. "Now you shall hear how Adam and Eve grew wicked," promised Mrs. Mortimer. There were woodcuts, fascinating by reason of their ugliness, but all this was supposed to make Belle Stewart a good little girl. But Belle herself said in later years that she was "mischievous most of the time."

It was a comfort to Mrs. Stewart that her daughter liked to go to church, however. In Jamaica, Grandmother Stewart drove to Grace Church attended by servants, as befitted a wealthy widow. When her little granddaughter was with her, Isabella sat by her side, enjoying the elegance and the glances bestowed upon her.

In New York, the Stewarts went to a different Grace Church—the one on the corner of Broadway and Tenth Street. The church was new, an example of that American Gothic soon to sweep the country. The high-vaulted roof was lath and plaster but nobody cared because it looked like cut stone. Stained-glass windows cast patches of brilliant color on a floor already decorated with geometric designs—and on satin and lace bonnets already colorful. Grace Church was famous for its well-dressed congregation. Sometimes Isabella's expression of rapt attention was not a tribute to the sermon but to the styles. Belle dearly loved fine clothes but she also loved ritual and the deep, satisfying color of clerical robes, varying from red at Christmas to purple at Easter. She loved the drama of processional and recessional, the light of candles, the coming and going of clergy and acolyte. Grace Church was famous for fine music and Isabella's soul thrilled to music. Her mother was greatly encouraged by Belle's good behavior in church.

And then, while walking home from church one day, Belle's shoes hurt her. So she took them off and walked in stocking feet.[13] People stared, and she enjoyed it—but her mother spanked her, Belle said.

On January 28, 1848, the Stewart's third child and first son was born—to be called David in honor of his father. The seven-year-old Isabella was probably sent to her Grandmother Stewart's, perhaps taking her five-year-old sister Adelia with her. But if Belle visited her grandmother when her brother David was born, it must have been almost the last time. Isabella Tod Stewart died July 26, 1848. Never again would a tempestuous-tempered little girl find an answering gleam of understanding in the older woman's eyes. But Belle kept and cherished everything that came to her from her grandmother.

There was the leather-bound notebook, the leaves printed with lines for music and on them hand-written notes with the words of a song below. On the flyleaf, the ink faded but still clear, was the name Isabella Tod. The imperious-looking portrait of her grandmother, painted by Thomas Sully, came to Belle eventually, and also the portrait by an unknown artist of the great-grandmother whom she resembled. There were handsome silver candlesticks and fine mahogany.

There was also a silver pitcher bearing the inscription: "Presented by the Agricultural Society of New York to Isabella Stewart, 2nd June, 1821." Belle had loved this pitcher of her grandmother's as long as she could remember, because on the other side of it was engraved a picture of a cow!

All these mementos eventually found a strange resting place. Belle placed them in the Short Gallery in the Isabella Stewart Gardner Museum in Boston.

Madam Stewart had two surviving children, Belle's father and Belle's uncle Charles. They inherited their mother's estate which included personal property valued at thirty thousand dollars—a goodly sum in 1848.[14] Only a year later, Charles Stewart died leaving no will and no heir save Belle's father. Once more, David Stewart was called upon to settle an estate,

16

this time containing personal property of about twenty thousand dollars. Gradually, he sold his inherited Long Island real estate to good advantage. Alert to the financial opportunities of his time, he used his capital well—especially in the iron industry. An "iron age" was in the making.

The Stewarts left Green Street in 1842 when Isabella was only two years old. David Stewart acquired the leasehold of Number 10 University Place, a handsome three-story house of brick with a two-story wooden ell. This "mansion," as his friends called it, was on the corner of Eighth Street, just north of Washington Square Park, and although University Place was spoken of as the home of many prominent families, there were also stables, fish markets, gasfitters and liquor stores along its length. Isabella said that the only thing she remembered about the house on University Place was the room where she took gymnastic exercises.

Belle was small for her age, and to her various lessons at home and at school, calisthenics was added in the hope of increasing her stature. Gymnastics had come into fashion and she gloated over advertisements showing girls wearing baggy trousers while doing wonderful trapeze acts, hanging head-down from horizontal bars and climbing rope ladders. What she must have wanted was to join a class at a gymnasium where she could enjoy competition and get into the act when exhibition time came. It was undoubtedly her mother who refused to hear of such a thing. So Belle learned to turn cartwheels and do handstands in the privacy of Number 10 University Place with only her father's laughing applause to sustain her. Eventually she would amaze a larger, if still private, audience. She never grew tall but she learned to walk as though she already wore diamonds in her hair.

Isabella was sent to a series of small private schools for girls, kept in nearby parlors by "ladies of respectability." French was taught, which Belle learned easily. There were dancing lessons and she loved to dance. When Belle Stewart of New York first became Mrs. Jack Gardner of Boston, Professor Papanti, Boston's famous dancing teacher, told her that she danced so beautifully, she must have been taught by a Frenchman. "I was," she said.

There were drawing lessons and some of the water color sketches in Isabella's notebooks show that she was not taught in vain. She had an accurate eye for color and handled perspective remarkably well. In later years she liked to pretend that she never set brush to paper, but that was when she was confronted by professional artists, such as John Singer Sargent,

17

and when she learned to appreciate old masters—and bought paintings by Titian, Raphael or Rembrandt.

Belle remembered no scenes of childish rebellion at the family piano. She was fond of music, could read it well, and her ear for music was as accurate as her eye for color. Strict as her mother tried to be, Mrs. Stewart was not puritanical and Belle was allowed to go to the opera. One opera company or another played in New York most of the time during Belle Stewart's girlhood. She knew whether music was played right or wrong—which many of her contemporaries could not say. But just as she preferred professional art, so professional music pleased her best and she cared little for amateur efforts —her own included. Isabella's intelligent appreciation made her the friend of Paderewski and other famous concert artists, while she also encouraged many a struggling unknown musician.

Looking back, on being pressed for memories of school days in New York, Isabella refused to be serious. "Did you study hard?" she was asked.

"Well, if it was against the rules, I did," she said.

And in what subject did she excel?

"I could run faster than anyone else in school," she declared.

Just down the street from Number 10 University Place, the crenellated towers of the University of the City of New York's new Gothic buildings rose above the trees. They faced Washington Square which was still called the Parade Ground. A wooden fence failed to keep out small boys and girls. From her house Isabella could hear martial music whenever the Seventh Regiment paraded and then, either with or without permission she would run to watch, for she dearly loved a parade. Little boys, out on the edge of the parade ground, "scuffed among the fallen ailanthus leaves and pranced about as cavaliers, whacking their steeds." [15] It struck Isabella that boys were more fun to play with than girls and she joined them if she felt like it.

In 1847, a four-year-old boy by the name of Henry James was brought to New York from Paris by his parents. He lived near the parade ground and rode a stick horse. But Belle never knew which boy he was and it was not until later, when they were both grown, that they met in Boston. Their friendship from that time was lifelong.

Henry James remembered that in 1851, the Hudson River Railroad was built through the streets of New York. There was "a riot of explosion and a shouting and waving of little red flags." Isabella was irresistibly drawn to scenes of excitement. She did whatever came into her head and she had a head full of ideas, so that it was impossible to forecast and forbid all her escapades. She arrived on any scene where there was drama and forgot to go home until sought and captured. Doubtless her mother spanked her, but her father understood. He loved trains as much as she did—and for additional reasons.

The coming of the Hudson River Railroad and the Erie showed David Stewart that he ought to shift from the importing of Irish linen to the iron industry. The Erie bought an iron steamboat in which to ferry its passengers across the Hudson and "183 iron locomotives" to carry passengers westward.

Belle was very close to her father when she was a child. It surprised him to have her excited over the discovery of gold in California—as a boy would have been. He talked to her about gold coinage, pleased that she could understand and remember such things. "I was much interested in one-dollar gold pieces that I had heard of," Belle Stewart recalled years later.[16] "On one of his journeys to California," Belle's father "told a friend there that his little daughter wanted a gold dollar. The result was that the California friend gave him for me four little gold dollars and a gold half-dollar. . . ."

Isabella Stewart of New York never thought much about ancestry until she married into the Gardner family of Boston. In Boston, she endured a good deal of fairly dull conversation on the subject, so, eventually, she had her Stewart descent traced directly back—all the way to King Fergus I of Scotland, a contemporary of Alexander the Great! She found that she "shared an ancestor with Mary Queen of Scots," so she joined the Order of the White Rose and had a costume made like that of the queen, in which to commemorate the queen's death with appropriate ritual.

After having the Stewart lineage engrossed and illuminated in colors on a long scroll, Isabella Stewart Gardner was in a position to make one of her famous, much-quoted remarks. She had listened to a monologue by a Boston dowager concerning that lady's American Revolutionary ancestry. "Ah yes," said Isabella. "They were much less careful about immigration in those days, I believe."

Nevertheless, Belle Gardner never repudiated the Smiths on her mother's side. She would have loved to visit her Grandfather Smith's tavern and stable in Brooklyn, had he not died long before she was born. Bostonians were to remember that

19

Mrs. Jack Gardner made no secret of this less-than-royal ancestor—while claiming kinship with kings and queens.

Upon her marriage, Belle Stewart's mother gave her an etiquette book entitled *A Lady's Guide to Perfect Gentility*. Her mother was genteel. Belle dutifully took the book to Boston —and broke all the rules in a most delightful fashion.

She also took with her a little child's pocket book. "In it I kept all of my financial treasure," she said. They were the gold coins her father had given her, which she loved—not because of what they would buy, but because of their beauty.

Isabella Stewart Gardner, the lady "in sweeping black" who opened her palace to friends in 1903, still had the coins— childhood playthings which were her first collector's items.

TWO

Gardner—Stewart

O<small>N THE SECOND</small> day of April in 1854, Belle Stewart's sister died. Adelia would have been twelve years old in just four days. Isabella never spoke of private grief, nor would she ever allow anyone to ask her questions concerning a deep personal loss.

Belle's father continued to prosper in business, but what can a man do with money when he has lost his little girl—except to give advantages to his remaining daughter? What can he do for his wife except to help her try to forget? So it was decided that Belle should go to a French finishing school and that her parents would go abroad with her and join her in a European tour when the school year closed.

Mrs. Stewart had misgivings about French schools. In the textbooks of her own girlhood the French were described as gay and Paris was noted for "magnificence and gaiety" [1]— points all too likely to please her flighty daughter Belle overmuch. As usual, Mrs. Stewart turned to her church for help and was provided with a small volume entitled *The School-girl in France, or the Snares of Popery; A Warning to Protestants Against Education in Catholic Seminaries.* [2] This remarkable work was written in story form and concerned two American girls, Caroline and Emily. It opened in a style Mrs. Stewart thoroughly approved.

"The feathered songsters of the grove were warbling their hymn to their Creator . . ."

"Dear Caroline's dark hair and eyes gave additional interest to the paleness of her cheek" while "Dear Emily" was her "blue-eyed, golden-haired companion." The snares of Popery to which the girls were exposed consisted mainly in being encouraged to kneel "to images" and being allowed to buy fruit, cream or pastry on Sundays. After Caroline had fainted numerous times and Emily had begun to enjoy kneeling to images they were transferred to a Protestant convent school. This school also got a poor press and the moral seemed to be that an English school would be safer than a French one.

Mrs. Stewart was well aware that Belle was not given to interesting fainting fits, nor was she a golden-haired angel so perhaps an English school frequently visited by Anglican bishops would be a wise choice. It is safe to say that Belle had ideas on the subject. She loved French and she wanted to go to Paris. Doubtless her father backed her up. In any case, when she was sixteen, her parents took her abroad and she entered a French Protestant school. The courses of study mentioned in *The School-girl in France* were Italian, music and embroidery, so probably, with the addition of French, Belle's studies were similar—none presenting any difficulty.

Nothing was said about Belle's eight-year-old brother David. Perhaps he went to boarding school back home in the United States but Belle's parents lived in Paris while she was in school there, dutifully seeing the sights, guidebook in hand. When the novelty wore off they began to be lonely, observing a life in which they had no part, hearing a language of which they understood little. They gravitated to places where Americans might be met with, and among these they found the John L. Gardners of Boston. Two of the Gardner daughters, Julia, a year younger than Belle Stewart, and Eliza, only ten years old, were in Belle's Paris school.

Gardner is not an unusual name. There were two families in Boston, one spelling the name with an *i*, one without. They were not related and were inclined to become annoyed if confused one with the other. So Bostonians called them the "one-eyed Gardiners" and the "blind Gardners." [3] The Stewarts had just met the "blind Gardners," remarkably clear-sighted people, as it happened.

Mr. John L. Gardner was formal in his manner but behind his spectacles with their oblong frames, his eyes gleamed with humor. He liked riding in the "Boy," as he called the Bois de Boulogne, to tease his womenfolk who were so serious about their French pronunciation.

Mrs. Gardner, a Peabody of Salem, was full of energy, an indefatigable sightseer always ready for one more excursion, no matter how strenuous. Her husband poked fun at her, affectionately, but he had come abroad for his health and he took care of it. He liked David Stewart of New York, and the two of them sat at café tables on the boulevards and watched the Paris world go by.

John L. Gardner owned sailing ships like his father, Samuel Pickering Gardner, before him. [4] Formerly of Salem, Samuel Pickering Gardner had come to Boston on the flood of the tide that eventually left Salem with only a phantom merchant fleet to dream about. Through his wife, John L. Gardner owned Roque Island and small adjacent islands off the coast of Maine, where the family went in the summer when not gallivanting off to Europe or enjoying their Brookline summer home. He had an office at 39 State Street and had taken his son George into business with him. But it was especially of his son Jack that John L. Gardner spoke with pride. All would go well at home because Jack had his eye on things, David Stewart gathered.

In 1857, it was time for David Stewart to take his daughter to Italy to see the art and antiquities for which her recent studies in Paris had presumably prepared her. News from the United States was not good, however. There had been reckless spending in the course of railroad building and there were rumors of misuse of railway funds.[5] Banks began closing their doors, and Mr. Stewart decided to take the next boat for New York in order to look after his business affairs. He left his family in Rome under the care of Lewis Cass,[6] United States Minister to Italy.

Mrs. Stewart was glad to find other Americans in Rome. The Waterstons of Boston were there, with their daughter Helen. And Louis Agassiz, the famous Swiss professor of geology, with his Bostonian wife, the former Eliazbeth Cary. They had Ida (a daughter by Agassiz's first wife) with them and it seemed to be second nature to Elizabeth Agassiz to organize study groups wherever she went. She got up an Italian language class for Ida, inviting Helen Waterston and Belle Stewart to join—and found a charming young man for their professor.

Isabella's quick mind and gift for languages amazed the slower, more serious Ida. Ida remembered that Belle, having mastered the fairly simple lessons, turned her attention to flirting with the young Italian teacher. Nothing loath, he joined the game, although with discretion, lest he lose his job. The girls whispered and giggled over it—while studying their Italian grammar.[7]

In New York, the panic of 1857 was in progress.[8] "Business everywhere went down like corn before a hurricane," but David Stewart weathered the storm. He leased his University Place "mansion" for business purposes and according to promise, returned to Rome to bring his family home.

It was a time of parting for the schoolgirls, Ida, Helen and Belle. They talked of what they wanted out of life, one night, imagining the adult world they were soon to enter as a sort of fairy tale, complete with the inevitable handsome young man with whom they would live happily ever after. At least, Helen and Ida confided such ideas. But Belle had just been to see the Poldi-Pezzoli Palace in Milan, filled with heirloom furniture, with paintings by great artists of the Italian Renaissance, with tapestries, books and ornaments of gold or silver-gilt. "If I ever have any money of my own, I am going to build a palace," she said, "and fill it with beautiful things."

The Waterstons went on to Naples, where Helen died of a fever—as so many young Americans did. Ida went home to Cambridge, Massachusetts, to teach in her mother's school for a time, and eventually to marry Colonel Henry L. Higginson. Ida never forgot Belle Stewart's desire to build a palace and wrote to remind her of it when Belle's dream came true.

The Stewarts returned to New York to live at the Hotel St. Germaine, on the corner of Fifth Avenue and Twenty-second Street. They decided that they liked East Twenty-second Street even though it was so far uptown—almost as far as Madison Square. New houses were being built of brownstone which seemed wonderfully modern, compared with the old red brick of University Place.

At Number 27 East Twenty-second Street, the Stewarts found just the place they wanted. The house was high and narrow—the width of only one room plus stair and hallway —with an iron balcony across the front parlor windows. Iron railings protected the areaway and kitchen windows were below the street level. Railings with brass ornaments flanked the high front steps.[9]

Within, Italian workmen, wearing little paper caps to keep the wet plaster out of their hair, molded the high ceilings at cornice and center with a riot of fruit and flowers. Brass chandeliers sprouted from plaster medallions. There were fireplaces, tomb-like with small openings framed in marble, and at the windows were shutters to keep the sun from fading the carpet.

Upstairs was a nursery and on December 18, 1858, James Stewart was born, the final addition to the Stewart family. David Junior was now nearly ten and Isabella was a young lady of eighteen, finished abroad.

As a rule, friendships made abroad fall apart when travelers return home to go their separate ways. But Julia Gardner of Boston invited Belle Stewart of New York to visit her and Belle accepted with pleasure. The two girls were opposites, Julia being pretty and calm in temperament, which was perhaps the reason for their congenial friendship. Her father had gone to New York on business, so Julia wrote to him: "We

24

have been very gay," she said, and then, lest her father imagine scenes of extravagant revelry, "although in a quiet way, small parties, etc." There was snow in Boston. "The sleigh *Cleopatra's Barge* called for us about seven o'clock and we drove out of town in company with some twenty other young people, all well bundled up, and all in excellent spirits. . . ." [10]

The sleigh *Cleopatra's Barge* had been calling at house doors for young people in Boston for a generation. It belonged, at least originally, to the Perkins family when they lived on Temple Place, and it was a familiar sight on Temple Place, Beacon Hill and Louisburg Square. It was "very long and curved up in front into a 'swan's neck' which leaned over backward, thus making a great cave and this cave and the whole body of the sleigh was lined with fur." [11]

The sleigh ride was properly chaperoned, as Julia Gardner made haste to assure her father. Mrs. Theodore Lyman, Mrs. Richard Fay and Mrs. Fred Sears "matronized" the party. They were very young matrons, however, all in their twenties. But it was Mr. Lyman who made news in Julia Gardner's letter. He was twenty-six—doubtless an advanced age in the eyes of Belle and Julia. He had been one of Agassiz's star pupils at Harvard and was already a trustee of the new Museum of Comparative Zoology—a most serious young man. Yet here he was on a sleigh ride, making everyone "laugh all the way" to the Forbes house in Milton, where he "danced, organized games and kept the fun going all the evening and finally sung all the way home." Even serious people had fun at parties, especially when Belle Stewart was along.

At the Forbeses' or at a small party given by the Gardners, Belle danced for the first time with Richard Sullivan Fay, the leading beau of Boston. He was considered the best dancer at the Assemblies, and he was not letting his marriage, now of about four months' duration, interfere with his social career. He was astonished and delighted to discover that Miss Stewart of New York danced beautifully, and he was to have the pleasure of dancing with her again, many times.

Julia did not mention her brothers in her letter to her father. But if she took them for granted, Belle did not. There was Joseph Peabody Gardner, nearly thirty-one years old and unmarried. Next came George Augustus, a little over a year younger but married these last five years to Eliza Endicott Peabody. And then there was John Lowell Gardner, Junior, unmarried, unattached and only twenty-one years old.

Young John L. had completed two years at Harvard. But

when it was decided that his father's health would benefit by a trip to Europe, John left college, in good standing—and went into his father's business. Joseph P. Gardner, John's older brother, was in business as a commission merchant with Thomas Jefferson Coolidge. George Augustus was already in business with his father's firm but it seemed they needed Jack. "Jack" they always called him because he had his father's name, but he was such a serious young man that the jaunty "Jack" never quite seemed to fit him.

Jack Gardner was tall—over six feet—with a thick, glossy black mustache that must have been the pride of his life. He had infinite patience, a sense of humor—and he could dance. Whether his conscience ever let him take much time for dancing was another matter. He loved to keep records, such as the time, daily distance traveled and precise cost of driving his father's horses to Stockbridge, Massachusetts. These records he would pass on, assuming they would help others and never dreaming that scarcely anyone ever paid as much attention to detail as he did.

At the Somerset Club, which had fine quarters next to his father's house on Beacon Street,[12] Jack Gardner was much beloved. He was the member who saw to it that the club had the finest chef in town and the best wine cellar—at the same time keeping the club staff happy in their job. If tempers were lost and members quarreled, it was Jack Gardner who mediated—calmly, tactfully.

Jack was so modest that he probably never realized that the girls all set their caps for him—in a discreet, Bostonian way. When he looked the girls over, he saw no one but cousins, some close, some distant, or daughters of his mother's friends whom he had known since infant school. No girl like Miss Belle Stewart of New York had ever crossed Jack Gardner's path before.

Belle was not pretty. In fact, she was probably one of the plainest girls Jack had ever known. Her hair was neither blond nor auburn, but a rusty red. Eyebrows and lashes were sandy and not even in Paris had she learned to do anything about them. But her blue eyes were audacious. When the other girls looked down demurely Belle looked up and laughed. Her eyes shot sparks of fun—and also of malice when she so inclined.

Belle had a pure white skin of which she was proud. But the slightest exposure to the sun turned her scarlet, with freckles to follow that many applications of lemon juice refused to fade. She had already learned to wear veils and

26

carry parasols. After dark, she showed as much of her white shoulders as her mother would let her and, in spite of the panic of 1857, her father had bought her Paris gowns. In Paris, hoop skirts had reached such dimensions that Belle astonished Boston when she dressed for the small party the Gardners gave her.

Perhaps Jack Gardner danced with Belle from a sense of duty—the first time. But how she could dance! To take her hand and lead her forward and back through the intricacies of the Lancers was pure delight. It made a man decide to try a waltz and then a polka—to place a white-gloved hand against her tiny waist and wish those swinging hoops would let him hold her closer.

At supper, Belle made Jack Gardner laugh. Other girls turned to look at her with suspicion, wondering what she had said, but Jack had the impression that it was he who was the witty one. This was a delightful sensation. Next thing he knew, he was talking to her about business and she seemed to understand. Her admiring questions made him feel quite a man and he was annoyed when the supper intermission was over and others came to claim a dance from the guest of honor. But Belle told Jack she wanted to hear more—next day, perhaps?

It was Eliza, Julia Gardner's little sister, who thought something was in the wind when Jack took Belle walking on Sunday morning. Down the steep slope of Beacon Hill they went, where recent snow and sleet made the brick sidewalks treacherous, even though thoughtful householders had sprinkled them with coal ashes. Belle was wonderfully sure-footed but Jack found that she was willing to take his arm. They walked as far as the lower edge of Boston Common until they came upon a scene of chaos and construction where once had been a mill-dam, with a road across it and mud flats below. Small trees had been set out in a row along an area to be known as the Public Garden and the tide which had recently come in as far as Charles Street was receding, fill winning against water.

In the mud flat had once been papers, bottles, discarded hoop skirts—with rag-pickers searching through the rubbish for something salable. But now clean gravel from Needham, nine miles away, was coming in by train over special tracks, to be spread on the dump, turning it into real estate. Trains ran night and day; and it was a pity it was Sunday, because Jack would have liked to have Belle see this earth-moving project in action. There was a new invention called a steam

27

shovel out at Needham, too. It had a high smokestack and did the work of a whole crew of Irishmen.[13]

But since it was Sunday, Jack could take Belle out along an unfinished street and show her the place where he would build a house of his own some day—out here in the Back Bay. The street was to be called Western Avenue, which had an adventurous, pioneering sound to it. But it would really be an extension of Beacon Street and eventually, Beacon Street would be its name. Jack wanted a lot on the water side with a view of the Charles River. He asked Belle if she liked Boston well enough to live here, for he was a businesslike young man who knew his own mind. He asked Belle if she would marry him.

Belle Stewart was said to have made the correct nineteenth-century reply. The young man must ask her father. But Eliza Gardner, looking at Belle's flushed cheeks and Jack's joyful face, thought everything had been decided between them by the time they got back to Beacon Hill.

Jack Gardner made the journey to New York, of course, and approached Mr. Stewart with a formal request for his daughter Isabella's hand in marriage. David Stewart liked the young man, but he had seen many an attractive, well-to-do husband go through his own, his parents' and his wife's money. He made stipulations and arrangements. At some time, either now or later, a "Stewart Fund" was set up which Jack Gardner was to administer with as much formality as though it had belonged to a stranger.

Mr. Stewart listened to Jack's enthusiastic description of the new Back Bay section of Boston and he probably went down to have a look. "One hundred and forty-five dirt cars with eighty men including engineers and brakemen" hustled gravel into the salt marshes to make "nearly two houselots" per day so that by October, 1859, an auctioneer "set up his station" at the corner of Berkeley Street and Commonwealth Avenue. He laid "boards across a rough fence" to make a platform from which to shout his "going, going, gone." [14] In November, Mr. David Stewart bought from the Commonwealth of Massachusetts the lot Jack Gardner wanted. He promised to build a house for Belle on it—but he kept title to the property in his own name. Mr. Stewart was a careful man.

Isabella's engagement was promptly an accomplished fact, and on February 28, 1859, she wrote to her future sister-in-law, Julia, describing herself as "one of the happiest of human beings." She was particularly gratified by the "very kind letters and expressions of satisfaction I have received from your family . . ." Her tone was so formal as to suggest that this was a letter she expected Julia to show her mother.

Soon afterward, Belle wrote a letter in a much more girlish vein, evidently intended for her "darling Julie" alone. "I am so *very, very* happy. . . . So you are engaged! Oh, it is *too* glorious! And to Randolph Coolidge of all others. . . . I am not in the slightest astonished. Do you remember a little talk we had together one night in bed? . . ." [15] Eighteen sixty was going to be a year of weddings in the Gardner family, for Joseph, eldest and confirmed bachelor though he was, had or would soon succumb to the charms of Harriet Sears Amory, twenty-five years old.

There were visits from John L. Gardner senior and his daughter to the Stewarts of New York, Julia Gardner being the historian, in letters to her mother. They went to the opera to see "Speranza make her debut in Traviata"; but Adelina Speranza was ill, and the opera was changed to *Il Trovatore* which was badly done. Poor Speranza's season was a failure and people made jokes—her name means hope in Italian— saying that the Academy of Music on Fourteenth Street should have "abandon Hope" written over the door.[16] But the Stewarts had a box and Julia Gardner "had a very agreeable young man to talk with almost all the evening." So the music seems hardly to have mattered anyway.

They went to the French Theatre on the corner of 14th Street and Sixth Avenue and saw "some amusing little vaude- villes." These were given on off nights and sometimes they were "intolerably funny. In costume, not elegant, but decided- ly low comedy, buffoonery in fact," according to the diarist George Templeton Strong, who was there and confessed that he was "weak enough to enjoy buffoonery . . . when it is free from essential coarseness and hints of dirt." [17]

Minstrel shows were going on in New York most of the time and Mr. Stewart consented to take Julia and Belle to one. But he got in touch with the management beforehand and requested that there be no vulgar jokes because Miss Gardner of Boston would be there. As a result the comedi- ans, during the show, kept admonishing each other: "Shh— Miss Gardner of Boston is here." Blessed with the reliable Gardner sense of humor, Julia laughed and told the joke.

The wedding date was set for Tuesday, April 10, 1860. Isabella Stewart would be twenty just four days after she be- came Mrs. Jack Gardner. Grace Church, famous for its high Episcopal ritual and the new bonnets of its communicants, was the place, the Rev. Dr. Taylor officiating. The groom's sister Julia must have been one of the wedding party; but the whole family had come to New York, so she wrote no story of the wedding for Gardners on Beacon Hill.

Although all this was a matter of record, one of the first Mrs. Jack Gardner legends was to the effect that she "climbed out of a convent window in Paris and eloped with Jack." She never corrected legends but only laughed at them, and sometimes it seemed as if the less people knew about her the more they talked.

The bride and groom went to Washington, D.C., for a brief honeymoon. It was cold at the South, the papers said. The British minister was putting his house in order to receive the Prince of Wales, who would travel in the United States incognito under the name of Lord Renfrew.

On April 21, according to Julia Gardner, "Jack and Belle have returned and are as happy as possible." Julia had been staying with the Stewarts, who had taken her out to see Central Park, which promised to be very fine; and she was going to see Tom Thumb. "Somebody shorter than myself," she said. As far as she could discover, the honeymooners spotted four other newly-married couples in Washington and they all seemed to have been very busy watching each other.

The young Jack Gardners lived with the senior John L. Gardners when they first arrived in Boston. The stone house on Beacon Street, with its square rooms, classic in detail and furnished in ancestral mahogany, made a fine place for a reception for the bride.

But before long, the Jack Gardners went to live at the Hotel Boylston, on the corner of Boylston and Tremont Streets, a location taken over later by the Hotel Touraine. The Hotel Boylston was "an apartment house," claiming to be the first in the country and so called because "the mode of living was in suites after the French and continental systems." It was an enormous pile of varicolored brick with a high-arched arcade at the street level and arched windows, row after row, culminating in a monstrous mansard roof. Some of the apartments occupied a whole floor, but all the kitchens were at the top of the building. It was the latest thing in modern convenience. There were also "passenger elevators." [18]

The big event in Boston during the autumn of 1860 was a public ball in honor of His Royal Highness Albert Edward, Prince of Wales. Belle was delighted when the John L. Gardners took a box at the old Boston Theatre, now refurbished and called the Academy of Music.

A dancing floor, built in sections so that it could be stored away, was bolted together and laid across the theater seats. Belle had a good view of the stage, "draped with crimson velvet," to form a tent, with the wall behind it painted to represent Windsor Castle. Here, at 10:20 P.M. on Thursday, October 17, the Prince appeared—a "nice-looking young man with light-brown glossy hair, blue eyes" and a chin which was "only slightly receding." [17]

Jack Gardner was somewhat concerned in the affair because the supper for the Prince was prepared "by the cuisine of the Somerset Club." It was a simple matter of thirty-eight courses, beginning with terrapin and proceeding through boar's head, veal in baskets, woodcock, lobster salad and on down to wine jelly and ice cream. But Belle did not care much for banquets. It was the dancing that she liked.

The Prince's dancing partners had been chosen by a committee who were afterwards the most berated of men. They chose the wives and daughters of politicians, for the most part, selecting the mayor's wife for the Prince's partner in the opening quadrille. After all, the City of Boston was paying for the party. But the governor's wife was thereby insulted, and the committee, in trying to please all factions, succeeded in pleasing none.

The Gardner family had little or nothing to do with politics and Belle knew she need not hope to dance with the Prince. There were a few socially prominent debutantes who did—Miss Susan Amory having the fifth dance and Miss Hattie Appleton the fifteenth, for example. These girls were inclined never to let people forget this honor, as time went by. Belle Gardner danced anyway and probably had more fun than they did. "Several sets continuously occupied the center of the floor" surrounding the Prince—and there was Belle, again and again.

It was a new and delightful experience, next day, for a girl never before in the limelight, to have her dress described in the papers. Mrs. Jack Gardner wore "green moiré antique, trimmed with point lace and green satin rouches." She had on "a costly Bertha; a green velvet head-dress, diamond necklace and ear-rings to match." It was all in the Boston *Transcript!*

THREE

"Too Young to Remember"

ON November 14, 1860, came the wedding of Joseph Peabody Gardner, Jack's older brother, to Harriet Sears Amory—the daughter of a "Cotton Whig." Then, on a cold and blustery day, December 18, 1860, Julia Gardner was married to Joseph Randolph Coolidge.[1] The wedding was in King's Chapel; the winter season a happy time for Gardner family festivities. But Julia had now acquired Southern marriage connections.

Not to be outdone by Belle's father, David Stewart, John L. Gardner, Sr., gave his son Joseph and his daughter Julia houses on the new Beacon Street in Back Bay. Eventually Belle, Julia and Harriet would be neighbors. In 1861 they were drawn together as friends with similar sympathies because their old schoolmates began to call them "Copperheads."

The Gardner family hoped ardently that the question of slavery could be settled without war. They belonged to the world of manufacturing and finance, rather than to the group of social reformers. Gardner men had voted against Lincoln and Belle agreed with them.

Springtime in Boston in 1861 was typical of New England's so-called temperate climate. On April first it began to snow, as though to play a thoroughly disagreeable April Fool's trick, and it snowed for three days. There was sleighing, which Belle and her sisters-in-law loved, but the sun was warm and the deep snow almost immediately turned to slush. The streets on Beacon Hill became icy torrents and Jack Gardner, coming from the Somerset Club to 126 Beacon Street (a house he and Belle had rented) arrived wet nearly to the knees.

"Mr. Appleton and Mr. Amory have decided to go to Charleston to see for themselves the true condition of affairs," Jack told her. Neither politics nor business were supposed to be talked about at home—the club was the place for that. But Jack Gardner already knew that Belle's habit of listening to what men said was not just an act. She was really interested, so he told her that the Appletons and Amorys were worried about the cotton supply for their mills. What these gentlemen saw "for themselves at the South" however, was the attack on Fort Sumter. They got home "by Savannah and Cincinnati without being stopped . . . although known to be from Massachusetts." [2]

In later years, some tactless person would occasionally ask Mrs. Jack Gardner for her reminiscences of the Civil War. "I was too young to remember it," she would say, with an ominous gleam in her eyes which indicated that this ended the question.

As a matter of fact, Belle Gardner was twenty-one the day that Fort Sumter was evacuated by Union troops. She remembered. But as in later years she was to say, "If I am not happy, do you think I would tell you!" so she chose to forget certain periods during her married life—and this was one of them.

"Jefferson Davis issued a proclamation offering letters of marque to anybody and everybody to attack our merchant vessels and pillage our commerce." [3] The men at the Somerset Club had the news before it appeared in the papers. "If we seize these pirates we cannot hang them because the South would order reprisals on prisoners of war that would mean mutual extermination." [4] Julia's husband had an "Uncle John" in the Confederacy and neither Julia nor any of her family wished to see him exterminated.

The Gardners took great risks from now on because they were shipowners. Fourteen sailing vessels had been registered under the name of John L. Gardner, Sr., as sole owner, six more belonged to John L. Gardner and Company, while new ones, just being built, carried Jack Gardner's name as part owner. The *Lepanto* was built in Boston in 1860 with Jack Gardner owning an eighth interest, his father five-eights and his brothers Joseph and George an eighth each. She was over 690 tons register—which was large for Gardner sailing ships —and she must even now be dodging Confederate privateers. Every night, when Jack came home from the office at 22 Congress Street, Belle looked at him anxiously. If he seemed cheerful, she knew that the *Lepanto* had not been listed under "disasters at sea."

In 1861, when his father and brothers built the 1053-ton *St. Paul*, Jack did not take a share. But in 1863, he ventured a sixteenth interest in the ownership of the *Arabia*, a beautiful, fast ship. She escaped the "Rebel pirate *Florida*," a privateer so successful as to be featured in Boston papers again and again. But her master reported that she had such a "fore

33

and aft pitch" that he was sure she would take a header and go down. She did well, however, until after the Gardners sold her, when—under a different captain—she sailed, never to be heard of again. In 1864, Jack Gardner took a quarter interest with his father and two brothers in the *Nabob*, a bark of only 536 tons.[5] She was his last venture, for he turned to railroads as a much better risk. This is not to say that he could get sailing out of his blood—but a man may buy yachts with railroad money. And this, Jack Gardner did.

Neither Jack nor any of his brothers volunteered to fill the quota when Lincoln called for militia from Massachusetts. There was no opprobrium attached to this—men stayed at home who did not want to go to war, and that was that. "Public opinion was divided in Boston. . . . The Democratic Party had been too long and too firmly united to the dominant party at the South to feel any sympathy with a movement" hostile to the South. "The Whig Party, though almost dead, was dying hard; and the Webster Whigs . . . the Everett men, the conservatives generally were for peace at almost any price," according to an observer on the spot.

By the morning of April 16, 1861 ". . . fifes and drums began to be heard, the streets were thronged with people, flags were displayed in every direction." Belle Gardner must have gone out to watch the parades on Boston Common that day and many another day.

The Gardner men, interested in banking as well as shipping, sat in conference—whether they heard drums or not. Boston banks offered the Commonwealth of Massachusetts a loan of $3,600,000 "in advance of legislation" to take care of the militia who were marching into Boston. From private donors, $30,000 was raised in three days "to aid in formation of a regiment of infantry." And now the bankers came up with another plan. If commanders of companies would "collect a portion of the money their men received . . . and transmit it to the Mayor of Boston," the savings banks would take care of the cash and pay it out to soldiers' families on request. There was as yet no such thing as an allotment, and until now no one seemed to care what became of the wives and children of men in service.[6]

In retrospect, it seemed as though abolitionist Boston sprang to the attack. As a matter of fact, Boston was a long way from being unanimously abolitionist, but the city was unionist and against secession. The three months militia went off lightheartedly, sure that the rebellion would be suppressed in a matter of days and by a mere show of force. "On the

19th [of April] a mob in Baltimore assaulted the 6th Massachusetts Volunteers as it passed through to Washington, and at once bridges were burned and railway communications were cut off between Washington and the North . . . the first blood was shed on the anniversary of the battle of Lexington and Massachusetts suffered in both cases." [7]   Belle Gardner was a naturally friendly, outgoing girl; but in her new home town of Boston she found herself increasingly shut out, especially by girls of her own age and women who were a little older. Without the loving welcome that her sisters-in-law, Julia Gardner Coolidge and Harriet Gardner, gave her, she would have been unbearably lonely. The political situation was largely to blame but there were certain social customs which gave Boston girls powerful leverage against outsiders if they chose to use it.

Assemblies and cotillions of any social standing whatever always took place at Papanti's Hall, where Beacon Street boys and girls had been taught to dance. This hall was not large, although it was a new one—with a dance floor set on springs! Since there was limited space, "a book was sent around to families considered eligible as subscribers" to all the dances, and "Boston was stern about who should and should not have their name on that sacred scroll." [8]

It would have been impossible to omit the name of a Gardner; but young Mrs. Jack never knew—at least at first—how fiercely her presence was resented at Papanti's Hall. She could dance better than most of the Boston debutantes; she had snatched one of the most eligible bachelors from under their noses—and, worst of all, she had a way with men which made the remaining bachelors forget their duty, which was to dance with unmarried girls.

When the girls snubbed Belle at assemblies, men rallied around her, at first from a desire to see fair play for the newcomer, but very shortly because they liked her. The girls and women had a citadel all their own, however, which they could hold against Belle Gardner. It was called the "Sewing Circle." Each year, as debutantes made their bow to society, a "Sewing Circle was formed for them" and in this tight little group they remained all the years of their life.

Until now, sewing had been "for the poor"; and Julia brought Belle to a meeting—since guests were permitted, looked over, and judged to be either delightful or impossible. There was time at the meeting to "sew two buttons on to the end of something" before a "lavish luncheon with six

35

salads" [9] was served and sewing was discontinued until the next meeting.

After the conflict over slavery began, the Boston sewing circles became much more serious. Girls and women worked hard and turned out many garments and dressings for the Sanitary, that forerunner of the Red Cross. But Julia Gardner Coolidge's circle did not have to invite young Mrs. Jack Gardner to join them if they did not want to. Belle pretended not to mind being left out and perhaps she never really knew how the girls talked about her behind her back. Sewing Circle members liked to say that young Mrs. Jack was snubbed unmercifully when she first came to Boston—a procedure which seemed to give them great satisfaction for years to come and of which even their descendants spoke with pride.

Belle had one small revenge. A matron's age could be accurately estimated by the Sewing Circle to which she belonged. Attached to no circle, Belle could seem as young as she pleased, and even if women guessed her age correctly, men did not. All in all, it was not surprising that Mrs. Jack Gardner was said to like men better than women.

As the Civil War continued, the ranks of young men at assemblies and cotillions diminished. Theodore Lyman, who had danced and kept the fun going at the Forbes' party before Belle was married, had been opposed to the abolitionists and did not vote for Lincoln. But he became aide-de-camp to General Meade, serving without pay. Robert Gould Shaw recruited his famous Negro regiment and died with them; their bravery the equal of his; their memory and his to be forever enshrined in Boston's heart. Richard Fay, that leading beau of Boston, did not join the army, but perhaps too often he selected Belle for his dancing partner. The Sewing Circle girls later wondered out loud whether Belle had anything to do with Fay's divorce.

The Gardner family stood by Belle during these difficult Civil War years of her early married life. She was spoken of as shy; and in view of her later career, this seems ridiculous. But as a matter of fact many a show-off is shy and many a fine actress has confessed to extreme shyness in private life. It hurt to be snubbed, but Belle had tremendous personal pride. Sometimes, as shy people often do, she overplayed her part of seeming not to care.

A picture of Belle, taken about this time, shows a painfully thin young woman, so frail that she actually seemed to need the support of the chair beside which she was posed. Her hoop skirt, enormous at the floor, narrowed as it reached her tiny waist, so that it hung in limp folds like a half-opened umbrella. She was smiling bravely as though overanxious to please.

Belle, as a matter of fact, was far from well. First of three Gardner brides, she had hoped and assumed that she would be the first to have a child—a son, of course, to carry the name of John Lowell Gardner to the third generation. But no: Joe's wife Harriet had a boy on September 17, 1861— named Joseph Peabody Gardner in honor of his father. On May 17, 1862, Julia had a son, named Joseph Randolph Coolidge for *his* father. Isabella Gardner was childless—so far.

Pregnancy was spoken of as an "illness" and Belle often hoped that she was ill. She would stay in bed until after breakfast which, in New England, was considered sheer self-indulgence unless sufficient ill health excused it. Peabody relatives on Jack's mother's side remembered seeing him carry his frail wife from the carriage to their parlor in Salem and place her on the sofa when they came to call.

At the first sign of pregnancy, Julia and Harriet disappeared from the social scene. Within a few months they never left the house except to take the air in the family carriage, carefully wrapping themselves in shawls to disguise their "condition." Belle hopefully missed a dance or two. But for her, disappointment followed a few days of hope. Young Mrs. Jack, having no reason to stay in bed and no "condition" to conceal, would go dancing again, attracting more men than any matron had a right to do.

In winter, Belle went skating on the pond in the new Public Garden—a graceful, dashing little figure in hoop skirts. Her father-in-law twitted her about New York girls being unequal to Boston girls, at least on skates, so she had to show him he was wrong. They were great friends, those two.

In summer it pleased the senior Gardners to have Belle and Jack come to their summer home in Brookline. "Green Hill," it was called, a rambling farmhouse rebuilt until it fitted the family like a living shell. It stood on a knoll overlooking fields and woodland. In the distance was the city of Boston with the golden dome of the State House clearly to be seen above the clustering Beacon Hill houses. Distance made it seem a scene in miniature, like an Italian hilltown landscape painted in tempera.

On summer mornings Belle could hear the clip-clop of horses below her bedroom window as her father-in-law, erect in his saddle, and her husband, handsome on his mount, set out for their Boston business office—a groom riding behind to take care of the horses after they dismounted on cobblestoned Congress Street. John L., Senior, insisted on this morning ride as a means of preserving his health. But on rainy days wheels crunched on the driveway and Belle knew that Jack was more pleased than otherwise to lean back on carriage cushions.

Belle rode horseback beautifully, and her father-in-law loved to see her well mounted from his Green Hill stables.

The War Between the States, although an ever-present cloud on the southern horizon, was less important to a girl in her twenties than her personal problems and pleasures. The Fourth of July, 1863, was particularly exciting. From Green Hill, the fireworks were plainly visible, although the set piece called "The Traitor's Doom" could not be properly appreciated. "A firey figure suspended by the neck to a gibbet spasmodically jerked its arms and legs and was particularly enjoyed by the juveniles," the Boston *Advertiser* said next day. There were only two accidental explosions on Boston Common. But the exhibition of the electric light, the "last and crowning glory of the day" was beautiful from Brookline. A light, mounted on the cupola of the State House, "could be revolved, elevated or depressed so as to throw its beams on any desired spot and at times was made to light up various portions of the Common . . ." Two other electric lights, one at the corner of Park and Beacon Streets and one "by the pond . . . produced magical effects," shining through colored glass. These were battery-powered arc lights and some people felt that electricity might be the coming thing.[10]

News of the Battle of Gettysburg had been "received over the telegraph" by the second of July but no one knew what to believe. It "could hardly turn out to be worse than a drawn battle," people thought, and "to an invading army a drawn battle would mean a defeat." Not until July 5 did "fragmentary tidings from Gettysburg" seem like "glorious news."[11]

On July 8 conscription began in Boston. "The operations were conducted with the utmost fairness and the names drawn are those of persons in all classes of society," said the Boston *Advertiser*. "There was a good deal of interest and excitement shown in the result and people, for once, were very anxious *not* to see their names in the newspapers . . . The Boston names were put in a large copper sphere which was made to revolve after each name was drawn. Deputy Provost Marshal William H. Gardner, having been blind-folded, drew the names and they were announced by Captain Howe."[12]

The name of John L. Gardner, Jr., was drawn the first day.

"To answer inquiries," the *Advertiser* printed the terms under which men between twenty and forty-five, if unmarried, or married men between twenty and thirty-five might avoid service, if drafted.

"First. Any person paying $300 under Section 3 of the Enrollment Act is thereby exempt from further liability under that draft.

"Second. Any drafted person furnishing an acceptable substitute is exempt from military service for the period for which the said substitute is mustered into service . . ." [13]

Unfortunately, Jack Gardner was never moved to write his reminiscences, but T. Jefferson Coolidge, a Gardner business associate and Julia Gardner Coolidge's brother-in-law, wrote an autobiography. "I paid seven hundred and eighty-five dollars for a substitute," he said, "and as much as one thousand dollars was paid." It is safe to say that Jack Gardner also paid for a substitute when he was drafted.[14]

FOUR

Jackie

A<small>FTER MORE</small> than two years of married life, the Gardners' house-building project was completed. In 1862 they moved into 152 Beacon Street, an address which was to be famous for the next forty years.

Built of cut stone, light brown in color, it was French with a strong Boston accent. A great tower ballooned outward from the front wall, rose four stories to be surmounted by a mansard roof. Squared-off windows behind a railing on the fifth floor of this bastion gave it the look of a lighthouse. Below the level of the street, kitchen windows peered into an areaway and beyond kitchens and pantries were wine cellars which it was Jack Gardner's delight to stock, especially with Burgundy.

The "house of Mr. John L. Gardner, Jr.," was deemed worthy of illustration in *Artistic Houses of Boston*, gotten out in 1894. Text was by an anonymous hand. "Mr. Gardner's house," said the article, "was designed by Mr. John Sturgis whose particular care has been line . . ." The entrance hall "was but a landing place for a noble flight of stairs, so easy of ascent that a modern elevator would seem a supererogatory convenience." (So much for "passenger elevators," pride of the Hotel Boylston.)

A balcony, inside the house over the entrance, was "filled with exotic plants that thrive in the abundant sunshine." Mr. John L. Gardner, Senior, gave Belle all the flowers she could use for her balcony and windows. His "gardens under glass" were the envy of his Brookline neighbors and Mrs. Gardner's interest in horticulture, perhaps aroused by her Stewart grandmother, was another bond between Belle and her father-in-law. But in the illustration for *Artistic Houses*, the Gardner "exotic plants" were represented by three palms and one rubber plant!

Ceilings were left "entirely without ornamentation," evidently to the surprise of the writer in *Artistic Houses of Boston*, who must have expected the gilded wreaths and garlands which had been the delight of a previous generation. The Jack Gardners, however, had not actually gone so far as to leave their plaster unadorned. A low-relief Renaissance border decorated the widest of a series of cornice moldings and a small triangular ornament occupied each corner of the white plaster ceiling.

There were fireplaces surmounted by mantelpieces of intricately carved wood, painted white, replete with little columns, shelves and niches, each "an architectural study of importance," the essayist of *Artistic Homes* felt sure. Balusters on the stairs were variously turned, elaborately carved.

On the second floor over the front door was a small sitting room which Belle Gardner called her "boudoir." It was entirely her own. Here she would entertain those she liked best, giving each guest the feeling, as he sat in a low chair by the fire, that the mood of intimacy was for him alone. Tea would be brought in, with wine for the gentleman if he preferred it. The decoration of this room changed with Isabella's changing moods, as time went by. It was for a while "more French than Paris" with golden-yellow brocade covering the walls. But it was variously described only by privileged guests and the representative from *Artistic Houses* never saw it.

Photographs not appearing in *Artistic Houses* showed the Jack Gardners' front parlor. Chairs and sofas were overstuffed until it seemed as if they must burst their many buttons; fringe modestly covered their legs. Most chairs were armless to accommodate the huge hoop skirts all ladies would be wearing. Table covers swept the floor and tabletops were crowded with signed photographs. Two gentlemen in high silk hats stood side by side; there were gentlemen with beards, gentlemen with mustachios and long or short hair, depending on their occupation on or off the stage. There were ladies in every sort of dress.

If ceilings were relatively plain, carpets were flowered and overlaid with oriental rugs. Gas fixtures were a jungle of brass flowers. Palms, doubtless from John L. Gardner, Senior's palm house in Brookline luxuriated in every more or less unoccupied corner. And there was a potted mimosa tree, ceiling-high. But it was by no means sturdy enough to support anything but the *legend* that Mrs. Gardner perched in its branches to receive her guests! All in all, the Jack Gardners had every reason to congratulate themselves on their new house; and the article in *Artistic Houses of Boston*, though flattering, hardly did justice to it.

It seemed as though Belle's first child had just been waiting for a home of his own. A competent nurse was engaged as soon as it was at all probable that Belle was not to be disappointed once more. A room was fitted up for a nursery with everything a baby could possibly require. On June 18, 1863, John Lowell Gardner III was born. Never had parents been happier, never had there ever been such a wonderful baby. They constantly invaded his nursery to see their child, to take him up and carry him downstairs to show their friends.

On December 3, 1863, Harriet Gardner had another little son, named William Amory in honor of her father. Julia was the mother of a second son, John Gardner Coolidge, born July 4, 1863. Belle Gardner could picture all the cousins growing up together, all going off to Harvard—her Jackie the most brilliant, of course, but all of them remarkable. It had been fun to be "Aunt Belle" to Julia's and Harriet's first boys but how much better it was to be the mother of a son! [1]

In March, 1864, Jackie was perched upon a chair to have his picture taken—a solemn baby with fair hair. By November he could talk, his mother said.

The senior John Gardners were again in Europe and Belle wrote to them about their grandson. Jackie "did not walk yet but pronounced any quantity of words very distinctly."

The weather had been bad in Boston. There was snow and sleet on the night of the "Grand Lincoln Torchlight Procession." Belle hoped the parade would not be postponed until the night when the McClellan parade was scheduled. The Gardners favored McClellan over Lincoln in the presidential campaign of 1864.

Jackie was ill with "a high fever for two or three days." The doctor thought it might be measles or whooping cough, both serious diseases of childhood for which he could do little or nothing. The Gardners were relieved when Jackie's illness "subsided into a bad cold aggravated by the coming of four double teeth."

Belle had been to show her parents their first and only grandchild. It was fun but she had been ill, she told her mother-in-law. She was "quite well again" and had "really accomplished wonders," making herself a new bonnet. The new one she bought in New York was "shockingly" expensive, "so I couldn't afford to have my old one made over by a milliner," she explained. She bought "a new-fashioned frame," therefore, and "turned out quite a respectable bonnet." [2]

Then it was the year 1865 and spring seemed to lag along more slowly than usual. Jackie would be two years old in two more months and his parents could take him to the senior

Gardners' Brookline home. There were the horses at Green Hill, and fields and flower gardens which a little boy of two would love.

But spring, that season of returning life, was the danger season for little children. Jackie had a cold that developed into pneumonia. On March 15, 1865, Jackie died and the light went out of Belle Gardner's life. She would not let anyone else touch her baby but dressed him herself for the last time and brushed his soft, fair hair.

The previous year, on April 10, 1864, her fourth wedding anniversary, Belle had been confirmed by Dr. Manton Eastburn, Bishop of Massachusetts.[3] With her careful religious upbringing, it was strange that she had not been confirmed before, but it might have been a sort of thanks-offering for the child she so much wanted. Her church sustained her now with its promise of eternal life for little children.

But spring, when it came, seemed cruel instead of beautiful. Of what use were flowers without Jackie to enjoy them! Summer came and Belle tried to take care of herself—because once more she was pregnant. There would never be another Jackie, the beloved firstborn, but she wanted children more than ever.

Harriet Gardner was also expecting a child—her third. The two young Mrs. Gardners were often together, for now they were neighbors in Back Bay. Harriet's third son was born November 5. His name was Augustus Peabody Gardner. But his mother died.

Belle Gardner "had been very delicate since the death of her child and was to be confined again some four or five months hence," wrote Mrs. John Amory Lowell, a friend of the family, to her son Augustus, who was in Europe. "But when Harriet Gardner so suddenly passed away, the servants ran to Jack Gardner, and being very near, they were there before Joseph.

"Belle Gardner did everything for Harriet that she had insisted on doing for her own child. She was constantly with Joe, the excitement and shock kept her up until after the funeral, when she was taken ill and remained so for four days . . ."[4]

The doctor was Henry J. Bigelow, Boston's outstanding surgeon, who was considered a genius in his time. He was a big man, and impressive; a professor of surgery at Harvard Medical School as well as a private practitioner.[5] Dr. Bigelow knew Belle Gardner personally and counted himself one of her admirers. He knew how much she wanted children—

which was something many people would never know. But after four days of "illness" the battle must have been lost as far as future children were concerned. He must have been thankful not to have lost his patient.

"Jack Gardner kept vigil beside his wife day and night," Mrs. Lowell wrote. And in another letter: "I don't think that Harriet's death was the same affliction to the Gardners that Belle's would have been. They are extravagantly fond of her and she is a superb person. We thought her so the summer we passed with the Stewarts at Sharon."

FIVE

Paris and Pearls

MONTHS PASSED and Belle Gardner did not regain her strength. Her mother-in-law, full of health and energy, murmured among her contemporaries the story of other girls with the same "illness" who became "sofa invalids" for life. Of course Belle's miscarriage was never mentioned outside a small circle. She had a "nervous breakdown," everyone else was told.

Dr. Bigelow was sent for again and again. Finally he laid his cards on the table. He could not cure young Mrs. Jack because there was nothing organically wrong with her. "A wit as well as a surgeon" and in later years, somewhat of "a vain old man," Dr. Bigelow managed to combine a certain amount of social life with surgery. He had watched Isabella dancing and had probably given her a whirl himself, so he indulged in gallantry, reminding her that there were still men in the world and that "so many gentlemen admire you."

Mrs. Gardner was not the only woman ever to be childless, her doctor may tactfully have told her. She must develop new interests. Reverting to a custom of previous generations, Dr. Bigelow prescribed a journey for health.

The Gardners in family conclave decided that Jack could be spared from his father's office. In the spring of 1867, an ambulance called at 152 Beacon Street, Mrs. Jack was brought downstairs on a mattress, placed in the ambulance, driven to the dock and carried on board ship. There was drama in this departure and Isabella must have felt a stirring of interest and pleasure.

The Jack Gardners arrived in Hamburg, Germany, on June 10—and nothing was said about a mattress and an ambulance when they went ashore. As Belle regained her old verve and enthusiasm, Jack must have been amused to see how much her capacity for sightseeing resembled his mother's. Guidebook in hand, she dutifully admired Thorwaldsen in Copenhagen, buying photographs of all his mighty works to mount in an album for the parlor table back home.[1] They spent six weeks in Norway, three in Sweden, a week in St. Petersburg, a week in Moscow, and then they went to Vienna. Jack Gardner's invalid wife was far less fatigued by it all than he was!

In Vienna, however, Belle put away her guidebook. She had found music—the first of the absorbing interests which were to crowd her future days. Music was not just a form of entertainment in Vienna, it was a way of life. Even the bells on the horsecars were tuned in harmony. Everyone sang, there was music indoors, outdoors, all day and more than half the night. Johann Strauss had been conducting open-air concerts in St. Petersburg and was now on his way to the Paris Exposition. "The Blue Danube" would be heard for the first time in Paris at the Princess Metternich's ball. But Vienna was already set to "music by Strauss." The Gardners lingered in Vienna, the perfect setting for this second honeymoon.

There was time, however, for a two-month stay in Paris and in 1867, Paris was exhilarating. Napoleon III had decided on an exposition to recoup national resources. The blockade of American ports during the Civil War had injured the Lyons silk industry because it partially closed the American market. Disastrous campaigns in Mexico further drained French resources. Napoleon's idea was that lavish spending would be the way to avoid bankruptcy—so he ruthlessly destroyed the old Paris by laying out broad boulevards lighted with flaring gas lamps. "Paris, the City of Light" was his creation.

The Empress Eugénie and all the ladies of her court were now wearing more yardage of Lyons silk per costume than women had ever carried on their backs before. On new avenues in the Bois de Boulogne, carriages circled every afternoon so that the Empress could show a new costume every day. And in the Bois was the circular Exposition building, all of glass.

The Gardners missed the height of the Exposition when Paris was overrun with royalty; the Queen of Spain, the Sultan of Turkey ablaze with diamonds, the King of Prussia, "overshadowed by the colossal Count Bismarck . . . in his dazzling white uniform and wearing a shining helmet with an enormous spread eagle on the top of it . . ." Prizes were given out at the Exposition in July as dignitaries sat under a glass roof in the blazing sun, the sultan wearing "a necklace of pearls"; and a Hungarian "encrusted with turquoise" the size of "hen's eggs." Americans came forward in black "dresscoats, without any decorations" to receive gold medals for pianos, sewing machines and beer.[2]

By the time the Jack Gardners arrived in August, the excitement had died down and Paris belonged to Frenchmen again. The Exposition building was still the great attraction and one exhibit in the French section particularly attracted Isabella. Street dresses, morning costumes and ball gowns of a startling design had all received awards. An evening coat of white satin covered with gold embroidery had won a gold medal. The designer's name was Charles Frederick Worth.

Mrs. Jack would perhaps have been surprised to discover that Worth was an Englishman. She probably never heard that he was the son of an unsuccessful lawyer, apprenticed as a boy in the drygoods trade in London. Arriving in Paris at the age of eighteen with only five pounds in his pocket, he was now forty-two and an absolute power in the field of dressmaking.[2]

Worth owed his success to the Princess Pauline de Metternich, a non-beauty with a tremendous flair for style. Worth saw her when she arrived at the court of Louis Napoleon, designed a dress for her and sent his attractive French wife around to sell it to her. The princess was to set the price and she paid 300 francs. The Empress Eugénie noticed the dress, asked who designed it—and Worth was made.

Belle Gardner had forgotten how much she liked clothes. Of what use were new clothes to a girl lying pale and weak upon a sofa—seeing no one but the family. Now she wondered how she would look in one of these daring new dresses and Jack took her right around to see Worth. It was fortunate that the Empress was out of town or Worth might have declined to receive the young Jack Gardners.

Worth was the first designer to make dressmaking big business in Paris. Carriages with liveried coachmen were constantly before his door at Number 7, rue de la Paix. Having been refused a raise by his first French employer, he had taken an old mansion in this famous street before any other merchants, except Guerlain the perfumer, were established there. He now employed 1200 people and his wife, a former fellow clerk, rode out in her own carriage every afternoon—wearing Worth gowns.

The Gardners mounted crimson-carpeted stairs, banked on each side with flowers. They entered a room where nothing was displayed except silks by the yard, in black and white. There were chairs and couches, excessively overstuffed, and in little glass-and-gold-leaf cabinets were enchanting bits of frivolity, such as snuffboxes and antique lace fans. These were not for sale; they were part of Mr. Worth's private collection.

In the next room were silks in all colors; products of Lyons looms, except for a few Italian brocades that Mr. Worth happened to like. The third room was devoted to velvet, the fourth to woolens—where English broadcloth predominated, Worth's early training at Swan and Edgar's of London standing him in good stead.

Only in the fifth salon were actual dresses displayed, on wooden forms against a mirrored wall. Customers gazed at them in silence, as though standing before great works of art in a museum.

There was one more room, called the *salon de lumière*, ablaze with gaslight and lined with mirrors. Here customers could be fitted and would see how a ball-gown would look under the gaslights of the Tuileries Palace. Mr. Worth sold pure white "rice powder" to his clients—a style of face powder which was to endure for more than a generation.

Everywhere there were attentive yet unobtrusive young men in tight-fitting morning coats, ready to answer a client's questions. Young girls, in black dresses designed by Worth, were always on call. They were models, ready to show the new designs upon request. While still a clerk, Worth had discovered that he could sell many an expensive shawl by draping it cleverly around the shoulders of the girl who was now his wife. He was the first couturier to use living models.

Behind the scenes, Charles Worth worked—not in glossy broadcloth like his young salesmen, but in smock and baggy trousers like an artist—complete with beret to cover his bald spot. He was growing portly as well as wealthy when Jack Gardner crossed his path. Naturally, he did not emerge from his workroom for every client, but he liked Americans because they had "faith, figures and francs," so he put his long dressing gown over his work clothes and came out to see what these Gardners of Boston were like. Mrs. Jack qualified on one point. In spite of the hoop skirt that she wore, Worth could tell that she had a "figure"—tiny but excellent. He looked Jack over and saw a man obviously not only possessed of francs, but in a mood to spend them. Now—had the Gardners "faith" in Charles Worth?

It was said that Worth introduced the hoop skirt or "crinoline." If so, he was now trying to get rid of a fashion that had lasted fifteen years. The hoop was kind to women who indulged in thirty-eight-course banquets, such as the one served the Prince of Wales in Boston. English-speaking gentility refused to admit that a woman had legs—only "limbs," not to be referred to unless absolutely necessary. Legs were covered with long voluminous drawers. Charles Worth showed Mrs. Jack Gardner his 1868 designs and watched her face to see if she would have "faith."

In came a model in a dress flowing smoothly over the hips! It could be seen that she had legs which moved gracefully under somewhat clinging silk. Gone was the look of little mouselike feet pattering under a bell; but pretty shoulders were bare, her bosom opulent though actually no more revealed than usual. There were still yards and yards of silk but it flowed back into an enormously long train which the model managed with grace and dexterity.

Would Mrs. Gardner wear a dress like that? She would, indeed! Her blue eyes shot sparks of mischief; and Jack, although preparing carefully to inquire into the cost of all this, smiled at the thought of how she would startle Boston. They would need several gowns by Worth, "as beautifully finished inside as out"—and designed especially for a small woman with a homely face and a pretty figure.

That eminent businessman Charles Worth knew how to sell goods. He designed a street costume, for example, having bands of sealskin with which a sealskin jacket, muff and hat to match were obviously desirable. A black velvet afternoon costume included hat, muff and tippet of Russian sable. Would Mrs. Jack Gardner wear a short dress on the street? Of course she would. A dress all of six inches from the ground would show her pretty feet and ankles. She would need custom-made bronze kid boots, silk stockings in colors other than black! Mr. Worth was in a position to supply them; Jack Gardner liked them. Masculine Boston was to observe with approval, while certain Boston ladies never forgave Mrs. Jack.

Hoop skirts were still advertised in the Boston *Transcript* when the Jack Gardners came home in October, 1868. But Mrs. Jack Gardner returned a changed woman—cheerful, self-assured and ready to become the talk of the town. Old friends such as Julia Coolidge defended her right to do as she pleased—others were either bitterly critical or plainly delighted. One matron said that it was all right to buy clothes in Paris but that she, personally, always put hers away for at least a year after she got home—so as "not to be conspicuous."

The masculine comment which was attributed to Tom Appleton was repeated for years until it became one of the "Mrs. Jack" legends. Belle was arriving late at a party and coming up the stairs as Appleton descended, the story went. "Pray, who undressed you!" Boston's famous wit was moved to remark.

"Worth," said Mrs. Jack. "Didn't he do it well?"

Before long other girls, most of them younger than Belle Gardner, "dropped" their hoops. They said it made them "feel naked," and it certainly meant that their dancing partners could hold them closer than the customary three feet or so.[4] There was of course the matter of the long train which was as new to Boston as a skirt without hoops. Worth equipped Belle's train with cleverly concealed loops so that she could hold it up and keep it out from under her partner's feet. Young Mrs. Jack was clever at this, and it was delightful to be constantly referred to as "graceful," at least by the men.

Dr. Henry J. Bigelow observed the results of his prescription—"a journey for health" and "new interests." He may possibly have wondered if his former patient had taken an overdose as he wrote to thank her for some hothouse grapes she sent him because she heard that he had been ill.

"No wonder so many men admire you. I hesitate to put on paper the way I feel about you, there are so many people about . . . The trouble is, you excite all those emotions in other peoples' bosoms and remain so perfectly hard-hearted yourself. I have seriously thought of trying a course of Jacqueminot roses,[5] now that the price has come down, if I believed they would produce the least effect . . .

"As it is, there seems to be no alternative but to sit on Oak Hill and think of the way your dress fits . . ."

The Jack Gardners probably timed their return to the United States to attend Eliza Gardner's wedding. On October 11, 1868, "little Eliza" married Francis Skinner, "merchant" and Harvard graduate, twenty-eight years old. Eliza was no longer the "petite amie" of French convent school days, who once begged Belle not to forget her. She was twenty-two, and would become exceedingly formal in her manners, increasingly critical of her gay, unconventional sister-in-law. Eliza Skinner seemed to take it as a personal injury when Belle was talked about, yet she was not above adding to the gossip.

The Gardner business interests often carried Jack to New York and Belle went along to visit her parents. Sometimes she stayed there, enjoying the theater and especially the music, while Jack went back to Boston. The spitefully inclined said that she stayed until Jack "had to fetch her home."

There was, as yet, no Boston Symphony Orchestra. Opera companies visited Boston but the so-called "Opera House" was as likely as not to feature minstrel shows or "performing dogs and monkeys." [6] Not that Belle disliked minstrels and monkeys, but Vienna had showed her how exciting music could be. New York was no Vienna but Boston, soon to experience a musical awakening, was as yet scarcely stirring in its sleep.

There was excitement in Boston in 1872, however, which had a bearing on Gardner family fortunes. This was the "Great Fire"—not by any means the first serious fire, but the most disastrous. On Saturday night, the ninth of November, "somewhere near nine o'clock . . . fire-bells began to ring." People living on the water side of Beacon Street went to their windows overlooking the Charles River—but the sky was not red over Cambridge. From windows on Beacon Street they saw a "column of light" that looked as though it came from the Hotel Boylston. Everyone went "over to Commonwealth Avenue for a better view." [7] But the fire was not in the modern French apartment house, it was in the newly built warehouses on Summer Street.

There was "no getting very near," but that night and most of the next day "the great high buildings seemed to melt away." Sixty-five acres of brick and stone warehouses, churches, office and bank buildings were destroyed, the loss eventually computed at seventy-five million dollars.

Curious coincidences contributed. The fire started in a warehouse of Quincy granite, supposed to be fireproof. But elevator shafts had been lined with wood and there were wooden partitions within the building and between each building and its neighbors. Coming on a Saturday night, the fire had a two-hour start because the warehouse district was deserted.

Epidemic at this time was a disease called "Epizoötic," which attacked draft horses. Oxen instead of horses had been hauling drays through the city of Boston. Now, at this moment of emergency, there were almost no fire horses and volunteer firemen had to pull engines to the scene, as in early days. "Suburban cities and towns appealed to . . . could get little apparatus on the road" for lack of horses. Moreover, "an engine stationed anywhere near the fire could not be got in working order before it had to be removed or abandoned, so hot was the blaze."

There was one more factor. The warehouses had been built on land once occupied by fine houses and gardens, among them, the "Mansion House with land and appurtenances . . . situate in Summer Street" which had belonged to Jack Gardner's grandfather. When the fine old houses were torn down, water pipes had not been replaced. They were small, with "hydrants of an old-fashioned pattern" so that no effective stream of water could be brought to bear upon the fire.

On Monday, "all the world within reach was looking at the wilderness of ruins" and the place to go was "the upper floors of Hovey's store on Summer Street" built by George Gardner, which "almost miraculously escaped." You could see Boston Harbor with its ships, because "everything was flat to the ground all the way to the water." [8]

Boston was stunned, but rebuilding began at once. Summer Street, Washington Street and others were widened "so that it would be impossible for fire to cross them," curious as the statement now seems. John L. Gardner, Senior, looked the situation over and decided that now was the time to buy up a bankrupt insurance company. On November 12, he wrote to his son Jack, who was in New York.

He had indulged in "too much beer and raw oysters" the night before and the women in his family had prescribed a mustard plaster, he said. Then he got down to business. He was going to put "50,000 dollars in the Washington Associates Company if the thing can be secured and at work at once. All depends on this. Good risks must be secured at once and there will be a great pick—as all Boston is worried at this moment. As many as possible must be taken—with good round premiums—million on million if obtainable—with the chance of total loss if another conflagration occurs —which will not happen with our water and fire departments.

"The risks are the best in the country. No small management will answer but holdings may secure great profits. It is not a thing for trustees, widows and children. No good will come of it if it is managed with the idea of avoiding risks." Jack was to "send daily advice and New York quotations and other news." [9]

T. Jefferson Coolidge wrote to Jack that same day. Although a younger man than Jack's father, his tone was much more cautious. "Your father authorized me to take 50,000 dollars Washington Associates Co. in his name. I put his name down for 30 m with the understanding that Mr. Bartlett should authorize the company for two ways.

"First, no liability for past insurance.

"Second, no liability for anything beyond the amount sub-scribed.

"I have no doubt the papers will fill up at once. If you think well enough of it . . . I'll put [your father] down for the amount he named, 50 m [$50,000] and increase my own.

"With common luck I think we shall be able to sell out 4 months hence at a 10% advance. Only 5% is cash, balance 12 month notes."

The Gardners' business prospered along with rebuilt Boston. By 1868, John L. Gardner, Senior, had moved to the corner of Clarendon and Beacon Streets, where he and his wife built themselves a new house. His old home, Number 7 Beacon Street, he had converted into a "hotel" where apartments were much sought after. In 1879 he became president of the Massachusetts Hospital Insurance Company, along with his other interests, which were "chiefly banking and financial transactions."

In 1873, Mrs. Jack Gardner, the future collector of European masterpieces, felt wealthy enough to buy her first picture—or at any rate, the first to be included in her final collection at Fenway Court. She bought it at Doll and Richards, art dealers, at 145 Tremont Street, and it was a mild enough affair—some sheep under a tree. But it was painted by Emile Jacque, a sixty-year-old Frenchman who had become a member of the "Barbizon School" by venturing out of his studio to paint in the open air.

Of course the young Gardners had talked of another trip abroad together, but the time never seemed right because Jack was increasingly needed in the family business. But in 1874, Jack Gardner made an entry in his pocket diary.

"Saturday, November 7. Left Boston by the 10 A.M. Springfield train. Many people to see us off." Jack and Belle were on their way to Egypt, Palestine, Greece and Turkey by way of Springfield, Massachusetts, New York and Jersey City.

Their steamer carried them to Liverpool over stormy seas. London was "bitterly cold" with "dense fogs." But before leaving London Jack Gardner bought of "Hancock and Company" a "very fine single-row pearl necklace consisting of 44 fine pearls" and a diamond "snap." He paid $4500 for the first of Isabella's famous pearls.[10]

53

SIX

Belle Gardner, Diarist

JACK GARDNER kept a pocket diary in which he jotted down brief notes; but Mrs. Jack began a journal [1] that was very different in style from her husband's line-a-day. She started her record on December 10 when the *Hydaspes,* after a fair passage from Brindisi, lay off Alexandria. It was color which impressed her first of all. "When I went on deck in the morning . . . I knew it was a dream for never had I seen such color as was the sea. There was no word for it—and on the horizon was a low stretch of sand and moving palms. I felt that it was Africa and from that moment everything was interest and enjoyment.

"The dragoman Bonicci [who was to travel with the Gardners for the next six months] came for us in a boat but instead of being anxious to get away on shore, we lingered to watch the mass of screaming, scrambling Arabs, men and boys, each more determined than the other to secure his prey. The next day we went to Cairo where the dream only became more colored with Eastern glow."

In Cairo it was the crowd that excited Mrs. Jack. "The people had stepped out of the Arabian Nights which were no longer tales that we had read, but were bits of real life happening with us looking on and we had truly come aboard and forgot ourselves."

Jack Gardner's entry in his diary [2] for the same date read, "Friday, December 11 (1874) Left Alexandria abt. 8½ A.M. Arrived at Cairo at 12:30 P.M. Went to Shepheard's hotel— very good—except full of fleas."

The Gardners set out for the pyramids on December 16. "There were several carriage loads—principally Americans," Mrs. Jack wrote. "I felt I was disappointed when I stood close to Cheops, hemmed in by the screaming Arab host— but when I got away from the carriage . . . and could lie on the sand near the Sphinx with the silent desert beyond and on every side—and the pyramids a little away from me—then solemnity and mystery took possession and my heart went out to the Sphinx . . ."

Four days later the Gardners "took up residence" aboard the dahabeah *Ibis*. As soon as they started up the Nile, Jack began carefully recording the distance sailed each day; whether or not they grounded on a sand bar and how their performance compared with other dahabeahs. He had brought along a camera. "Took two photos and made failures of them," he wrote.

"The *Ibis* spread her wings and flew South," Mrs. Jack said. She was "charmed" with their dahabeah. "After a few touches the little parlor became very pretty and as we could spread ourselves all over the boat we were quite comfortable with our separate dressing rooms, bath rooms, etc. After dinner, we went up to our sky parlor," which was equipped with "Eastern rugs, couches, plants and awnings . . . The crew, with their turbans and many-colored robes, squatted in a circle around their lurid, flickering fire, cooked their coffee and chanted their low, weird songs to the tapping of the tarabooka . . ."

Belle Gardner illustrated her journal with watercolor sketches, many of them remarkably good and all of them creditable. While Jack stayed at table over his coffee and claret, she "sat alone on deck" and this was her favorite time for sketching. Among her best were those with a subdued, after-sunset look; a delicate lavender sky reflected reddish-gold in a foreground of brown water. Palm trees seemed really windblown, boats with triangular sails contributed to good composition, while rows of columns disappearing into the distance showed that she understood perspective. She wrote in her journal during many a peaceful hour, and sometimes she watched "palm groves in the early moonlight," letting her "thoughts fly away with the many white-sailed caiques that floated out into the fading light."

The Gardners often left the *Ibis* for excursions on the banks of the Nile. When they traveled to Memphis on donkey-back: "The donkeys were so small we could only see their ears and tails and the donkey boys seemed as happy as the most favored children of the sun could be . . ." Little could be "seen to tell of the past of glorious, regal Memphis, still to me it will always be a memory of surpassing loveliness." They rode "through the palm groves, with the earth more green than it ever was painted elsewhere, with caravans camping here and there" by the oases, "and the graceful women coming and going with water jars on their heads . . ."

Although knowledge of ancient Egypt had been increasing, little excavation and archaeological study had as yet been accomplished. "Tempted ashore" three days later, it gave Belle "quite a dreadful feeling to see scraps of mummies lying about" among "old brick fortifications." For the most part, she left archaeological study to the experts and contented herself with sights and impressions. "The *Ibis* and we dozed through the day" before Christmas. "I went up as usual alone, after dinner and found the steersman at his prayers . . . As I lay upon the couch with the fragrance of frankincense stealing over me, the wake of the moon was a fit path by which my thoughts went straight to Cleopatra and I forgot that it was Christmas Eve." On the twenty-fifth she "tried hard not to remember it was Christmas Day." There was "no wind in the morning," so after visiting "a small town full of life" she made one of the best of her sketches: a boat without sail in front of a tan-colored cliff reflected in water below, with blue sky also reflected. "J. gave me a silver talisman case" for a Christmas present, she said.

Next day, the wind was intermittent. "We tracked (poled or rowed) and sailed and late in the afternoon passed a curious old convent . . . but long before we reached it, the monks swam out to us, begging. I hope they were as innocent of sin as of clothes." On New Year's Day, Belle went on deck to find the *Ibis* decorated "with palm branches and flags." For a New Year's gift Jack gave her "a pair of tinkling bracelets" she had "fancied in Cairo."

Jack Gardner, in his pocket diary, said on January 14 that he found a man who could help him "abt. photography," and from now on, Mrs. Jack's journal was illustrated with photographs as well as sketches. They were doing serious sightseeing now, taking excursions "via felucca, men's arms, donkey, ferry boat and donkey." Mrs. Jack read her guidebook faithfully but lost her heart to little "Hassan, aged 4," who was "steersman" of the felucca, and to "little Fatima, who had scrambled over the rocks with a water jar on her head" and while the Gardners had a picnic lunch, "watched from behind some ruins, each mouthful that I ate." Belle gave the little girl "a necklace of red and gilt beads and her eyes lighted and her teeth shone."

From time to time, American friends in their dahabeahs passed the *Ibis* on their way north to Cairo. Tom Appleton came along on the *Rachel* and "we hurried on deck and had a yell with him," Mrs. Jack wrote. "Hailed and conversed," wrote her husband, referring to their fellow Bostonian with proper dignity. "The Biddles" in the *London* passed going down.

The Gardners were now approaching the first cataract. On January 25, 1875, they "got off pretty well" at four-thirty in the morning. Jack stood on deck encouraging his crew, as though competing in an America's Cup race. He had "3 English and 1 American" boats against him and "until noon" he thought he would be first at the cataract. Then the wind dropped and he "came in next to last."

This meant a long wait but Jack took his defeat philosophically. "General McClellan's two boats came down" and they and the Gardners exchanged calls. Jack saw crocodiles just before dark. To pass the time they "lounged about the town of Assouan," where they saw "instead of antiquities, leopard skins, ostrich eggs," as in other towns, "live, tiny monkeys, [and] poisoned spear heads for sale."

There was as yet no Aswan Dam, and the Gardners, starting "about 9" in the evening, on donkey-back, rode to the narrows in the midst of which lay the Island of Philae, not yet inundated. They took a boat to the island, landed and then passed through "five miles of weirdest waste, with the deceptive moon lighting up rocks and tombs" till Mrs. Jack could fancy she saw "the ghouls" of Arabian Nights tales. The island was "entirely covered with the ruins of temples . . ."

On Monday, February 6, they "hoped and expected" to pass the first cataract, only to be told that "the governor would not allow it as Prince Arthur was expected and the cataract must be kept clear."

"Mrs. G." rode "a little way into the desert on a camel," Jack said. While she was gone he prepared a present for her but it was she who told about it.

"On my return I found on deck the dear little monkey I had wanted to buy. It was meant as a surprise for me and there he was, tied to a house made out of a claret box."

Mrs. Gardner's monkey almost bit the "Sheikh of the Cataract" before the "Shellalee," a tribe with exclusive rights as cataract pilots, took the *Ibis* through. Belle described the passage. "Four mummies with their bandages more or less unrolled, stationed themselves on the upper deck in charge of the helm. A maniac placed himself on the gangway and jumped up and down, waving a stick and shrieking . . . The commanders and commanded yelled and screamed." It was a most exciting time, not that the cataract was anything wonderful or terrible, but the Shellalee were like the inmates of an insane asylum let loose. At one point as they stood on the rocks, pulling the dahabeah, they "dropped the ropes and, rushing at each other, had a tremendous fight . . ."

Now it was on to Wadi Halfa with quite a good wind and Mrs. Jack thrilled to the idea of Nubia. Her husband's journal entries, although of a different sort, expressed equal satisfaction. "We led the fleet handsomely all afternoon," he wrote on February 19. On the twenty-second, "We had a fine race with the *Nellie* and arrived at Wadi Halfa at 12 almost neck and neck. Our bowsprit was a trifle ahead but the *Nellie* was inshore of us and we could not head her off."

In Jack Gardner's pocket diary there was no mention of his crew having had a fight with the crew of the *Zingara*, a rival dahabeah. His wife told that "J. was obliged to take away their weapons with his own hands." From time to time he rewarded them with a whole sheep which they roasted on shore at night when the *Ibis* tied up.

The McClellans had warned the Gardners not to go overland from Wadi Halfa to Abonseer, the rock from which to see the second cataract. The way to get there was by boat, "so we sailed and rowed . . . in the very craziest of crafts, —our ordinary row-boat; a mast manufactured out of odds and ends, one of the linen sheets for a mainsail and a flying jib made out of an awning," wrote Mrs. Jack. "After . . . threading our way thro' the thousand islands of the second cataract, a little climb . . . [brought] us to the top with no end of Nubia in one direction and black rocks jutting up in the rapids . . . at our feet." Mrs. Jack "hunted amongst the carved names for those of friends and found several, as well as historical ones."

While "J. was busy scratching 'Gardner,' I had the top of the mountain all to myself and there was nobody to laugh at me for being absolutely unhappy because our journey was over and our faces were to be turned north in half an hour . . ."

They got back to Wadi Halfa at noon and boarded the *Ibis*, whereupon "one of those children, the crew," quarreled about "the oar he was to have rowing down the river . . . The *Ibis* [was] in a wretched enough plight, shorn of her feathers, her pride and our delight, the beautiful big sail being stowed away and everything cleared for action." The childlike crew cut "up all kinds of pranks in their rowing and when bed-time came, they each had a hole to sleep in that was made by planks being taken up between the rowers and when they sat up in their white garments it looked like the resurrection morn. I can't bear going down the river," Mrs. Gardner added. But the "crew were happy" to be on the way back to Cairo.

There were more side-trips to ancient ruins, more sketches and several quite impressive photographs. Belle Gardner's "Nile Voyage" ended on April 12, 1875, but her travels were not half over. Day-by-day accounts continued, written more hastily and without watercolor sketches, once the leisurely days aboard the *Ibis* were over. Her mood of wonder and delight deepened, however, for now she was on the way to Palestine. Scenes in the Holy Land proved to be more than sight-seeing; they were a religious experience. She was often close to a state of exaltation.

Belle's health had been perfect, but now it failed her. "Delicious cakes" were sent to the Gardners on leaving Cairo. Mrs. Gardner enjoyed them on the train journey to the town of Suez, "a long hot ride." At seven A.M. next day they "left in a tiny boat for Port Said, through the Canal. J. and I sat out in front. Extraordinary mirage over the desert," she wrote. But by the time they got to Port Said she was "quite ill," with a high fever and passed "a wretched night." Next day she was "too ill to move."

The cakes had been presented by an American lady, resident in Cairo, who had been "very ill" for some time. But no one seemed to question the kitchen sanitation or any kindred subject, such as the safety of unboiled milk or water. Belle had recurring "wretched" times with fever but she ate any sort of food offered, the more "native" the better, and drank from wells of doubtful purity, sacred to religious tradition though they might be.

From Port Said, after eighteen hours of heavy seas, the Gardners reached Joppa. Belle was "weak but not seasick," she recorded with pride.

The ship anchored two miles out and the Gardners "dashed through the waves in a small boat" over a "passage in the reef only ten feet wide" with "jagged rocks" on each side. On reaching shore, they were "hauled up the cliff" to get to the town. It was "beautiful" and "very exciting," said Mrs. Jack, who "almost fainted" but was not afraid.

They had planned to set out on horseback for Jerusalem but Belle was so weak that Jack hired a carriage for her. The road, she said, was "sometimes jolting and rough but generally delightful." The people were "Russians mostly," who had left Jerusalem and were "on their way to catch the steamer at Joppa and who plodded along on foot, clogging the road" so that the Gardners' carriage horses "went at a walk."

Toward evening the weather "turned cold and bitter—a thunderstorm creeping over us" and then it was "a race down the hills, enveloped in darkness and the lightning flashing on the walls of Jerusalem."

The hotel in Jerusalem was "dirty, but the people kind and attentive—quite troubled at my being ill and wanting to do no end of things," Belle wrote. She was so weak that she could hardly stand, but every day, if only for a short time, she went to the Church of the Holy Sepulchre. "There I sat, alone, the church almost empty, but for the Greek pilgrims who came singly or in families.

"I watched them as they dragged themselves on their knees to the Holy Tomb . . . Then came the hour for vespers. The bell of the Latins was rung and their monks with lighted tapers and books formed a procession and were followed by a few well-dressed English-looking pilgrims, each also with a book and taper. They went to all the most holy spots, lingering for a short service at the most holy. From where I sat, as they wound among the different passages and up to Calvary, the chanting would almost die away at times and suddenly burst out as if quite near . . ."

On Ascension morning the Gardners took a carriage and "rode up to the Mount of Olives. On our way, a pretty girl suddenly handed me a rosebud," Belle wrote. "Everyone carried flowers. We rested under an old olive tree and read the Epistle and the Gospel for Ascension Day . . ."

Jack Gardner had been busy organizing a small army to travel in Palestine. There was still Bonicci, their courier from Nile journey days, and Jack also hired "old John, such an intense, good old Catholic," a cook, a head muleteer with four mule-drivers under him—eight horses, five mules and two donkeys to carry "bags, baggage and cooking utensils," tents included. Jack searched Jerusalem for a horse with an easy gait and found "a little chestnut mare" for Belle to ride. They left Jerusalem "over the Mount of Olives, the road by which David fled when Absalom rebelled."

Into her saddlebag went Belle's Bible and her prayerbook and when they stopped at noon, she read aloud the story of the good Samaritan. They were on the road to Jericho. Their tents were pitched just outside the walls of Jericho that night, and at five next morning they started for the Dead Sea.

"In the distance" the Dead Sea "looked like a Swiss lake

with its clear greens and blues. When they reached it, the Dead Sea was "the saddest, most desolate spot," with "whitened driftwood lining the shore." Belle and Jack, however, took "the most delicious bath," an event recorded in the diaries of both of them. Then, in "about an hour" they reached the banks of the Jordan, where they had lunch, "tormented by flies." The item about the flies was in Jack's record only.

Mrs. Jack drank from the River Jordan and filled a bottle with river water. This she would take home to keep as a sacred relic along with some desert sand from Egypt, which she had already collected in another bottle.

Mrs. Gardner found Bethlehem "a pretty town nestling in the hills—*the* hills over which shone the star." She "drank the waters of the well at Bethlehem" and ate "a dish of delicious sweets" a Syrian offered her. Goats were pastured on a hill behind the Gardners' tents and she drank goats' milk "hot" from the she-goat a little boy milked for her. The illness recurred, which seemed a mystery to everyone.

On the twenty-fourth of June the Gardners' Palestine journey ended. Again, Belle was ready to weep, this time at leaving scenes that had changed little in over a thousand years and which she had peopled with actors in Biblical history she knew so well. But Syria was "not disappointing after all" and "Tyre was the climax." Their tents were pitched on a height "overlooking the sea, the columns of old Tyre in the water" below, "the waves washing over them."

Damascus was to be the next stop; but Ahmet, one of the muleteers, rode ahead and brought back a letter from the consul telling of "real Asiatic cholera having appeared and the people leaving." Ahmet also brought back letters from America for the Gardners.

"Thank God, good news," Mrs. Jack wrote. Somehow, she had been feeling anxiety about the family at home.

They paused "on a hill over Damascus," to "breakfast and feast our eyes, then pluck up strength of mind and turn our backs," Mrs. Jack said, much disappointed to miss seeing the city. But Baalbek made up for this loss. They camped for the night in the grand courtyard of the Temple and when they left at four next morning it was still moonlight. Two days later, their tents were pitched under the cedars of Lebanon. "It was glorious to be under the shadow of these kingly trees and to smell from them the delicious fragrance," Belle wrote, looking about her for the last time at a place described in the Bible. In her diary she pressed a leaf and a small pink flower.

The Gardners reached Beirut at ten in the morning on the

twenty-eighth of June, to find that an Austrian Lloyd steamer was leaving at seven that night. "With some hurry," they "settled accounts and went on board." Their voyage to Smyrna was punctuated with cholera scares at every intermediate port, for the yellow flag was run up to indicate that they were to be quarantined. But each time, authorities decided there was no cholera aboard their ship. There had been a mysterious death on the ship and it seems possible that the authorities had their palms crossed with silver, perhaps by Austrian Lloyd representatives.

At Smyrna, the Gardners went ashore to await a steamer bound for Piraeus. Mrs. Gardner indulged in her favorite dessert, vanilla ice cream in "hot and dirty Smyrna. I was wretchedly—not seasick" she wrote, but she recovered quickly this time.

The "solid comfort" of the Hotel d'Angleterre in Athens was much appreciated but the early rising habit acquired in the Holy Land persisted. Getting up a little after five, Mrs. Jack put a roll of bread in her "pocket" then she and Jack set forth on foot to explore the modern and then the ancient city. At the Temple of Theseus they found "coffee tables in the open air, clustered around the ruins." Workers in the city were eating breakfast, so the Gardners sat down and ordered coffee to go with their roll of bread. They made friends in sign language, smiled at the dark, smiling mustachioed faces around them as they sat "between the pillars of Jupiter Olympus." Then they "rambled over the theater of Dionysus and sat in the old marble arm chairs that the old swells used." Those chairs, carved for the priests of Dionysus, delighted them.

There was another early breakfast at the Temple of Theseus among the workmen who now seemed like old friends. A day was spent on the Acropolis and another day, carriage-riding to the foot of Mount Pentelicus where horses were waiting. Mrs. Jack rode to the top of the mountains "straddle-legged" on a saddle "made of pieces of wood." These were companionable times for the Jack Gardners—on their own together with no crowd of retainers, no courier, no chattering guide.

A rough voyage brought them to Constantinople, "beautiful and very like New York," at least at a distance, Belle thought. But here, in a sense, this happy journey ended. "Jack went for letters" and "found the two terrible telegrams about poor Joe." Jack's brother Joseph Gardner had died on the night of June 11, at the age of forty-six. The news

62

reached them on the sixteenth of July. Joe's three boys, especially dear to Belle since their mother's death, were now fatherless and Mrs. Jack's anxiety about news from home seemed to have been a premonition.

In her Nile Journal, Belle had told of a visit to an American Presbyterian mission school. The schoolboys sang in Arabic, "There is a happy land, far, far away." This was "one of the hymns the dear boys sang those Beverly Sundays" when she had visited their father's summer home. "It quite startled and affected me," she said at the time. Now she wanted to go home to the boys and she continued her sightseeing with only half her heart.

Santa Sophia was disappointing. While riding in a carriage past the Sultan's summer palace, Belle was "obliged to put" her "parasol down" which seemed a "strange etiquette." The Sultan's treasure was "full of such diamonds, pearls, rubies and emeralds" as she had "dreamed of" but it was good to be traveling on—toward home. They listened to "music in the Volksgarten—Edward Strauss" in Vienna—and reached Paris by the middle of August.

Paris was a sadly changed city since the days of the Exposition in 1867. The Empress Eugénie was now in exile in England, Napoleon III was dead, and their palace of the Tuileries lay in ruins. Anyone was welcome to fragments of the palace who would carry them off and Worth, who had loved his lost empress, loaded wagons with statuary for the garden in his private home. He had seen Frenchmen shot down in the street in front of his rue de la Paix establishment and had brought the wounded inside in an attempt to save them. All that was over now, but he was more than grateful for foreign clients, Americans especially.

Mrs. Gardner was not in a mood to order gay clothes. Her oldest brother, David Stewart, had died just before she left America and now she grieved over the loss of her husband's brother Joe. But Worth made especially beautiful dresses in black, their distinction depending upon line. Mrs. Jack Gardner's black gowns were to be commented upon.

SEVEN

The Intellectual Mrs. Gardner

THE GARDNERS' first concern, on their return to Boston, was the welfare of their three orphaned nephews. Joe was fourteen, "of a supernormal sensitiveness, of nervous structure." [1] Amory was not quite twelve and Augustus, not yet ten. Their uncles, George Augustus Gardner and John Lowell Gardner, Jr., had been named in their father's will as their guardians. And as a result of family conference, they were "given" to the Jack Gardners because Belle was childless. She already loved and wanted them—this they knew.

Mrs. Gardner took her responsibility to her boys seriously. There were Boston matrons who thought of her as affected, frivolous, utterly devoted to a social life. It would have astonished them to know how John Jay Chapman, future Harvard classmate and traveling companion of the Gardner boys, thought of their Aunt Belle's discipline. She gave them "such training as one connects with the idea of a British nation," Chapman said. "It was a mixture of devotion and rigor." [2]

In summer, the Jack Gardners now lived at least part of the time in Beverly, where the late Joseph Gardner had bought a large estate soon after his wife's death. Horseback riding was an indispensable part of a gentleman's education and Aunt Belle rode every day with her three nephews, supervising their form and style. They were allowed only "a blanket and girth"—no saddle, no stirrups, so that they would develop a firm seat. Of course they were thrown occasionally and Amory remembered that once he "showed symptoms of scare" when he was "thrown rather hard." He was punished by being "left at home every day for a week when the rest of the family pranced forth." [3]

The three boys now lived in winter with the Jack Gardners on Beacon Street. Maud Howe Elliott remembered Mrs. Gardner "in the old Music Hall attending the Thursday afternoon concerts" given by the "Harvard Musical Association," forerunner of the Boston Symphony Orchestra. Mrs. Elliott (who was at this time Miss Howe) said that "the concert would be incomplete without [Mrs. Jack's] elegant figure, her expressive face as she glided quietly to her seat escorted by —to be exact—*escorting* three conspicuously well-dressed, very young tow-haired gentlemen, Mrs. Gardner's orphaned nephews." [4]

The boys went to Hopkinson's School in Boston where they slaved over Latin and Greek, as required by Harvard, but to the detriment of wider interests, their Aunt Belle felt sure. She began to read Dickens aloud to them once a week. When she finished *Pickwick Papers*, the boys asked for more, so she read them *Oliver Twist, Nicholas Nickleby, David Copperfield* and *A Tale of Two Cities*.

This reading aloud was a pleasure for all concerned. Mrs. Jack always loved the theater and eventually she asked a young actor, Leslie Buswell, to "read with her to improve her diction." She discovered that she had a beautiful speaking voice—which she cultivated as a singer practices scales.[5]

Confronted with the responsibility for "those brilliant boys," as Henry James was soon to call her nephews, Belle Gardner embarked upon a course of self-education. Attending lectures had always been a favorite indoor sport among Boston matrons but hitherto Mrs. Jack had scorned the pastime as unutterably dull. Now she tried on the intellectual life as she might try on a costume by Worth. To her amazement, she liked it. It was still the fashion for a woman to conceal her brains, if any, and Mrs. Jack sometimes hid her attainments all too well. But Professor Charles Eliot Norton, supremely gifted as an awakener, gave Isabella Gardner a new, if sometimes secret, world to live in.

Norton was now in his early fifties. He had been briefly in the East India trade, had lived in India, traveled in Egypt, Italy and France—always seeking out scholars, artists and writers to make lifelong friends of them, wherever he went. During two years in Rome, Norton began the study of Dante which was to become a consuming interest. But while abroad, his wife died in giving birth to her sixth child, and Norton came home to "Shady Hill" in Cambridge, Massachusetts. It was his cousin, President Charles Eliot of Harvard, who suggested that Norton lecture.

Norton's lectures were an immediate success, for he had great personal charm as well as scholarship. The public often occupied seats in his Harvard lecture room, which was always crowded, and when Mrs. Jack Gardner joined the circle, he soon noticed that she never missed a lecture. They met, and he was like no one who had ever crossed her path before. In all probability, knowing her was an equally novel experience for the professor. Their friendship lasted until his death.

Charles Eliot Norton suggested to Mrs. Jack that she collect something other than Worth gowns, bazaar bracelets or pearls. His idea was that she should buy rare books and manuscripts and he showed her his collection of various editions of Dante that he had picked up in Italy. Isabella, the daughter of a Scottish merchant, had a sense of cash value, although she hardly realized it as yet, and she began collecting, under Professor Norton's direction. Although aware that her purchasing power was far greater than his own, Norton rejoiced when she bought something he would have liked to have for himself. He took especial pride in her volumes of Dante, some of them without duplicate in the United States.

In 1879, Mrs. Jack was faced with a dilemma in regard to the education of her nephews. Joe was seventeen and ready for Harvard, which was all well and good. But Amory, at fifteen, was also prepared, being blessed with total recall. He was too young for college, his Aunt Belle decided, and she decreed a year of music, German and French. Perhaps to cheer a disappointed Amory, the Gardners decided to take him abroad—with his younger brother Gus for company. On March 28 they reached England, only "Gussie" being with them because Amory had stayed behind to take his Harvard entrance examinations. He passed brilliantly and joined his aunt and uncle in London.

Mr. and Mrs. Henry Adams were in London, and "Clover," as Marian Adams was always called, went to see Mrs. Jack Gardner. She wrote her father, Dr. William Hooper of Beverly, who knew the Gardners and their nephews well, being summertime neighbors. The Gardners "are all so fascinated with London that they've been here ever since they landed and don't know when to leave," [6] Mrs. Adams said on Sunday, July 13.

The following evening Mrs. Adams was at the Grosvenor Gallery; "two long rooms perhaps a hundred feet by fifty, panelled with crimson brocade." The gallery was "that refuge of the pre-Raphaelites," for whom Mrs. Adams cared little, and she thought the exhibit contained "many shocking daubs, with now and then one to redeem the rest. Mrs. Jack Gardner was there and we had some twenty minutes side by side in the vestibule waiting for our respective broughams."

Ruskin had just attacked James McNeill Whistler, the expatriate American artist, whom he accused of "flinging a paint pot in the face of the public." Mrs. Adams and Mrs. Gardner had both come to see Whistler's portrait of Connie Gilchrist. But only Mrs. Adams thought Ruskin had been right about Whistler.

Connie Gilchrist was an American dancer whose various marriages had been food for gossip in New York. "Connie has a red flannel vest reaching to her hips, a handkerchief, bag and satin boots with high Louis XV heels; is jumping rope with red handles. Any patient at Worcester who perpetrated such a joke would be kept in a cage for life," Marian Adams said, describing the portrait.[7]

Apparently, Mrs. Jack said nothing. But as an amateur artist she could not help noticing that the red jump-rope handles picked up the color of Connie's vest. The young dancer, although far from beautiful, had an impudent, devil-may-care look that was appealing. Whistler had not been throwing paint around and even Mrs. Adams's objections had all been leveled at Connie's clothes. Mrs. Jack liked eye-catching garments.

Mrs. Adams was introduced to Whistler at Lady Lindsay's party. She found him "more mad away from his paint pots than near them." Mrs. Jack also met him—and liked him. When she was again in London, they became friends.

A Little Note in Yellow, Whistler was to call his pastel portrait sketch of Mrs. Gardner. She bought of him, at the same time, his *Violet Note*, a nude sketch of his model, Lyse Vazaeti. The two pastels were alike in size, so that eventually the gossips had it that Whistler had painted Mrs. Jack in the nude. Enjoying the joke, she hung the two sketches side by side at Fenway Court.

Lady Lindsay, who gave the party for Whistler and other artists, was "a young and not pretty woman," according to Clover Adams. She was a niece of Baron Rothschild; her husband, Sir Coutts Lindsay of Balcarres, was an artist, and she owned the Grosvenor Galleries. She made the opening of an exhibition a social event of the London season—or a "smash" as Henry James described it. And Mrs. Jack Gardner went to Lady Lindsay's party "on the arm" of Henry James.

In all probability Mrs. Jack and James had met before— perhaps in Cambridge, through Norton. In any case, James now remembered "those agreeable days in London and Paris —those talks and walks and drives and dinners—with a tenderness which the past, directly it recedes a little, always awakens in my sensitive soul but which, in this case is altogether of exceptional softness. All those were delightful hours

—not only pleasures but treasures of memory . . ." [8] he told her.

James proceeded in his best embroidered style for page after page. Brought up among businessmen and their associates, married into a family of merchant princes, Isabella Gardner had little or no experience of flattery, elegantly administered by a man of letters. At first, she liked it altogether too well.

The Jack Gardners broke away from London in August and took the nephews on a tour of English cathedrals. Reporting proudly to his father, Jack Gardner said that the boys were "very good and intelligent and interested in the things they saw. What Amory doesn't know about ecclesiastic architecture isn't worth knowing. But he knew more about it when he started than most people do when they are through."

Jack had noticed in the London papers that "iron in America had begun to advance." He had borrowed some money to invest in the iron industry before he left home, and now "I am much obliged to you for renewing my notes," he told his father. "Before long we may get profitably out of our speculation and I shall be able to reduce my indebtedness." But he did not believe he would buy a boat. Jack had been "pricing steam-launches and found on looking into them that it was too expensive and impracticable to get even a small one." [9]

The Gardners next took their nephews on a tour of French cathedrals. Gus had a good time and Amory applied himself to a study of French Gothic. He "had a phenomenal memory and the conscience of an anchorite," his future classmate, John Jay Chapman was to say of him. "He was the victim of his memory and of his conscience; and in his later years had to be humored when he talked; you could not detrack him; you had to let him unwind."

Guidebook in hand, Mrs. Gardner attended to her French sightseeing, but once in Paris, the conscientious Aunt Belle gave way to the frivolous Mrs. Jack. Styles were changing much more rapidly. The ever-plastic female figure must now be molded into a "straight-front corset" but in the rear a lady protruded with an increasingly sizable bustle. Girls who felt naked when they dropped their hoops developed into matrons who, at least for a while, would consider it indecent to go around without wearing a sort of pincushion behind. Worth was the man to see about all this. He was still the leading Paris dressmaker.

The Henry Adamses were also in Paris and on September 21, 1879, Clover Adams wrote her father. "Henry and I were

68

presented in great form to the great Mr. Worth by Mrs. Gardner. Mr. Worth ordered one of his young women to parade in a gown designed for the Grand Duchess of Würtemburg" and Mrs. Adams "so far yielded to Henry's wishes as to order a duplicate gown in dark green merino trimmed with black." Worth still had plenty of titled clients but it was "a compatriot" whom Clover Adams and Mrs. Jack watched "hefting the silks to be sure he was getting his money's worth" for his "fat wife." They imagined he was "a prosperous grocer from Iowa." The prices were actually quite as reasonable as dressmakers' prices in Boston, both ladies agreed.[10]

Mrs. Jack had taken good care of her girlish figure, eating little at Belshazzar feasts she and her husband were bidden to, and proceeding with caution at ladies' luncheons which seemed to be contests between cooks to see which of them could use the most whipped cream. Worth was genuinely glad to see her, complimented her figure, and without appearing to notice that she was older, suggested something sophisticated in ball gowns. Belle was now thirty-nine.

As for Worth, himself, he had grown still heavier but his puce-colored dressing gown concealed this to a certain extent. "Puce," or flea-color, was all the rage. Worth had twin black spaniels, each occupying a green velvet chair, in the room where he received the Bostonians.

Henry James was in Paris. He had just finished his "little book on Hawthorne," he said, and he was in a mood to celebrate. He went with the Gardners and the Adamses to an open-air restaurant and then to the Cirque, to see the "angelic blonde," Mademoiselle Jutan. They finished their evening with ices on the boulevard.

James remembered "the *plaisirs* and the gingerbread at St. Cloud" the next time he wrote to Mrs. Jack. She had "the little Hawthorne" by this time and had pleased him by saying she liked it. "Do you remember the day it was finished?" he asked—a question he knew was rhetorical. He had "a happy faith that we shall Europeanize together again in the future," he told her. "But doubtless before that we shall Americanize as I hold fast to my design of going home . . .

"Look out for my next novel; it will immortalize you," James promised.[11]

The Gardners reached home long before the Adamses. They hastened to Beverly to enjoy the last of the season and there Dr. William Hooper met Mrs. Gardner. He wrote to his daughter, Clover Adams, telling her to be sure to buy herself one of those "skin-tight costumes of English stockinette" that Mrs. Jack looked so well in. Mrs. Jack had a way with doctors, it would seem. Dr. Jacob Bigelow, her faithful admirer, had died in January, 1879, but his son William Sturgis Bigelow—also a doctor, even though he never practiced—joined Mrs. Gardner's circle of younger men.

"The dances of the upper ten" during the winter of 1880 "are the waltz (danced in quick time) the polka and the heel and toe polka with now and then a Lancers as a sop to the Cerberi, whose dancing days are supposed to be over.

"The German is simply a combination of figures which allows each couple dancing it a turn every time and permits them to choose other partners and give favors—but only the three round dances alluded to are permitted." So explained *Andrews' American Queen,* one of the first society papers. "The waltz done in quick time" was such a favorite that eventually it became "The Boston"—the joy of the younger generation. It was the joy of Mrs. Jack, who danced with her Harvard nephews and their friends, calmly taking her place among their generation. She was gay; she was fun—only the women made remarks about her age.

Henry James made good his promise to Americanize with Mrs. Gardner. It was early November, as he recalled it, "that I paid you that little visit . . . in the sweet, sunny American autumn with just a little growl of approaching winter in it. I remember the sea, the woods, the color of the rocks and the sound of the waves; also the color of your sofas and ottomans and the sound of your conversation . . ."

A few weeks later, James was in New York, writing to Mrs. Gardner about "a pleasant feast with three lovely ladies without their lords." In this daringly unconventional situation, "the ladies were charming," he said, "but what made the most impression on me was that we talked of you—they had heard that you were so original. I gave a sketch with a few original touches—then they sighed and said to each other, 'Ah, if we only knew how to be like that!' " [12]

Henry James was hoping at the moment to take up his writing career in New York. But he had been socially successful in London, a charming bachelor willing to pay court to homely ladies provided there were no danger to his state of bachelorhood. Men liked him—he belonged to a good London club and lodgings and service were within his means abroad. New York, with its hustle and its newly-rich, was a disappointment on all counts.

It was at the end of January, 1882, that James received

news of his mother's fatal illness. He tried in vain to reach Boston on the night train from New York but arrived in Cambridge too late for "a last farewell."

"I thank you for your tender little note," James wrote to Mrs. Gardner. He was much touched by it, having been "passionately attached" to his mother. He now took "bare and ugly rooms" on Mt. Vernon Street, walked every morning across Boston Common to the Parker House for breakfast, and then tried to get on with his work. There had been one thing commendable about New York—the theaters. James decided to write for the stage. He sat writing till three or four o'clock in the afternoon and then, time and again, he walked down Beacon Hill in the winter darkness and called at 152 Beacon Street.

Henry James would find Mrs. Jack Gardner sitting behind her tea-table, the tea urn steaming gently over its alcohol lamp. There would be thin-sliced bread delicately spread with butter, English style, cakes, French style—and conversation with Mrs. Jack, very American.

James was writing a dramatized version of *Daisy Miller*, by far his most popular novel to date. He knew that his work brought him more criticism than praise in America—although it is to be hoped that he was mercifully unaware of a remark by Clover Adams that went the rounds. "It's not that he 'bites off more than he can chaw,' but that he 'chaws more than he bites off,'" she said.[13] Mrs. Gardner made no such remark but gave James the praise he craved.

If he would read her his play, she could hear it undisturbed in her private sitting room upstairs, she told him. There would be a fire in the grate in the "boudoir"—she would instruct the butler to say she was not at home.

"I think with extraordinary tenderness of those two pretty little evenings when I read you my play," James wrote several months later, when he was back in England. "They make a charming picture in my mind and the memory of them appeals to all that is *raffiné* in my constitution. Drop a tear—a diminutive tear (as *your* tears must be—small but beautifully shaped pearls) upon the fact that my drama is not after all to be brought out in New York (at least for the present). I had a fundamental disagreement with the manager just before sailing. It is possible it may see the light here—I am to read it to the people of the St. James Theatre next week. *Please don't speak of this*.

"London seems big and black and horrible and delightful —Boston seems only the last named. You indeed could make

71

it horrible for me if you chose and you could also make it big; but I doubt if you could make it black. It would be a fair and glittering horror of icicles and white fur . . ." [14]

James had tried to say goodbye to Mrs. Gardner on his last day in Boston but found that she was still in New York. He pictured her as "contributing the harmony of your presence and the melodies of your toilet to the din of Wagnerian fiddles and the crash of Teutonic cymbals . . ." [15]

Mrs. Jack had listened with profound attention when James talked to her about his work. She had praised his play when he was at a low ebb and needed to be reassured. Later, he was to say that she overdid the rapt attention act.

Henry James was Mrs. Gardner's first literary lion. It had been perfectly safe for her to flirt with him, for he was mortally afraid of being seriously involved with a woman. His gallantries were understood by his generation and his various "dear lady" friends soon found that he would use even more adjectives getting out of an entanglement than into one.

Mrs. Gardner's next literary lion was not safe. But she had the joy of considering herself his inspiration. He gave her the hand-written manuscript of his first novel and she wrapped it in a lavender silk envelope brocaded with pink roses, lined with gold-colored silk and fastened with three silver buckles. His letters to her she tied in packets with ribbon, first cutting away and destroying whole pages which none but she must read. He was F. Marion Crawford, American novelist born and brought up in Italy.

Henry James, writing to William Dean Howells, bemoaned his fate. "I am surrounded by the social desolation of Boston," he said. "The one feature here is Mrs. Jack Gardner's flirtation with F. Marion Crawford, the American novelist of the future . . ." [16]

EIGHT

"Chandeliering"

CRAWFORD WAS twenty-seven years old when he arrived in the United States in 1881. His mother, the former Louisa Ward of New York, had been an heiress; but her fortune was now almost gone as a result of speculation on the part of an uncle, a cousin—and her brother Sam Ward, "King of the Lobby" in Washington. She still referred to her son Francis Marion as "the Boy" and she had borrowed more than two thousand dollars to pay his debts in Rome and send him to America. As a last resort, Louisa was turning to her sister, Julia Ward Howe, and her brother Sam to see if, between them, they could induce Frank to earn a living.[1]

The twenty-seven-year-old boy was not at all worried. He had returned to his mother's home in Rome after working briefly for the *Indian Herald* in Allahabad—the first serious job he had ever attempted in his life. A quarrel with the native proprietor of his paper had injured his pride so that he quit his job. But he knew a young American heiress who was going to marry him, he felt sure. This would solve all his problems.

Frank had met Mary Perkins for the first time in Rome when she was five years old. Mary came with her parents to a birthday party of his and he threw her doll out of a high window in the palazzo where he lived. This would seem an inauspicious beginning, but it did not bother Frank Crawford. He subsequently wrote a story about it, called "The Doll's Ghost" and recent encounters with Mary convinced him that she was in love with him.

Crawford's "vanity was of the simplest," wrote his cousin Maud Howe. "He would pose before a mirror quite openly, rejoicing in his strength and beauty like any other animal. He was six feet tall and perfectly proportioned."[2] His mother, in a letter to him, referred to his "beauteous head" and his "luminous look."

Although the son of American parents, Francis Marion Crawford was born in Bagni di Lucca, Tuscany. His father was Thomas Crawford, famous sculptor in his day, and Frank was three years old when his father died. Frank was brought up in Rome with only brief, unhappy experiences of schooling in England, Germany and the United States. Italian was his first language and he spoke English with a trace of foreign accent which was typical, his sister "Mimoli" said, of the expatriate child. She thought it set such people apart so that they felt slightly alien when they went to America—that strange country which their parents insisted on calling home.

Frank "had a most imperious temper combined with a stubborn resolve to do nothing for himself that other people could possibly be coerced into doing for him." This was his sister's opinion. She said she spent years "picking up his toys and handing them back to him." [3]

Crawford never had any doubt about his charm for women. To be sure, his first love affair had been unhappy. But that was before he was twenty; the girl was older, and her family arranged a marriage for her to a titled Italian. Frank understood this. Marriages were always a matter of arrangement among the upper classes in Italy. Very early in his life he learned that there were girls with whom arrangements could be made where marriage was not part of the bargain.

Applying his Italian point of view to the American situation, Frank Crawford first visited his Uncle Sam in New York for a while, then his Aunt Julia in Boston or Newport. Finally, he went around to see Thomas Handasyd Perkins, Jr., wealthy Boston merchant, to ask for his daughter Mary's hand in marriage.

"If Mary wants to marry you, Mr. Crawford, I have no objection," Mr. Perkins was reported as saying. Frank considered the matter settled, although Mary was traveling abroad and had not, apparently been recently consulted.

Frank relaxed. There was much in America that he deplored but it did not seem to concern him. For example, a young man was supposed to occupy himself gainfully even though he might have inherited wealth. Young men of wealth who merely played around were few, at least in Boston, and were not applauded. The pursuit of an heiress was not considered a sufficiently honorable occupation. Frank's cousin Maud Howe explained this, and his Aunt Julia lectured. His Uncle Sam Ward tried to get him a job.

Frank spent his first summer, or what remained of it, at his Aunt Julia's comfortable but old-fashioned house at Newport. "Oak Glen" was too far from the Casino and the huge brown-shingled "cottages" of the wealthy to be much fun. But as a charming young bachelor at a fashionable resort full of girls, Frank had no difficulty in getting invitations. There was competition on weekends when young men, so unaccountably employed, came to Newport from Boston and New York. But Frank could put up with that—he had his Mary.

When the Newport cottages closed and Aunt Julia stayed on, industriously writing articles to augment her income, Frank left and went to New York. His Uncle Sam was indignant because his sister and his niece Maud had been left without their "protector." But Mary Perkins was coming home, and Frank, the impatient suitor, explained that he must be in New York to meet her. He arrived the day her ship, the *Serbia*, left Queenstown.

"I have blown new life into Frank," his uncle wrote. Sam Ward had gotten some assignments from editor friends of his and had made Frank "work six hours at my room yesterday, during which he knocked off two articles for *The Critic*, both excellent, which I delievered this A.M." An interview had been arranged for Frank with Hurlbert of the *World*.

Sam Ward, a master of persuasion himself, had succumbed to his nephew's charm. "He is indolent but not lazy and if he had a little more push would make quite a man . . ." Sam thought. He had been told about Frank's "sentimental entanglement" but felt less than confident of the outcome. It was to be "tied or untied when the *Serbia* arrives. But for that I could drive him well to success . . ." [4]

Frank Crawford was on the Cunard dock, handsome and impatient when the *Serbia* came in. He saw Mary Perkins at the rail—but she was not looking for any ardent young suitor ashore. She was with another man, a young surgeon, Dr. Frank Watson, of Boston, to whom, either now or very shortly she was engaged. Her behavior toward Francis Marion Crawford was easily explained. It had been nothing more than a "flirtation."

Crawford was profoundly humiliated. What he did was his own affair, but his cousin Maud Howe wrote that "the next day Marion returned to our house a sick man. He stayed in bed for twenty-four hours. He never slept nor touched food or drink . . . Severe pains wracked his poor body and a great swelling developed on his back." Frank refused to see a doctor and Maud said that she was "his only nurse." He would not let her see the "swelling" but had her "apply the cold bandages over his sleeping garment." [5]

Later, Maud's older sister, Florence, tried to explain "the meaning of the half-playful, usually quite harmless flirtations" of American girls. She said that foreigners used the word in a graver sense than we do and misjudged American flirtations, which were not really a dangerous pastime. Frank neither understood nor believed a word of this.[6]

It was decided that the Boston home of his Aunt Julia would be the best place for Frank. Plain living and high thinking were the rule there and since a literary career seemed to be the only line he was in any way fitted for, he would find plenty of encouragement.

In April, 1881, Sam Ward bought the "Rollins Morse house" and gave it to his sister Julia—Number 241 Beacon Street. His Wall Street ventures were going well and it was not until reverses followed that she discovered that the gift was heavily mortgaged. She loved the house and somehow, by means of lectures and writing, she managed to hang onto it. Number 241 became as famous, in its very different way, as Mrs. Gardner's Number 152 Beacon Street.

Mrs. Gardner's younger and only remaining brother, James, died on April 15, 1881. He would have been twenty-three the following September. James had never married, nor had his brother David, so that Isabella was now her father's only surviving child. Mrs. Jack would never be a "Bonanzaine," as wives and daughters whose fortunes came from gold-mining ventures were called—but she now had prospects of inheriting a comfortable fortune. Officially in mourning and also genuinely grieved, Isabella spent a quiet summer.

In the autumn, new neighbors, the Howes, moved into 241 Beacon Street. Maud called on Mrs. Gardner, bringing a cousin to meet her. Maud Howe was one of the great beauties of her time and Mrs. Gardner was always attracted to beauty. The cousin was Frank Crawford—even handsomer than Maud; his "complexion like a child's . . ."

Frank was well aware of Mrs. Jack's admiring glance. Of course admiration and rapt attention were Mrs. Jack's methods of harmless flirtation, but this seemed not to have occurred to F. Marion. He agreed all too completely with her apparent estimate of him and he needed to prove to himself, now that he had lost Mary Perkins, that he was irresistible.[7]

Mrs. Jack's situation seemed perfectly clear to Frank. She had a husband who was hardly ever in evidence, who spent his days at his office, lunched and often dined at his club. It was the life of a serious American businessman, but to Frank Crawford it added up to neglect. Mrs. Jack must be lonely and starved for affection and her flirtatious manner could be nothing short of an invitation to an affair. In Italy, affairs

76

with married women were not frowned upon if carried on with discretion. The only sin was in being caught.

Music ought to be a sure avenue of approach, for Mrs. Gardner was said to be musical. During the previous summer Crawford had studied voice with George Henschel, first conductor of the Boston Symphony Orchestra. So Frank would stand at the piano at his Aunt Julia's, "with head thrown back" and sing:

> *"Once I loved a maiden fair*
> *But she did deceive me . . ."* [8]

It seemed strange to him that Mrs. Gardner did not ask him to sing at her house.

Frank said he was studying for a career in opera and it was true that he had a beautiful, powerful voice. But he could not stay on key and eventually even his teacher despaired of him. His Aunt Julia, who in her girlhood had a fine voice and perfect pitch, felt humiliated. And Mrs. Jack, who had an ear for music, suggested that there were careers other than grand opera.

Frank had better luck at dances. He observed that Jack Gardner escorted his wife to many a German and that the large bouquet she carried was his gift. But Mrs. Jack carried other bouquets from other men all at the same time, and a curious custom was explained which he never understood. A gentleman wrote a formal note to a lady, asking her to dance the German with him at the next party. This note he enclosed with flowers. If she had already promised to dance the German with someone else, she declined but kept the flowers and brought them along to the party, together with other bouquets she had received! If she were married, it was not expected that her husband would dance the German with her, but with some other lady, to whom he gave flowers. He gave his wife flowers too, "prudent husbands giving larger bouquets to their wives for the sake of domestic harmony." [9]

Jack Gardner danced a dutiful German with some matron he had known as a child. He was growing a little portly and after a quickstep waltz with Belle, he would be off to the card room where other men of his age had gathered. Jack was forty-four in November, 1881—not feeling old, but glad to settle down. Dowagers watched the dancing. Young matrons hoped for partners. Belle danced.

It was utterly confusing to a young man brought up in Rome. But Crawford soon discovered that Mrs. Jack Gardner would dance the German with him if he asked her first. To be sure, the flowers were exasperatingly expensive, but he thought he was making progress.

"Fashionable society was bestowing the significant epithet, 'Chandeliering,' on the practice of persons who make themselves the central ornament of the ballroom" by waltzing continually in the center of the floor. So said the Boston *Transcript* during the winter of 1881–1882. Mrs. Jack Gardner was seen "chandeliering" with Frank Crawford more often than with any other man. She wore a "Worth gown of white uncut velvet," [10] she loved the center of the stage—and so did he.

When winter came, Frank Crawford, who longed for Rome, described snow in Boston. "Horse-cars moved slowly along like immense white turtles ploughing their way through deep white sand. The sound of bells was muffled . . . and the scraping of the Irishmen's heavy spades on the pavement . . . followed by the regular fall of great shovelfuls . . . as they stacked the snow, sounded like the digging of a gigantic grave." [11] Sidewalks were spread with coal ashes to keep people from slipping on the ice. Coal furnaces were poked up and rooms grew chilly with coal-burning grates constantly to be replenished. One dreary winter afternoon, Frank discovered that Mrs. Gardner had no "day" when she was "at home." Mrs. Jack was at home whenever she pleased and to whom she pleased from about five in the afternoon until it was time to dress for dinner.

Sometimes Crawford found others in Mrs. Jack's parlor. His cousin Maud went there often and that American, Henry James, with his British-cut clothes. Sometimes a young girl would be sent to a window seat with a huge album of foreign photographs to show a young man. The book made an excuse for sitting close together, and Frank saw, with what he thought was perfect understanding, that Mrs. Jack was romantic. But there were comparatively few men callers during the daytime. Frank was often the only one.

To Crawford's surprise, he discovered that the apparently purely social Mrs. Gardner had studied Italian and was interested in Dante. He had already spoken French with her and told his Cousin Maud that her French was excellent. Now he knew what to do. He brought over his edition of Dante to compare with one of hers and she asked him to read a passage to her. His Italian was pure music and his speaking voice was deep and moving, even if he could not sing.

Belle decided that she would like to study Dante with Crawford and of course serious study should take place where there would be no interruptions. As she had done with Henry James, so she now did with F. Marion Crawford. She invited him to her private sitting room upstairs, telling the butler to say she was not at home. The "boudoir," as she liked to call it, was frivolous, with its walls of yellow silk, its French furnishings and low chairs beside the fire in the grate. She spent not "two pretty evenings"—as with James—but many hours with Crawford.

In all of Frank Crawford's experience, no lady had ever received him so intimately—without ulterior motives. He annotated the margin of his copy of Dante and hers. Passages which he would particularly enjoy explaining to her, he knew all too well how to find.

Meanwhile, Frank's family required bulletins of progress. "The future looks black," he had written his Uncle Sam in September, 1881. "I will work as a proof reader, or a farm hand, or I will go west and fight Indians rather than be dependent on anybody." He received a sympathetic reply and told his uncle that he was "ready to go into a business office —into yours if you are willing . . ." Although he was living with his Aunt Julla, free of charge, he needed pocket money —to buy flowers, for example. "I cannot live by writing articles but I can gain some reputation in that way and yet be going on with a regular employment . . . I compose everything I write before I put it down, so that the time needed for mere writing is very insignificant," Frank said.[12]

Sam Ward was at this time a Wall Street plunger. Generous-hearted and extremely fond of his nephew, he had to be warned not to spoil "the boy" by giving him money. But it could have occurred to him that Frank would be very little use in any business office if he were composing articles in his mind all day so as to have them ready for mere writing during some insignificant time or other, at night.

As the winter advanced, Frank's letters to his uncle began to cause concern. "I have been in a whirl of dinners and parties and concerts, seasoned with a certain amount of work, necessarily less in these days of the [social] season than at any other time," Frank said, in explanation of his having finished only two book reviews, both of the same book! His uncle summoned him to New York, to "dine with Thorndike," editor of the *North American Review*. Sam Ward was ever optimistic. He had arranged the interview "in the hope that it will be the beginning of a profitable career."

To his sister, Julia Ward Howe, Sam wrote reproachfully —"I always feel anxious when I hear that he [Frank] is going out a great deal, as he is naturally convivial and I fear that too much of the sensual will coarsen the fibre of his spirituality . . ." [13]

The Boston season was "short but merry, while it lasted," Crawford discovered. He was always trying to learn rules of etiquette such as governed Roman society, and some of his findings were curious. A lady "may go out with a man in a sleigh," but "couldn't possibly go with him on wheels—on the same road, same man, same everything except wheels," he wrote! [14]

Spring came and Mrs. Jack Gardner's shining black sleighs were put away. Her small, fast-trotting black horses were harnessed to a carriage and she took Frank Crawford riding.

All too soon, the Beacon Street houses were closed for the summer. Gone were the flowers that made Mrs. Gardner's bay window so bright. There were no lights in the drawing room at night. The Gardners went to Beverly, and Mrs. Howe went to Newport, taking Maud and Frank Crawford with her. Frank wrote long letters to Mrs. Gardner. "You make me think of summer days and flowers and wind-blown water and the happy rustle of spring leaves . . ."

Eventually, there was a letter written during the winter of 1883 with an enclosure to which he gave an earlier date. He told of his work—his plan to write "stirring tales of the Moslem conquest" of India. Belle Gardner had constantly encouraged him, earnestly assured him that he could be a novelist; and there were pages of this long letter which she kept. Pages were taken out, also, and destroyed. But the ending she could not bear to part with.

"Goodbye, dearest, till we meet again—and soon, I hope. This is not a goodbye at all, you know. There is only to be one goodbye between us, and I do not think it will be spoken aloud, nor written, for it will come when one of us two reaches the end, and it will be very long before that. Goodnight then, and sweet dreams. You have been long asleep for the day is almost breaking—while I say goodnight, dear." This was followed by a page entitled:

SONNET

My lady late within my chamber tarried
In the sweet dark vesture, all her fair hair flowing
In ripples o'er her shoulders she carried
Her beauty with such royal air, so sowing
Her path with jewels from love's treasure quarried
That I was awed and low before her bowing

Felt all my body by sweet love-strings harried
And all my soul with silent pleadings glowing.
Such love doth surely purify and hallow
The earthbound spirit from all common dross.
Such blossom, bursting forth in life's green fallow
Blooms heavenly red, as roses among moss.
The heart's sweet soil is not so scant or shallow
But it may feed a rose—or hold a cross.

Below these lines were the initials "F.M.C." and the date,
May 13, 1882.[15]

NINE

"No Goodbye"

ON FEBRUARY 11, 1882, Crawford wrote his Uncle Sam Ward that he would like to go to Japan, China and India the following summer. Frank thought that Uncle Sam might come along and they could collect information about Buddhism. "A lady and her husband think of going there and we might join forces and make a square party," Frank said.

But by March, Frank was in New York, "a good deal upset by some news from Boston," and his uncle devoted a whole day to soothing him. In his next letter, Uncle Sam spoke for the first time of a certain anxiety in the family. "I don't know what will be the outcome of his [Marion's] present *affaire du* [sic] *coeur*. It seems to stimulate him to good effort. But is the stimulus a healthy one? Can he work better in Boston than here?" Crawford was not getting along well with Jack Gardner, Sam Ward's awareness of this being expressed in a letter written when Crawford seemed to be getting on better.[1]

Frank himself knew that he and Mrs. Gardner were being talked about, and, dating his letter March 26, 1882, he told his mother, "If you hear rumors of my attachment to a certain married lady, do not be distressed. She has been a good friend to me in trouble and is one of the purest and best women living —in spite of the slandering tongues of petty Boston . . ."[2]

Frank Crawford and his uncle lunched together at the Brevoort at about this time. Their guest was George Brett, who had been "in the retail shop of Macmillan's" but had now moved into the editorial department. Frank told the story of Mr. Jacobs, the diamond merchant of Simla, whom he had encountered during his stay in Allahabad. "You must make this into a novel," Brett remembered saying. And so *Mr. Isaacs*, F. Marion Crawford's first novel, was conceived. Afterwards, Uncle Sam Ward remembered that he himself was the one who suggested the subject. He may very well have directed the conversation. As usual, the whole family was mobilized to get "the Boy" to work.

The Howes went to Oak Glen as usual. "In front of our house was a small enclosure, surrounded by a thick hedge of cedar that screened the interior from the road. A tall nut tree shaded the place," Maud Howe explained. Her mother called it the "Green Parlor." There was a rustic seat at the foot of the tree; a deal table was brought out and here F. Marion Crawford "wrote the book that was to make his reputation. . . . He used a large pad so that the wind should not blow away the sheet he was writing on. Day after day, he sat in the Green Parlor, under the nut tree, writing and writing." [8]

Frank Crawford finished page 202 of minute handwriting on various kinds of paper. Eventually he printed THE END in large block letters, wrote "F. Marion Crawford" and the date, June 15, 1882. Then he took his manuscript to New York and read it to his Uncle Sam, who was delighted with it. They added a title page as follows:

Mr. Isaacs
A tale of Modern India
by
F. Marion Crawford
18 Clinton Place, New York
U. S. America

"Note to publisher. The writer will [be] ready to expunge any expression considered too offensive to an English public in case the ms is accepted." [4]

"Marion Crawford sent off his novel to London to undergo the Macmillan ordeal," Sam wrote to Maud Howe on June 28, 1882. "He is not sanguine. I am." [5]

After amusing himself in New York for a bit, Frank went back to his Aunt Julia's, where he began his second novel, *Dr. Claudius*. It was to include a character affectionately and flatteringly reminiscent of his Uncle Sam Ward. But around the middle of July, Frank fell ill. "Marion has a bilious sore throat," his Aunt Julia told her daughter, Maud, "which I attribute to his great imprudence about draughts of air and partly to his having the key to the wine cellar in his possession." A week later, Frank made his own report to his uncle.

"The doctor says it is not liver or any form of similar trouble but an elaborate cold, which has produced a soreness in the mouth so severe that I have lived on liquids entirely . . ."

On the twenty-first of August, Sam Ward wrote joyfully to his sister Julia. "Hurrah for Marion! Macmillan has accepted

Mr. Isaacs . . . It goes straight to press and will appear simultaneously here and in London. I telegraphed Marion, directly I got the news . . ."

The Macmillan telegram was treasured by Mrs. Gardner, along with the original manuscript of *Mr. Isaacs*, which Frank gave her. She also kept the fragment of a letter of Frank's, concerning this first novel, which was published in America the following December. "I think of it as someone else's work; as indeed it is, love, for without you, I should never have finished it."

In Beverly Mrs. Gardner had "a little cabin-boudoir" which Henry James remembered. He hoped she would be lonely there, he wrote—and would read his latest novel.

Frank Crawford and his cousin Maud made a visit to Beverly in August, 1882, and Frank observed that Jack Gardner spent most of his summer days at his office in Boston, his nights at his club, usually coming out to Beverly only on weekends. How would it be possible for a man already so wealthy to be so devoted to business!

"I have not heard from Marion but twice since he got to Beverly and he owes me three letters," Sam Ward complained to Maud, who, it would seem, had gone back to Newport. "The love of pleasure makes all men selfish and I fear he is no exception . . . Yet I have constantly sent him books and magazines which remain unacknowledged."

Finally, Frank wrote his uncle as much as he thought Uncle Sam ought to know about Beverly. "The life here is everything a man could desire to nurture body and soul. I bathe often twice a day, generally row several miles on the bay and in the afternoon I ride with Mrs. Gardner. I need very little sleep here, and so in the morning hours I have done a good deal of writing. *Dr. Claudius* progresses and Mrs. G. thinks the work better and more highly finished than *Mr. Isaacs*, tho' not so striking as yet. . . ." [6]

To be the inspiration for a young novelist was exciting, but there were too many inquisitive Beverly neighbors to watch the process. Little Eliza Gardner was now Mrs. Frank Skinner, prissy to a degree, a member of the Beverly summer crowd but not necessarily a popular one. She spread gossip as Mrs. Jack was eventually to discover, and the stories grew until Henry James wrote to William Dean Howells, "Crawford appears to act his novels as well as write them."

Mrs. Jack could not stand the sight of a fat man and Frank was overweight. She particularly disliked overindulgence in wine, which she personally did not care for. By September, Frank had "grown as thin as a rail with temperance and exercise," [7] his relatives observed. He had also finished *Dr. Claudius*. Although his uncle predicted that it would be a great success, he thought the plot needed to be "quickened by some such cataclysm as we thought of." It is hard to imagine how the plot could have been any sillier than it finally turned out to be—whether "quickened" or otherwise. However, it pleased the public taste for sugar-coated nonsense.

Mrs. Jack Gardner was now a collector of items concerning Frank Crawford, for he gave her the manuscript of this second novel, and she cherished a letter to him from Thomas Bailey Aldrich. "If you have anything as admirable as your admirable *Mr. Isaacs* I should greatly like to print it in the *Atlantic Monthly*," Aldrich wrote. "I am in want of a serial story, or a series of short stories for the coming year. Would it suit your convenience to call to confer with me on the subject?" [8]

Frank went to work at once on *A Roman Singer*. It was to be one of the best things he ever wrote, and he dashed it off at white heat, payment on receipt of manuscript being part of his contract with the *Atlantic Monthly*.

In a novel as yet unwritten, *The American Politician*, he described spring in Boston. "The Public Garden is a carpet of bright flowers and on the walls of Beacon Street the great creepers have burst in blossom and are stretching long shoots over brownstone and iron balconies. There is a smell of violets and flowers in the air and down on the little pond the swan-shaped boats are paddling about with their cargoes of merry children and calico nursery maids while Irish boys look on from the banks and throw pebbles when the policemen are not looking, wishing they had the spare coin necessary to embark for a ten minutes' voyage on the mimic sea." [9]

Talk of a trip to the Orient was being revived. Frank Crawford's sister Mimoli had married Hugh Fraser, a British diplomat now in Japan. His tour of duty there would soon be over and it was Maud Howe's perfectly logical idea that she and her mother should visit Japan while they could be guests at the embassy. Mrs. Jack Gardner would go with them, cheerfully paying the bills. F. Marion Crawford was to be a member of the party.

Then, without warning, there came a letter to Maud from her mother. It was headed 241 Beacon Street and dated April 7, 1883. "You are not, darling, to say one word about Marion's departure. I will explain the reasons why. He has determined to go to his mother's. The other party will wish him to go to Japan. He had his reasons for wishing to keep very quiet about his movements. I am thankful that he has decided as he has. Cannot say any more on paper. *Mum's* the word." Next day, Mrs. Howe had further confidential news. "Marion has decided to sail for Italy in the *Florio* steamer of May 12. I have had some worriment about him but am very glad the Japan trip has been given up, at least by him." [10]

On April 16, 1883 Frank wrote his uncle, who had gone rather precipitately to London because of an unhappy turn in his stock-market dealings. "First of all, let me tell you that I have delayed my departure until some time in May. The Gardners will go to Japan, and I go to Rome. The resolve was made hastily, and the sudden execution of it turned out impossible, but it is now all quite settled. . . . I cannot by letter enter into details but I will ask you not to mention my plans to Madame, if you write to her, as you sometimes do write. There is a time in a man's life when certain things must stop and I think the time has come. Help me, dear uncle and father —and keep my counsel." [11]

The Howe journals indicate that Jack Gardner had not been planning to go to the Orient with his wife. Mrs. Howe expressed regret on Maud's account and relief on her own part, that now she would not need to go to the Far East to chaperone a romantic lady, aged forty-three, and her nephew, not quite twenty-nine.

Maud Howe described her cousin's last evening in Boston. Proofs for *A Roman Singer* had arrived on the afternoon of May 12. No one paid any attention to them until night, when Maud was "drafted to help."

"We sat beside the soft coal fire in the library with the pile of corrected proof sheets mounting higher and higher. There had been company at dinner. Marion was in evening dress with a red rose in his buttonhole. Midnight came and passed, the gray of dawn found us finishing the task. There was a hurried breakfast by gaslight and then Crawford and my brother Henry Marion Howe carried his belongings to the waiting hack and drove off to the Cunard docks in East Boston." [2]

Among the belongings was "the watch and case" Mrs. Gardner had given Frank. Among the letters from him which she kept were these lines, torn from a larger sheet: "I am rambling and talking nonsense when I had just sworn I would not. So I close this worthless note. It takes tenderest greetings from him whose only worth is that he loved you so long and so dearly." But this letter was written either in New York or

Italy long afterwards. In 1883, Crawford departed with "no goodbye." [13]

Jack Gardner's part in the situation is entirely a matter of conjecture. He had apparently never objected to any of his wife's previous dancing partners. They saved him the trouble of having to dance too much himself. The extravagant compliments men paid to her were nothing but gallantries, as he knew perfectly well. There would always be those who addressed Belle as "Dear Lady" and wrote her a lot of nonsense.

Crawford had been different. A man of no occupation, he was always underfoot. In exasperation, but also in good faith, Jack Gardner offered him a job of writing "on the political economy of railroads." Plenty of material would be made available at offices down on State Street, where Frank could work from nine to five or later, like anyone else. To show the Howes that he was *"aux mieux* with Jack Gardner," Frank told them all about this, but never took it seriously for a moment.

The reason for the secrecy of Crawford's departure is understandable. He wanted to avoid a scene. But "the resolve was made hastily," he wrote his Uncle Sam Ward, and there is a temptation to speculate upon the possibility of Jack Gardner's having a part in the haste. Frank's half-sister Margaret later wrote her own version of the story.

"Mrs. Gardner had a much-talked-of flirtation with Marion Crawford from which he escaped by following us to Rome. Maud was sent for and had to spend days at her [Mrs. Gardner's] house." [14]

People said that Belle Gardner had "a nervous breakdown." It was true that she talked to Maud, who sat "in the little low chair in the boudoir" and perhaps told her too much. It was to Maud that she wrote, "Dear, dear girl, how sweet and dear you were and always will be, I know . . ."

Then pride came to her aid. Her heart hardened, never to be worn on her sleeve again. She would play the flirtation game and take revenge upon the unwary. The invincible Mrs. Jack, laughing at gossip, denying nothing and doing as she pleased, was on the way to becoming a reality. Her husband —standing solemnly and solidly behind her—took out a forty-thousand-dollar letter of credit and carried her off alone with him to the Orient.

Book Two

ONE FIFTY-TWO
BEACON STREET

TEN

Cambodia for a Broken Heart

THE CARRIAGE THAT took the Gardners to the railroad
station in Boston was "followed by two others filled with
flowers, farewell offerings from Mrs. Gardner's admirers"—or
so it was said. This was no funeral cortege, however, although
it must have looked like one. Belle Gardner was very much
alive, for all her broken heart. The Gardners crossed the
American continent to San Francisco and embarked for Yokohama.

The death of her child and of her hopes for another had
been Belle's deepest grief. Jack had taken her away from familiar scenes. Now she had sustained an injury of a very different sort, but painful in the extreme. And Jack was standing
by her. "We are leading a perfect holiday life," [1] she wrote. It
was a good way to show gratitude—by seeming gay, the way
Jack liked his wife to be.

Sturgis Bigelow was in Yokohama. Gallantries from Bigelow were as harmless as those from his father, Belle's doctor,
had been, or from Henry James. Bigelow, like James, was a
confirmed bachelor, ready to escape at a hint of seriousness.
He "always carried local color around with him," Belle wrote,
on discovering that Bigelow was now wearing Japanese costume.

The young man, studying to become a Buddhist, wrote notes
to Mrs. Gardner in his new Japanese manner, to the effect
that his "heart was a handful of dust" when other engagements prevented him from taking her to the "choicest shops
and shrines." When they went shopping together, Belle loved
to "kick off her shoes . . . and sprawl in stocking feet." It was
a "bewitching life." She was "wild with excitement."

News from home was good. The nephews, whom the Gardners missed the most, were well and happy. Joe was having
himself fitted for a cadet uniform. He wrote twenty-page letters to his Aunt Belle. At the Hasty Pudding show at Harvard,
Amory's singing had been a great hit, as well as his mincing

steps in his part as an old maid. The boys went sailing on the *Scorpion*.

John L. Gardner, Sr., wrote with affectionate humor of his wife. "Your mother is looking forward to great doings this afternoon," he told Jack early in June. "She reasons thus—that this is the last week before breaking up in Boston—and as the azaleas are very fine, she will have a reception in the garden." He, personally, was going to "start for Brookline forthwith."

"Union Wharf pays a dividend," Mr. Gardner added before he made good his escape. "Amoskeag has had a very successful 6 months—they pay 7% but made over 11%." Jack was to have a good time, therefore—and give his love to Belle.

In July, Mrs. John L. Gardner, Sr., went to Roque Island, off the coast of Maine. This lively lady seems never to have visited the islands before, although they were part of her Peabody heritage. Her stamina during the journey from Bar Harbor to Roque, by steamer, horse and wagon and rowboat, was remarkable. She stayed at a cottage Jack Gardner had built and wrote "in appreciation of all the comfortable and tasteful and I may as well say luxurious appointments" of his "island home." The island itself was more beautiful than she had supposed but she was doubtful of a project to promote the sale of lots on nearby Campobello Island, in spite of its "two first class hotels." It would never be a second Bar Harbor because of "Bay of Fundy fogs" and "distance from rich and populous regions," and it would be "a long time before Jack got any of his money back."

The senior Mrs. Gardner was seventy but in her zest for living she seemed much younger. She told with amusement of a contemporary in Boston "who drives with Tiger and liveries." Jack would "think Boston is going ahead."

"While you have been in Japan your mother has been deep in 'Miss Bird,' the 'Comte de Beauvoir' [and others] so that she will be able to converse quite understandingly with you when you return," Mr. Gardner wrote on September 1, 1883.

The Jack Gardners were in Peking on September 25 when a letter came "enclosing the telegram with news of Mrs. John L. Gardner's death." It was "a terrible blow." She had seemed so alive, the heart attack completely unexpected. Mrs. Jack "went to get mourning things" and Jack attended to the dispatching home of packing cases in which, it was heartbreaking to remember, were presents that he and Belle had selected for his mother.

The Gardners journeyed to the Great Wall of China. They went "to see Ming tombs—tremendous solemn place," and

Belle went into a temple where "women have rarely been admitted." She was fascinated by China but saddened by the news from home.

It was the end of October when John L. Gardner next wrote his son. "Until now I have hardly put pen to paper," he confessed.[2] His children and grandchildren had been devoted but he had left Brookline only twice. Julia and Eliza had been "prompt to decide and unwearied in carrying out what they believed would have been their mother's wishes." He took pleasure in telling Jack matters he personally attended to, however.

"A handsome sum in money has been given to all our servants, gardeners, clerks etc. beside complete suits of mourning to all. Some money also to my children's servants . . All the servants remain, even the seamstress and the kitchen maid. The seamstress will make Julia's dresses." Mr. Gardner wanted his son to "continue your travels, find much to interest and amuse you." He sent his "finest love to Belle."

John L. Gardner wrote a New Year's letter with affectionate wishes for happiness to Jack and Belle. Mr. Stewart had sent $4000 to be credited to Belle's account, but business in general was bad. The elder Mr. Gardner still hoped to distribute $30,000 among his children this year, but "it will not come from my income—but from property I fondly thought I possessed a year ago," he said. "I think my valuation must be reduced at least $200,000." The newspapers would keep Jack "informed of the changed conditions of all investments since you left us. There are as yet not many outward signs of reduced estates—but judging from ourselves there must be some pinch in every family." He had just "engaged to be interested to the extent of $200,000 in a syndicate with Drexel etc. for supplying $8,000,000 for the purpose of relieving the Oregon and Transcontinental railroad."

The senior John L. Gardner, who would be eighty on February 8, 1884, sent his son Jack a month-end report for January 31. "My largest losses were in the Valency Cattle Yard, $20,000, Willard Stock, say 45,000 and very heavy on Factory stocks—besides mining, some railroads, etc. etc." He set this against a $63,000 profit, most of it in real estate, the previous year. And then he wrote, "We have a good deal of money on hand and I believe George is to remit to Barings to keep plenty there for you."

Only one sentence that Mr. Gardner wrote revealed that he was growing old. "Sometimes I ring the bell and when the servant comes I find I have forgotten what it was I wanted."

93

The Jack Gardners spent July and August, 1883, in Japan. Jack found the weather hotter than he liked, but Belle never tired of sight-seeing and shopping. She bought brocades for herself and for Maud Howe, gifts for Mrs. Howe and many other friends. At the last minute she bought herself a red teapot.

September and October were spent in China and in November they started for French Indochina. On shipboard they acquired two delightful traveling companions, the Viscount de Barré and Baron Durant de Fortmagne, young career diplomats. De Barré was connected with the French Protectorate in Saigon and Fortmagne reported to the Belgian consulate there. Affairs of state occupied them only mildly in comparison with their immediate interest in Mrs. Jack Gardner. She liked de Barré, the younger man, best. The day after they met, de Barré had so far fallen under her spell as to show her "his charm for good luck." It was a "watch chain made of a hangman's rope!"

De Barré began "politely saying all he could do to persuade us to think seriously of going to Angkor Wat," [3] Mrs. Gardner wrote in the new travel journal which she began in Shanghai.

These great ruins, deep in the Cambodian jungle, had been only recently uncovered. Except for Siamese and Cambodians, very few people had ever visited Angkor and some who went there never returned. Marco Polo mentioned the place but did not visit it, and Mrs. Jack Gardner, although not surprised, was delighted to surpass Marco Polo. As soon as they reached Saigon, "J. and I went ashore to try to arrange to go to Cambodia," she wrote. It took five days of negotiation.

At last, the Gardners boarded a small steamer, bound along the coast of French Indochina and then up the Mekong River to Pnompenh, residence city of Cambodia's "First and Second Kings" and of numberless queens. Naturally, both de Barré and Fortmagne found that their diplomatic duties required them to go along.

Mrs. Jack thoroughly enjoyed the coastal and the river journey. "Started at 8 P.M. Tuesday, November 13. Beautiful night but no sleep," she wrote. The next day was very hot. Leaving a trail of smoke, the steamer passed "low banks, tremendous vegetation and white birds like ibises." They stopped several times and at one tiny port Mrs. Gardner laughed with glee to see a fat old woman who came "down to the wharf in a cart, drawn by two men!"

When they reached Pnompenh everything was *en fête* and Mrs. Gardner felt that they were in great luck. They could see the finals in the royal boat races. Jack looked up the agent of the Shanghai-Hongkong Bank, who took them to the King's Pavilion, where "a huge Dragon boat with chairs in it for Europeans" was provided.

"Soon the door from the Pavilion opened and the king appeared, small and nice-looking." Excitedly, Mrs. Gardner jotted down impressions of His Majesty. "Plain black clothes tight to his throat. A sort of Scotch cap of black silk with a diamond buckle on one side of it, a large emerald pendant and a belt with a diamond clasp. Also chains."

The king "had with him his favorite child, a little girl dressed in a beautiful dull yellow sarong—six gold chains over her body from left shoulder to right hip. Nine gold bracelets on each arm and two on each ankle. The two walked forward under a yellow umbrella.

"(I say nothing of a horrible contrast between the savage Cambodians and the dreadful French women in cheap finery)," Mrs. Gardner interpolated, looking over her fellow foreigners in the Dragon boat. The king noticed her maid, Mary, standing outside, "so he went up to her, shook hands, invited her into the boat." Mary, as well as Mrs. Gardner, would have something to tell friends in Boston!

Mrs. Jack thought the royal races were "the most extraordinary and exciting" she had ever seen, and she had seen many a boat race. Only two boats raced at a time. They were "long, narrow dug-outs with forty, forty-two and forty-four men paddling. A frantic person excited them by singing and dancing. A man in the bow waved a pole to beat the stroke."

Monsieur de Barré had gone straight to Protectorate headquarters to organize the trek into the jungle to reach Angkor Wat. "Mr. Hunter, the Interpreter" agreed to come along. The equally devoted Fortmagne stayed with the Gardner party and the next day their steamer started up the Mekong River, then turned into a narrow tributary. About three in the afternoon, the captain of the steamer retired to his cabin and went to sleep. The man he had left at the wheel promptly lost his course and turned into a narrow creek. "We steamed right into the forest," Mrs. Gardner said. Then "pilot to the rescue, wheel reversed, crash, crash among the trees—no end of French from the awakened captain—and we were out again."

They entered Lake Toule Sap, a lake seventy miles long and twenty miles wide—dry except in the rainy season. At this time, the village of Taona was afloat, each bamboo house on its raft, anchored in the lake. The houses were "all nodding and bowing to each other in the wake of the steamer," but soon they would rest on mud, and then on dry ground. Leaving Mrs. Gardner's maid, Mary, here, they "got into small boats, M. Fortmagne, J. and I in the one with the cover.

"In about two hours the boats could go no farther, so bullock and buffalo carts were got ready with much talk and wait, and off we started again."

At Siem Reap there was an empty shed with bamboo floors, where the Gardners had breakfast from their stores. While they were eating, a messenger arrived and made them a long speech. No one understood a word he said—except "Mr. Hunter, the interpreter" who was "invaluable." It seemed that the governor of the province wanted to see the foreign visitors. He had sent a gift of pomelos and coconuts.

The Gardners set out in procession, escorted by the governor's brother, his nephew and seven Cambodians who carried the presents the Gardners had prudently provided themselves with for just such an occasion. They reached the governor's palace, which had a brick wall around it, an open theater and a hall of audience. Mrs. Gardner saw the governor's many ladies, peeping at them "through doors and chinks" in the wall of the audience chamber.

The governor came in. He had already given them "boats, bullock carts etc."—and now he promised elephants. He passed around coconut milk and took the presents. Then they started out on a rough track only recently cut in the jungle. Mrs. Gardner rode in a bullock cart, lying on her back, looking up at the tropical forest.

In two hours they reached another shelter with bamboo roof and log floor. Their luggage was gotten under cover just in time before a short but heavy downpour hit them. Peering out from under the shelter, Mrs. Gardner saw a great temple. They had arrived at Angkor Wat.

The gray stone central tower of Angkor Wat is 213 feet high, more or less pineapple-shaped, carved and decorated all the way to the top. Partially ruined steps, "high, narrow, difficult and dangerous," led forty feet upward to the sanctuary. Needless to say, Mrs. Jack promptly climbed these stairs.

But she wrote first of the scene: "Tropical forest all about us. Buffaloes and their men wandering about. Directly on our left the four great stone gryphons and a huge tree, leaning on them. . . . M. de Barré sitting at the table making out the menus for all the dinners we are to have here. The others putting up the beds, a little fire nearby, water boiling, chicken and ducks lying about, another fire lighted," and at the far end of the shelter "the nephew of the governor squatted à la turque [dressed] in red and pink."

When the rain stopped, "we all went to see the ruins, walked leisurely through but had no time for examination. Then back for dinner. . . . Fires, cattle and carts grouped about. Early to bed. Moon rose." And by moonlight Mrs. Gardner saw "occasional glimpses of gryphons, camp fires and carts."

Next morning they were up at five, had coffee and were off to "Angkor Thom's gateway." Built about the ninth century A.D., Angkor Thom was larger and perhaps three hundred years older than Angkor Wat. It was an abandoned royal city. Mrs. Jack "tramped through the jungle" to see the "great towers, . . . each side covered with huge Buddha heads. In and around these, the banyan tree . . . has tied its roots and stems," she said. "Such a scramble to get through the jungle and every now and then we came upon ruins." At ten that morning they found themselves at the "bamboo-plated house" of an old man who had lived there forty-eight years. "We had siesta, breakfast, a visit from his wife." They gave Mrs. Gardner a little image, presumably picked up among the ruins— "an Indra," the god who presides over the "middle realm—the air."

The governor's two elephants arrived to take the Gardners back to Angkor Wat, and the next day was devoted to examining bas-relief sculptures on the great temple. Where spaces were long and narrow, processions were carved, featuring the progress of kings, their multiple queens and their elephants. On high walls was told the story of the battles of the monkey king with dragons and with man, some of them carrying shields reminiscent of archaic Greek armor. The death of the monkey king, with his conical crown, surrounded by many monkey queens each with a pagoda-shaped crown, was impressive and strangely pathetic. There was ornament, curiously Roman in effect, but most of the carvings were flamboyantly Oriental, replete with seven-headed snakes, flying dragons and elephants, against a jungle background. Mrs. Jack was fascinated as well as frustrated because no one had as yet been able to decipher the inscriptions and no one could explain to her the mysterious, dreamlike story the walls were trying to tell.

De Barré and Fortmagne spent their time hunting Buddha's treasure, Mrs. Gardner said. Tradition had it that the temples at Angkor Wat had been the repository of gold and rubies from mines still worked in Cambodia. They found nothing, and it was Mrs. Jack who returned with a kind of treasure none could steal—her experience of the place. She took "a long last look" when it was time to leave and then it was "elephants and bullock carts and away."

When they got back to the banyan tree where they had left their boats they dined and sat about on logs and cushions and smoked and talked. A Cambodian slave-boy, naked to the waist, fanned Mrs. Gardner.

Mrs. Jack was now among the few who had ever seen Angkor Wat, and she almost became one of those who never returned. "Finally we started in our boats," she said. "An elephant of the governor's had gone mad and escaped and was just plunging for the river when out boats got there! Two moments later and he would have been in the water and there would have been an end to us."

Only now were they told that "no native boats can go up or down the river" on account of the crazed elephant, which had already killed several men. "The steamer was waiting for us, steam up, so we got on board and immediately off we started down the lake." Next morning they had "champagne for breakfast," perhaps an idea of de Barré's to celebrate what Mrs. Jack admitted was "a narrow escape."

Back at Pnompenh, a dinner was given for the Gardners at the palace of the French Protectorate. Mrs. Gardner ate her first peacock. "After dinner a little tiger was brought in for us to see, a dear, wild, savage little thing which growled all the time" at his keeper, "who held and stroked him."

An audience with the two kings of Cambodia had been arranged, so "J. and de Barré put on evening dress," about three-thirty in the afternoon. De Barré had "gilded waistcoat buttons and his blue and white ribbon" but Mrs. Jack was caught, perhaps for the first time in her life, with nothing suitable to wear. "I in my dirty old white and black foulard and black lace bonnet" was the way she described herself. "But to make a glitter, I [put on] my diamond and pearl dog collar, my two white diamonds on my bonnet strings and my yellow diamond on the front of my dress."

They went to see the Second King first. The entrance to the palace was "through a red brick archway of which only the sides" remained because there had been a flood and debris was everywhere. They waited "under a tree, outside the inner gate and suddenly appearing through the gate a neat little man, purple stockings on his pretty little legs . . . It was the Second

King, himself. So we were presented, then and there under the tree."

The French Protector came to take the Gardners to the First King. They found the king waiting at the head of his palace steps; and Mrs. Gardner sensed that he didn't like the Protector very much. But Monsieur de Barré stepped forward and asked if they might see the palace.

Norodin I, King of Cambodia, walked through the palace and the gardens with Mrs. Jack. He asked her about her yellow diamond and said he had no such thing himself. Being an absolute monarch accustomed to receiving tribute, he probably expected her to give it to him. Many years later, Mrs. Jack Gardner did indeed give away the yellow diamond, but to Nellie Melba, famous opera star, and not to the king of Cambodia.

As they walked along, she made mental inventory of the king's jewels. He had a diamond buckle in his black silk cap. Around his neck he wore a gold chain with "emerald and diamond pendant and a superb sapphire ring." Mrs. Gardner "alone, was presented to five wives."

On Friday, November 23, Mrs. Gardner was up at six and ready to go on board the steamer to leave Cambodia at seven-fifteen. Mr. Hunter, the interpreter, arrived with a sketch of Angkor Wat and flowers for her; the day before, he had given her "a beautiful little Vishnu." De Barré and Fortmagne still found it their duty to follow Mrs. Jack.

At about five A.M. Saturday, November 24, Mrs. Gardner "saw the Great Bear upside down" and the Southern Cross. They were back on board the little steamer, returning to Saigon. The French mail steamer had left before they arrived and the ever-attentive de Barré suggested that they might as well go to Java.

Both heat and humidity were intense. Although Mrs. Jack was supposed to affect daring costumes, hers was still a generation that wore layer upon layer of clothes and so far she had made no concession to climate. However, she now bought "thin stuff for jackets." They went "to see the Java steamer and decided to go by it" although it was "a boat for merchandise—never clean, a dog, a monkey, chickens, augh!" was how Mrs. Gardner described it. The captain gave her his cabin but she spent the night on deck. They crossed the equator, watched flying fish; but there was no escape from the smells—"and nothing smells like ducks . . . !"

Arriving at Java at last, some "pretty boats with lateen sails come out to the steamer. We and luggage get into three of them and sail away"—with "never a Surabaya in sight," Mrs. Gardner said, on December 5. They reached the water-level city and visited "the customs, where they politely take away de B's gun" and we start again for the Hotel des Indes, down a long canal . . ."

Mrs. Gardner had greatly admired the naked torsos of men she had seen on her recent travels. But the Dutch in Java wore the strangest clothes since Eden. The men in pajamas, the trousers made of fantastic sarongs and the women (ladies?) in sarongs, no-heeled slippers, loose white jackets (absolutely nothing else) and hair down their back." She spent a sleepless night at the hotel—"people right next door . . . up until 3 AM talking and laughing—mosquitoes—at 4 AM . . . children with drums." Then, next day, between tropical showers, "J. and I went to some shops," she said, "I in white loose pongee wrapper and no hat! And it didn't seem at all strange."

Mrs. Jack had often startled Boston, but now she surprised herself. She asked the hotelkeeper what she should wear "to the opera." It would be the pongee wrapper again, he assured her, and "as from his women," whom he consulted, "I ought to wear a flower or ribbons in my hair!" It is to be hoped that a loose jacket or two had been made for poor "J.," who suffered from the heat more than his wife did and was much more conservative as to dress. But Mrs. Jack made no comment about her husband's costume.

De Barré, working hard at his diplomatic duty, arranged for an audience with the prince, whose palace was at Solo (Surakarta). They went there on the once-a-week work train which had "every square inch occupied" and people "hanging on the steps." De Barré foraged for food and brought their "first mangoes—really delicious."

The prince was "a nice young fellow with beautiful diamonds." The Gardners "made three bows in the proper places" and sat down with him.

But Mrs. Gardner, sensitive as always to a dramatic scene, felt a strange sense of impending doom. "Dim lights, rain pouring in the outer court of the palace," she wrote. "The Sultan's women squatting on the floor, one with his cuspidor, one with his sword, one with a shield, one with a cane. Women dwarfs in attendance who played most strange music with a strange fascination—the whole thing under one's breath as if something were going to happen."

To the great disappointment of de Barré and Fortmagne, the Gardners decided not to go to Bangkok, because time for India was growing short. De Barré had taken charge of baggage, he had been entertaining, and they would miss him. The apparently silent and retired Fortmagne was a friend they also enjoyed, although it was always "de B." who brought flowers to Mrs. Gardner. He gave her "a belt clasp as a bet," but she didn't say what the bet was about and his parting gift to her was a tiger claw.

The Cambodian adventure was over. At a time in the future, when Mrs. Jack was back in Boston, some ladies asked her to luncheon. They conspired together to study some strange out-of-the-way place so that they could talk about it and make sure that for once Mrs. Gardner would have nothing to say. They chose Cambodia!

ELEVEN

Heart-Whole Return

$\mathcal{A}$FTER A STOPOVER in Rangoon to see the pagoda, it was "goodbye to the country of men with tattooed legs and women with skirts open down the front," Mrs. Gardner wrote. The Gardners arrived in Bombay on January 3, 1884, and found that all the talk was of the coming installation of the Nizam of Hyderabad—but that tickets to see the spectacle were by now unobtainable.

Alexander Agassiz, son of the Swiss-American scientist, was in Bombay, however. He already knew Mrs. Gardner because he had been obliged to disappoint her about some rattlesnakes she wanted to see! They had been "sent off to the London Zoological Society," having "got out once or twice" [1] at the Museum of Comparative Zoology in Cambridge. Alexander Agassiz now made up for this by getting the Gardners tickets to the installation; and he characterized Mrs. Jack as of "unbounded energy, a perfect traveler, incapable of fear and wishing to see everything that ought to be seen."

After traveling all day in the train, the Gardners despaired of finding a place to stay in Hyderabad but ended up in tent Number 7, Public Gardens. Next day they met Agassiz and went to the installation, there being only twenty-five European ladies present. It was "after tiffin" when they saw "that which pales everything before it . . . the native princes paying allegiance to the Nizam. On the road, princes and retainers, a vast mass." [2] Artillery was drawn by elephants at the military review.

Another all-day train journey brought the Gardners to Madura to see the great complex of towers and courtyards that made up the temple. Life-sized figures covered the walls, somewhat reminiscent of those at Angkor Wat, but painted in every color, some of them whitewashed, some gilded.

Mrs. Jack was traveling too far too fast to have leisure for her journal, but one incident she found time to record. Leaving Madura, the Gardners took the train to Trichinopoly, found a note from Agassiz at the railroad station "handing over rooms and guide—he off for the hills." Agassiz had made an appointment for the Gardners to see the jewels at the temple, which were "quite wonderful." Priests welcomed them and crowned them with "double garlands of pink flowers," giving them a bouquet to hold in each hand. "J. was a sight," Mrs. Gardner wrote. If only his friends of the Somerset Club could have seen her balding husband with a crown of pink flowers on his head!

When the Gardners left Bombay, seven men of assorted ages, American and British residents, went out in the steam launch to say goodbye to Mrs. Jack. They bore gifts, "a superb bon voyage basket . . . a beautiful Kashmir silver and gold box with chocolate champagne bottles inside," numerous bouquets of flowers. Mrs. Jack, at the age of forty-four, could not be blamed if she felt like a young girl again.

All during her Oriental journey, Mrs. Jack wrote long letters to Maud Howe, her "dear, dear girl." She thanked Maud for her letter with its "little glimpse of Beverly and the Higginsons" and wanted to know if Mrs. Skinner (her sister-in-law Eliza) had been "pleasant" to Maud. She asked the name of "Crawford's new book," asked what it was about and who published it, and when it would come out. Maud was to send a copy. "In the midst of Boston society," Maud was not to "get intimate with any horrid women. Keep my place for me," Belle said.

Not that it would do even now for Isabella Gardner and Maud Howe to call each other by their first names. Maud was "dear Bacchante" or "Beautiful girl and very dear friend." Isabella was "Bianca."

F. Marion Crawford was in Constantinople during the first week in March, 1884. He had gone there because General and Mrs. Berdan were there with their daughter, "the beautiful golden-haired Bessie." Sam Ward had introduced Crawford to Bessie Berdan, either in New York or on Long Island, and they must have met again in Boston, where Bessie's mother brought her to visit two maiden ladies on Beacon Hill. The elderly ladies fell victim to Bessie's charm and, under her mother's tactful prodding, supplied her with furs to go over her ball dresses and with pearls for her pretty neck. Her mother hoped that Bessie would meet a wealthy Boston bachelor who would marry her. Nothing of the sort happened, however, and the Berdans set off on a European tour.

General Berdan was reputed wealthy, but most of his fortune was in an uncollected debt against the United States for use of the Berdan rifle during the Civil War. Crawford must have thought he had found his heiress at last when he told one of his sisters that "the lovely Bessie favors me."

"Every door is open to me, everyone has read me, even to the Sultan's Turkish aide-de-camp . . . Little men in gorgeous uniforms, talking broken English, assured me that they had never read anything like *Mr. Isaacs*," Crawford told his sister.[3] The lovely Bessie did indeed "favor" him. F. Marion Crawford and Bessie Berdan were married in Constantinople in 1884. Sooner or later, Isabella Gardner would have to hear the news. It was good that Cambodia seemed to have healed her broken heart and that her mind was fully taken up with new scenes. Almost ten years passed before Crawford crossed her path again.

The Gardners paused in Egypt, foregathering in Cairo with English and Americans at Shepheard's Hotel. "Very great changes since our last visit, nine years ago," Mrs. Gardner wrote. "Great ruin and before long it seems as if these beautiful monuments will have utterly disappeared." Among new friends were "the Berkleys," the future Sir George, chief engineer of the Indian Peninsula Railroad and consultant for other railroads in India. Mrs. Berkley played chess with Jack Gardner while "Mr. B. taught me Polish Bezique," Mrs. Jack said. This was the only time she mentioned playing cards. She was glad to be on a dahabeah again, if only to make a call.

On May 13, 1884, the trip to the Orient had ended. The Gardners were aboard ship, the sea was like oil, and there were yellow and red sails and Venice was "afar off, looking like a city in a dream." Mrs. Jack admitted that she was exhausted. Her weight was down to 115 pounds and what she wanted now was to float lazily in a gondola.

Isabella Gardner had just arrived at a city that was to capture her heart, to give new direction to her life, and to call her back year after year. On their first evening, "J." and Mrs. Jack "went to Florians for ices and coffee." They sat out of doors under the great arcade at the edge of St. Mark's Square, watching the people. Across the square, St. Mark's, with its Oriental domes and Gothic arches, seemed a perfect blend of experiences just past with a different kind of beauty now to be enjoyed. After a while they took a gondola to float along the Grand Canal, listening to music. This would become their almost daily routine.

The following evening, "to Palazzo Barbaro" to call on the Curtises, Mrs. Gardner wrote. She was seeing for the first time the Venetian Renaissance palace that was to be their home, summer after summer.

Jack Gardner knew the Curtises well. They were an ex-patriate Boston family, by reason of an incident taking place sometime in the late sixties and still told around town in various versions. Three men had been coming into Boston by train from their country homes and they turned a seat so they could sit facing each other. A few stops farther on, a large man carrying a toy baby carriage came into the car and took the fourth seat. When this stranger got up to go, he said that one of the three commuters was "no gentleman!" The commuter referred to, Daniel Curtis, "proved he was a gentleman by hitting the stranger in the face, knocking off his glasses." Other observers said that "Dan Curtis pulled the nose" of the stranger, who proved to be Judge Churchill. The Judge brought suit, and Curtis got a Boston neighbor of his, Lewis Stackpole, to defend him. Stackpole tried to make a joke out of the whole thing; but the court did not think it was funny to pull a judge's nose, and Curtis went to jail for three months.[4] After serving his sentence he left the country, vowing never to return. He was married to an English lady of considerable pretension to gentility, and their son Ralph had been born in Boston in 1854. Daniel and Ariana Curtis now rented one floor of the Palazzo Barbaro on the Grand Canal.

Mrs. Jack Gardner looked about her with delight when she entered the great, ornate Italian drawing room. Brought up to admire what Edith Wharton was to term the "upholsterer's" style of interior decorating, Mrs. Gardner liked plenty of ornament; and this room was frescoed, molded and gilded enough to please her. But it was not cluttered. Tables with marble tops had no covers to reach the floor and conceal their curved golden legs. Chairs stood about with their frames exposed, instead of hidden deep in brocade-covered down. But what fine lines—what ancient gold leaf and delicate painted flowers adorned these chairs that enthroned a lady, rather than submerging her!

Simultaneous with the discovery of the Palazzo Barbaro was the discovery of Ralph Curtis, son of Daniel and Ariana—now thirty years old. Tall, blond, with the ends of his mustache delicately waxed and upturned, his hair curling slightly, his chin cleft—he was one of the most charming young artists ever overlooked by fame! His parents called him "Rafe."

On the second day in Venice, Mrs. Jack found a teacher of Italian, Miss Maria Holas, who for three francs an hour would come to the Hotel de l'Europe to give a lesson. She would take her apt and interested pupil to shops and museums, conversing all the while in Italian. Before long it was

Jack Gardner who took lessons with Miss Holas while Mrs. Jack went with Ralph Curtis to watch him sketch his red-haired model against a Grand Canal background and to study *la lingua di Dantë* with the young artist whom she called "Rafaello."

With her guidebook, her Ruskin—and with Ralph Curtis by her side—Mrs. Jack saw every Tintoretto, every Bellini, every Veronese, whether starred as important or otherwise, that she could find in Venice. Ruskin said that Carpaccio was admirable, so Mrs. Jack mounted ladders to see some Carpaccios, reserving the right to call them "funny." When Ralph Curtis took his model to San Nichole to pose, Mrs. Jack began a sketch of her own.

Jack, meanwhile, had been ordered to bed, because of a "bad chill and a feverish night," soon after arriving in Venice. The doctor gave him a purgative, which made him feel even worse, and eventually decided that he had erysipelas. Nearly a month later, on the thirtieth of May, after many anxious notations, Mrs. Jack was at last able to write, "J. much better."

Jack's first activity on recovering was to look for a new maid for his wife, "Mary having gone home." [5]

"Engaged Agnes, 2½ Napoleons per month in Europe, 3 Napoleons in America, extra pay being in lieu of wine or beer —return passage if she stays a year," Jack Gardner wrote in his pocket diary.

On Monday, he wrote: "Agnes, maid, came."

On Tuesday: "Agnes, Maid, left." Mrs. Gardner was exceedingly demanding as an employer and she became more so as time went by. "Maria Costa" arrived, lasted nearly three weeks, and left. Yet, there would always be servants who loved and understood their imperious lady.

The Gardners dined with the Bronsons, new acquaintances destined, like the Curtises, to become lifelong friends. There was no visible Mr. Arthur Bronson. He had been ill a long time, "his mind having died before the death of his body." His wife, the former Katherine de Kay of Newport, lived in winter in a palazzo on the Grand Canal with her daughter Edith. She was soon to buy "a little scrap of a house" to please Mr. Browning, at Asolo, a mountain village, and Robert Browning often visited her there. In his last book, *Asolando,* "To Mrs. Arthur Bronson," he would write, "To whom but you, dear friend, should I dedicate verses—some few written, all of them supervised in the comfort of your presence . . ."

Mrs. Gardner had written to Henry James asking for a letter of introduction to Mrs. Bronson. He told her that none was needed, Katherine de Kay Bronson being "so absolutely easy to know." Her palazzo, with its red-cushioned balcony overlooking the Grand Canal, was a favorite rendezvous for friends, Edith's age and older, Europeans as well as Americans. "The music was good," Mrs. Gardner said—and there was almost always music at the Bronsons'. After dinner they all went to the Hungarian Café to hear Hungarian music.

The Princess Metternich called on Mrs. Jack Gardner and Mrs. Jack had herself presented to the cardinal. Jack contributed to the cardinal's charities. There was always enough to do in Venice and yet there seemed to be no hurry about anything. "Tea in gondola" became one of Jack's almost daily entries in his pocket diary, as well as "Music in the piazza." But on the twenty-fourth of June it was time to leave Venice. Passage home from Liverpool to New York was engaged for July 26.

Only eight days were allotted to Paris. Worth must have been distressed, for hurried fittings were the enemy of good workmanship. There was time, however, for a visit to "Boucheron of Paris," dealer in fine pearls. Jack Gardner and Mrs. Jack carefully selected "39 pearls," their average weight being 16⅔ grams, their luster of the finest. A "small" two-carat diamond was chosen for the clasp.[6]

In London, the Gardners were met at the railroad station by their nephew, William Amory. He had been in Europe with John Jay Chapman, that "tall young man with dashing good looks." Both boys had completed their senior year at Harvard —Amory graduating with "highest final honors in the classics" and with a Phi Beta Kappa key to hang on his watch chain.[7] He would be twenty-one in December. His income from his father's estate was ample and he could have a gay time in Paris, if so minded. But it was at this time that his traveling companion, John Jay Chapman, with one hundred dollars a month (probably the gift of his grandfather Jay), remarked rather sadly that "Amory had the conscience of an anchorite."

Mrs. Gardner had written from the Orient to Henry James suggesting that they meet in Venice. He answered the letter on the second of May while the Gardners were still in Cairo. "It is true that I haven't the excitement of believing that you miss me—on the lagoon—for I know too well that you don't miss anyone or anything in this preposterously pleasant career of yours. You have everything, you do everything, you enjoy everything and if you don't happen to find an extra post-horse at Venice to pull your triumphant car—to tow your gondola

—you may be sure that the next poor patient beast will be waiting at the next stage. In other words, I shall be waiting in London and shall get into harness when you arrive. In the meantime, have pity on the place where the collar rubbed. I wear a collar always: *que dis-je?* I wear half a dozen. They are piled up around my poor old head and when you see me you will scarce distinguish the tip of my nose. I am a ruminant quadruped, too, and I turn it over in my mind that really, I, at least, am too good a friend of yours to lend a further hand—or hoof—in spoiling you. I have heard about the King of Cambodia—and the Hyderabad—about all your adventures and entertainments and I feel kind of savage at the thought that you have had this lovely time while I have had a rude workaday life jolting and scraping from one dull day to the other . . . ."

Mrs. Gardner did not like the letter. Since Henry James made a point of destroying all letters he received, her reply can only be conjectured but when he wrote again, "Don't really say such cruel things to me!" he began. "I am certainly not unkind—I am soft and humane—and I don't think I am frivolous. I assure you I never dreamed of saying anything that would not seem to you essentially friendly and if I took a jocose and evasive tone it was partly to conceal my irritation in not being able to get away from London." Someone in Venice had told Mrs. Gardner that Henry James had not been working half as hard as he said he was. This must have been a woman, James was sure, and he hoped that "by this time" this person had "caught typhus fever or been drowned in the lagoon or tumbled from the Campanile."

James said he still hoped to be in London when the Gardners arrived. "And if you will tell me that I am not frivolous and unkind but serious and tender I shall be here also when you depart! I will drive you in the gondola of London, the casual hansom [cab]." [8]

Henry James underestimated Mrs. Gardner's intelligence. She knew he was not merely "jocose" when he spoke of her having everything and being spoiled. He envied her wealth, as he often envied the wealth of others who made his life pleasant for him in London and at their country houses.

James wrote to Grace Norton in late July or early August. "Mrs. Jack Gardner has just passed through London at the close of her universal tour and on me *her* hand too was laid: but very discreetly. She is worn and tired by her travels, but full of reminiscences and in despair at going back to Boston where she has neither friends nor lovers, nor entertainments, nor resources of any kind left. She was exceedingly *nice* while here and I pity her." [9]

The Gardners left London for Liverpool on July 25 and sailed next day, taking their nephew Amory with them. They arrived off Sandy Hook on Sunday, August third. There was "delay at quarantine—got ashore in a tug about 9 PM." That was all that John L. Gardner recorded in his pocket diary. Belle had ceased writing her journal on the first of June in Venice, her last entry telling of a "hail storm" and "wonderful fireworks."

There was no notation of sad news from home, but John L. Gardner, Sr., had died in Brookline on July 24.

On July 26, 1884, the Brookline *Chronicle* described John L. Gardner, Sr., in its obituary notice. He was "a man of modest demeanor and quiet tastes, spurning ostentation, dignified, affable, courteous to all who were brought into relations with him." All this was true, but he had constantly sent "finest love to Belle," the daughter-in-law he particularly loved. She was of gay demeanor and startling tastes; she had no objection whatever to ostentation in the form of fast-trotting horses, sable furs and liveried servants. She was dignified, affable and courteous whenever she felt like it but she was also capable of turning cartwheels or losing her temper in a blaze of fireworks.

John L. Gardner gave 147 Beacon Street to his daughter Julia, along with the Brookline cottage. He gave Eliza Number 200 Beacon Street, and Number 51 Commonwealth Avenue went to his son George. But he had loved his Brookline place above all. Green Hill he gave to Jack and Belle, knowing it would prosper under their care. It was good to think of Belle living there for at least part of every year.

It would have pleased her father-in-law that Belle Gardner first turned her attention to the greenhouse and gardens in Brookline. As a rule, Mrs. Gardner would not talk to reporters and refused to have anything personal written up. But a young woman of an aristocratic type of beauty and great charm approached her. She was Hildegarde Hawthorne, granddaughter of Nathaniel Hawthorne, and she wrote "A Garden of the Imagination" for the *Century Magazine*—after visiting Green Hill. The "garden was not so much one as many, folded one within another like the petals of a rose," Miss Hawthorne said. "The accents are soft and gradual, and the ways that lead from one charming spot to another so winding that the realization of being on a hill comes only when you finally look about you and perceive that the ground slopes down on every hand and you see only the tops of trees. It is this effect of mystery and surprise that characterizes Green Hill—this and the touch of the imagination as when, for instance, you encounter a mass of starry jasmine, the perfume barring your path . . . rousing memories of moonlit fountains . . . of Tasso and Petrarch.

"The Italian garden is above all else notably simple, with the simplicity of coherence and perfection. Particularly notable is Mrs. Gardner's fearless use of color," Miss Hawthorne said, her eye caught by "long, narrow beds of petunias of every shade." Impressed by petunias, she apparently missed the orchids under glass which startled Mrs. Jack's contemporaries. Still to be designed were the Japanese gardens full of iris such as everyone said would never bloom in the vicinity of Boston. Mrs. Gardner had her iris beds heated. It was a pity that Hildegarde Hawthorne was not at Green Hill when young Japanese artists set up their easels to paint iris, or when a young American attempted rhododendrons. In mid-winter came the Parma violets Jack Gardner eventually had a greenhouse filled with—just because his wife loved them.

"The house belongs intimately with its surroundings," Hildegarde Hawthorne continued. "Low, wide and spreading, the charming building is an incident, a happy accessory of the outdoor world it inhabits . . . its little balconies with their low railings made to lean on, link the outside and inside world and every window looks ready to let you step out into the sunny air . . ." This was true. And yet the house itself, especially after the Jack Gardners built a music room, was a happy place in its own right. Rain must fall, if the gardens were to prosper—and on a rainy day at Green Hill, no one felt trapped inside the spacious rooms with their Chinese wall hangings and Japanese screens.

The Gardners were fond of The Country Club, in Brookline. But this is not to say that there were any women members at first nor that anyone, as yet, played a curious Scottish game called golf. There was a rented farmhouse, with stalls, kennels and a curling rink. In 1881, hounds were brought in and live foxes were hunted in Brookline.

"I have just bought a cob to gallop over the country with you, but I don't believe he can jump," Thomas Jefferson Coolidge wrote Mrs. Gardner on May 19, 1884, while she was still on her around-the-world tour. "We have the first meeting at The Country Club today. A full band and pigeon shooting but unfortunately it rains."

What Mrs. Gardner liked best at The Country Club was the

sort of program that opened the season in 1885. There was "a show of private hacks and they were put through their various accomplishments by their different owners." This was followed by "a race over hurdles placed across the half mile track at regular intervals, with a basket of potatoes midway between each hurdle. Riders, who were mounted on their own hacks, were obliged to jump each hurdle, then alight at each separate bag of potatoes, take one potato, remount, clear the next hurdle and so on to the finish." First prize was fifty dollars.[10]

But the open country around Brookline was disappearing fast, and in 1882 kennels were built in Hamilton, near the North Shore. The Myopia Hunt Club, so called because so many of the members wore glasses, was closely associated with The Country Club. Myopia leased a hundred acres in the vicinity of Hamilton, and the younger men gravitated in that direction.

The Gardners returned home with just enough of the summer left, in 1884, to spend a few weeks in Beverly. There was time to go out on horseback, looking at land for Joe. In March, 1885, nephew "Joseph Gardner of Beverly" bought 235 acres and a homestead estate and farm in Hamilton.

In 1885, the Myopia Hunt Club ball was "the handsomest, most elaborate entertainment given in Boston." The men wore their pink coats, a splendid sight. "Dancing did not end until 5 o'clock, the cotillion beginning at half past three." [11] Boston's younger social set was moving at a faster pace and Mrs. Jack would keep up with her nephews.

In July, 1885, James Russell Lowell wrote to Mrs. Gardner expressing regret that he had been "called to Washington" and could not come out to Beverly for a visit. He was coming later, "and when I do I shall be sure to look you up," he wrote her—"if it were only to find out if your hair be as gold as ever." Of course he knew perfectly well that Mrs. Jack's hair was now permanently gold. His own, he said, "has accepted all the heresies of the Bland bill and gone in for the cheaper metal." [12]

TWELVE

Music and Diamonds

Town Topics, on December 1, 1887, devoted a great deal of space in its New York weekly society magazine to Mrs. Jack Gardner of Boston. The article was unsigned, as always, the tone more complimentary than ever before.

" 'Mrs. Jack,' as she is familiarly called, is easily the brightest, breeziest woman in Boston. Though hardly beautiful in the fleshly sense of the word, she is the idol of the men and the envy of the women. She throws out her lariat and drags after her chariot the brightest men in town, young and old, married and single. She dazzles them by her sparkling wit, her charming coquetry and her no end of polite accomplishments."

Leaving Western lariats and Roman chariots, *Town Topics* went on to greater efforts. "Let the wives of giddy and wayward husbands scold and stamp their feet in protest as they may, the spell of Mrs. Jack's enthrallment cannot be broken. The possessor of large wealth in her own right, as well as in that of her husband . . . she dispenses it in a manner to delight her admirers. Her carriages and horses are the finest that can be had and her coachman, footman and groom tally with their traps. Her out of town house in Brookline is a gem of beauty and its gardens and hot houses and lawns are as famed as their mistress. Her Beacon Street house is really two houses turned into one, and its conservatories and fittings throughout are in keeping with the elegant hospitality of the place."

The "two houses" referred to had been joined together in 1880 when Jack Gardner bought the house next door. Entrances were cut in the common wall. There was a difference in floor levels, but the architect contrived divided stairways, steps up and steps down, with attractive results. Out of former front and back parlors or other small rooms in the newly acquired house, a music room was achieved large enough for private concerts. The walls of this room were painted white, potted palms stood in corners, and over one door and on a wall were large plaster casts of della Robbia's angels and boys singing and playing instruments, from the marble friezes created for the organ loft at the Duomo in Florence. That Mrs. Gardner, the future collector of original masterpieces, should at this point cherish plaster casts was really not surprising. Casts were popular, especially as wedding presents. That she loved these so much as to place them in the future music room of her still undreamed-of palace was a little more remarkable, except that she was always fond of certain objects, regardless of their intrinsic value. Delicate little wooden chairs in the Beacon Street music room were also to find their way later to the larger Fenway Court music room.

The Beacon Street music room could double as a ballroom, and on December 22, 1887, "Dancing Parties at Home" was the headline in *Town Topics*. "To recur to one or two of the notable events in Boston's social calendar for the past week, the first of Mrs. Jack Gardner's dancing parties fully satisfied everybody's expectations, which is the same as saying it was characteristic of its graceful hostess, gay, brilliant, magnificent. The beaux were out in full force, of course. Mrs. Jack always attracts all the festive stags, including those who are bored to death with everybody else's dancing parties. There were not wanting scores of pretty women, however, and buds were there galore, likewise. Conspicuous among these latter was Miss Olga Gardner, the youngest daughter of Mr. George A. Gardner of Commonwealth Avenue." Olga was "not accounted a raving beauty," but she was "the bright particular belle of the evening," just the same.

Olga's mother had been Eliza Endicott Peabody of Salem, "one of the handsomest brides ever seen." The words "Peabody of Salem" conjured up a picture of extreme New England gentility, and these sisters (Olga's two aunts) more than once tried to put a brake on Mrs. Jack's social gyrations; but with all their art and artlessness, Mrs. Jack was too much for them.

In March, 1886, Mrs. Gardner entered the imposing store of Tiffany and Company in Union Square, New York City— at the corner where the horsecars in a double curve made the traffic so dangerous that a flagman was employed to guard the crossing. Mrs. Jack already possessed two large white diamonds and a yellow one, which she had worn when she met the two kings of Cambodia, but she was now shopping for something bigger and better. Tiffany had just what she wanted and, dating their bill March 27, 1886, they itemized:

1	Brilliant 25½ kts.	$35,100
1	" 12⅜ kts.	11,700

Mounting as necklace and hair pin	100
Expenses of man to Boston	13.75

$46,913.75

The diamonds came "from the estate of the late Mrs. Morgan," Tiffany said. They did not give the names "The Rajah" and "The Light of India," although among Mrs. Gardner's friends it was understood that the diamonds were so called.[1]

On the back of Tiffany's bill was a note in pencil. "Paid by Mrs. I.S.G. from money given her by J.L.G." The man from Tiffany's must have arrived in Boston with the diamonds in time for Isabella's birthday, on April 14. She would be forty-six years old.

It was the setting as a hairpin that caused the most private comment concerning Mrs. Jack's latest jewels. Each diamond could be attached to a tortoise-shell hairpin, and observers remembered that between the hairpin and the stone there was a gold spiral wire. A man who as a young boy sometimes occupied a box at the opera near Mrs. Gardner's described how she looked. "We could see Mrs. Gardner right close. She wouldn't exactly take a prize for beauty, you know. She had a kind of crown she wore and it had two long wires with great big diamonds on the ends of them. They'd bob and shine when she talked. We'd hear her laugh."

In a photograph of one of Mrs. Jack's parties on Beacon Street, the crown on her head seems to be a twist or braid of hair and the two diamonds are firmly fastened in it. Perhaps Tiffany later contrived the long golden wires!

Everyone was building music rooms as the dreary wastes of Commonwealth Avenue were filled with fine houses, but Mrs. Gardner's was unique, in that it was more often used for music than for dancing. Instead of just "trying to get a man to play," as one of her marriage connections put it, she selected musicians in whom she had faith as artists and then actually introduced them to her guests, instead of dismissing them by a side door, along with the extra help.

When she first opened her music room in 1880 Mrs. Jack relied heavily on students from the New England Conservatory of Music. She remained their chief hope of early recognition as she gave them their chance to be heard in society and extolled their genius to her friends, doing her best to make them fashionable.

Often, Mrs. Gardner's faith was misplaced. She tried to infuse stamina into the spineless and to drive her own energy into the slothful. Of course this never worked, but she rarely dropped a protégé as some wealthy patrons did. She was too stubborn to give up, too proud to admit defeat and, when all was said and done, too loyal to go back on a friend—whatever her enemies thought of her.

Among the first of Mrs. Jack's musical discoveries was Clayton Johns. An excessively shy young man of distinguished ancestry, he "refused to study law or become a parson," according to his own account, and his family refused to let him "become a fiddler or a dancing master"—synonymous in their minds with a musical career. So he studied architecture and on coming of age asserted himself by studying musical composition at Harvard. He was a fine pianist and in 1885 made his "first bow in public before a Boston audience" with a group of songs which he had composed while studying in Berlin. He was twenty-eight, boyish, dark, with regular features. Except that he was not blond, he was otherwise exactly the type that Mrs. Jack Gardner found irresistible.[2]

Johns was fortunate in meeting Miss Lena Little,[3] a socially correct and also beautiful girl of about eighteen—a fine contralto. She sang his songs to his accompaniment. Clayton Johns hated playing in public and "never got over a temperamental nervousness," he said. The only kind of concert he liked to give was "before about twenty-five people in Mrs. Gardner's music room."

Lena Little became the second of Mrs. Gardner's close women friends, Maud Howe still holding first place in her heart. As for Clayton Johns—Mrs. Jack immediately acquired him for her growing collection of favorite musicians. There was no need for her to throw out her lariat and drag him after her chariot. Clayton Johns was her willing slave.

In his time, songs by Clayton Johns were immensely popular. "One has yet to hear of a summer hotel in this broad land that has not echoed to 'I cannot help loving thee' or 'I love and the world is mine,'" wrote a contemporary. He "set French texts to music in the dainty 'Peu de Choses,' the beautiful 'Roses Mortes'—the somber 'Il pleure dans mon coeur.'" His "Berceuse" and a "Scherzino" for strings were played by the Boston Symphony Orchestra.[4] Of course, there were always those who said that Johns had Mrs. Gardner in mind when he wrote "I cannot help loving thee"—and that he did not love in vain.

Johns gave lessons, as all musicians had to do if they planned to eat regularly. One very young (and extremely pretty) girl was not allowed to go to his studio without a chaperon because he was supposed to be adored by Mrs. Jack. There were pictures of Mrs. Gardner all over his rooms, the still pretty but safely married lady remembered long afterward.

Music was at a low ebb in Boston in 1880 when Mrs. Gardner built her music room. The great organ at the Boston Music Hall, once the talk of the town, had begun to be a bore. Spoken of in 1863 with pride as having cost sixty thousand dollars, it was sold in 1884 for five thousand dollars.[5] "It lent itself to adventurous combinations," William Apthorp remarked. "I remember one evening when a fantasia . . . was played as a duet for mouth harmonica and the Great Organ; a combination, as the programme informed us, 'never before attempted in the history of music.' "[6] But a more sophisticated day had dawned. The organ was sold just to get rid of it and make more space for the Boston Symphony Orchestra.

There had been room enough on the Music Hall stage for the "Harvard Musical Concerts," forerunners of the Symphony, to which Mrs. Gardner had faithfully taken her three nephews. John Sullivan Dwight, editor of the *Journal of Music*, explained the purposes of this organization. "It had no motive but good music and the hope of doing a good thing for art in Boston." It guaranteed "pure programmes, above all need of catering to low tastes," giving "at least one set of concerts in which one might hear only composers of unquestioned excellence and into which should enter nothing vulgar, coarse, 'sensational,' but only such as outlives fashion."[7]

For seventeen years, Boston was protected from vulgar music—but, of course, it was next to impossible for a living composer to be heard. Mrs. Jack had enjoyed the pure concerts, but she greeted Henry L. Higginson's Symphony Orchestra with joyous enthusiasm. It was literally Mr. Higginson's orchestra because he paid the salaries of his sixty musicians out of his personal funds, which gave him "the right to all their time needed for rehearsals and concerts."

There was controversy—Boston would not be Boston if there had not been. The Harvard Musical Concert musicians had never been able to afford time enough for sufficient practice and Mr. Higginson had to go abroad to find a leader and performers of sufficiently high quality. Of course there were those who felt that American musicians had been affronted. Mrs. Jack Gardner sided with Higginson, caring nothing for the criticism this brought upon her.

Higginson decreed that his musicians "could give in Boston as many serious concerts of classical music as were wanted and also give at other times and more especially in summer, concerts of a lighter kind, in which should be included good dance music." Mrs. Jack became as ardent a patroness of the Boston Pops as she was of the Boston Symphony. Among her contemporaries were those so pure as to be shocked by her enthusiasm.

Given a day when there was no symphony concert and a time when there was no rehearsal, Higginson's musicians were free to play at private concerts. Some of them joined together to perform chamber music. The Kneisel Quartette was the most famous and these musicians played for Mrs. Jack Gardner frequently. But she seemed to like soloists best—first violins in particular.

And first among her favorite first violinists was Charles Loeffler.[8] He was born in Alsace, his father a writer who "engaged in government work" which took his family to Russia and then to Hungary. Loeffler was a professional violinist with orchestra experience in Paris when he came to New York in 1881 to play under Leopold Damrosch and Théodore Thomas. He had been in New York for less than a year when Mr. Higginson hired him for the new Boston Symphony. First violinist with Kneisel, Loeffler played in the Boston Symphony until 1903 when he "resigned to become a composer," according to the official word. Actually, he departed heartbroken because his fellow musicians refused to accept his compositions, which he had been at work upon for many years. But it was as a composer that Loeffler was eventually known, his memories of his childhood, his impressions of poems by Maeterlinck becoming tone poems and symphonies in a new manner to be played by the Boston Symphony and eventually recorded by the Eastman-Rochester Orchestra and others.

Loeffler was only twenty, but with a distinguished musical career already behind him when he crossed Mrs. Gardner's path. He resembled many of her past and future favorites in that he was young, blond and handsome, especially in profile. But there the resemblance ended. He was not boyish, but already very much of a man, age having little to do with this quality. No adoring mother hovered over him, nor would he tolerate such a relationship or the pretense of it on the part of an older woman. Mrs. Jack was genuinely excited over Loeffler's compositions. Her taste in music was much more advanced and modern than her taste in art ever would be. Loeffler played his music for her—often she was the first to hear it. He discussed in letters some of his musical problems and asked permission to dedicate his "Divertimento" to Mrs.

Gardner. "No conventionality may be looked for in the piece," Loeffler told her. "It may stir your imagination by astonishing your ears for I believe in tone coloring lies principally the possibility of future compositions. The orchestration therefore, I have given great thought [to] and there is many a new effect in the score I am sure."

Loeffler frequently thanked Mrs. Gardner for her kindnesses to him—something there is little evidence that many others did. Although he had small cash resources, he sent her modest but choice gifts—"this autograph of the frères de Goncourt" on New Year's in 1883, for example, because, in his words, the brothers Goncourt "were after all a great factor in modern French literature." And later (in 1898): "Pray accept this little book and autograph from me with my best wishes," the book having "belonged to Edmond de Goncourt, who like you was a 'précieux' and loved beautiful things." [9]

Loeffler was genuinely fond of Mrs. Gardner, but never did he call her "dear lady" and drop everything to run to her side when she summoned him. Sometimes she summoned in vain and there were a few stormy periods in their friendship. The result was that she respected him above all others—with a few exceptions, such as Wilhelm Gericke.

Gericke was the second conductor of the Boston Symphony —George Henschel, the first conductor, having served for three seasons adequately but without any remarkable brilliance. Critics were bored, and one of them wrote, "I believe that a large number attended the symphony concerts simply because it was fashionable."

Gericke put new life into the Symphony, but after two concerts, he came to Henry Lee Higginson and said, "You have not an orchestra here. There are some musicians but hardly an orchestra." He proceeded to drill the musicians—and at the end of the season twenty non-musicians departed. Gericke replaced them with Viennese, whom he could depend upon to work hard.

Vienna was "steeped in Wagner; Liszt and Verdi were visitors, Brahms was in process of composing his symphonies" when Gericke left the Viennese world of new music and came to Boston. He was disappointed not only in his orchestra but in the reaction of his audiences—to Wagner, especially. There was a tendency to laugh at Gericke, the new conductor with the black hair, the "uptwisted mustache and a parted, silken beard." Gericke spoke very little English. He would stand "off stage at Music Hall with his great gold watch in hand, walk stiffly to his place and raise his baton just as the hands of the clock at the rear of the balcony pointed to eight. At the seemly hour of 9:30 (or if the program warned, at precisely 9:35) the concert would end." [10] Perhaps it was at this time that Mrs. Jack Gardner began to add the word "precisely" to the hour given in her invitations to concerts in her own music room.

Mrs. Gardner was on Gericke's side from the beginning. If foreigners could do a better job in the orchestra than Americans, they should be hired. But she hoped always that young Americans would emerge from the New England Conservatory able to hold their own. She became an ardent Wagnerian —while her husband sided with those who thought that Wagner made too much noise.

Gericke was thirty-seven when he came to Boston—unmarried and very shy with women. "Mr. Gericke's English lasts only about fifteen seconds and then runs dry," a critic remarked. But during his seasons with the Boston Symphony, when he raised that merely good orchestra to the status of one of the best in the country, he became a personal friend of Mrs. Jack Gardner and her husband.

In 1889, in somewhat failing health, Gericke returned to Austria, expecting to remain there. But in 1896 he was back with the Boston Symphony. It was during his interim abroad that he wrote to Mrs. Gardner, his English by no means drying up but proceeding page after page in an idiom and spelling all his own. In Vienna, probably in 1890, he wrote:

"From here I cannot tell you any especiall news; we have now carneval where all people is dancing—except my own person—and in this time the musical season more or less stopped, untill Strauss has turned to death all the boys and girls which are finding that music is only to be made and written for the dance. This poor people does not know the wonderful history about Tristan and Isolde by [sic] King Marke . . ."

Mrs. Gardner promised that she and her husband would see Gericke in Bayreuth within two years. She wrote him news of his friends and he replied with affection as well as humor.

"To wait more than two years for the next meeting is to much for a man who is so devoted as I am to Mr. and Mrs. Gardner. You say in your letter that Brookline was so beautiful this Spring. Oh! I know how beautiful it is there. I have it in my memory as it is in reality . . . They are all three friends of my; but I really envy those three fellows which are going to Green Hill without me, to play for you. I am still always the old and good-natured man as I was in formerly time;

119

if not I would like to fight with them and kill one after each other!" [11]

The three fellows to go to Brookline were Clayton Johns, Loeffler and Tim Adamowski. Tymoteusz Adamowski was born in Warsaw and joined the Boston Symphony in 1884, when he was twenty-six. He was a violinist, tall, blond and handsome in the pattern Mrs. Jack found so pleasing. More given to flattery than her other musical young men, he was not her favorite, perhaps for this reason. Adamowski became the conductor of the Boston Symphony's Pops Concerts and not a little of the popularity of this summer series was the result of his personal charm.

Gericke was pleased to hear that Adamowski "is leading the Summer concerts in Boston! This is a great surprise to me and I like to hear it, he is going on in every way." But Gericke thought Adamowski "should have a care for his health . . . because it hurts sometimes in the stomach to lead an orchestra and Mr. Adamowski is in this case besides other things very sensitif."

Mrs. Jack never missed a summer concert if she could help it, dropping everything at Beverly to go up to Boston no matter how hot the weather. Her husband, though well educated in music and sufficiently fond of it, could live without Pops. He hated to miss yacht races—even when he was in Europe, letters from T. J. Coolidge to the effect that "In the yacht race last Saturday, Harry Hovey's boat won easily" but was, to look at her, "very ugly" made him wish he were back home and could get out to the Eastern Yacht Club.

During the summer of 1885 the Gardners were at home; and Jack Gardner had a stake in the America's Cup Race—to the extent that he was one of a syndicate of ten men who built the American defender.[12] They chose Edward Burgess, a young amateur naval architect just turned professional, to design their yacht, which was built in a Boston yard. Burgess's largest sloop to date had been 38 feet, but their Cup defender, *Puritan,* was 94 feet, with a broad beam, 22 feet 7 inches. She carried 8000 square feet of sail and she had a 51-foot keel holding 48 tons "of outside lead through which her centerboard worked." She was 140 tons and built of wood. Meanwhile, the New York Yacht Club was building a rival defender, *Priscilla,* all of iron. Jeeringly they called the Eastern Yacht Club's entry the "Bean Boat" and made fun of her broad beam. But at Newport the Boston boat, *Puritan,* "walked away from all her rivals." According to the rules, the America's Cup defender had to come from the New York

Yacht Club but one man in the Boston syndicate was a New York Yacht Club member, so all was well.

The first race with the British contender, *Genesta,* was called after five dull hours of fog and calm. In the second, *Puritan* tried too late to cross the bows of *Genesta* at the starting line. *Genesta*'s bowsprit ripped into *Puritan*'s mainsail and snapped her bowsprit. "The *Puritan* was promptly slapped on the stern by the judges and disqualified." There were damages to *Genesta,* which Jack Gardner's syndicate offered to pay for, but the British owner refused. He also preferred a "sail-over" to winning by forfeit.

The first completed race went to *Genesta* as far as the half-way mark but *Puritan* crossed the finish line 16 minutes and 19 seconds ahead.

A light wind favored *Genesta* at the start of the next race but when the yachts started "to beat home, a fresh autumn nor'wester blew up." *Puritan*'s crew had experience of heavy seas off Marblehead and their yacht could point closer to the wind. "The skipper of the *Genesta* made the mistake of crowding sail on her, putting her lee rail under most of the time." This slowed *Genesta* and *Puritan* came tearing along "leaving a wake like an ocean liner" to win by one minute, 38 seconds.

Jack Gardner was not to underwrite another America's Cup defender. The *Puritan* was sold at auction for $13,500; J. Malcolm Forbes (one of the ten syndicate members) bid her in for use off his family's island of Naushon. Eventually, she became a passenger packet between New Bedford and the Cape Verde Islands—flying the Portuguese flag. Jack Gardner had yachts of his own he liked better. He always kept at least one at Roque Island, and every summer, when he was not in Europe, he tried to find time for a cruise with assorted nephews, friends and relatives—an all-male crew. Isabella, left stranded at Roque, was not cast down. Singly or in groups her favorite young men, musicians, artists and writers, visited Roque.

During the summer of 1886 the Jack Gardners sailed for Europe taking with them "J.P.G."—Joseph Peabody Gardner, eldest of the three nephews who were so much their own boys. Joe was leaving his "homestead estate and farm" near Hamilton, acquired in March of the previous year. In the light of coming events, it would seem that something had gone very wrong with Joe.

Possibly Joe had bought a homestead in the belief that a girl he loved was going to marry him. Certainly he never married. Joe's father had been subject to periods of melancholy—with good reason, for he had early lost the mother of his boys. Something in Joe's private life was making him intolerably unhappy, and this journey may have been planned, at least in part, on Joe's account.

Arriving in Liverpool on July 1, the Gardners took the Midland train to London to stay at the Albemarle Hotel in Piccadilly. The Albemarle, according to Baedeker's Guide to London, was "largely patronized by royalty, the diplomatic corps and the nobility. Wines and cuisine are excellent." In 1886 the hotel was "largely patronized" by Gardners, for Jack's brother George Augustus was already there with his daughter Olga.

The Gardners gave a luncheon for Henry James, who should at least have appreciated the cuisine. A new figure in Mrs. Jack's tapestry of friends appeared at the party; Miss Violet Paget, who wrote essays under the name of Vernon Lee. She later took Mrs. Jack shopping for books, commenting with surprise that the American lady knew a collector's item when she saw one. Professor Norton would not have been surprised.

Henry James complained, of course, writing to Grace Norton: "All this time I am supposed to be looking after Mrs. Jack Gardner, Mrs. Bronson, the Daniel Curtises and about 30 other Americans now in London who are all holding by my coat-tails." The Curtises met and liked young Joseph Gardner.

On July 22, Jack Gardner went to Paris, via Folkstone and Boulogne, according to his pocket diary. The next day, "W.A.G. arrived in Paris from Germany in the morning." Evidently, Jack Gardner had gone to meet William Amory and the following day "Mrs. G. and J.P.G. came from London via Boulogne."

There was no reason given for Mrs. Gardner's staying over a day and then coming to Paris with her nephew Joe. They "all drove to St. Denis & back via Bois de Boulogne" on the 26 of July and then, on the 27th, "J.L.G., I.S.G. & W.A.G. left Paris at 8:10 P.M." in the sleeping car bound for Hiedelberg.

Did Joe see them off, and then return alone to London? There was no mention of him again—until October 17, when the Gardners were back in Paris after an Austrian tour followed by a short stay in Venice.

On October 17, 1886, John L. Gardner's pocket diary entry read, "Rec'd telegram (early) of death of J.P.G."

This was all. Not another word referred to the eldest of the Gardners' three nephews. Only one letter of condolence was kept. It was from Ralph Curtis, who had not been in London with his parents and had never met Joe. "My father was so particularly charmed with him that he has spoken frequently to me about him," Ralph said.

Joseph Peabody Gardner died at the age of twenty-five years and one month—almost to the day. The cause of his death was never mentioned but his college friend John Jay Chapman, in his *Retrospections*, said, "Jo, the wittiest man of his epoch, committed suicide in early life." [13]

THIRTEEN

The Sargent Portrait

A NOTE WAS DELIVERED at the Albemarle Hotel just before the Gardners left London. It was dated October 26, 1886 and it was from Henry James.

"I am writing to Sargent to say to him that we will come and see Mme Gautreau on Tuesday about 3:15." Time was "short to prepare Sargent's mind and Mme Gautreau's body," James told Mrs. Jack. "Don't answer this," he said. "I only send word in advance to give you a timely warning and let you know that the bolt is levelled at the susceptible young artist." [1]

It was just Jamesian banter to please Mrs. Jack, who was amused but rarely deceived. John Singer Sargent was neither very young nor particularly susceptible. The son of American parents, he was born in Florence in 1856, and it might be imagined that Isabella Gardner was about to meet a second Italian-American charmer in the style of Crawford. But such was not the case. Sargent's mind was firmly fixed on building a solid career in painting, on supporting himself and assisting his parents and sisters if need be. He was curiously American for a man who never saw the United States until he was twenty. His father was the impecunious, impractical one, who retired early from medical practice and drifted about Europe on dwindling assets at the behest of his wife. John Singer Sargent, supremely gifted as a draftsman and as a colorist, had inherited the spirit of some Gloucester seafarer ancestor. He was determined to wrest a living from art—more difficult than the sea, if not as dangerous.

Madame Gautreau, whose body Sargent was to "prepare" for Mrs. Jack, was not a model, nor was she in London in person. It was her portrait—in no need of preparation but long since finished—that James referred to. Sargent had exhibited it under the title *Madame X* at the Paris Salon in 1884.[2] Brilliant in color contrasts, dramatic and third-dimensional in the handling of light and shadow, it was the pose which in fact made this portrait sensational. Knowing nothing about the lady, spectators were bound to judge her to be beautiful but brazen, hard and probably heartless.

The trouble was that everyone in Paris knew who Madame X really was—an American, born Virginie Avegno of Louisiana. Her father, General Avegno, raised the "Avegno Zouaves" during the Civil War and was killed at the battle of Shiloh. Her mother then took her to Paris, where she married a wealthy Frenchman named Gautreau. She had a strange "lavender" complexion, which people suspected to be the result of using cosmetics. Visitors to the Paris Salon, standing before Sargent's portrait, were heard to laugh and say that it was "a painting of a painting."

The pose of a Sargent portrait invariably caught more of the character of his sitter than the expression of the mouth or eyes, of which sitters themselves and their relatives were apt to complain. Sargent did justice to Madame Gautreau's enchanting profile, her arms and shoulders. Her dress, although sleeveless and low-cut, covered her adequately. It was the way she stood that was brazen. The frail chains that held up the bodice of her velvet gown neither slipped nor slid, but she held herself as though willing to break them. People stared, then meditated on the stories they had heard about the lady.

No one seemed to notice the draftsmanship or the brilliance of this painting. Sargent, angered and hurt by the press and private comment (or so it was said), broke up his Paris studio and established a studio in London, taking the portrait of *Madame X* with him, since her husband refused to buy the picture. Sargent's reputation increased as women in high society sought him out and he was besieged by sitters—some of whom he painted to look like the hard, haughty, overdressed females that they really were.

Mrs. Jack Gardner liked the portrait of Madame Gautreau. Her inborn sense of merchandise told her that Sargent's work would sell and should be collected. Sargent had painted a sketch, oil on wood, called *Madame Gautreau Drinking a Toast,* and had given it to the lady's mother. In 1919 when it came on sale in Paris Mrs. Gardner bought it, hanging it eventually at Fenway Court.

But on the occasion of her first meeting with John Singer Sargent, Mrs. Gardner started a collection of painters, rather than their works. She saw that here was a most attractive man; but there was no time for her to have Sargent paint her portrait because the Gardners' return passage had been engaged for November 5.

There was time, however, for Mrs. Jack to visit James

McNeill Whistler's studio in London. It was now that he made his little sketch of her and that she bought the sketch of his model.

Not particularly pleased with the pastel portrait, Whistler wrote: "Your visit has been most charming to me—and I only wish you had carried away a more brilliant proof of my appreciation. However, you rather beat me in the hurry of things this time! but you must give me my *revanche* when I come to Boston. . . ." [3]

Whistler was not coming to Boston, however. He, too was an expatriate, born in Lowell, Massachusetts, but he once told a stranger who had irritated him by claiming the same birthplace, "I shall be born when and where I choose . . ." He chose "Baltimore or St. Petersburg!" He was fifty-two when he sketched Mrs. Jack—the only painter older than herself with whom she established a personal friendship.

It would seem that European musicians were flocking to the United States and that American painters all lived abroad. If Mrs. Jack wanted a Boston collection of both, she would find it hard to fill up her ranks with artists of note. But artists of promise would do, and she had already found one.

Denis Miller Bunker had arrived in Boston in 1885. In December, he was taken to a house where he "talked to the daughter of Julia Ward Howe, . . . a delightful and sympathetic person." [4] They discussed St. Gaudens—at that time a controversial sculptor, conventional though he now seems. Maud Howe was "solid on St. G. so I naturally froze to her at once," Bunker said—having come to Boston with preconceived ideas of the coldness of society. "I have seen gallons of the blue blood of Beacon Street," he wrote. "It's not so chilly as I thought." But in "late afternoon rambles through this atmosphere of wealth and respectability, thawed by an occasional cup of tea, I sometimes feel supremely ridiculous."

Dennis Bunker was the son of New England Quakers who had moved to New York City. He was about seventeen when he began to study art at the National Academy and the Art Students League in New York. With difficulty, he persuaded his parents to send him to Paris. Funds were limited, so after an experience he thoroughly enjoyed he came home spelling his name "Denis" [5] in the French fashion, tossing French phrases into conversation and letters, certain that his ancestral name must have been *Bon Coeur* and that his soul was French. It seemed a harsh fate that his body must find sustenance in America.

A new venture, called the Cowles Art School, [6] was starting up in Boston with rooms at 145 Dartmouth Street. Bunker got a job there, teaching drawing and painting, all the while despising his students, whom he described as "some dozen or sixteen old maids and the usual complement of raw boys."

In Boston, Bunker was "melancholy [because of] the way people troop to church here Sunday morning, the streets are black with 'em, it looks like a fire." But very shortly he began a portrait of Madame Nordica, a prima donna of the first magnitude, now only twenty-six. Her name had been Lillian Norton; she was born in Farmington, Maine, and it was her French voice teacher who thought up her stage name of Nordica. She had already scored a success in Paris and New York as Marguerite in *Faust* but she was now Mrs. Gower, unhappily married and temporarily retired from the stage. Nordica's great career as a Wagnerian soprano was still to come, as were several more marriages, but meanwhile she made Boston infinitely more fun for Bunker. She took him to the theater, to restaurants—and to places far from frigid, where there were singing and refreshments. The *Nordica* portrait seems never to have been finished and the affair ended abruptly. When questioned about it by his friend and fellow artist Joe Evans: *"J'en suis bien aise. Elle est bien trop exigeante,"* Bunker wrote. It seems probable that Madame Nordica had already become "too demanding" and that Bunker had tired of her before Mrs. Jack Gardner appeared on the scene.

Denis Bunker was another most attractive young man. In his photograph his regular features, his center-parted, softly waving hair and his wistful expression make him look like a boy, mysteriously sad. Sargent painted him as having slightly heavy eyelids, a more flamboyant mustache and hair artistically disarranged.

Mrs. Jack had suffered a severe shock in the loss of the oldest of her three nephews. When she destroyed all of Joe's long letters to her (as she seems to have done) she was erasing him from her memory, putting him out of her mind forever. But of course no one can do that. She must have felt that she had failed Joe, or he would not have taken his own life. But here was a young man of the same age (actually just nineteen days younger than Joe), gifted, witty—and melancholy. If Mrs. Jack could help Denis Bunker to become a great painter it would be a sort of expiation for the tragic failure with Joe. Not that anyone ever dared to express such conjectures—Mrs. Jack would have been furious. The thing to do was to be the brightest, breeziest woman in Boston, playing with a young man and pretending to be his own age.

Bunker and Mrs. Jack were now seen at the theater together constantly. He took her to the restaurants and the late supper spots which he had discovered with Nordica, and Mrs. Jack was delighted to go to places her friends had never heard of. Bunker aided and abetted her in one of her ideas that was to become a legend—along with so many others.

The story was told by Jack Sheean, veteran boxing referee. Women were never allowed to see a boxing match but "back there when their skirts were long and they all wore bustles, some of the highest hostesses in society, some of them bearing Boston's bluest blooded names, used to be smuggled in through side doors by their husbands or their escorts to view . . . private prize fights" held in men's clubs. "And they often had a bottle of champagne on the side, too," Jack Sheean declared. But not all high hostesses had as good luck getting escorts as Mrs. Gardner and not all husbands were amenable to smuggling ladies through side doors.

"Why I remember refereeing a fight one time before an exclusive audience of Boston society women," Sheean said. "There wasn't a man in the place besides me, the fighters and their seconds. It was Mrs. Jack Gardner's idea and she put up the money. It was for a purse of $150 and I matched Knucksey Doherty of Donegal Square with Tim Harrington of Cambridge and told them to be themselves.

"The battle was held in a studio in the old studio building on Tremont Street. There was so much furniture and statuary and bric-a-brac in the place we had to spend an hour clearing a space for the ring.

"When all those sedate, quietly-dressed society women arrived, I grew nervous. I figured some of them would scream or faint but the vestal virgins in the Coliseum never looked on with more calm as a gladiator bit the dust, than these high and haughty dames watched these two babies murder each other. In fact, they were cheering before the bout was half over . . ." The fight went for seventeen rounds, "with a full quota of gore and knockdowns." Sheean thought the ladies rooted for Harrington because he was good-looking but "sympathized graciously with Doherty when he broke a hand and had to take the sponge."

It was said that Mrs. Jack invited a prizefighter to come to 152 Beacon Street, strip down to fighting trunks, and stand behind a screen so that his shadow would delight her lady guests one afternoon. According to the story, the ladies wanted to dispense with the screen and the fighter thereupon came out and flexed his muscles for them. It was entertainment like this which helps to explain the remark of a prim lady from Brookline: "Of course Father never let us go to Mrs. Gardner's parties!" Father could never feel sure whether the party at Mrs. Jack's music room was for Mozart or muscles.

Still more often told was the encounter between the great prize-fighter John L. Sullivan and Mrs. Jack. The scene was South Boston, where streetcar workers with a grievance were milling around in an ugly mood. Mrs. Gardner had been to dinner at Perkins Institution for the Blind, and on her way home her carriage was stopped by the crowd. It was a brougham, some said, and she rolled down the window and leaned out to see what was the matter. On her head were the two famous diamonds.

The crowd became menacing. Then a huge man stepped forward. "Don't be afraid, Mrs. Jack," he said, walking beside the carriage while people parted right and left to let him through. The man was John L. Sullivan.

In other versions of the story, Mrs. Jack was sitting in an open carriage, wearing evening clothes and all glowing and gleaming with pearls and diamonds. However embroidered the story, Mrs. Gardner knew John L. Sullivan. She probably saw him display his diamond belt, his name composed of 250 stones, the belt considered to be the largest piece of flat gold ever seen in this country, according to his own story. Although never a suffragist, Mrs. Gardner asserted women's rights to sit at the ringside if they wanted to. After Sullivan's day, however, her interest in prize fighting seemed to diminish in favor of artists.

Almost the whole Gardner family was mobilized to sit for portraits by Denis Bunker. He wrote Mrs. Jack many letters reporting his progress among the Gardners. "Mr. Gardner (George) seems on the whole to like his picture now. I have repainted part of it. Mr. Gardner (George) wants me to paint his son (John) . . . Mr. Gardner's son George and brother of John wishes me to paint his wife, next winter—I shall wear a decoration—painter in ordinary to the Gardners of Boston." Bunker also painted Olga, sister of John and George, who looked as if she wished the whole ordeal of sitting for a portrait were over with. "Miss Olga" sat very straight, her bustle curving behind her and her skirt much draped in front.

"I'm going to paint Mr. Higginson (Henry L.) all over again tomorrow morning," Bunker told Mrs. Jack. " 'Cause why? 'Cause he ain't red enough in the face." He had finished

"Mr. Montgomery Sears," he said in a later letter. "He and the pretty lady are both delighted with it, for which I thank Jove and my lucky star . . ."

Bunker was actually happiest and at his best in landscape, however. He was to paint a brook in Medfield, Massachusetts —a grass-grown, watery track deep in meadow grass which was a miracle of greens and blues. Neither slavishly realistic nor strictly impressionistic, Bunker quietly solved many problems where a lesser artist would have failed. Mrs. Gardner bought the Medfield picture in 1889 and included it in her final collection at Fenway Court, with another landscape by Bunker.

Although it might seem as though Mrs. Jack spent all her time with Denis Bunker, this was far from true. She had not forgotten her old friends, Maud Howe among them. On December 30, 1886, Maud's mother, Julia Ward Howe, was "Much worried about Maud's precipitate intended marriage." But Mrs. Jack was not worried at all—Maud was going to marry John Elliott, an artist of considerable ability, born in Lincolnshire. He had met the beautiful Maud when her mother took her to Europe in 1877, had faithfully pursued her—bitterly aware that her face entitled her to marry a fortune and that he had none. Jack Elliott had just arrived in the United States "with the sapphire ring," [7] and the incurably romantic Mrs. Gardner was delighted that Maud had decided in Jack's favor.

On Monday, February 7, 1886, Mrs. Jack Gardner went early to 241 Beacon Street. Flowers she had ordered from her own greenhouses had arrived. She and Jack Elliott together "made a bower of hibiscus and laurel" in Mrs. Howe's parlor for Maud to be married in.

Mrs. Howe, romantic herself, was anxious only about her daughter's happiness with a masterful man. She wrote "a bridal song" for Maud, which was sung by Maud's brother and three men friends. Further music was composed by John Sullivan Dwight, sponsor of those pure programs by the Harvard Musical Concert group. Then Maud "parted the bamboo veil"—a curtain between rooms, probably one of Mrs. Gardner's gifts from the Orient—and "in queenly loveliness, stepped forth, taking Elliott's arm and walked to the bower . . ." [8]

Elliott was a muralist and both Maud Howe Elliott and Mrs. Gardner tried hard to get him commissions. It was probably Maud, on one of her lecture tours, who persuaded Mrs. Potter Palmer that she needed an Elliott mural for her dining-room wall on Lake Shore Drive, Chicago. He painted *The Vintage* for her, "exuberant with the spirit of youth," someone said. Mrs. Gardner probably used her influence to get Elliott to submit a sketch for a mural in the projected Boston Public Library building on Copley Square. Elliott's sketch won a contract and he painted *The Triumph of Time* —in the course of which time almost triumphed, for he needed many months to finish it. He carried Maud off to Rome, where studios could be rented at low cost and models were easy to come by. Eventually the Jack Elliotts were among the attractions that brought Mrs. Gardner to Rome.

In her enthusiasm for artists, Mrs. Gardner did not forget her comparatively recent interest in lectures. Mrs. Julia Ward Howe was speaking at the Concord School of Philosophy in 1887 and Mrs. Jack proposed to go to Concord to hear her. It must have startled her, therefore, to receive a letter from Mrs. Howe promising to visit in Beverly and bring "the Aristophanes Lecture" but at the same time saying, "You must not go to Concord. You would take people's minds off from their difficult themes and abstractions. You would play the very devil with the *indifference* which is necessary for the pursuit of philosophy. My hair stands on end at the thought of the mischief you might work in that sacred place . . ."

Professor Norton had no such misgivings. He admired the three-volume Boccaccio which Mrs. Jack had just brought home from Florence and the forty-seven volumes of Goldoni's comedies she had bought in Venice. It was probably Norton who introduced a young man named Bernard Berenson, in 1886,[9] perhaps early in the year before the Gardners went to Europe with their nephew Joe.

Bernard Berenson ardently desired to win the Parker Traveling Fellowship at Harvard. His marks were high, especially in languages, and he knew that he and only one other student were being considered. The other man won.

Perhaps feeling that injustice had been done, four of Berenson's professors "and a few friends subscribed several hundred dollars to give Berenson a traveling fellowship." The Gardners were among the friends. As in all their projects of this sort, Jack Gardner and Belle decided how much to give, how to give it, and to whom. They were always generous and always completely secretive about it. Jack signed the checks and let Belle handle the personal side of the matter, so that it often seemed as though she alone were responsible for her protégés.

Berenson gave Mrs. Gardner a photograph of himself, his

hair a mass of curls so long that they reached his coat collar in the back, his profile turned to the camera to show an almost Grecian nose and a mouth that could only be called childish. He was born in Lithuania; brought by his parents to Boston when he was about ten, and the curls were ritualistic. They could have been ritualistically cut when he was thirteen, but he was still wearing them now that he was twenty-one. The following year (1887) in a picture taken among contemporaries at Harvard, the effect of Berenson's center-parted long hair gave him a look reminiscent of Oscar Wilde.

During his boyhood, Berenson experienced poverty, which instead of crushing him or making him the enemy of society, fired his ambition. His first escape from "flat" and "ugly" South Boston was into the public library, where his reading ranged widely and joyfully into realms of mediaeval history. His parents sacrificed themselves and their other children to keep him in school, Boston University being within their means. But after one year there, Berenson set his sights on Harvard.

When Berenson called on Mrs. Gardner in 1887, it was to say goodbye. He was on his way to Europe on what might be called his Gardner Traveling Fellowship, if the Gardners had been disposed to mention facts and figures. He wrote to Mrs. Gardner in August, 1887, when he had already been several weeks in Paris—a most lonely, homesick young man—"plunged so suddenly into the most horrible of solitudes, a great city, where you do not know one friendly soul." He had taken refuge in books but was still further depressed by Tolstoi's *Confessions*.

"What shall I do? What is there for me to do? For others, there is a living, as such. What care they if thousands like them have lived? . . . But as for me, I feel that I have no right to live but for what I shall write; and that whatever I may write, it will always be about myself. . . ."

Patiently, Mrs. Gardner answered these boyish effusions; but it is said that Berenson eventually destroyed all her letters.[10] It would be interesting to know if she took up the challenge when Berenson referred to Dante as "crude and vulgar." Mrs. Gardner, through Professor Norton, was financing publications of members of the Cambridge Dante Society. When Berenson wrote that he was doing no work, that "time slipped through" his fingers, Mrs. Gardner's reply can be imagined. She had little use for people unwilling to work.

Berenson at this period was not ungrateful, however. "I thank you so much for the interest you take in me," he wrote. "I feel so often that I have a hold on nothing and that no one cares a whit for me; me, in myself. Your letters always bring with them a feeling of encouragement and assurance to myself." [11]

So wrote the very young man who was to play an important part in Mrs. Gardner's life as an art collector. But in 1887 she was still a collector of artists; and when John Singer Sargent [12] arrived in Boston, Mrs. Jack promptly invited him to visit her in Beverly.

"I am working on time and cannot leave," Sargent replied, from Newport. He would soon be "going to Boston to paint a portrait, where I must look forward to meeting you." Sargent would be in Boston "a good part of November," painting Mrs. Edward Boit and staying at her house, Number 170 Beacon Street.

Edward Boit was an artist and a great friend of Sargent's. The Boits had been living in Paris where, five years earlier, Sargent had painted their four little girls, each wearing a white pinafore, the youngest sitting on the floor with her doll. It was a most appealing picture, so full of dramatic contrast that visitors to the Museum of Fine Arts, where it now hangs, stop in their tracks to look at it.

Mrs. Boit had just come to Boston to launch her second daughter in society; and Sargent painted this lady, elaborately dressed, triumphantly sure of herself, with a confident smile —and narrowed eyes.

Mrs. Jack Gardner arranged for sittings to Sargent. It was the custom for an artist to stay at the house of his sitter, but when Sargent went to 152 Beacon Street, *Town Topics* saw a story in it. "That fascinating young American artist, so popular in Paris, has lately been the guest in Boston of Mr. and Mrs. E. P. Boit, Jr. Mr. Boit was recently called out of town I hear, and Mrs. Boit, not caring to have such a bewildering young man in the house, suggested to Mrs. Gardner that she take him in charge in the interval. This proposition was enthusiastically accepted by the festive Mrs. Jack who, on the appointed evening called for him in her carriage, and the staidest quarter of Boston saw them drive off triumphantly to Longwood, amidst a shower of slippers and rice, quite like a *lune de miel,* as it were." This burst of eloquence, misinformation and humor was followed in a week by another item.

"I hear that John S. Sargent, the eminent portrait painter, who had all of artistic and aesthetic Boston at his feet, is now engaged on a portrait of no less a subject than Mrs. Jack Gardner. Fortunate artist with so fascinating a woman for his subject! Of course Mr. Sargent can never hope to transfer her most bewildering charm to his canvas, but I fancy it will be the portrait of the season, nevertheless, and society will be sorely disappointed if it is not exhibited in some of the club galleries. I wonder if the dainty white slipper with its diamond buckle which stole out from beneath the petticoats at a recent reception in Boston, will be one of the features of the portrait?"

While Sargent was the guest of the Gardners, they took him out to visit Groton School. They were always glad of an excuse to see their nephew Amory, who, the year before, had built a house for himself on land adjoining the school. A student who had recently entered the school was Ellery Sedgwick, a New York boy who was to become a famous *Atlantic Monthly* editor. Young Sedgwick saw a memorable scene:

"The time was a lovely Sunday morning in the late '80s. There were two hours before church, and I well knew the danger of running across a master and hearing his suggestion that there is nothing like a Sunday morning walk in God's sunshine. I had other views, and with a copy of *Ben Hur*, which had just burst on my excited world, I slipped into the gymnasium and, piling two wrestling mats, rolled them up in one corner, tucked myself securely behind them, and was lost to the world. For an hour I was buried in my book, when suddenly the gymnasium door was thrown wildly open and a woman's voice thrilled me with a little scream of mockery and triumph. Cautiously I peeked from my concealment and caught sight of a woman with a figure of a girl, her modish muslin skirt fluttering behind her as she danced through the doorway and flew across the floor, tossing over her shoulder some taunting paean of escape. But bare escape it seemed, for not a dozen feet behind her came her cavalier, white-flanneled, black-bearded, panting with laughter and pace. The pursuer was much younger than the pursued but that did not affect the ardor of the chase. The lady raced to the stairway leading to the running track above. Up she rushed, he after her. She reached the track and dashed round it, the ribbons of her belt standing straight out behind her. Her pursuer was visibly gaining. The gap narrowed. Nearer, nearer he drew, both hands outstretched to reach her waist. In *Ben Hur* the chariot race was in full blast, but it was eclipsed. 'She's winning,' I thought. 'No, she's losing.' And then at the apex of my excitement, 'He has her!' But at that crucial moment there came over me the sickening sense that this show was

134

not meant for spectators, that I was eavesdropping and, worse, that I would be caught at it. There was not one instant to lose. The window was open. Out I slipped and slithered to safety.

"For me that race was forever lost and forever won. The figures go flying motionless as on the frieze of the Grecian urn.

What men or gods are there? What maidens loth?
What mad pursuit? What struggle to escape?

I knew not then whether it was lost or won. What I did know was that the Atalanta of that Sunday morning was Mrs. Jack Gardner and Milanion Mr. John S. Sargent. It was that same year he painted the famous portrait of her with her pearls roped about her waist, her beautiful arms glowing against a background that might have been the heart of a lotus." [13]

There was another observer—at the beginning of this episode who said that Mrs. Gardner had twitted Sargent because he was gaining weight. She had challenged him to a race once around the track at the gymnasium. But everyone was willing to let the race remain forever lost and forever won.

Sargent painted Mrs. Gardner in black, her slippers (barely showing) having ruby buckles. He painted at her home on Beacon Street, not at Longwood or even in Brookline, for the month was January and the Brookline house was closed. He chose for background a sixteenth-century Italian or Spanish velvet brocade, deep red with tan ground of metal threads much dimmed by time. The design of the textile, Sargent greatly enlarged, working out a pattern of circles and semicircles repeated by Mrs. Gardner's famous pearls, which it was his idea to have her wear around her waist. Her lovely arms and hands, whose beauty she was proud of, he had her clasp lightly below the pearls.

The effect of the circles in the textile was to make people ask if Sargent had painted Mrs. Gardner with "a sort of aureole about her head"—and to laugh. Photographs brought out what looked like a little crown upon her head—a fitting symbol for the future Queen Isabella of the Gardner Palace —but no one noticed this.

It was said that Sargent had great difficulty with the face and that Boit urged him to give up the project of painting Mrs. Gardner. Evidence of scraping and repainting can be detected and Sargent's sure but sometimes too hasty touch is absent. The public doubtless expected Sargent to paint Mrs.

Gardner with the gloss and hard brilliance of his average society portrait. But instead, he showed a woman leaning forward a little as if anxious to please, a woman a little unsure of herself, not entirely happy, but friendly and not in the least arrogant.

The portrait was full-length—the dress draped in front and doubtless gathered back into a bustle like Olga Gardner's in Bunker's portrait. Perhaps both ladies bought their gowns at Worth's when they were in Paris the previous summer.

Mrs. Gardner's dress was heart-shaped at the neck, cut low but by no means as revealing as some of those of Boston ladies Sargent was currently painting. A short string of pearls encircled her throat, from which hung a ruby. To come upon this portrait with the afternoon light on it at the far end of the Gothic Room at Fenway Court is to come face to face with Isabella Gardner—enigmatic, experienced—a *"presence,"* as Okakura, another artist was later to say.

The portrait was exhibited, beginning February 1, 1888, at the St. Botolph Club, then on Newbury Street. Mrs. James T. Fields, widow of the publisher and Miss Sarah Jewett poured tea, during the opening afternoon—both ladies in black, their hats adorned with ostrich plumes, their bosoms with violets *en corsage*. The Boston *Herald* described Mrs. Gardner's portrait as the "gem of the collection" which "thirteen hundred people" crowded in to try to see, but their reporter said that Mrs. Gardner had been painted "in a rich white satin gown, very *decolleté* . . ." The *Town Topics* writer said the portrait was "a capital likeness," patronizingly corrected the *Herald,* but said that Mrs. Gardner's dress, besides being "cut very low in the neck," was "sleeveless"—neither statement being true—and that Sargent had painted "a rather dazzling display of diamonds," which of course he did not do.

On December 8, 1887, *Town Topics* had revived Boston's memory of F. Marion Crawford. In discussing the possibility that William Dean Howells would leave Boston, the editor speculated that Mr. Crawford might take his place "in the domain of letters," and then piously remarked, "The fact that he is no longer a bachelor will, I fancy, lessen the cordiality of his welcome by some of the Boston women who had rather desperate flirtations with the author of *To Leeward* when he was here last. However, if Mr. Crawford behaves himself, and has no affairs with married women other than his wife, he won't have the doors of Boston's really best society slammed in his face when he goes to make a call, as was more than once the case when he formerly tarried in Boston."

Crawford did not return to Boston at this time, but almost forgotten gossip was revived and repeated. John L. Gardner overheard a story that was going the rounds of the men's clubs. Using the name of the popular resort in the White Mountains, "Sargent had painted Mrs. Gardner all the way down to Crawford's Notch," the story went. Jack Gardner said he would horsewhip the author of the witticism if he knew who it was. Of course, no one admitted knowing anything about it and Mr. Gardner committed one of the few errors in a circumspect career. He withdrew the Sargent portrait from the St. Botolph Club exhibition.

Critics had prophesied that Sargent's portrait of Mrs. Gardner would win a gold medal at the next Paris Salon, but when Sargent asked leave to show it, he was refused. Mr. Gardner had decreed that the portrait should never again be publicly exhibited and it never was during his lifetime. Mrs. Jack, however, continued proudly to say that it was the best Sargent ever did.

Of course speculation ran wild as to the supposed indecency of the portrait and the witticism was widely circulated. *Town Topics* printed it but in terms too vulgar even for a scandal sheet.

As before, when the hounds of gossip were on her trail, Jack Gardner stood by his wife. "Some surprise has been manifest at Mr. Gardner's departure from the country at this time, in view of the troubles that have overtaken the Chicago, Burlington and Quincy Railroad," the papers said. Mr. Gardner was one of "the three managing directors" and "largest stockholders." But Jack Gardner was again taking his wife abroad, this time to Spain.

FOURTEEN

La Donna Isabella

SPAIN WAS comparatively undiscovered country for Americans in 1888, London, Paris, Rome, the Riviera—that was the beaten track. Accommodations in Spain were still primitive; traveling was often dangerous by reason of bandits. Jack Gardner's pocket diary contained frequent notations such as "hotel dirty," or even "hotel awful," but Belle Gardner made no complaint.

Ever since her schooldays, Isabella had made it a habit to copy down passages she liked from books or poems that she read. In a notebook to which she still added, she had recently written a sentence she attributed to Bernadin de Saint Pierre which went, "There is in women an easy gaiety which scatters the sadness of man." Both she and her husband must have left the United States angry and unhappy because of the innuendo concerning what should have been a long-buried past. But Belle's "easy gaiety" soon returned. In Spain she was "seeing beautiful things" and was "in a heavenly frame of mind," she wrote.

In Burgos it was "snowy and very cold," the lace-like Gothic spires of the cathedral all frosted over like wedding cake. They "went to museum" in Madrid, according to Jack Gardner's record. And then at last they were in warm and sunny Seville.

The city, after an orgy of lenten penance, was prepared to celebrate Easter with what, to Spaniards, seemed most fitting —a splendid bullfight. The Gardners had a front-row box and Mrs. Jack was honored by having a bull named for her. She was as happy and gay as a Spanish señora—until the ceremonial proceedings got under way. Picadors on horseback planted spears in the neck of the bull and Mrs. Gardner shuddered. She had always loved animals; this was anything but fair play and she found herself on the side of the bull. Then the bull gored a horse. Amid cheers and shouts of "Olé," they dragged the horse from the ring, and Mrs. Gardner loved horses. It was too much for Belle, who said that she got down on the floor in the box, shut her eyes and put her fingers in her ears.

It was not true that John Singer Sargent had a rendezvous with Mrs. Gardner in Spain. The story that they had a clandestine love affair is pure fabrication, from beginning to end. Sargent was in Spain only twice in his life, once when he was twelve years old and again in 1879 when he was twenty-three. For a man so often remembered for his paintings of Spanish dancers, this seems remarkable, but on his second visit he was sketching constantly, as also the following year during his trip to Morocco. Love of Spain had entered his blood, never to leave him.[1]

In 1888, Sargent planned to be in Italy but did not go there, either. Mrs. Gardner had persuaded Sargent to let Denis Bunker come to watch him paint her portrait; the two men had struck up a friendship and it was Denis who told Mrs. Gardner about Sargent's plans.

Bunker had sailed from Boston with Gericke, who was bound for Oberammergau, while Bunker was to paint in Sargent's company. "Sargent's father was ill and ordered to Italy where we concluded to spend the summer," Bunker told Mrs. Gardner. But in a subsequent letter Bunker said that the elder Sargent was "now better and has been ordered to go to England where we . . . expect to spend the summer. So the world, or Mr. Sargent père wags me and my plans, from one part of Europe to another . . ."

Mrs. Jack may have written to Sargent suggesting that he meet her and her husband in Spain. She was always summoning friends to meet in Europe in some choice spot, where she thought both they and she would most enjoy sightseeing together. Henry James wrote many a page easing himself out of such invitations, and so did Bernard Berenson, even at this early date. Bunker said he could not leave his painting to go to Oberammergau, got scolded evidently, and excused himself for "being so lazy about the performances at Bayreuth" on the ground that he "has not lived long enough yet in Boston."

Ralph Curtis, summoned from Venice, met the Gardners in Seville where he sketched Mrs. Jack, who was wearing a lace mantilla. He gave her the sketch, inscribing it "Seville, 20 April, '88."

It was while watching a solemn religious procession in Seville that Mrs. Gardner was seized with a violent, constricting pain in her chest. She could not catch her breath and turned so white—almost blue—that Jack thought she was going to die. Then the pain abated, the color came slowly back into her face. It was an attack of angina, terrifying in every way. The constriction around her heart and the almost intolerable pain left her just as a great crucifix was being carried by in the street. Mrs. Gardner's maid was certain that here was a miracle wrought by the sight of this cross—and people told the story.

The Gardners bought their first important antique painting in Seville. It was a *Madonna and Child* by Francisco Zurbarán, painted in the seventeenth century and representative of Zurbarán's early period. Mrs. Gardner was to hang it in her own room on Beacon Street, rather than in one of her parlors downstairs for everyone to stare at. When Fenway Court was first built, she kept it in her private quarters. But when she altered Fenway Court, she had a Spanish chapel designed for it. On the walls, the words "In Memoriam" were carved, for the Christ Child in the painting looked remarkably like one of the photographs of her little son.

In June, when the Gardners reached Venice, there was a new young artist waiting for Mrs. Jack Gardner to collect and add to her permanent gallery of people. He was Joseph Lindon Smith, who in 1887 had been teaching the decorative art classes at the Boston Museum School of Fine Arts as assistant to C. Howard Walker. Mrs. Jack had not met him in Boston—perhaps because she was so taken up with Bunker, who taught in a rival school, and with Sargent, who overshadowed everyone.

Mrs. Gardner first encountered Joe Smith in the Square of St. John and St. Paul, Venice, at the equestrian statue (high on its marble pedestal) of Bartolommeo Colleoni. Smith himself told the story.[2] "I had taken advantage of a ladder, placed against the statue and not yet removed after some repairs to the head. No one had protested as I mounted it and I returned to climb it again with a roll of canvas and paints. Three days later I had completed the picture" of the head of Colleoni "without being ejected by officials. I was about to roll up my canvas when a cultivated woman's voice called up to me, asking what I was doing. 'Painting [a] portrait . . .' I answered.

" 'Come down and steady the ladder for me!' she said.

"Her manner was that of a woman with the habit of command. I obeyed at once and stood beside her, impressed by the elegant simplicity of her gown and the magnificent ruby at her throat and above all by the charm of her personality.

"She went up the ladder without effort and perched in the

uncomfortable seat I had vacated. It was almost half an hour before she rejoined me.

" 'You caught the strength and courage Verrocchio got into the features and the delicious green patina of the bronze,' she said. She ordered me to bring the picture and any other studies I had," to her hotel. " 'I am Mrs. John L. Gardner,' she turned to say, and was off."

Mrs. Gardner always called Joe Smith "Colli" in honor of their meeting. He was a most entertaining young man, with a great gift for the writing and staging of pageants and dramas, for painting of antiquities—and for enjoying life. About twenty-five at this time, he had come into Mrs. Gardner's life to stay and to help her when her serious collecting days began.

This time, the Gardners made only a ten-day visit to Venice. After they left, Ralph Curtis wrote to Mrs. Jack, "I wish I had your comely self beside me and could hear your musical, mellow voice so suited to confidences by moonlight in Venezia." He suggested that she read Casanova, in eight volumes!

The Gardners were off for Bayreuth, where they met Gericke and Clayton Johns. They heard Madame Materna, the "greatest of all Brunhildes" and Gericke took the Gardners to a party at "Wahnfried," Wagner's house, one evening, after a performance of opera.

"All the opera singers were there," Clayton Johns said. "Frau Cosima received us graciously, particularly Mrs. Gardner. Materna sang a scene from *Götterdämmerung* and other stars obliged with selections until it was early morning." [3] Jack Gardner was at this party with his wife, but it would be irreverent to wonder how he stood this Wagnerian jam-session.

In September, the Gardners were in Paris. They called at Boucheron's, the jeweler, where Mrs. Gardner chose "1 row, 37 pearls weighing an average of 17.5 grains each." Boston friends might think that they had already seen Mrs. Jack's jewels but she had not finished collecting them.

"Welcome home to the world that loves you best," Henry James had written to Isabella when he heard she was coming abroad. "What a wonderful Mrs. Jack-in-the-box you are, popping up in all sorts of graceful effects and surprises, purely your own, in the most unexpected parts of the universe. And always on the way to something delightful. I envy you Spain—and I envy Spain you . . ." It was one of *his* most graceful effects. But when the Gardners reached London in

August, it was the height of the social season and James was irritated at having to bother with Gardners. Behind Mrs. Jack's back, he caricatured her as "a locomotive with a pullman car attached."

James was telling the truth when he said he envied Mrs. Gardner. He could not help envying many of his friends who had money and freedom to do as they pleased, and he did not always love the desk at which he was doomed to sit for many hours in order to make only a modest living. Mrs. Gardner, on her part, failed to understand James or any other author completely. She knew when a musician was working because she could hear him practicing. An artist could be seen scraping off paint to make a new start. But she could not see a writer developing a new plot. She knew that James was a constant weekend visitor in English homes, a clubman and a diner-out. Why couldn't he give her more of his really delightful company! If he had been less lavish with excuses and less flattering, she would probably have understood him better.

The Gardners reached home in late September, 1888. The Myopia Hunt Club ball was the big event of the 1889 season, and Mrs. Jack was there. The ball was in the new Cotillion Hall in the Mechanics Building on Huntington Avenue, where skins of tiger, fox and bear had been hung about the walls—as though the hunting out at Hamilton had yielded a rather remarkable bag during the past season. Debutantes put rouge on their cheeks, a new fashion by no means accepted as yet among dowager patronesses. "The belle among the married women was decidedly Mrs. Jack Gardner who was exquisitely attired in primrose satin, and silver-dotted tulle." She wore her pearls and "diamonds . . . and a huge bouquet of Russian violets from her own conservatory." *Town Topics* had come over to her side again after failing to injure her with innuendo concerning Crawford.

There was time for concerts in the Gardner music room by Franz Kneisel and his increasingly famous quartet and for concerts by Adamowski, "society's favorite musician." Then all too soon it was Lent. "Mrs. Jack Gardner is the most vigorous observer of Lent among society leaders . . ." the papers said. "She wears black serge garments fashioned after the manner of a sisterhood, with a double row of black beads at the waist . . . and she drives several times a day in her elegantly appointed carriage, with subdued Lenten liveries to the Church of the Advent for various services."

Mrs. Gardner was an ardent supporter of the Church of

the Advent, where "peculiarities of faith and worship" made the church "a prominent and interesting object in the life of Boston." Rectors of this church avowed that prayer may be addressed to the Virgin Mary and that auricular confession was both allowable and profitable. The Episcopal Bishop of Massachusetts once descended upon the Church of the Advent in wrath, demanding that they give up their "superstitions." They refused. In 1878 they built a new church on Brimmer Street (selling their first church on Bowdoin Street), with quarters for the Sisters of St. Margaret behind it. Mrs. Gardner gave a carved reredos to the new church. Although confession was "allowable and profitable" nothing was said about penance. And then, one Sunday morning Mrs. Jack Gardner arrived with a pail and proceeded to wash the granite steps at the front door of the Church of the Advent, in penance. A choir boy watched her along with a crowd of spectators. Others said that it was the altar steps she washed and that a pretty young girl helped her. Actually, this girl's penance was to walk all the way from her father's house in Cambridge to the church in Brimmer Street instead of riding in her carriage. One would surmise that her sin was worldly pride. But a lady who knew insisted that it was not—"it was flirting." [4]

Some thought that it was Mrs. Jack who invented her own penance and imposed it on herself. No one remembered the date except to say that it must have been between 1883 and 1890. Everyone agreed, however, that Mrs. Gardner's sin might also have been "flirting"—but with whom? Opinions differed.

However that may be, when Lent was over in 1889, Mrs. Jack was at the Artists' Festival where she was "conspicuously elegant . . . in a Renaissance costume cut extremely décolleté back and front." She wore her finest diamonds and pearls. Her train was carried by "a tiny African in Malay costume and in default of a panther, a tiny white poodle completed her equipment." [5]

It was in this costume that Denis Bunker painted Mrs. Gardner's portrait, the canvas inscribed "Denis Bunker 1889." The costume was a harsh pink which matched his sitter's over-made-up mouth and cheeks. The hair was brassy and the expression of Mrs. Gardner's face was arrogant.

This was so different a portrait from Bunker's usual style that it is baffling. Had he and his patroness quarreled? There was no indication of that in the letter he wrote, asking to keep the costume. "As soon as I can get through with that costume I will leave it at 152—probably next Wednesday. I think tho' that you had better sell it to me again—I don't believe you'll ever use it . . ." It may be that this was a hint to the lady that her too-bright dress, too insistently youthful air, were unbecoming. It is to be feared, however, that Bunker's portrait was merely much too truthful. The habit of arrogance had been growing until sometimes only Jack Gardner could make Mrs. Jack behave.

They told how Jack, coming home one night, met his butler coming out, suitcase in hand. "Now where do you think you're going?" Mr. Gardner said.

"Madam has dismissed me," the butler replied.

"Go back and get ready to serve dinner," Mr. Gardner told him. The other watching, listening servants saw him walk into the living room; heard him say, "Belle, I hire our servants and I fire them—nobody else."

"I won't leave this house till the man goes," Mrs. Gardner was supposed to have said.

"Then you'll have to stay home a long time," her husband told her.

"She had an awful temper," one of the Gardner staff always remembered. "Some little thing she didn't like and she'd fire us. Of course we took our time about leaving and Mr. Gardner would come home and straighten things out."

The papers loved to get hold of an incident and expand it into a paragraph about Mrs. Gardner. ". . . at the Boston end of the Boston and Albany Railroad, a telegraph dispatch was received addressed to the president of the company, Mr. William Bliss. The messenger made a vain search for him at his office, at his house and among his several favorite haunts . . ." Mr. Bliss was finally located, playing poker. "The exhaustion of the messenger and the long search . . . suggested a portentous importance for the message and Mr. Bliss . . . gravely proceeded to examine it . . . and then with a yell of laughter, tossed it on the table and called 'Jackpot.' Everybody [at the club] came in. The telegram read, 'Mr. Bliss, Pres. B. & A. R.R. The porter of car 204 refuses to open the ventilators.' It was signed, 'Mrs. Jack Gardner.' "

Anyone able to remember the stuffy Pullman cars of the period can only sympathize with the lady.

In 1890, John Singer Sargent returned to the United States. He had acquired a Spanish dancer by the name of Carmencita whom he was said to admire extravagantly. She was the toast of New York. Sargent had painted her and now he wanted to sell the painting because Carmencita made him pay for his admiration in pearls—or at least so went the story. Sargent sent a message to Mrs. Jack that "by hook or by crook, here or in Boston, you must see Carmencita." He would arrange for Carmencita to dance for Mrs. Gardner, except that he had no place.

"I should have liked you to come and see her at my studio before this," Sargent wrote. But in the New York studio he was using there was only "one gas jet and the gas man said he could not put in another. Could you have it at your home in Fifth Avenue? If so, might I go and see whether the floor or carpet would be good and whether there is a chandelier against which she would have to break her head."

The answer was a definite no. That house on Fifth Avenue belonged to Mrs. Gardner's father, David Stewart. Her mother had died in January, 1886. Her father had come to Boston in April 1887, and "in consideration of love and affection and a sum of $1.00 in lawful money," he had deeded to Isabella the house he had built for her on Beacon Street. It might appear that he had finally decided to trust Isabella's husband and such was the case, doubtless—but not the reason. David Stewart had decided to marry Mary Elizabeth, a sister of Edgar S. Hicks, a business associate.[6] Isabella was not pleased. She still visited her father once in a while, but the Fifth Avenue house would never be hers, nor would she ask favors of her stepmother.

William Merritt Chase, an older artist, popular for Venetian fishing scenes and the like, had a large studio on Tenth Street in New York. Sargent wrote Mrs. Gardner that it was "a capital big place"—they could have the party there. "I will contribute wine and supper," Sargent said. Chase would only want to ask two or three friends and Sargent wanted permission to "ask a few."

"The Carmencita with two guitars will cost you $120, which is her price, en ville," Sargent wrote Mrs. Gardner. He wanted to know how many guests she would invite "from the point of view of sandwiches."

In his next note, Sargent accepted "with pleasure for Delmonico's"—evidently a dinner the Gardners were giving before Carmencita's stage appearance. Her exhibition dance would come afterward. And now he told Mrs. Jack that she "must come to the studio on Tuesday at any time and see the figure I am doing of this bewildering creature." At the studio, ". . . we will sit on the model stand and make this Carmencita sing a seguidilla or two and dance à la flamenca. This is a secret because we don't want to augment our party do we,"

145

Sargent said, but added, "Please extend my invitation to Mr. Gardner."

This "secret" party may or may not have come off. The 120-dollar performance went badly—everybody there telling the tale in different versions, but Joseph Lindon Smith's eyewitness story was the best. He was now in America, teaching again probably and most certainly amusing Mrs. Gardner and her friends with his pleasant company.

Carmencita arrived with her hair curled tightly in what she doubtless felt to be a fetching new style. Sargent was furious and took a wet brush to it in an endeavor to restore it to the straight, raven-wing effect that was part of her beauty. Now *she* was furious. When Sargent told her to play up to Mrs. Gardner—the small woman with the golden hair and the long strings of pearls—Carmencita threw a rose in Mrs. Gardner's face and made "a rude gesture." Joe Smith picked up the rose, however, pretending he thought it was meant for him, and put it in his buttonhole. "Colli" Smith could be depended upon to do this with an air, and Carmencita was mollified.[7]

Mrs. Gardner did not like Sargent's painting of Carmencita and it went eventually to the Luxembourg Museum in Paris. The painting of a Spanish dancer by Sargent that Mrs. Jack had already set her heart upon was *El Jaleo*, exhibited at the Paris Salon in 1882. This was one of the most dramatic scenes Sargent ever evoked—it was Spain itself as Sargent had seen it in 1879 and as Mrs. Gardner now knew it. But her connection by marriage T. Jefferson Coolidge owned the picture.

Sargent could see that Mrs. Gardner was not going to buy any other painting of a Spanish dancer, having set her heart on the unobtainable *El Jaleo*. He had his commission to paint a mural for the Boston Public Library, so he went off to Egypt to sketch white-robed figures for his frieze of the prophets. He left Carmencita in New York, and eventually she came to Boston to dance for the benefit of the Cadet Army Fund, to the tune of $800.

Mrs. Jack had nothing against the girl personally. Carmencita danced for Mrs. Gardner and people said that, "excited by the marvelous agility of Carmencita and carried away by the spirit of the occasion, Mrs. Jack executed, in the pauses, her world-renowned *pas-seul* . . ."[8]

Without doubt, Mrs. Gardner had a good time at the party she gave, whether she did a solo dance herself or not. What most people did not know and would not have believed, however, was that, at this time, she was also interested in Robert

Browning! Her friend Mrs. Katherine de Kay Bronson had just written to her from Casa Alvisi, Venice.

"I enclose you, dearest, a tiny lock of hair—which dear Mr. Browning allowed me to cut at Asolo. He seemed to wish me to cut a large quantity and said, 'Take it all—just as much as you want—don't be afraid,' but I was so nervous that I only dared take a little. The thought flashed over me, he thinks this will be the last time anyone asks for his hair." [9]

Isabella put Browning's hair in a moonstone locket and asked Mrs. Bronson to get her a Browning autograph. Mrs. Bronson had wanted Browning to meet Mrs. Gardner because "he would be interested in your octagon character" as she put it. She sent Mrs. Jack "the last autograph" Robert Browning "ever wrote for anyone," the poet having died December 12, 1889. "Surely no woman ever had so pure and holy a love given to her as his to me," Mrs. Bronson wrote. "He loved me so! And I am left lonely at heart without his everlasting affection." In 1890 it was time for the Gardners to be off for Europe again and they would go to Asolo to comfort the bereaved Katherine.

As always, Jack Gardner kept his line-a-day record of the trip—mentioning coaching parties in England with the Appletons and the fact that he went to a "dog and flower" show in Paris and also to "the Poker Club." "Mrs. G." visited galleries and listened to concerts. Clayton Johns appeared on the scene in time to go to Oberammergau with "the Shattuck girls, Mrs. G. and maid." But Jack Gardner gave Wagner a miss. Instead, he "horse-carred and walked"—two pastimes he was fond of.

On Friday, August 2, 1890, Jack Gardner's usually laconic record expressed emotion. "Arrived Venice 6:35 P.M. Angelo and gondoliers met us at station. Installed at Palazzo Barbaro. Hurrah!"

"La Donna Isabella" was Katherine Bronson's name for Mrs. Gardner, who lived up to the title from now on. The *sala* on the second floor with its balconies overlooking the Grand Canal was the room Belle Gardner loved best. French doors leading to the balconies could be left open, doors with Venetian blinds closed during the noonday heat—soft air stirring through the louvers. All doors could be opened at night to make the view of a great sweep of the Grand Canal seem part of the room. Only late at night could the faint lapping of the water below be heard in the *sala*. The rest of the time, the canal was alive with the put-put of steam launches, the shouts of men who poled produce boats, and the songs of the gondoliers, who sang to please the tourists—part of the time —but more often just for the joy of singing as they moved along their water Main Street.

The murky tide below threw green and gold reflections on the ceiling of the *sala*. Plaster cupids disported themselves at the cornice over huge wall paintings or over doors and wherever cupids could perch or fly. All was white or faded gold but for the dark paintings. Crystal chandeliers and great candelabra standing on the floor in corners, held hundreds of candles and the servants gasped with shocked delight when Mrs. Gardner ordered all the candles lighted every night—as if for *festa*.

But of course it was *festa* every night when the Donna Isabella was there. The *sala* was a room built for parties—gilded chairs stood about as if awaiting guests in evening clothes— and the room was so large that the floor was always uncluttered, the grand piano never in the way.

Mrs. Gardner's pearls never looked so right as they did by Venetian candlelight. She brought life and vigor to the *sala*, such as it had not seen since the days of its glory.

Other rooms, some as large, some smaller, were furnished with Venetian pieces, bow-fronted, painted the shade of green that copper turns when corroded. There was an upstairs library and another on the lower floor. Some rooms looked out upon an inner courtyard planted with flowers and fruit trees —a spot Jack Gardner chose for his Italian lessons with Miss Holas. When a trip to Siena to a *festa* was planned, it was Miss Holas who took "Mrs. G. to Sienna," while Jack Gardner remained peacefully behind.

The Palazzo Barbaro had more or less recently belonged to the Contessa Evelina Pisani, daughter of a Scottish professor and a Greek lady. The contessa's husband was Count Pisani, who was in the Italian Navy, and who had inherited real estate but no cash. His Scottish-Greek wife sold for him his "immense Palazzo Pisani," getting a good price, bought the Barbaro, repaired and furnished it and rented it to the Daniel Curtises. For a while the contessa lived on the top floor and Mrs. Gardner knew and liked her. Eventually she sold the Barbaro to the Curtises, who—without admitting it—found summer rental money from the Gardners and others to be welcome. "Rent of Palazzo Barbaro. Venice (amount fixed by myself) pd. D. S. Curtis, July '90 £200#" Jack Gardner wrote.

The Curtis staff of servants went along with the deal and were a delight. In charge was the butler, Arcangelo and an

148

archangel he seemed to be. Fernando, the cook, obeyed the butler but exerted himself to the utmost when he found that the American gentleman appreciated fine food and that the Signora, although a light eater, had guests who did justice to high art from the kitchen. The gondoliers, Batisto, Tito and Fernando, were as handsome as Mrs. Gardner could wish. One of them was always on duty at the water entrance at the foot of the great stone staircase.

Mrs. Bronson received the Gardners with open arms and thanked John L. for his "magnificent gift" of wines. The Contessa Pisani found Mrs. Jack something of a kindred spirit, while Cardinal Agostini promised to pray for the Gardners in return for their "great charity." All this made Venice a second home. The smiling, devoted servants, however, were not a small part of the pleasure of living at the Palazzo Barbaro. On September 2, they left Venice after handing out carefully recorded gifts: "Arcangelo, 100 francs," all the way down to "young girl, 20," and all wished the Gardners a happy return.

In Paris, Mrs. Gardner acquired her fifth and final necklace, having the same magic number—thirty-seven—of seventeen-and-a-half-grain pearls. The clasp was especially designed so that the strings could be locked together or taken apart to vary their length. These last pearls were "bought by I.S.G. with her own money," according to John L. Gardner's notation on the bill. They cost $13,056.[10]

Collecting of art and manuscripts proceeded in a very modest way, in 1890. Mrs. Gardner bought a page of a letter by Jean François Millet, written in Barbizon in 1873—for four dollars. At Christie's gallery in London she bought a Turner, *Roman Tower*, painted in 1819 when Turner made a tour of the Rhine Valley. Since much of Turner was already in public galleries, out of reach, it was a find.

Jack Gardner also did some shopping in London. He bought "stable things: head collars, night collars, stable cloths and rubber coats." From Italy he had shipped "71 bottles of Chianti Stravecchio"—old and ripe Chianti wine.

The Gardners returned to Boston by the middle of October, 1890, and at a reception in Cambridge, given by Professor Norton and his daughters, "Mrs. Gardner came, very splendid in pearls," Sara Norton said.[11]

In November, 1889, Denis Bunker had become engaged to Eleanor Hardy and *Town Topics* had more or less gone to town on it. "An engagement announced last week in Boston has mildly agitated society there, mostly because of the prominence given the fiancé by the fact of his being one of Mrs. Jack Gardner's 'Little Brothers of the Rich.' " Eleanor's father was a Boston lawyer, they had met "at amateur theatricals at Mrs. Billie Apthorpe's," in which Mr. Bunker and Miss Hardy appeared in Howell's *Mouse Trap*. Mrs. Jack had given a dinner for Eleanor at the Somerset Club.

Denis wrote to Mrs. Gardner while she was abroad. "I often think of you in your Venetian state—while I am at Medfield," he said. He was staying with Martin Loeffler, whom he heard downstairs "working over his composition, playing over one phrase hundreds of times and days at a time.

"Do you wear your red and gold dress I wonder—and wear your hair à la Tintoretto?" Bunker expected to be married before Mrs. Jack returned to Boston and assumed she could not be at the wedding. "I shall think of you when I am married (perhaps not at that instant) and how you'd have chuckled to see the bad Mr. Bunker meekly swept into the ranks of the good by the almighty broom of fate."

Bunker was married in October, 1890, and went to New York to set up a new studio—where his chief subject was his beautiful wife, Eleanor, whom he painted in many poses. Without Mrs. Gardner to help him, portrait commissions were few. He and Eleanor came back to Boston for Christmas and while at the home of his wife's parents, Bunker developed pneumonia and died December 28, 1890. "It is a mistake to have only one life," he had once written to Mrs. Gardner. "As for me, I am only rehearsing this one—I might be a painter if I could live again and begin afresh. We ought to be given three tries like the baseball men."

One of the most promising among young American artists, Denis Bunker left little work behind him. Mrs. Gardner went around to the Cowles Art School where she bought drawings he had done when a student in Paris. Eventually she included them with the landscapes by Bunker in her Isabella Stewart Gardner Museum. Once more, she had lost a gifted young boy whom she loved.

FIFTEEN

Queen of Holy Back Bay

IN 1891, MRS. GARDNER met Thomas Russell Sullivan and added him to her collection of admirers. Sullivan, encouraged by the success of some short stories he had written, had just abandoned a business career and had set himself up as a writer, in bachelor quarters at Number 10 Charles Street. Mrs. Gardner's collection of people, at this point, included many musicians, several artists—and only a few literary men. She needed Sullivan, and, very fortunately, Sullivan kept a journal.[1]

Anecdotes people told him that might be short-story material went into the journal and he wrote of literary hopes and disappointments. Mrs. Jack Gardner appeared in his pages for the first time on the eve of 1891 as he saw the old year out at "the great ball given by Mrs. J. E. Lodge for her daughter Constance." Mrs. Gardner was there, "in white, with an array of precious stones, large and small, but all rubies." [2]

Constance Lodge had become engaged to Augustus Peabody Gardner, youngest of the three nephews whom the Jack Gardners called their own boys. He was now twenty-five, handsome, likable, a commanding figure in the saddle who had magnificent mounts to ride.[3] After a year at law school, he had decided that the law was not for him and had become "a farmer and landowner" in Hamilton. Fox hunting was one of his chief duties as farmer and landowner. Always a little envious of his brother Amory's intellectual prowess, "Gussie Gardner" finally found success in a military career in 1898 during the Spanish-American conflict. He became Captain, then Major Gardner. The only one of the three nephews to marry, Gus was also almost the only Gardner ever to become interested in politics. Eventually he went to Congress.[4]

Thomas Russell Sullivan made little mention of Constance Lodge or of her fiancé in his journal. His attention was taken up with Mrs. Jack. On February 6, 1891, he had lunch with "Mrs. J. L. Gardner, in her boudoir, which might be called 'the chamber over the gate.'" Sullivan had never seen this room when the walls were covered with yellow silk brocade and the furnishings were French. All was now Italian in style with dark wood wainscot, above it "a frieze of portrait heads" that Mrs. Gardner was to place above a dark wood wall in the Gothic Room at Fenway Court, where they would intrigue the visitor and puzzle the experts. All the same small size, all in mediaeval dress—head and shoulders only—who painted them, who were they? Mrs. Gardner told Sullivan that she bought them in Venice, and perhaps she told him more, but all he did was to count them and write down that there were "thirty in all."

Sullivan asked about other things he saw in the boudoir. "A little Bartolozzi print in one corner once belonged to Byron," Mrs. Jack told him, while she stood "arranging orchids in a glass," pleased to have her new young man roam around asking questions. "Everything here is a remembrance," she said.

T. R. Sullivan had been invited to luncheon before a concert where "Scharwenkl, the Polish composer played a concerto of his own"; so there was no lingering in the boudoir, for Mrs. Jack was never late to music. That same evening, Sullivan was at "the Cochrane ball in their superb house. Everything and everybody at their best, with Mrs. Jack Gardner in all her pearls." [5]

Sullivan progressed rapidly, from the formal "Dear Mrs. Gardner" in his notes and letters, to the all too usual "Dear Lady" of other admirers. Then he came up with "Carissima Cugina," which was his own invention. He and Mrs. Jack had discovered a mutual love for Italian and had scraped up a distant kinship, so that "Dearest Cousin" pleased them both. Later, he guessed right and thanked her for anonymously proposing him for membership and paying his dues in the Dante Society, in which Professor Norton was so prominent.

On February 18, "Mrs. J. L. Gardner, Mrs. John Gray and Mary Cochrane took tea" in Sullivan's rooms and were "very affable." He had been "drawn lately into breaking" his rule against reading an unpublished manuscript aloud, but his story "The Anatomist of the Heart" was to come out in August in *Scribner's* magazine and when the ladies begged him to read something to them, he got it out. "I thought I might as well be hung for a sheep as a lamb," he said, "so he read this same story "on three distinct occasions to three clever women," pledging each to secrecy—wondering if each would

152

keep her word. "Awkward if they should happen to confide in each other, also amusing," he wrote. The ladies didn't tell.

Sullivan's story began with "a graceful woman with black lace about her head" who "reclined alone in a gondola" during a Venetian *festa*. This Italian marchesa had married for a title and being now happily widowed, had come in search of her old flame, an American bachelor. She confessed her passion for the hero, who rejected her because of her "motive of self-interest" in her first marriage; remained true to his own first love, a "tall and fair" American who would have none of him.

Mrs. Gardner said she "would like to write a sequel" showing the hero "dissatisfied" with that American girl "after getting her," and she thought that Sullivan had been most unjust to the marchesa. " 'Of course she married on the European system—how could she help it!' " Her opinion of his story was the only one Sullivan wrote down.[6]

While in England the previous summer, the Gardners had spent a weekend with the Neville Chamberlains, where they met "A. I. Mountenoy Jephson," as the young man styled himself. He had been with Stanley on his African expedition of 1887 and was more than willing to tell of his adventures.[7] Mrs. Gardner asked him for some poisoned arrows and he gave her several. In 1891, Jephson and Hamilton Aïdé, also a member of the African expedition, arrived in Boston. They had come to the United States with the white-haired Stanley and his young bride—this time on a lecture-tour safari.

Mrs. Stanley told reporters that they had been invited to twenty-two dinners in Boston. They had "refused most of them" but accepted one "given by the venerable Julia Ward Howe," her daughter Maud Howe Elliott assisting. Mrs. Jack Gardner was there, and so was Jephson, now described as "Mrs. Jack's adoring lieutenant."

The papers claimed that Mrs. Stanley was critical of the décolleté of Boston ladies' dresses. They were the most daring she had seen in America, Mrs. Stanley was supposed to have told an interviewer. At dinner, she had been seated opposite "the unique, the only Mrs. Gardner, exposing as usual a generous surface of her famous flesh tints." When asked if she had met Mrs. Gardner, "the woman of all others to see," Mrs. Stanley was quoted as saying, " 'Oh yes, and she was good enough to let me see a good deal of her.' " It would appear that not all the poisoned arrows had been given to Mrs. Jack—some were aimed at her.

Jephson and his fellow explorer Hamilton Aïdé, a future

novelist, got to Boston ahead of the Stanleys. A letter from Aïdé reached Mrs. Gardner still earlier. "Mrs. Hamilton and I want to play a harmless practical joke on Mr. Jephson," it said. In various places, all over the United States, people had turned up announcing kinship with the Irish-born Jephson: "a milliner, who claimed he was a long-lost nephew, etc." Aïdé wanted Mrs. Jack to play the part of "someone to claim him in Boston." It could be done "at dusk," Mrs. Jack to be suitably costumed and disguised. Mrs. Stanley would do it, except that "her height would betray her."

Mrs. Jack probably refused the assignment—the only part she cared to play being her own. But Jephson took great pains to tell her all about his ancestral castle in Ireland and his noble descent, while Aïdé wrote a novel about Americans, wherein "Mrs. Courtly" seemed to Bostonians to represent Mrs. Gardner.

The Stanleys departed but Jephson stayed on in Boston as the guest of the Gardners. Mrs. Jack asked him to go out to speak to the boys at Groton School. Her nephew William Amory Gardner had found his lifework in this famous school, beginning in 1884–1885, when Dr. Endicott Peabody and Sherrard Billings lived and had their classrooms in Brooks House. Amory taught mathematics and Greek; Mr. Billings, Latin and English; Dr. Peabody, "miscellaneous subjects."

Jephson felt that he lectured badly to the boys when he went out to Groton with Mrs. Gardner, but she reassured him. Snow began to fall, the Irishman's "first experience of a real American blizzard that raged all that Sunday." When the storm ended and the moon came out, Amory had a sleigh harnessed, and Jephson remembered, eleven years later, "our sleigh ride after dinner with Amory Gardner and Howard Cushing, through the fir woods laden with snow, our stopping on the high bridge to tell stories, with the snow-bound, moonlit landscape all around us and the dark river rolling below." It all came back to him in "a series of little, bright, happy pictures, all of them associated with you; for you, dear Lady, were the gracious center figure of them all . . ."

Augustus Gardner had come home from Europe ahead of his aunt and uncle—fired with enthusiasm for driving a coach. He was determined to start a "four-in-hand club" and by spring drove four fast-stepping horses, sometimes tandem, sometimes two by two, along the narrow country roads near Boston, passing his one-horse friends at a gallop. Luckily, his fiancée, Constance Lodge, immediately became a coaching enthusiast.

The New York Coaching Club had been in existence since 1875; but now the Myopia Hunt Club decided that what Boston needed most was a coach or coaches. The *Independence* was accordingly acquired. Freddie Prince was considered the best "tally-ho tooler in Massachusetts." Freddie Prince of the jaunty white top hat and "Gussie Gardner," handsome but more conservative, took turns in "navigating the *Independence* coach from Beacon Street out to The Country Club races [in Brookline] without fracturing the limbs of the passengers or being dragged down on the backs of the wheel horses."

Sometimes "the natty Mrs. Prince" was on the box with her husband and Mrs. Gardner was reported as arriving at The Country Club in her own victoria, wearing furs and "smothered in violets from her own conservatory."

People said that Mrs. Jack also liked the roof of the coach and that a lady sitting behind her made faces at her because she had wanted the front seat for herself. Various courses were laid out for the *Independence*. They might start from the Hotel Vendôme on Commonwealth Avenue, with a great fanfare on the horn; pick up their first relay in Brookline at The Country Club; and proceed through Auburndale to Wayland, their destination. Here, all the passengers had lunch at the Wayland Inn.

During the summer of 1891 a new coach was to make its first run, starting from Prides Crossing. Mrs. Gardner reserved a seat "on the roof for herself and escort" who happened to be her husband. The Gardners were in Boston and on the day of the run they missed the train to Prides Crossing.

Great was the consternation when the train from Boston brought no sign of Mrs. Jack and escort.[8] There was nothing left to do but go on without this particular attraction, and the coach had started away from the railroad station toward the grade crossing just beyond when "frantic shouts from the railroad crossing tender made every head turn. . . ." Down the tracks came a wild engine, whistle hooting, bell clanging. The engine stopped and in the cab sat Mrs. Jack.

Finding that no scheduled train would get them to Prides Crossing in time, Jack Gardner had hired an engine, just as he would have called a cab for a trip downtown. *Town Topics* had it that Mrs. Jack "sat cosily tucked up beside the engineer," but it seems more likely that she had the fireman's seat and that it was she who pulled the whistle-cord and clanged the bell.

People remembered that Mrs. Jack had been dressed all in white and that when she climbed down out of the cab, her costume was smudged with soot. As usual, she was "the sensation of the party."

Plenty of people believed that Isabella Gardner was sensational only for escapades, and she herself disclaimed any reputation for wit. She had briefly her Boswell in the form of Thomas Russell Sullivan, however. Invited to spend three nights in Brookline, along with Clayton Johns, in May, 1891, Sullivan first recorded the beauty of his hostess's gardens and then the sparkle of her dinner conversation.

"The flowers in the spring garden" were all in blossom and there was "a hillside sown with tulips, springing up singly through the grass, the prettiest sight imaginable." The Kendalls had been playing in Boston and at dinner the talk turned to Hamlet's "Give me that man that is not passion's slave."

Mrs. Jack brought a laugh all around the dinner table when she exclaimed, *"I* like men best when they *are* passion's slaves."

One of the guests "asked of Mrs. Gardner, 'Are you a happy woman?'

" 'What an absurd question!' she exclaimed. 'If I were not, do you think I would tell you!' " [9]

On the first day of July, Sullivan was again at Green Hill with Clayton Johns, Ralph Curtis and Jephson. This time, he admired the famous Japanese iris, in their flooded beds, which were in full bloom and made a superb show. Mrs. Gardner had just been awarded the medal for them by the Horticultural Society at a special meeting—a trophy to set beside those won by her grandmother Isabella Stewart. Sullivan recorded no repartee of Mrs. Jack's but paid unconscious tribute to her gift of lending her guests to talk of themselves. Ralph Curtis told all about his recent trip to India, Burma and Japan. Jephson talked about Africa, and Sullivan spoke of his writing. Sullivan liked Jephson and left "with a desire to know him better."

Jephson had been in California and was on his way home, but he had written Mrs. Gardner indicating that he would like to see her again. "I hope things are not too gay, just now," he had said, "for I've absolutely not clothes to wear and I should bring disgrace upon the Queen of Holy Back Bay by going shabbily, so if you go out much you will have to leave me at home and Mr. Gardner and I will smoke unlimited cigars together and talk about the frivolities of women."

In London, Jephson had given Mrs. Gardner a photograph of himself, signed "Bubarika," his African name. He appeared in heroic pose, gun at rest, one foot on an imitation rock supplied by the photographer. His low-crowned hat with a veil wrapped around it was set at a rakish angle; he wore white knickers and a white shirt with sleeves rolled up. He seemed to consider himself a great hero but he returned to Massachusetts a changed man.

Jephson later described coming to Brookline, "alone from California, beaten and sad with all that miserable, huge mistake weighing upon me." He never went into details, at least in writing, but he seems to have made a disastrous investment, perhaps in gold-mining or ranching property. "You were so sympathetic to me and so silent, even though you felt it was all wrong and could never bring me anything but unhappiness. How good you were to me, and full of tact," he was later to write to Mrs. Gardner. In 1900, he wrote that he had "paid off slowly and with great difficulty, three-quarters of those California loans."

Mrs. Gardner took Jephson to Beverly because he said he wanted to rest. Then they went to Roque, which Jephson described as "that enchanted island where we were out of doors the whole day long and you read Walt Whitman to me and his 'Song of Joys' till the shadow that was over me lifted a little, and I seemed to feel quieter and better.

". . . Do you remember, too, the voyage of discovery in the canoe round the island, when we glided along and crept in and out so silently that we came upon the herons fishing before they were aware of us, and the sleeping seals upon the sunny rocks, who plunged into the sea almost under the bottom of our boat?" Jephson remembered an Isabella Gardner that few who had seen her only at balls, glittering with jewels would believe even existed.

Then, while Jephson was with Mrs. Gardner, a telegram arrived by rowboat from the mainland. David Stewart, her father, was staying at a hotel on Lake Champlain. He had suffered a heart attack—Isabella must come at once.

Jack Gardner was not at Roque. It was mid-July, 1891, and he may have left on a sailing cruise with friends, cousins and nephews—such a cruise as often started from Roque for a few days among other deep-water islands still farther north. There was no time to lose, so Mrs. Gardner set out with

Jephson. "I remember that breathless night journey across the country to Lake Champlain," he wrote, "our arrival dirty and travel-stained in the early morning with only a toothbrush between us, our walk through the dewy garden up to the hotel, with the sun just rising over the lake."

David Stewart died July 17, 1891. His death was spoken of as sudden and no one told whether or not his daughter reached him before the end. Isabella and her father had been close, in spite of his second marriage which had caused his daughter some twinges of jealousy. She had been her father's traveling companion on winter trips to Florida and each had known the grief of losing children.

No longer in need of an escort, Mrs. Gardner gave Jephson "the little Indian arrowhead scarf pin [she was] wearing at the time. I have it with me now at this moment," he told her, sixteen years later.

Jephson saw Mrs. Gardner again in New York. "I recollect coming to see you to say goodbye when all was over in your father's house in Fifth Avenue where I found you sitting sadly at the window in your deep mourning, looking out into the deserted street—for it was late summer and New York was a desert waste."

Of course there was immediate speculation as to the amount of Mrs. Gardner's inheritance from her father, and outsiders imagined that he had left her a tremendously rich woman.[10] In terms of the immense fortunes of New Yorkers like Morgan and Vanderbilt, this was not so; but according to the appraisal for taxation of the estate of David Stewart, he left "his daughter Isabella Stewart Gardner $1,625,800.69." This included "certain objets d'art," valued at $2000, and $100,000 in cash. He left his second wife, Mary Elizabeth, $1,532,882.69 plus the Fifth Avenue house, "certain paintings, furniture, silver, jewelry, horses, carriages, sleighs, harness, stable equipment etc." Isabella's additional $100,000 was evidently intended to equalize the division of the property. David Stewart's total estate came to $3,429,705.38; and he named a good many minor beneficiaries, such as "Theodore F. Hicks [his] faithful clerk, $25,000," along with the "leasehold property" at Number 10 University Place. Mr. Stewart's coachman was given $3000.

Mrs. Gardner was always strict about withdrawing from society during periods of mourning. But when, in December, Paderewski appeared in Boston "like a musical meteor," as Clayton Johns put it, she asked him to give a small private concert in her Beacon Street music room for a few friends.[11]

Unfortunately, Paderewski had just survived an unhappy experience in New York. "The recital, or 'at home' in private houses was not so popular in New York as it was in London," he said, but he was prevailed upon to give four private concerts in William Chase's studio—that big studio where Sargent's Carmencita had danced for Mrs. Gardner.

The crowd was so great "that people were actually sitting next me so close that they almost prevented me from playing," Paderewski said. He "felt suffocated . . . In fact it was dreadful"; and he was not going to let that happen again. He was sure that "it was just a lionizing stunt—a stunt so often indulged in by ladies in search of celebrities" [12] when Mrs. Gardner asked him to play at 152 Beacon Street, so he refused. Finally, Mrs. Gardner proposed that he play for her alone, for a fee of one thousand dollars. Paderewski consented.[13]

Word got around that Mrs. Jack wanted Paderewski all to herself—just to show what her money could buy. Clayton Johns, who should have known better, seemed to believe this. "Before the recital, Mrs. Gardner, out of the kindness of her heart, smuggled me into an adjoining room where I sat and listened behind the tapestries," he wrote. "After the music was over, I was invited to join the supper party which was composed of Mr. and Mrs. Gardner, Paderewski and myself." [14]

As Johns remembered it, he was the only guest; but years later, Mrs. John C. Munro,[15] who lived across Beacon Street from Mrs. Gardner, told a different tale. She and her husband were invited over, she said. They sat "on a short bench . . . not directly opposite the door" of the music room "and could not see into the music room at all." But they heard "three voices, all familiar; Mrs. Gardner's, Paderewski's and Clayton's . . ."

In the course of negotiations, Mrs. Gardner persuaded Paderewski to give another concert, for which Jack Gardner handed him another one-thousand-dollar check. This concert was for Boston's musicians and students at the New England Conservatory of Music. The hall was a sort of "amphitheater," Clayton Johns said, with Paderewski sitting and playing "in the pit while the audience filled the seats in rising tiers." No tickets were sold, only students were admitted; and "it was certainly a splendid offering on the part of Mrs. Gardner," Johns thought.[16]

For better or worse, George Proctor appeared upon the scene at this point to become Mrs. Jack Gardner's most troublesome protégé. He was just eighteen but seemed younger—his blond, boyish good looks as yet unspoiled. George played for Paderewski, who was asked if the boy showed promise.

Politely, Paderewski said that Proctor had talent. Where and with whom should George study, Mrs. Gardner wanted to know.

Paderewski said that his own piano teacher had been Leschetizky—a man whose name appeared more and more often as musicians at this time told of their training. Leschetizky took only advanced pupils who played for him once a week in "the class," which was really "a kind of concert" with other students as audience. The master sat "at the piano, ready to pour out his wrath and fury upon any pupil who failed to measure up . . . He showed no mercy . . . He would storm and shout but was really kind and good . . ." Leschetizky's wife, Madame Essipoff, took care of pupils "not sufficiently competent to come under the master."

Mrs. Gardner was much impressed and told George Proctor that he could go to Vienna to study under Leschetizky. It was John L. Gardner who signed the checks, a total of seven thousand dollars in 1892 with more to come, and Clayton Johns agreed to go along with George and to take care of the money.

Mrs. Jack Gardner knew little about Proctor at this time, but in 1895 he wrote her an appealingly boyish letter. "When I was twelve or thirteen, I used to go down on the Kennebec River in Maine and spend summer on a farm. I did lots of things such as row heavy boats, a fine thing for a pianist's fingers! . . . When I was fourteen or fifteen I was a choir boy and sang solos, and was from time to time petted by people who liked to hear me sing . . . At sixteen, I did not sing any more but played the organ in church, piano at the New England Conservatory where a lot of silly girls made me rather vain for a short time, and at eighteen was organist in the same church where I had sung as a little boy . . . When I got here [Vienna] I thought I was fairly on the way to do something fine . . . I worked, experienced some hard knocks but kept on and at times basked in the sun and cheered myself as best I could with the thought that I would accomplish what I wanted."

This letter ended with the request that Mrs. Gardner be his patroness in Boston, doing as much for him as she had for Clayton Johns. "I should be in great spirits for I am sure a 'boost' from you cannot be less in effect than being put in a large cannon with a dynamite cartridge." [17] Mrs. Jack Gardner would never fail this boy; but in all his three years in Vienna he never learned how to work hard and no amount of dynamite could ever change him.

The winter months passed quietly for the Gardners. On the second of April, 1892, they boarded *La Touraine,* bound for Le Havre, and went to Paris, where they settled down at the Westminster Hotel on the rue de la Paix. They hired a carriage and coachman and began a round of luncheons, dinners and theater parties with Americans as their guests, so that they might as well have stayed in Boston. After a brief descent upon London they made a leisurely journey toward Venice.

Once more, the pleasure of being in Venice brought forth what amounted to a lyrical passage in John L. Gardner's pocket diary. "Palazzo Barbaro, enchanting," he wrote.

This time, Henry James accepted Mrs. Gardner's invitation to visit her in Venice. He arrived from Bologna about two P.M. July 7 and was met at the station by the Palazzo Barbaro gondola. The upstairs library with pink chairs and lemon sofa, the ceiling painted in "arabesques and medallions, the marble floor of polished perfection," was awaiting him. There were little white papers on the clean shutters to keep out the noonday sun.[18]

James was free to work or go out in a gondola with "the little lady," as he called Mrs. Gardner. Rather reluctantly, he spent a day at Asolo with Mrs. Bronson, "the big lady" at the "top of a stable"[19]—which was the way he described the Asolo country house Mrs. Bronson was so fond of. He had thought he did not want to go to Venice, but he was sorry to leave on July 24, when Jack Gardner escorted him to the station.

"The Barbaro is a phantom and the Donna Isabella herself but an exquisite legend," James wrote Mrs. Gardner after his departure. He referred to his "bleeding heart" and in a second letter described her as he remembered seeing her, "with your hair not quite up—neither up nor down, as it were, in a gauze dressing gown, on a sea-green (so different from pea-green!) chair beneath a glorious gilded ceiling, receiving the matutinal tea from a Venetian slave . . . don't tell me you are *not* seated there in the attitude and costume which it was apparently my sole privilege to admire—I mean only *my,* not my only privilege . . ."[20]

The "Donna Isabella" could not help being pleased by the letters although she by now knew better than to suppose that James's heart was bleeding for her. He was to visit her again.

The Gardners made a trip to Paris, arriving on October 22, and the Daniel Curtises took back their Palazzo Barbaro. On November 7, the Gardners were back in Venice, this time staying at the "Hotel Europa—both front suites." "Ralph and gondoliers" had met them at the station, there were "flowers and messages of welcome" at the hotel. They had returned for the first performances of the opera *Atenaïde* by Pier Adolpho Tirindelli, director of the Music Lycée in Venice and one of Mrs. Jack's most faithful admirers.

Two days later, the Gardners "lunched early" and then "Mrs. G. went to rehearsal with Tirindelli." She went again in the evening and every day thereafter for the next week. Sitting alone in the empty theater, she was thrilled with watching the process of creation on stage as the opera was hammered into shape. There was a "press rehearsal" on November 17, to which Jack also went and then they all went to the first three "representations." "Hand-kissing extraordinary" took place whenever Tirindelli met Mrs. Gardner.

Mrs. Jack wrote to William James Stillman, of *The Times* of London, to come to the opening of Tirindelli's opera. He was then in Rome but had another assignment, he replied— and he invited Mrs. Jack to send him a review of *Atenaïde*. She telegraphed her opera report and Stillman sent her a gold half-sovereign. "Don't laugh," he wrote. It was not everyone who got that much out of *The Times*.[2] Mrs. Jack had the coin pierced to hang on her "chain of thought"—an invention of her own, pre-dating the charm bracelet.

It was in November that Mrs. Gardner and her husband sat to Ludovick Passini for their portraits. Mrs. Jack, looking graceful and appealing in a light summer dress, wore her pearls exactly as Henry James had his heroine Milly Theale wear hers in *The Wings of the Dove*, twice around the neck and then "hung, heavy and pure, down the front of the wearer's breast." Like Henry James's heroine, Isabella was "holding and fingering a part" [22] of her necklace, but in the Passini portrait a ruby pendant, on a slender diamond-studded chain, hung below the pearls.

On June 17, 1892, according to Jack Gardner's Venetian line-a-day notes, he "walked out with Mrs. G. . . . & went to R.R. Station and got ruby drop." John L. Gardner "wrote to Boucheron [enclosing] Mrs. G's cheque."

The story of rubies went back to the Gardners' visit to London the previous May, however.[23] Boucheron the Paris jeweler was also in London, where he showed them a five-carat ruby solitaire ring. This ring was "Bought by Isabella S.

Gardner with her own money," according to Jack Gardner's notation on the Boucheron bill. She began at once to wear the new ring but she also bought a pear-shaped ruby pendant which had to be given a new setting. Boucheron had just sent it to Venice.

While the Gardners were in London, Boucheron also showed them a still more beautiful ruby. He did not own it; it was held on consignment, and he explained that it was "necessary to wire to Calcutta and from there to the interior of India" to know if "the Indian people" would accept an offer of $55,000 for it. Mrs. Gardner said she would return her five-carat ruby solitaire and take an eleven-thousand-dollar credit toward the cost of the nine-carat stone if the Calcutta people would sell it. Time passed and Boucheron had "no answer for the ruby." Of course he would not show it to anyone else who might make a higher offer—"the stone is put in one sealed envelope and nobody can see it," he wrote. He hoped to see Mrs. Gardner later in Paris, with better news.

At last, while the Gardners were still in Venice, the news from Paris was that "after many long negotiations . . . the Indian people . . . agree in taking the offer . . . This magnificent ruby is one of the finest I have ever seen, and I don't think there is a better one," the jeweler declared.

Jack Gardner wrote to Boucheron to hold "the big ring" for his wife. The ring she planned to return for a credit of $11,000 she would keep until they reached Paris, because the "trouble and risk of sending such valuable stones was considerable." He enclosed Mrs. Gardner's "cheque for £8,910."

Isabella had been wearing her five-carat ruby ever since she bought it in London in May and she had grown fond of it, so she did not return it after all. Jack gave it to her along with the nine-carat Indian ruby. He also gave her another string of pearls.

These were the final additions to Isabella Gardner's famous collection of jewels; for the Gardners both had acquired an entirely new interest in 1892. They had become serious collectors of antique art.

SIXTEEN

The Gardners: Art Collectors

V ENICE IN 1892 "is as romantic as ever but in the depths of poverty. With the exception of the manufacture of antiques, there is almost no occupation for the people and the old palaces, standing on the canals are tumbling down for want of repairs or are hired for a few months of the year by strangers." So wrote T. Jefferson Coolidge, the Gardners' kinsman by marriage, who was now American Minister to France.

In October, Coolidge made a visit to "Mrs. G.," who "held a little court in the Palazzo Barbaro . . . surrounded by musicians and artists, some of them of distinction." [1] He found both Jack and "Mrs. G." enthusiastically buying antiques. They acquired furnishings from ancient palaces, carvings in wood and some of the stone carvings which had been about to drop into the Grand Canal. Prices were too low to resist—some of the pieces too beautiful to be allowed to disappear in dust and decay. It was true that Venetian craftsmen, seeing a market for their skill, "manufactured" antiques, and the Gardners bought a few of them, taken in by careful faking. But for the most part Dalla Torre, Richetti and the other dealers sold them fine things. It was Jack Gardner who went most often to the "antiquity shops" while Mrs. G. went to churches to look at pictures.

Up to this time, the Gardners had bought few pictures that could be classed as old masters. But Mrs. Bronson said she knew "an old man of illustrious family" who needed money and would sell his *Adam and Eve,* which he claimed was by Lucas Cranach, a Germanic painter, born in 1472. Carrer, the picture dealer, showed it to the Gardners.

Eve was just handing the apple to Adam while a very large snake looked down out of a tree. Adam and Eve, having yet to eat the apple, were not wearing clothes; and Belle Gardner could visualize the expression on the faces of certain Bostonians when she hung this picture in her Beacon Street parlor. The Gardners offered ten thousand lire for it and the old gentleman of illustrious family was delighted. The picture, which

Mrs. Gardner afterwards hung in the Gothic Room at Fenway Court, is now listed as "from the workshop of Lucas Cranach"—a good antique if not the prize it was supposed to be.[2]

Favenza, another Venetian picture dealer, doubtless hearing of Carrer's sale, offered the Gardners a portrait of a handsome young boy with long brown curls, dressed in armored breastplate over court costume. The boy was the young Duke of Monmouth, illegitimate son of Charles II of England, the portrait by Justus Suttermans, a Dutch painter born in 1597 —so everybody said. The Gardners were urged to take it on approval—which they did, hanging it in the Barbaro. But just before they left Venice, Jack Gardner returned it.

He bought, instead, a Madonna by "Antonio dalla Corna, pupil of Mantegna," for 2500 lire.

After the Gardners got home to Boston, Ralph Curtis wrote that the Empress Frederick of Germany wanted the portrait of the young Duke of Monmouth because it was "a family picture" but that Favenza would prefer to sell it to Mrs. Gardner —doubtless for a better price than the empress cared to pay. Mrs. Jack replied that as a descendant of Stuart kings she had a better right to the picture than the empress, and she bought it. Jack Gardner told her that she need not return "the little Madonna"—he would give it to her for Christmas.

Many years later, art experts decided that the young boy was by Suttermans but could not have been a portrait of the Duke of Monmouth. The little Madonna, with its curiously Oriental treatment of clouds, was "a contemporary copy of a lost Mantegna," Bernard Berenson said later. But in 1931 the British expert Philip Hendy declared it a "Bono da Ferrara," an artist recorded at work "in 1442 to 1461"—and a rare collector's item.

In 1892, however, there were few art experts. Berenson had yet to achieve his great reputation, and the Gardners bought what they liked because they liked it—believing or disbelieving the dealers' stories as they saw fit. They were remarkably successful in choosing good things—The Concert, by Vermeer, bought in 1892, being one of the finest pictures in what was to become the Isabella Stewart Gardner Museum.

The Gardners had reached Paris when The Concert by Jan Vermeer went on sale at auction at an old mansion which had been turned into a dealers' gallery, the Hôtel Drouot. Vermeer was almost unknown and unappreciated as yet, but on looking over the items at the auction preview, The Concert was the only picture Mrs. Gardner wanted. It was an intimate little

Dutch exterior, exquisite in detail, luminous with subtly reflected light. A young girl sat at a keyboard, another girl stood singing; a man was seated between them. The girl, with her round Dutch face, was not pretty, but she had charm. Mrs. Gardner might have seen not only perfection in painting but a reminder of herself, as Belle Stewart, at the piano.

Robert, the Paris picture dealer, agreed to bid on the Vermeer for Mrs. Gardner. He asked her how high he should go. She told him to reserve a seat for her at the auction; she would hold a handkerchief up to her face and Robert was to bid until she put it down. If the bidding slowed, he was to raise his bid suddenly by about two hundred francs.

Jack Gardner's line-a-day record provides a laconic account of the result. On Monday, December 5, "lunched at Café de Paris. Had Ralph [Curtis]. Went to sale at Hôtel Drouot. Mrs. G. bought the van der Meer for frs. 29,000." (Vermeer was also called Jan van der Meer van Delft). The price would amount to about $6000. Only about thirty-six Vermeer canvases are known to exist; and eventually a Vermeer was sold to an American for, allegedly, $350,000. During Mrs. Gardner's lifetime the value of her Vermeer rose to at least $200,000—and Ralph Curtis advised her to "tell Georgie [her nephew] that he can't make investments like that in State Street."

Americans who bought antique art were often severely criticized for letting contemporary artists starve. But Mrs. Gardner had not deserted her friends. During their stopover in Paris in April, 1892, the Gardners met the Whistlers, according to John L.'s diary, asked them to dinner, and very promptly dined at a restaurant as the Whistlers' guests. They were soon seeing the couple frequently.

James McNeill Whistler had long been a bachelor, although there were rumors of a red-haired mistress. But in 1888, when he was fifty-five,[3] he married Beatrix Goodwin, widow of the architect who had built a house for him in England. Whistler had spent a good deal of money in the course of legal battles; he had sold his home and gone traveling and painting. He had now just arrived in Paris and had found what Henry James described as "a queer little gardenhouse off the rue de Bac where the only furniture is the paint on the walls and the smile on the lady's [Mrs. Whistler's] broad face."

At Whistler's studio, Mrs. Gardner saw a painting she wanted. It was called *Harmony in Blue and Silver*.[4] Whistler had painted it in 1865 at Trouville, the small silhouetted figure in the foreground being Courbet—Whistler's teacher. But the picture was not for sale.

Returning to Paris in the autumn, Mrs. Gardner saw *Harmony in Blue and Silver* again and still wanted it. The legend is that she took T. Jefferson Coolidge from his ministerial duties to go to Whistler's studio with her. On the way she told him that she was going to ask him "to take a certain picture down to the carriage." He was to "pick it up and take it without any fuss," while she distracted the artist's attention; and according to the story, "Mr. Coolidge was somewhat disturbed but obeyed." A slightly different version tells that Whistler followed down the stairs and had the picture brought back so that he could sign it.

Sir Rennell Rodd told still another version of this tale. "I remember at this time taking Mrs. Jack Gardner of Boston to acquire one of his pictures," [5] he said. The reason given for Whistler's reluctance to sell *Harmony in Blue and Silver* was that it had once been given to a friend.

Into this scene, then, complicated by the presence of T. Jefferson Coolidge and Sir Rennell Rodd, comes John L. Gardner! "Nov. 9. Snow storm. In afternoon went to Whistler's studio. Met Lady Archie Campbell there." The next day Mr. Gardner received a letter from Whistler, dated November 10, 1892. "Dear Mr. Gardner, I have an idea that I ought to give you a formal receipt for your cheque for the picture—so I enclose it—and also the consular paper." The receipt was for "six hundred guineas for picture: Harmony in Blue and Silver, Trouville." [6]

John L. Gardner's record accounted for every day in Paris, mentioning his wife's whereabouts when they were not together. "Mrs. G. went to lady luncheon," for example. Of course there may have been some playful running up and down with the canvas, for which Jack Gardner's line-a-day had no space.

Town Topics caught up with what they supposed was a story, "regarding the recently developed fondness of the artist, Whistler, for the inimitable Mrs. Jack Gardner of Boston who is sojourning abroad and the lady's reciprocation thereof." They had not yet discovered that Mrs. Gardner was collecting pictures and for years to come they would assume that she had nothing but so-called flirtation on her mind.

The Gardners delayed their return to Boston until after Christmas in 1892. Thomas Russell Sullivan had been writing faithfully to Mrs. Jack, giving her news from home. At Prides Crossing, Manchester-by-the-Sea and Beverly there were "band concerts on our lawns in the moonlight . . . We disport ourselves and try to be Venetian in our sweet Puritanical way. Dr. Holmes comes frisking in . . ." And in Boston, Nikisch, now conductor of the Boston Symphony, "wakes the echoes of the Tavern Club with your Steinway." Mrs. Gardner had sent her Steinway to the Tavern Club so that it would not suffer from disuse during her absence abroad.

When Boston began to come back to life in the autumn, Sullivan wrote of 152 Beacon Street. "Yet over all hangs the blanket of the dark . . . because there are no flowers in your window and the lamp before the Madonna does not burn."

The World's Columbian Exposition at Chicago was scheduled for the summer of 1893 and preparations were in progress when the Gardners reached Boston early in the year. There was to be a "stately Palace of Fine Arts," and Henry James suggested that there ought to be a "Mrs. Jack's Building," so interested was she in the whole project. The Committee on Fine Arts asked her to lend a picture and she sent to Chicago *The Interior of the Cathedral of St. Denis* a picture she had just bought of the artist, Paul César Helleu, in Paris at Sargent's suggestion. It was very modern for its time, an example of pointillism, with color in tiny dots.

The Fine Arts Committee invited the Gardners to come to Chicago to the Exposition before it opened and Mrs. Jack was wandering almost alone through the gallery of Swedish art when she saw a painting she liked. *The Omnibus*, it was called—not a picture of a bus, as the name suggests, but rather a close-up of several people sitting in one.

A man was supervising the hanging of a painting and Mrs. Gardner asked him if he knew who had painted the one she liked. Well, yes, he did: he had painted it himself. His name was Anders Zorn. Nothing could have pleased both of them better than this introduction. Mrs. Gardner bought *The Omnibus* by Zorn and later entertained Mr. and Mrs. Zorn in Boston and in Venice.

Anders Zorn was Swedish Art Commissioner to the World's Columbian Exposition, a young man who at thirty-three had already made a name for himself in etching. He liked to refer to himself as a peasant; and when his portraits were in fashionable demand he made the most of his homespun qualities, which the world of fashion found delightful.

Mrs. Gardner paid $1600 for *The Omnibus,* cajoled friends into having their portraits painted by Zorn, and saw to it that the Boston Art Museum gave him an exhibition.

"I hope you have got a fine Zorn," Ralph Curtis wrote Mrs. Jack. "He ought to do your Beverly shore and you, bathing in the gloaming with a corn-colored moon rising behind your pearly back." Mrs. Gardner bought a small Zorn painting of a nude young woman and a child bathing at the seaside which she displayed in her Beacon Street parlor, and as time went by, people speculated about it, wondering if they had heard somewhere that it was Mrs. Jack.

During the summer of 1893, Henry James wrote to Mrs. Gardner that "Paul Bourget and his quite exceptional young wife sail for America today"—August 5. "They will be very vague and helpless and hot, just at first . . . They want to go to Newport; but I fear its complications for them—and about all ways and means their minds are a touching blank. She is a very exquisite little French madonna—and he is everything that is admirably sophisticated and sophisticating. Therefore, dear Mrs. Gardner, look out. Look out for them, I mean. I wish I could tell you to look out for me . . ." [7]

Writing in French, "My dear Henry James told me too much about your charm and goodness for me not to have expected your so cordial invitation," Paul Bourget told Mrs. Gardner on August 26 while he and his wife were at the Cliff Hotel, Newport.

Apparently, Bourget's bride had also been told too much. It was said that Minnie Bourget burst into tears when she heard that they were going to meet a lady who would be sure to steal her husband! But Minnie and Mrs. Jack became friends at sight.

Bourget was forty-one, but looked younger—Minnie was twenty-five, "beautiful, refined and charming," according to Thomas Russell Sullivan, whom Mrs. Gardner sent to the Somerset Club to help entertain the Bourgets.

In Beverly, Mrs. Gardner asked Oliver Wendell Holmes, a Beverly summer resident, to come to dinner with the Bourgets, and later she described the scene to Sullivan. Holmes was exhausted by recent festivities in honor of his eighty-fourth birthday. People had come flocking to Beverly, bearing flowers and carrying away his autograph—but after dinner, at Mrs. Jack's request, he was happy to recite "The Last Leaf."

Bourget, who had a little trouble with the English language, didn't get quite all the words, so Holmes recited "The Last Leaf" a second time and gave "The Chambered Nautilus" as an encore. This was "so touching on the part of a much-loved old gentleman who had seen so many 'swift seasons roll' that there were tears in everybody's eyes when it was over." [8]

Of course Bourget was writing a book about America. When *Outre-Mer* came out in 1894, he seemed to have forgot-

169

ten about an elderly gentleman poet and a touching scene. Instead, he described a portrait—"that of a woman whom I do not know," he said. He then proceeded to describe Mrs. Jack Gardner's portrait by John Singer Sargent which he could have seen only at Mrs. Gardner's house.

"It is a portrait such as fifteenth century masters painted," Bourget wrote. ". . . The woman is standing, her feet side by side, her knees close together, in an almost hieratic pose. Her body, rendered supple by exercise, is sheathed—you might say molded—in a tight-fitting black dress. Rubies, like drops of blood, sparkle in her shoes. Her slender waist is encircled by a girdle of enormous pearls . . . The head, intellectual and daring, with a countenance as of one who has understood everything, has for a sort of aureole, the vaguely gilded design of one of those Renaissance stuffs. The rounded arms are joined by the clasped hands—firm hands . . . which might guide four horses with the precision of an English coachman. It is the picture of an energy, at once delicate and invincible, momentarily in repose, and all the Byzantine Madonna is in that face, with its wide-open eyes.

"Yes, this woman is an idol, for whose services man labors, which he has decked with the jewels of a queen, behind each of whose whims lie days and days spent in the ardent battle of Wall Street. Frenzy of speculation in land, cities undertaken and built by sheer force of millions, trains launched at full speed over bridges built on a Babel-like sweep of arch, the creaking of cable cars, the quivering of electric cars, sliding along their wires with a crackle and a spark, the dizzy ascent of elevators in buildings twenty stories high . . . — these are what must have made possible this woman, this living orchid, unexpected masterpiece of this civilization."

Mrs. Jack Gardner, this orchid woman, after giving the Bourgets dinner at the Somerset Club took them to a Harvard-Yale football game. She explained the intricacies of football to Bourget, who was appalled by "the roughness of this terrible sport." During the contest he heard "a distinguished and refined woman," next to whom he was seated "crying out 'beauty!' at the sight of rushes that sent five or six boys sprawling on the ground."

"Farewell dear lady and friend," Paul Bourget finally wrote to Mrs. Gardner. After a year in the United States, he spoke a mixture of French and English, called the United States a land "des elevators, des fast trains, des hands-up, des smash-up, et des pet 'gators." He hoped they would soon meet in France, the country "des diligences, des fiacres . . . et des cannons Krupp." [9]

Minnie Bourget inquired about "The Isabella Club," as she called Mrs. Gardner's group of young men. Recalling her visit to the Gardners in Beverly, "What does John L. eat for breakfast this time of year?" she asked. "Always your devoted friend and I kiss you fondly," the girl who had been afraid to meet Mrs. Jack Gardner, reputed stealer of husbands, signed herself.

While Mrs. Jack was adding new literary lights to her collection, an old one was heard from. Frank Crawford wrote her that he would be in the United States "in all probability from October till May." Complaining that her letters to him were never longer than a line or two, "Dear Sister Brevis," he addressed her. "You have heard, perhaps, that my father-in-law died very suddenly . . . That will make it necessary for me to be much in Washington, as the appeal on a big claim of his comes before the Supreme Court in April—or should . . ."

Crawford's letter was anything but brief. "I have the old watch with me. Do you laugh? It will tumble into the sea some day and then I shall have lost my last ragged little bit of sentiment about *things*." He had finished his twenty-first book—he was "going southward for a few days in the felucca —along the Calabrian shore." He sent "many greetings, tender and unforgetting."

In December, 1893, Crawford was in Boston lunching with Eliza Perkins Cleveland, who described him—and also passed judgment.

"Frank alias Marion Crawford . . . is here reading selections from his writings . . . I should not have known him in the street. Tall and spare, with broad muscular shoulders, iron grey hair very thin and [cut] short, an almost black mustache, light blue eyes, sad and far away in their expression . . . He seems a man of 48 rather than 38 and when one thinks what a name he has made for himself, of his miserable youth, his absolute repentance (he never touches wine now, refused it at lunch & said he only drank water) his religious convictions (for he is a devout Roman Catholic) . . . and how good has triumphed over evil, one remembers that 'there is joy in the Kingdom of Heaven over one sinner that repenteth.' "

The pious Eliza Cleveland said that Crawford "warmed up more about his books and children than anything—and he seemed sad . . . He brought out pictures of his children, charming creatures evidently, two boys and two girls . . ." [10] She would have been shocked to know that Crawford was bringing Mrs. Gardner a copy of Boccaccio, which he promised to mail to her as soon as he arrived.

Crawford said that Boccaccio's *Decameron* was published in Florence uniform with the small Dante which he and she so well remembered. The stories "are not food for babies, but they are beautifully told," he informed her. "Some of the love speeches seem to me to be the best ever written," and he referred her to "Ghismonda's defense when Tancred discovers her love for Guiscardo." He marked the page—" 'tis most true that I have loved and still love Guiscardo and while I live shall continue to love him . . . To this I was induced by no frailty so much as his superior virtue . . ." [11]

It might appear that Crawford intended to blow upon old embers. But Isabella Gardner was a different person from the woman he had left with no farewell ten years earlier. Travels in the Far East, studies with Professor Norton and a growing knowledge and love of music had filled the interval. She and her husband were now collecting fine art together. And it just so happened that Mrs. Gardner already owned a rare copy of Boccaccio. She could look up Crawford's references herself if she wanted to—there was no need for him to educate her.

Mrs. Gardner cordially invited Crawford to visit her in April. The Gardners would be in Brookline; Clayton Johns and assorted musicians would be there, perhaps Bourget—certainly Sullivan. Soon, of course, she and her husband would be off to the Columbian Exposition.

By August 19, 1893, Crawford had yet to meet Mrs. Jack. He was glad "the little books" had reached her safely—and for the first time he addressed her as "Dear Lady," just like all the rest of her entourage. "Just let me turn up some morning at Beverly," he suggested. And he wondered if he might have marked the wrong page in her Boccaccio for her!

Finally, "if you will let me come for a day about the first of November, and if there is to be nobody else there, I think I could manage it," he wrote. "Will you forgive the proviso about there being nobody else? It sounds arrogant—which I am, perhaps—and rude, which I am not except under provocation . . ." He had been "working furiously" on "these big three-volume novels."

When November first was agreed upon, "my homage at your feet, dear lady," Crawford wrote. After their meeting, he addressed her as "dear friend" and a friend to F. Marion Crawford, Mrs. Gardner would always be to the end of his life. She read his books, replied, if briefly, to his long letters, which were often full of self-pity.

"The world is an inkpot, I am the pen and the Devil dips me," Crawford told her, and this summed up the later, harried, debt-ridden years of his life. Crawford brought from Brookline a Dante, a large and presumably rare edition, together with the little copy they had once read together. He had them interleaved and bound in soft olive-green leather with silver decorations designed by himself and executed by Tiffany—a vine with quatrefoils.

About the middle of November, Crawford met Mrs. Gardner in New York, at her hotel, and they spent the afternoon and evening together. She had asked him to find out when vespers would be and later he wrote, "I think I shall go to the Paulist Church on Sunday—in spite of the music! And sit in the same seat. Who says I am not sentimental?"

On the tenth of January, 1894, Crawford wrote to Mrs. Gardner. "This is my fifteenth day in bed, gentle lady . . ." He had been "suffering so much pain" from an "old strain" that he decided "to undergo an operation which was performed on December 27th." It was "perfectly successful but the healing process [was a] long one." She was not to be "at all anxious" and not to "tell anyone lest it get into the papers . . ." Mrs. Gardner must have written to say she would come at once, for Crawford suggested "Sunday morning between 10 and 1 o'clock" at the New York Hospital.

After considerable correspondence, Crawford came to Brookline once more—in April, 1894. The Brookline garden was "full of flowers and sunshine" and they read "the dear green Danté with its clasps and its Gothic corners." He arranged to come again in June. "I should be glad if I could so manage it that no one should know (in Boston) that I was there," he suggested. "It would obviate the necessity of going to spend an evening with my aunt . . ." Then, on July 17, 1894, "It was lovely and peaceful with you in Brookline. I shall always remember those clear, quiet days—as we have many good ones to remember in years gone by. May there be others to come! And thank you for them with all my heart . . ."

SEVENTEEN

Enter Berenson

THE GARDNERS HAD established a pattern of spending alternate summers in Europe. In 1894, however, they decided to go abroad to stay for more than a year. "The marvelous quarter century," the period between 1875 and 1900 has been called. It was a time during which the United States "doubled its population, trebled in wealth and cut the national debt to less than half." [1] John L. Gardner may or may not have trebled his personal wealth by 1894, but he was feeling no anxiety about his income. No Federal income tax was required of him, and his nephew George had become a capable businessman, qualified to look after the family interests.

Mr. Gardner's pocket diary began with a compliment on reaching Le Havre early in June, however. "Each passenger can bring into France only 300 cigars apiece," he wrote. He had to pay duty on the rest of his supply, which cost him "a little over 2 cents" per cigar!

Mrs. Jack had several times suggested that Berenson meet her somewhere in Europe, since he was not planning to come back to America. He always replied that previous plans made this impossible; he was to be in Holland while she was in Spain, in Germany when she proposed Venice. It was not until this 1894 residence abroad that they met. "Dec. 12. After lunch, Berenson and Mrs. Costelloe to Bernoski's to see collection of Japanese and Chinese bronze," John L. Gardner wrote.

Mrs. Costelloe had been Mary Smith, a girl whose Pennsylvania Quaker parents lived in England. Mary had become a Roman Catholic when she married Benjamin Costelloe, a London barrister. In 1899, when she was twenty-five and Berenson twenty-four, they met and "fell in love at first sight," according to her brother, Logan Pearsall Smith. "Divorce was impossible," so Mary left her children with her parents in England and traveled with Berenson as "his pupil and his secretary," taking down his every word, keeping a record of his observations, deductions and attributions in Italian art. [2]

174

In a letter from Berenson to Mrs. Gardner, dated 1889, Berenson wrote that "a friend here quite surprised me with an offer of enough money to keep me abroad another year." [3] Far from being the homesick boy of his early letters, he now found the United States far too crude for his taste. He would be "like one who, after living in Rome for three years of our second century was returned to Colonia."

The traveling scholarship money had run out. Berenson would be forced to do "almost anything for a living" in America—even teaching, which would be a last resort. Because of this surprise from a friend, however, Berenson could live in Italy. Mary Costelloe had money of her own.

Berenson indicated, in a letter written in 1894, that Mrs. Gardner had lost touch with him. "I venture to recall myself to your memory apropos of a little book on Venetian painters which I have asked my publishers to send to you. Your kindness to me at a critical moment is something I have never forgotten and if I have let five years go by without writing to you, it has been because I have had nothing to show you that could change the opinion you must have had when you put a stop to our correspondence."

In several of Berenson's earlier letters he had expressed a desire to spend his life acquiring culture, with no further end in view. Mrs. Gardner had not contracted to support him indefinitely, however, and she may very possibly have enclosed a final remittance in a letter which she said would be her last —until Berenson produced some tangible results of his foreign study. Whatever the cause of the rift, Isabella Gardner, although famous for her sharp tongue, was always ready to forgive a protégé. Her correspondence with Berenson was not only renewed but became prolific as Berenson found that he could act as agent in selling Mrs. Gardner some Italian masterpieces.

Discovering her fondness for her own name and her willingness to buy any portrait of an "Isabella" or any item belonging to one, he played up that theme. Fortunately, history was full of Isabellas. Each picture that Berenson recommended was positively the most wonderful that he had ever seen and Berenson was completely unabashed at making this claim again and again. He did not scruple to hint that rivals would snap up his bargain unless Mrs. Gardner bought quickly and at his price. As time went by, Berenson's technique improved and he became a super-salesman. His friendship with Mrs. Gardner had its ups and downs, as might be expected.

"How much do you want a Botticelli?" Berenson asked

Mrs. Gardner during the summer of 1894. "Lord Ashburnham has a great one—one of the greatest, a 'Death of Lucretia.' I understand that although the noble lord is not keen about selling it, a handsome offer would not insult him. I should think it would have to be about £3000. It would be a pleasure to me to be able, in some way, to repay you for your kindness on another occasion when I needed help . . ."

Through Berenson, the Gardners bought *The Tragedy of Lucretia* from the Earl of Ashburnham for about $16,500. It was their first example of an Italian Renaissance painting of the early period. As a young man, Botticelli had painted altarpieces full of simplicity and unworldly charm—his client, the clergy or the pious churchgoer. *The Tragedy of Lucretia* was painted about 1500, late in Botticelli's life, when scenes from Roman mythology together with an architectural background displaying all the new mathematical skills in perspective were the fashion. His clients were now the Italian nobility grown rich from looting their neighbors.

Small armored figures swarmed into the center foreground, surrounding the dead Lucretia. Other acts of the tragedy took place under porticoes, left and right. Mrs. Jack could study the picture long at a time, enjoying this scene and other classic scenes painted into arch and frieze in the background, for *The Tragedy of Lucretia* was a splendid illustration for the history of Italy which she read constantly these days.

The Gardners bought nineteen paintings during their long stay in Europe in 1894. Nine were by contemporary artists, ten were old masters acquired through Berenson.

After enjoying a few weeks of the London social season, the Gardners' purpose was to go to Austria to hear music before settling down in their beloved Palazzo Barbaro in Venice. But Mrs. Jack was suddenly "weak and thin." [4] She wrote "dispirited" letters to friends instead of her usual brief but gay ones and "fainted at the dressmakers." Her husband grew anxious about her. Friends spoke enthusiastically of a health resort at Schwalbach, Germany, so Jack Gardner made reservations. On July 28, 1894, he wrote, "The doctor examined Mrs. G., told her to rest, and prescribed treatment to begin Monday." And when Monday came, "Mrs. G." went to the building housing the reputedly medicinal spring and "drank 3 fingers of water," Jack said.

The doctor also prescribed "bed at seven" for Mrs. Gardner, so that she recovered her health in plenty of time to attend the Opera in Frankfurt, and again in Munich. The *Götterdämmerung* lasted from 6:30 in the evening until

10:30, Jack Gardner noted, with an air of resignation. He was still not a Wagnerian. At a mountain town called Ischl, much favored by musicians, Clayton Johns joined the Gardners.

Gericke, who had left his post as conductor of the Boston Symphony in 1889, was living near Ischl at a village called Stein Kogel. In 1890, he had gone to Bayreuth, meeting there Paula Flamm, daughter of the court physician, "an intelligent musician, a good pianist—a Wagnerite of course." Gericke fell in love and after a prudent two-year engagement, he married Paula. "Gericke married!" exclaimed the Boston musicians. They could hardly believe the news.

The Gardners reached Ischl by carriage from Ebensee, "meeting Gericke and his baby" (a little girl named Katherine) "on the way." Next day, they drove to Stein Kogel to lunch with Mr. and Mrs. Gericke.[5]

Making the comfortable hotel at Ischl their headquarters, the Gardners settled down. "Mrs. G. went with Johns to café to look at Brahms & Co." Jack Gardner wrote. They "took tea with Mr. and Mrs. Strauss etc."

Brahms had a cottage near Stein Kogel and Gericke took Mrs. Gardner and Clayton Johns to call on him. Johns told the story. "Gericke, leading the way, cried out through the open door, *Amerika kommt.* Brahms thought he said, 'Mrs. Gardner *kommt,*' so by the misunderstanding, the ice was broken. We stayed only for a few minutes. Brahms spoke no English and Mrs. Gardner no German, so Gericke became interpreter. I don't remember what anybody said, but we *saw* Brahms in his little roadside house . . . and that was the main thing." [6]

George Proctor was still abroad studying music and John L. Gardner was still signing one-thousand-dollar checks, payable to Clayton Johns, for Proctor's support. George was now at Ischl and called on the Gardners at their hotel the minute they arrived. The next afternoon, after lunching with the Gerickes, "Mrs. G. went to hear Proctor play." That evening she went to hear Proctor play again.

George had been writing faithfully to Mrs. Gardner since 1892, when he arrived in Vienna and he was to remain abroad until 1896. At first, the great Leschetizky refused to accept him as a pupil, telling him after a tryout that he played "like a drunken fellow or a woman." George was sent to Madame Essipoff to practice five-finger exercises and he felt that he had been allowed to form careless habits at the New England Conservatory. At the end of January, 1893, "I am with Leschetiz-

177

ky at last," George wrote in triumph. He was to "prepare a sonata and two preludes to play in class."

Then the day came when George was scheduled to play for Leschetizky before all the famous piano teacher's other pupils. And he had not worked on his assignment! "I sneaked out of the parlor when he was not looking and went upstairs to Madame Essipoff's room and commenced to practice," George wrote to Mrs. Gardner with remarkable frankness. "I stayed as long as I dared. The class had lasted four hours and I was beginning to think that he had forgotten me." So back went George, sure that Leschetizky had never missed him.

"A lady with the strength of an ox played the Chopin Polonaise in A♭ and then Leschetizky (he was in a jolly mood that day) said, 'Now, my dear scholars, we will hear from somebody weaker—Mr. George Proctor.'

"Ye Gods! What I went through at that piano! The class fairly howled for half an hour. He played everything after me, made the most horrible faces, struck the notes wrong and acted like a monkey." George remained "cool as an ice cart." Leschetizky said the boy had no temperament and was sleepy.

In a burst of honest self-appraisal, "I have wondered why it is that Mrs. Gardner is so good as to send me here," George said. He felt that "a clerkship at Jordan's would be more suitable" to his abilities. Mrs. Gardner could not resist this disarming candor and wrote to comfort and cheer the boy. She asked Gericke to go to see him and find out if there was anything he could do to help. Clayton Johns went to Vienna to see Proctor every year—probably at the Gardners' expense.

In 1893, George Proctor's letters must have given Mrs. Gardner great pleasure, they were so full of naïve enthusiasm for the opera. "Every piece is done here on the same grand scale, regardless of the cost of labor and time," George wrote. He was so carried away one night that at the end of an aria he "jumped up and shouted 'That was bully'" and "everyone laughed."

The Gardners took George to Venice with them in 1894, where he met the musicians who always gathered at the Palazzo Barbaro. He was treated like an honored guest and almost like a son, seeing for himself what a young man of modest beginnings might aspire to if he proved to be a fine artist. "My Venice trip was not to be compared with any pleasure I have ever had or ever expected to have in my life," George wrote to Mrs. Gardner. "It was more than I ever supposed mortal man enjoyed." The Gardners escorted him to the railroad station when it was time to leave and Mrs. Gardner gave him "a history of Venice" to read on the train, he told him "not to look back" when she left him. George made no report of progress in history but wrote, "I wanted to give you a good hug but American proprieties might have been shocked so I restrained myself."

It is possible to infer from part of Proctor's letter that Mrs. Gardner had been disappointed in his progress as a pianist. She gave him some advice and he answered her argument. "In regard to the 'great big, real love affair' which you hope will come some day to knock everything and me into the bargain to pieces for my own and art's sake, I can only reply that 'my sake' would probably just as soon remain whole."

After Proctor left the Barbaro, Anders Zorn, the Swedish artist, and his wife arrived. A festival was in progress, so Mrs. Jack took them to the regatta in a big gondola with four rowers and in the evening she hired a piano and musicians, loaded them all into another gondola to follow her and her guests along the Grand Canal.

There were fireworks every night which could be watched from the balcony of the Barbaro. Tirindelli, the violinist, and Agostini, the cellist and nephew of the cardinal, came to dinner while Clayton Johns was still a house guest. Johns played the piano and they "trioed after dinner," as Jack Gardner put it.

Mrs. Jack went out on the balcony to watch the fireworks. Suddenly, she thrust open the balcony doors leading into the drawing room and stood in the archway, arms outstretched. "Come out—all of you," she cried. "This is too beautiful to miss."

"I'm going to paint you like that," Anders Zorn exclaimed —and this he did, beginning the following evening. Mrs. Jack, her hands pressing apart the glass doors, seemed to come forward joyously. Her pale yellow dress echoed a distant golden flare against the night sky. The famous pearls hung far below her waist and at the end of them a ruby glowed, while in the sky behind, the color was repeated in the red streak of rocket. Zorn did not flatter Mrs. Jack overmuch—she was neither pretty nor too young—but a woman, full of vitality, in love with Venice and in love with life.

Contemporary critics were unkind about the picture. A mere sketch, they called it—just an impression, "impressionism" being at this time a scornful term. That Zorn finished his picture in two evenings was held against him, but the verve and color, the effect of motion in the portrait were not accidents but art.

John L. Gardner made no comment concerning his wife's latest portrait, but he kept the record straight. "Oct. 22 . . . Zorn finished picture of Mrs. G. in window."

Hitherto, Rome had not interested the Gardners, but Maud Howe Elliott and her artist husband were living there—as were innumerable other Americans. On January 3, 1895, the Gardners arrived in Rome to be "met at the station by Mrs. Story" and taken in her handsome carriage to the Grand Hotel. There were two young sons of William Wetmore Story, Waldo and Julian. It was probably Emma Eames, wife of Julian, who met the Gardners, because Clayton Johns had just been singing her praises—she having sung his songs in London a few months previously. "Emma Eames was a woman of unusual beauty, with a beautiful voice," Johns said. "She became a star shining over two continents . . . many people remember how beautiful she was as Juliet" when she made her New York debut—"radiant and just nineteen." She married Julian Story that same year, but Johns did not mention her artist husband, whose portrait of her is said to be his best work.

William Wetmore Story, patriarch of the family, was now eighty-five years old but still handsome and impressive. He represented the Roman-American social life of Hawthorne, Thomas Crawford and Charles Eliot Norton. His daughter Edith was now the Marchesa Peruzzi di Medici, a social leader in a second generation of Roman-Americans, many of whom had been American heiresses in search of a title. This new group cared little for art or letters, stepped faster, spent plenty of money—and often sold family art treasures when the money was gone.

Henry James, after expressing his purely imaginary regrets that he could not meet Mrs. Gardner in Rome, told her, ". . . but *my* Rome is buried in the past. May this find you perched on new conquests." [7] Then, writing to Mrs. Daniel Curtis, who was now in her own home, the Barbaro, he said, "The mere distant image of Mrs. Jack 'going it' on the graves of the Caesars and the lifts of the Grand Hotel, makes me huddle close to my fireside and groan over what might have been. She may capture the Pope but I think she is too amiable to become really fashionable. I see her succeeding better at Grand Hotels than at grand manners. She tries too hard and listens too sympathetically—bless her innocent (after all) heart." [8]

James never characterized Mrs. Gardner better, nor did anyone else, for that matter. He was among the few who knew that her heart was, after all, innocent. She had listened

180

too sympathetically to his own abortive play in Boston and he had been annoyed rather than grateful but he said she was to believe him her very affectionate old friend—and in his way, he was.

F. Marion Crawford was not in Rome, nor even at his "Villa Crawford" in Sorrento, but in Sicily. He gave Mrs. Gardner his opinion of the Rome of 1895. "Poor little Rome, I am told, is on its very little hind legs with excitement over your coming. It has still some historical interest but you will find it a nasty, dirty, snivelling, sneaking little hole."

Crawford to the contrary, Mrs. Gardner found Rome full of historical interest as she went around "to see things found in excavations" and attended lectures on archaeology. She had a wonderful time socially.

Queen Margherita was very affable when Mrs. Gardner was presented to her by Isaac Wayne MacVeagh, American Ambassador to Italy. The king's birthday followed shortly, to be celebrated with much pomp and public parading. Mrs. Jack sent him a huge basket of red roses. The story went that His Majesty told an equerry to find out what sort of lady this Mrs. John L. Gardner might be and what her intentions were before he ordered the gift acknowledged. The story was picked up by *Town Topics* in New York—they said Mrs. Jack told it herself, and laughed.

Maud Howe Elliott was writing a Rome letter for the Boston *Transcript*. She mentioned Mrs. Jack Gardner, "with wonderful costumes from Paris and such furs—sables and chinchillas." Mrs. Jack needed all her costumes, for there were balls at *palazzi* and hotels, dances at the American Embassy. The John L. Gardners went to the Marchesa Chigi's party, met the marchesa's daughter Margaret and soon Mrs. Jack was chaperoning Donna Daisy Chigi at the races. It is quite possible that at the Chigi family palazzo in Rome, Mrs. Gardner saw a certain Botticelli Madonna—eventually to be for sale.

Fox hunting on the Campagna was a favorite Roman pastime. The Gardners went to the meet several times, riding on top of a coach behind four galloping horses. "Mrs. Gardner invited me to go to the meet but I was afraid to do so," wrote Mrs. Barrett Wendell, wife of the Harvard professor of English, who was in Rome with her children. She overcame her fears, whatever their nature, and accepted a third invitation. "Perfectly beautiful view," she wrote. "Certainly 500 people there. Gay scene." [9]

Henry James had suggested that Mrs. Gardner might capture the Pope and in a way, she did. She was presented to the Pope and people said she had demanded a private audience. This was not strictly true, but she told Thomas Russell Sullivan all about it and he wrote down her account when he got home from a dinner at 152 Beacon Street after Mrs. Jack's return home.

"She has the power of presenting such scenes very vividly with individual feminine touches," Sullivan said. "On her way to Rome, she waited over in Paris while Worth put all his art into the dress designed for the Papal interview . . . a costume of black, magnificent but very simply made. Upon her arrival in Rome she expressed her wish to Schönberg, the Pope's chamberlain," and "after many days" the invitation arrived.

What Mrs. Jack did not tell Sullivan was that during the "many days" she and her husband wined and dined the Baron Schönberg and made formal calls on Cardinal Rampolla.

For her audience with the Pope, Mrs. Gardner wore the specially designed dress, "a veil, no gloves, but at the request of Rampolla, her wonderful pearls . . . She found herself one of eighteen in the antechamber" at the Vatican.

"Then appeared Schönberg who said, 'I have news for you; His Holiness grants you a private audience.' "

Mrs. Gardner was "taken by surprise and asked, 'What must I do? How am I to behave?' "

" 'You have only to follow me when the time comes,' " the baron assured her. " 'The doors of the Pope's apartment will be thrown open and then closed behind you. You will find yourself alone with His Holiness and may do as you please."

Mrs. Gardner "soon stood within the closed doors of a long room lighted by one large window. Far off at the opposite end, under the window, sat the Pope in the lowest armchair she had ever seen. She hesitated a moment. *Viens mon enfant,*' the Pope said very gently and she went forward, kneeling instinctively at his feet . . . He asked her many questions about America and there was much admiration of her pearls."

Mrs. Gardner told the Pope "that she owned a *Book of Hours,*" printed and illuminated in 1514, which had once belonged to Mary, Queen of Scots. The Pope said she must bring it with her to show him, next time she came to Rome.

The interview lasted twenty-five minutes and Mrs. Gardner said it seemed long. The Pope asked her if there was any favor he could grant her and she said she would like to come to his private mass in his own chapel.

"'Ah, we will see if that can be arranged,' he said and summoned an attendant and finally, 'Come next Sunday morning,' he told her."

Mrs. Gardner said that the mass in the Pope's private chapel was "very impressive. Only nine attended and the Pope's method of celebrating it" seemed to her "spontaneous, as if done for the first time." [10]

During the audience, the Pope asked Mrs. Gardner if she were Catholic. *"Anglican Catholic,"* she had replied and she remained loyal to her Church of the Advent, although word went around Boston that she had become Roman Catholic. Years earlier, Thomas Jefferson Coolidge had playfully suggested in a letter to her, "I think you ought to turn Catholic. I think I should immediately turn priest to hear your confessions." Mrs. Jack enjoyed the humorous touch, seriously religious though she was.

The Gardners indulged in considerable domestic debate from time to time, and guests were sometimes embarrassed by their fierce arguments. But they saw eye to eye on the purchase of antiques. "Went to Simonetti's, the antiquario. Selected chairs and stuffs which Mrs. G. purchased afterwards," Jack Gardner wrote. And then, "to Villegas and bought for Mrs. G. the things she had selected." They often went to "bric-a-brac" shops together.

Two Roman pavements, recently uncovered, were for sale and Jack Gardner went to see them. "One about 5 metres square in about 26 small pieces, say 5 pcs wide and 5 or 6 long" attracted him. "Middle piece abt 1 metre square. Design—Gorgon's head in middle arabesque & a few birds in outer pieces" was the way he described it in his pocket diary. It was "owned by a lady, together with an antiquarian" and the "asking price for the two pavements was 30,000 lire." The lady had already borrowed 9000 lire on these fragments from a Roman villa. Mr. Gardner wanted only the one with the Gorgon's head and the birds, and so negotiations fell through. But in 1897, the Gardners bought a Roman pavement very much like the one described and perhaps the same. It became the chief ornament of the beautiful inner court at the Isabella Stewart Gardner Museum.

Early in April, after a swift descent upon Naples and a return, the Gardners left Rome for Venice. Sargent had been in Venice, sharing Ralph Curtis's studio and painting masterly watercolors of the watery city. He "recommended Mancini," whom he thought "a man of genius," to paint Jack Gardner's portrait.

Antonio Mancini had been a popular painter but now his work was going out of style. Ten years earlier, the Gardners had bought his sentimental portrait of a boy in fancy dress, called *The Standard Bearer of the Harvest Festival* which Mrs. Gardner eventually hung over the case where she kept Crawford's letters, in her museum. They now bought a similar item called *The Little Groom,* and Jack Gardner obligingly sat to Mancini, who needed money. Most of the fee, however, went to the artist's creditors.

Maud Howe Elliott, arriving at the Palazzo Barbaro to visit the Gardners, described the artist at work. "Mancini's method was to put a network of squares in front of the canvas and to paint the picture through these squares. You can sometimes see traces of these in Mancini's work."

Some years later, Joseph Lindon Smith tried to help Mancini and succeeded in getting him a commission to paint the American Ambassador to Italy. The likeness turned out to be good, but Mancini asked for more time to add finishing touches, and when the portrait was delivered, black lines forming squares had been added so that the Ambassador seemed to be peering through a tennis net. People said poor Mancini had gone mad—although it might have been said that he had gone modern.

In part of the background of the John L. Gardner portrait, lines in squares can faintly be seen—not black, but pale gray, where unpainted canvas seems to show. "Mancini made a crayon sketch of me and decided how to paint the portrait," Jack Gardner wrote on Sunday, April 21. One of the decisions was to paint him with his hat on to conceal the fact that he was now disastrously bald.

Mancini did a creditable job, showing a pleasant gentleman with an alert, not to say wary eye, a Roman nose, and, under an adequate but no longer luxuriant mustache, a mouth with a hint of humor. Jack Gardner was seated out of doors, his fedora worn with an air, his hand upon an elegant walking stick. He seemed to be enjoying a spring afternoon in a thoroughly European, gentleman-of-leisure manner and he looked as though he would like to see a pretty girl come by.

The faithful Sullivan had been keeping Mrs. Gardner informed of doings in Boston. In January, 1895, "Melba is here, and yesterday at a popular matinee with the Symphony Orchestra, she dragged from the Green-room, C. Johns esq. and sang, 'I Love and the World is Mine,' to his accompaniment." She made Clayton Johns take a bow with her.

"Tim Adamowski is now Melba's slave, having, as Monty

Sears says, 'hitched his wagon to a star.' I have met the lady and understand the fascination which isn't Bostonian the least bit."

The Gardners had missed a reception at the new Boston Public Library in Copley Square, on April 25, 1895. Only the Abbey murals and the Sargent frieze of the prophets were in place but "we had a great time here in our humble way." It was a private party, where McKim, the architect, "received with Abbey and Sargent. Forty noble dames came over from New York, headed by Mrs. Harry White and Mrs. Canfield, with all their jewels and nothing on their shoulders. The great staircase looked as it can never look again in our Republican age . . ."

Sullivan told Mrs. Gardner that "the Sargent decorations are overwhelming. He has never done anything in the way of single figures, so strong as his frieze of the prophets . . ." As a sort of private memorial to a young artist of promise, now dead, Sargent had used a study he had made of his friend Denis Bunker for the figure of Joshua among the prophets.

The Gardners sailed for home on July 29, 1895. Mrs. Jack, deserting Worth for Paquin, stopped in Paris for a few new clothes. Thomas Russell Sullivan soon saw her in Beverly, "all in white, wearing her crown jewel, the great ruby."

Trunks and packing cases cleared customs in Boston and were forwarded to 152 Beacon Street. During the coming year, the Gardners bought pictures through Berenson from photographs he sent them, along with his wonderful selling letters. On February 6, 1896, Berenson wrote, "I am now sending you the photograph of a picture which was always called a Titian until the breaking up of the great Scarpa collection where it belonged. Of course it is not a Titian; it is almost certainly by his best follower Polidoro Lanzani. You can judge from the photograph of the attractiveness of the picture. What makes it to the highest degree valuable is the fact that it is the portrait of the greatest and most fascinating lady of the Renaissance—your worthy precursor and patron saint,—Isabella d'Este, Marchioness of Mantua. I can get you this portrait for £600 and I trust you will not let it escape."

Mrs. Gardner did not instantly rise to this bait, however. She studied the photograph carefully and objected to the painting of the right hand. As a matter of fact, it looked like a badly stuffed glove with no thumb. On March 25, "I am cabling you that in the picture Isabella's hand is not at all offensive," Berenson replied. ". . . Purely and solely as a picture, I should not be urging you to get it. But you will find her decorating a wall well and besides she has potent attraction as the portrait of an Isabella."

There still might have been no sale—except that Mrs. Jack had taken up horse racing! [11] Green Hill Stable was registered with the Jockey Club in 1894, the colors, green with yellow cap. "My horse Halton," Mrs. Gardner wrote proudly, on a newspaper clipping telling how Halton "got away poorly," but "after a drive, won by a length." Before Mrs. Gardner bought him, he had entered only two races, winning one and losing the other. She bought Halton in 1894 and that year he ran in seventeen races, winning four. During the following season, he ran ten races and won none of them! Probably Mrs. Gardner was advised to get rid of him, but in 1896 Halton ran four times and won twice. Mrs. Jack was jubilant. With her winnings—or just because she felt like celebrating —she bought *Isabella* and when the picture arrived, summoned friends to see it.

"In the first place, let me thank you for your genial, cordial, warming letter," Berenson wrote, "wherein you spoke of the reception given Isabella d'Este, the music and the incense. And then I heartily congratulate you over your triumphant horse."

The portrait of Isabella d'Este had been sold to a European dealer in 1895 as a Titian. Berenson's refusal to attribute the picture to Titian caused the value to fall, so that a good deal of comment among dealers and their clients resulted.

In 1907, Paul Bourget wrote a satirical story called "The Lady Who Lost Her Painter." This told of an imaginary visit of an expert to an ancient castle to see the owner's particular pride—a painting by an old master. The expert disauthenticates the picture so that the lady of the portrait loses her supposed painter. But there were friends of Mrs. Gardner who, never having read the story, assumed that she was the "lady" and that the "painter" was Sargent!

Experts argued fiercely over Mrs. Gardner's *Isabella d'Este,* proposing four artists other than Lanzani and ending up by saying "Perhaps by Francesco Torbido (Veronese, *ca.* 1483–1561)." In the course of the argument the identity of the sitter was lost! No longer *Isabella d'Este,* she became merely *Lady in a Turban.* At the future Gardner Museum, Mrs. Jack would always remember that she had never liked the lady's queer hand.

But Berenson had gone right to work to sell another picture. This time, the painting was actually as beautiful as he said it was and completely authentic. "Now I come to the point of this letter," he wrote in an unusually long communication, even for him. The date was January 19, 1896. "I am sending you a photograph of one of the most precious pictures in existence, which, if it is not sold by February 18, goes to the National Gallery. Owing to a number of fortunate accidents, I am in a position to offer you a chance of buying it.

"The picture in question is not only one of Rembrandt's very earliest pictures, but the earliest portrait of himself, executed as the dates indicate, in 1629 when Rembrandt was 22. The condition is perfect, the colors . . . of that greyish green, prevalent in all early Rembrandts. This masterpiece you can have for the comparatively small sum of £3000."

Berenson wanted Mrs. Gardner to cable "Yes, Rembrandt" or "No, Rembrandt." She cabled "Yes."

On March 10, 1896, T. R. Sullivan wrote in his dairy, "Dined tonight with Mrs. John L. Gardner, one of a *partie carrée* which included Lily Codman and Joe Smith. Our hostess showed us her newest treasure which came only this morning, a portrait of Rembrandt by himself, in a green velvet doublet and gold chain, a hat and feather. It is a younger Rembrandt than we know—a masterpiece.

"The picture has been for many years in the gallery of Stowe House. The owner, dying, left instructions that if it did not bring a stated price within his time-limit, it should pass to the National Gallery. Mrs. Gardner, hearing of this, cabled the money two days before the time expired and henceforth the Rembrandt will hang in her drawing-room, cheek by jowl with her Van Eyck, her Van der Meer, her Botticelli, her Lippo Lippi, her Lucas Cranach—fine examples, all . . . So day by day, the wonderful little *Musée* Gardner gains in values."

EIGHTEEN

Art and Lions

W HEN MRS. GARDNER appeared at the New York Horse Show in November, 1895, immediately after her long stay in Europe, *Town Topics* had a comment more perceptive than most. "Mrs. Jack Gardner, Boston's most cherished institution, was on view. She did not cause, of course, either the thrilling interest or the solemn hush with which her movements are watched in her own city. She is too intelligent and not rich enough for New York."

It would almost seem as though the anonymous reporter knew of the negotiations going on, as Mrs. Gardner's remarkable art collection began to take shape—and to overflow the Beacon Street house. Berenson was not yet certain how far his client would be able to go in the matter of price but he was soon at work trying to sell her Gainsborough's *Blue Boy.* On March 22, 1896, he wrote Mrs. Gardner to tell of the *Blue Boy* and *Lady Siddons as the Tragic Muse* being for sale. "I must beg you on your honor to keep the strictest silence," he said. "The price will certainly not be under $100,000."

It did not surprise Berenson that Mrs. Gardner should care little for *Lady Siddons as the Tragic Muse* but be definitely interested in the *Blue Boy.* He had already observed that she loved portraits of charming young boys and perhaps he suspected that this might be because she had no son of her own. On April 26, 1896, he wrote, "For the last ten days I have nothing decisive to write you regarding the 'Blue Boy.' For several days the news that came to me only was of the most despairing kind; that the Mrs. Siddons was to be had; but that the 'Blue Boy' was not even for sale—that this was a misunderstanding. At last I have news of a better sort, although negative enough. This is that it may be possible to treat of the matter of the 'Blue Boy'—on a basis of about £30,000. I may be able to get it for a couple of thousand pounds less; we may have to give a couple of thousand pounds more."

This was at least as good a way as any of finding out whether Mrs. Gardner would be able to pay about $150,000 for a picture. "My conscience more than permits me to urge you to spend that much on it—provided you want it badly enough. And I doubt whether, in the whole realm of possible purchases there be such another prize. So my advice is BE BOLD." Berenson urged Mrs. Gardner to cable YEBB— "Yes, Blue Boy."

Mrs. Gardner agreed to buy the *Blue Boy* and then, on May 10, Berenson had to tell her: "The owner of the Blue Boy seems to have wanted to see what serious offer would be made for his picture and this having been made—£30,000 —he then firmly said that he had not the remotest intention of selling and that no price could possibly tempt him . . . Do forgive me for having excited you in vain. Your disappointment cannot be greater than mine. The only consolation is that in our lifetime the Blue Boy will not leave its present owner without its going to you if you continue to want it. Of that I can assure you." In 1921, Gainsborough's *Blue Boy* was sold to H. E. Huntington, through Duveen, for $620,-000.

Berenson, meanwhile, went right to work to sell Mrs. Gardner another picture. "Now on bended knee, I must make a frightful confession," he wrote in his letter of May 10. "Just a week ago, I thought the Blue Boy was so certainly yours that I did something in consequence. 'Tis a tale with a preface, and this you must briefly hear.

"One of the few greatest Titians in the world is the Europa which was painted for Philip II of Spain, and as was known from Titian's own letter to the king, dispatched to Madrid in April, 1562." The picture became part of the dowry of Philip IV's sister upon her proposed marriage to Charles I of England. It was packed up to be sent to England and when the marriage negotiations were broken off the picture remained carefully packed, which Berenson thought probably accounted for its marvelous preservation. It came "in the last century into the Orleans collection. When that was sold some hundred years ago, the Europa fell into the hands of a lord whose name I forget," Berenson said, "then into Lord Darnley's and now it is probably to be bought for the not extraordinary price of £20,000." [1]

Knowing full well that Mrs. Gardner had a genealogical report tracing her father's line directly back to the royal Stuarts, the *Europa* was a "far greater picture, great and great though the Blue Boy is"—it was also "intended for a

189

Stuart," he told Mrs. Jack, "and should at least rest in the hands of one."

The "frightful confession" came when Berenson explained that he had offered the picture to Mrs. S. D. Warren, thinking that Mrs. Gardner would not have money enough to buy it, if she bought the *Blue Boy*. This part was hard to bring up tactfully but Berenson did his best. He had only wanted to be sure that the Titian would "go to America and if possible to Boston"—his love for the city of his youth having increased, apparently, now that he was sure he would never have to live there.

"But you have forbidden me to bring you into rivalry with anyone else," Berenson continued. "Yet I have given you my reasons and I trust you will consider the exceptional circumstances. I am under no obligation to Mrs. Warren. If you cable as soon as possible, . . . your decision will, in a perfectly *bona fide* way, come before Mrs. Warren's and then the Europa shall be yours. Cable, please, the one word YEUP—yes Europa or NEUP—no Europa, to Fiesole as usual." Almost as a postscript, Berenson added that the *Europa* is on canvas, 5 feet 10 inches high, 6 feet 8 inches broad and signed "Titianus Pinxit."

Mrs. Gardner was not to speak of the *Europa* to anyone "until she reaches you, so as to spare me with Mrs. Warren," Berenson said—quite understandably anxious about standing in the middle in case of a quarrel between the two Boston ladies. The Samuel Denis Warren fortune came from the manufacture of paper and the present Mr. S. D. Warren was president of the Boston Museum of Fine Arts. The Warrens' path and Mrs. Gardner's would cross with increasing frequency from now on, with John L. Gardner keeping the peace but with no great love lost between the ladies.

Mrs. Gardner cabled $100,000, and a large wall space to the left of her drawing-room fireplace had to be cleared for the Titian. In the lower right-hand triangular section of this painting, a decidedly sturdy girl had toppled over on the back of a bull who was swimming hard in deep water and rolling his eyes. Guests with a knowledge of art extolled the blue in a cloud-flecked sky, the marvelous impression of depth and distance which are a part of this Renaissance masterpiece. Certain Boston ladies tried hard not to stare at the voluptuous Europa, with her scanty drapery, while Mrs. Gardner had fun watching their faces.[2] Thomas Russell Sullivan very correctly called the picture "large and important . . . splendid in color and composition."

It was really fortunate that Mrs. Gardner had failed to buy the *Blue Boy* but had acquired Titian's *Europa* instead. The Titian gave direction to her collection, and hereafter she specialized in Italian art, with emphasis on middle Renaissance but with some of the best of the earlier periods as well: a Giotto, for example, and a Fra Angelico. The handsome, forthright Gainsborough would have been out of place among Italian subtleties and would only have proved incongruous.

"Why can't I be with you when the Europa is unpacked?" Berenson wrote. "America is a land of wonders but this sort of miracle it has not witnessed." He felt that the Titian *Europa* was "the finest picture that would ever again be sold" but of course this did not prevent him from offering Mrs. Gardner many another painting, each the "finest" of all. His enthusiasm was hard to resist.

Although she was now a serious art collector, Mrs. Gardner did not disappoint her public—as represented by *Town Topics*. In 1894, just before she left for Europe, she made this paper because she sneezed!

It was the last day of May and the second Boston Pops concert was about to begin at Music Hall. "Everybody was there, scattered about at little tables and feeling very un-Boston indeed with cigarettes and beer . . ."

Tymoteusz Adamowski, Pops conductor of the Boston Symphony Orchestra, "had almost succeeded in hushing the great company into an appropriate silence for the 'Lohengrin prelude' when some one dropped a heavy cane . . . The titter raised by this untoward occurrence had scarcely subsided when Mrs. Gardner sneezed, which started a giggle all over the house. Adamowski, who was by this time rapping fiercely with his baton and quite red in the face from this second outburst, looked around to discover the delinquent, little realizing that it was his loyal friend and devoted patron, Mrs. Jack!"

The management of the Boston Pops concerts had decreed the little round tables—the air of Viennese informality. Of course no one would have dropped a cane and not even Mrs. Gardner would have sneezed at Symphony during the formal season! "Light alcoholic beverages and smoking" were allowed in the hope that "a partially indifferent public" would learn to like music "to the accompaniment of tobacco and other solaces." Mrs. Jack had beer brought to the special table which she had reserved for the season. She drank her beer and smoked her Turkish cigarette, aware that she was being daring.[3]

In the autumn of 1895, when the Gardners came home from Europe, it was time for the winter series of Symphony concerts. Mrs. Gardner paid eighty dollars at auction for her favorite pair of seats—this being considered a record price. A season ticket entitled the holder to attend public rehearsals, and people as interested in music as Mrs. Jack enjoyed them almost more than the concerts. The atmosphere was intimate. The little group of devotées, women and girls for the most part, felt as though they knew the musicians personally, and some of them formed friendships not always approved by husbands or fathers.

Town Topics held forth on the subject of Boston Symphony rehearsals. "The first symphony rehearsal is now one of the most solemn religious fashions in Boston," they wrote, in October, 1895. "Thrills trickle through the bosoms of Back Bay—if one may speak of the bosoms of so respectable and proper a community—and even Brookline is guiltily conscious of a titillation in its midst. Jamaica Plain chirps with unwonted gaiety and the calm Lords of Nahant feel the ice around their feet daring to melt a little. Chelsea steals in on evident galoshes and remote suburbanites nibble sandwiches and lift their souls into the aether. Last week's rehearsal brought out the usual eager crowds . . . [when] Adamowski, accoutered in a long Polack frock coat and sparrow-hued trousers, took his old seat amid the first violins and threw a silver smile to the happy place where Mrs. Jack Gardner sat, with score on knee and trusty Tirindelli by her side, then the whole house became two mighty hands . . ."

The trusty Tirindelli was the Venetian violinist whose opera *Atenaïde* Mrs. Gardner had watched through many rehearsals in Venice. Most people seemed to think that she had brought him home to Boston with her, as a sort of human souvenir, "to make the little fellow's heart glad by her beneficences." This was not true—he had come earlier under his own power. His musicianship was immediately recognized and he got a job as a first violinist and eventually as concertmaster in the Boston Symphony.

Although he had been director of the Venetian Symphony Orchestra and was knighted by the king of Italy, honors would not pay his bills. He "seems not to have left in Venice what is generally called a happy memory," one of Mrs. Gardner's friends wrote her. "The poor man had no talent for arithmetic and never realized the difference between addition and deduction. But a talent cannot be given a man for every branch of activity and an artist is not bound to be a bookkeeper." [4]

The guaranteed salary of Boston Symphony musicians looked large in terms of pay in Venice. Mrs. Gardner knew that Tirindelli would need still more money, however. "There is quite a twitter among the Boston elect over the first appearance in a public concert tomorrow of Mrs. Gardner's latest and most interesting protégé, Tirindelli, the Venetian violinist," *Town Topics* said in December, 1895. "Tirindelli is to play at Miss Little's concert. Miss Little, too, is one of Mrs. Jack's favorites and through this lady's friendship has become the accepted concert singer for that ultra swell coterie. It is rumored that Mrs. Jack, in a ravishing costume, will distribute the programs as she did at Clayton Johns' recital . . ."

And, as at Clayton Johns's concert, Mrs. Jack did indeed stand at the door of the public concert hall, clad in elegant black, and hand out programs. She greeted her friends, enjoying being stared at by strangers, and it seems never to have occurred to her that she was, as usual, doing something shocking.

Not all the musicians Mrs. Gardner tried to help were as successful as Clayton Johns and Tirindelli. In January, 1894, Busoni gave a concert in Mrs. Gardner's music room on Beacon Street. Ferruccio Busoni's charge was $200; but his American tour was a disappointment and in October of that same year he asked Mrs. Gardner for the loan of $1000—sure that he could pay it back when he made a success of his concerts in Berlin. She sent him the money at once. He thanked her "from the depths of [his] heart" and hoped not to disappoint her, "either as a musician or as a grateful man." It does not appear that he was ever able to repay the loan, but Mrs. Gardner's friendship continued, the help she gave him strictly confidential. He had been working on an edition of Bach, Busoni wrote Mrs. Gardner in 1896. He had also composed a collection of pieces for the piano which he wanted to dedicate to Mrs. Gardner and hoped she "would not refuse this modest sign" of his "attachment and esteem. . . . Respectfully and affectionately," he kissed her hand.

Newspaper reporters liked to imply that Mrs. Gardner was in love with every musician she ever sponsored. She minded this not at all and enjoyed driving around Boston with a new protégé in her brougham with coachman and footman in light-colored liveries while people turned to stare at her in the streets. She loved to show off, but she also hoped ardently that some of her young men would succeed in a great career. Only total strangers in Boston ever had to ask who Mrs. Gardner was.

"How many hearts have you broken and how many hearths have you robbed?" wrote Minnie Bourget in 1896, going along with the game. Mrs. Gardner was now nearly fifty-six and *Town Topics* observed her "done up à la Madonna in spotless, diaphanous white, all afleck with silver—a clinging sort of gown." Sometimes she "wore a jeweled sun on the back of her head," and in January, 1896, "Mrs. Gardner had the oddest arrangement on her head at Mrs. Nathaniel Thayer's dinner cotillion, Thursday night. It looked for all the world like a setting sun, the rays tiny spikes of diamonds, spreading out so as to be brilliantly conspicuous if not becoming. Her gown was white."

At a dinner dance at the Algonquin Club, Mrs. Jack had "a halo-like arrangement on her head—gold wires tipped with diamonds that made her look like a cross between a Burne-Jones and an Aubrey Beardsley."

The Boston Artists' Festival came in the middle of Horse Show week in 1896. Mrs. Montgomery Sears, Mrs. William Apthorp and Mrs. Gardner were among the few who were loyal enough to art interests to leave their horse-show boxes on Wednesday night. The Art Festival was a costume affair, the subject, *Arabian Nights*.

"Mrs. Sears' get-up had one peculiarity to which she held exclusive right. She wore through her nose, or apparently so, a genuine jeweled nose ring and she wore it with as much unconcern as if it had been her habit to have it there. Oddly enough, it was rather becoming. Mrs. Apthorp, all in fluffy white and peacock's feathers, was gorgeous as to fabrics and coloring.

"Mrs. Jack Gardner, however, outshone everybody and at her grand entrance she fairly stopped one's heartbeat. She was arrayed in a costume she had brought from Egypt . . ." and was dressed as a "nautch girl . . . tightly swathed round and round with layers of gauze, gold embroidered; a broad band of same made the bodice . . . and her famous diamond and ruby necklace, with her ropes of diamonds bound her throat. But it was upon her head that eyes were fastened with breathless admiration and awe. Everything was covered but her eyes which made it, as some facetious person remarked, 'such a becoming headgear!' Her chin was swathed in soft mull as tight as a bandage; two big diamonds held strings of jewels with a pendant in the center which hung just above her nose . . . It was a wondrously artistic costume and one which probably no one else could achieve . . . or could wear so well!"

In spite of all this publicity, Mrs. Jack's current enthusiasm for lions attracted more attention than her fondness for odd ornaments, strange costumes and jewels. Now that the Boston Public Library had moved to its new building in Copley Square, its old quarters on Boylston Street had been taken over by a man named Bostwick who had a zoo. His lioness Queen Victoria gave birth to twins and Mrs. Gardner went right around to see them. Their keeper let her play with them and when they were a few months old she took them out in her carriage. This must have been an open carriage, rather than the brougham, because everybody in Boston seemed to have seen her riding around with lion cubs on the seat beside her or in her lap.

Now and then Mrs. Gardner took the cubs home to Beacon Street with her—it is to be hoped that they were housebroken! She put a red ribbon on the one she liked best and Mr. Bostwick named it Isabella. Some observers said that the ribbon was not red, but pink. In any case, Mrs. Gardner and her lion cub were seen and talked about.

Schoolchildren could go into the zoo for a dime and one little girl always remembered several afternoons when she saw Mrs. Jack Gardner all wrapped in elegant furs, taking one of the lions for a walk on a leash.[5]

Lion stories grew and spread. Eventually it was recalled that "in Boston, Mrs. Gardner terrified crowds in the main hall of the Boston Zoo by romping with a lion called 'Rex.'" A less friendly report had it that the whole thing was an advertising stunt put over on Mrs. Gardner by Bostwick and that Rex was a very old lion with no teeth.[6]

Society reporters never had any trouble filling up their columns with items as long as Mrs. Gardner was at home. But during the winter of 1896–1897 it was reported that, although she came to dances, she was not dancing. Then, as winter hung on and spring seemed to have forgotten Boston, there were no concerts at 152 Beacon Street, no dinner parties for Thomas Russell Sullivan to write about. Those spasms of pain which had frightened Mrs. Gardner when she was in Spain were back again. She never liked to admit that she was afraid but a few friends were entitled to an explanation.

"I am distressed to hear of your long illness, dear lady," wrote F. Marion Crawford. "You speak of having had a touch of influenza some time ago and now you say you have been ill for three weeks . . . I have not the slightest doubt that you got it by some horrible imprudence, probably carrying a wet lion through a snowdrift in satin slippers . . ."

Crawford's letter was dated March 1, 1897. Mrs. Gardner was well again by April, for she was in her box at the Horse Show with her favorite niece, Olga, daughter of Jack Gardner's brother George. Among the guests was George Monks, a nice young man who had gone to Harvard with the Gardner nephews, then to Harvard Medical School, and who was now a surgeon.

"The most notable engagement of the week and one that caused quite a flutter of excitement was that of Olga Gardner to Dr. George H. Monks. . . ." Miss Gardner had "been out for several years," but she was "one of the most prominent of the older society girls—not pretty but extremely attractive." Olga was twenty-eight and was a serious volunteer worker at Children's Hospital and the convalescent home connected with it.

Dr. Monks had been such "an unflinching advocate of bachelorhood that he was long ago given up by scheming mammas . . ." He was "a leading light at the Tavern Club, very popular with both men and women and a right good fellow."

Sullivan was invited out to Brookline on May 18. He and Mrs. Gardner "drove over to Cambridge for the annual meeting of the Dantë Society" and then, next day, they "strolled about the grounds at Green Hill. The lilacs in the spring garden were in full blossom, the tulips almost gone. Later, George Monks and Miss Olga Gardner joined the party. Happy lovers! Their rapture was delightful to see." [7]

Sullivan was to be an usher at the wedding; Clayton Johns, best man. The ceremony was at "St. Steven's Church in a little off-street in Boston," a ceremony "notable for elegance and exclusiveness." Reporters forgot about Mrs. Gardner while writing of Olga's engagement; but now they forgot the bride's gown while describing Mrs. Jack's! "The bodice of Mrs. Gardner's pale green and white gown was adorned with her much-exploited milk-white pearls. She was in great feather from the top of her head to the sole of her white shoe . . ." Only young girls were supposed to wear white, and white shoes were daring even for debutantes.

The Gardners' collection of priceless paintings was growing —all unbeknownst to the public. Only their real friends such as T. R. Sullivan were allowed to share their enthusiasm. "I have just seen at Mrs. Gardner's, her latest purchase, an extraordinary Velazquez, the full length portrait of Philip IV painted for Olivarez. It takes away one's breath," Sullivan said.[8]

The time had now come for the Gardners to go abroad again. Their purchases during this short stay were different from those of any other period and would have puzzled anyone not understanding their purpose. In Paris, they bought a French Gothic double door, bound in iron, and a fifteenth-century "tambour"—not a drum, as the word would indicate, but a carved wooden screen for a circular staircase, ten feet high. More than forty items were packed in Paris for shipment to Boston.

Richard Norton, son of Charles Eliot Norton, was in Rome, excited over the project of starting an American Academy of Art and School of Archaeology, similar to the one connected with the French embassy. The Gardners' project delighted him and he began to act as agent, selling them Roman antiquities and mediaeval Italian fragments from ruined palaces. In Orvieto, Norton found for them a beamed, paneled and painted ceiling decorated with coats of arms and fascinating little scenes from the Bible and Roman mythology. No one knew much about it, but Dick Norton theorized that it came from a painters' guildhall and that the scenes, each by a different hand, had been painted by apprentices as a sort of examination before admission to guild status. To Boston it went, along with a Spanish wheel window and the Roman mosaic pavement with the Gorgon's head.

There must have been a gleam of humor in Jack Gardner's eye when he bought stone lions for his wife in Florence. It was a purchase Mrs. G. would be sure to approve, and two "Romanesque stone lions" would look well, set into a wall. Two "13th or 14th Century lions" had formed the base of columns from a demolished Italian church and were listed as "lion with crouching man" and "lion standing over man," as they started on their way to America.

The usual excursion into Germany and Austria was on the itinerary. Jack Gardner found Wagner loud and lengthy, as usual, but this time he visited all the antique stores with new enthusiasm. In Munich he bought a painted wooden figure of a man on horseback. The horse would never have taken a prize at the Myopia show but the doughty rider could well have belonged to the Somerset Club. In Paris, Jack Gardner had already bought a "St. Martin" on an even funnier horse. The two wood carvings would make a handsome pair!

Anyone who had been entertained recently at 152 Beacon Street would have wondered where the Gardners were going to put these purchases. The brownstone house with the bow window was already filled to capacity and the Brookline gardens would soon be strewn with statuary till there was hardly room for lilacs. In Beverly, the house called the Alhambra, in honor of a gay music hall in London, was no place for carvings of either wood or stone. It was a shingled structure, ugly to a degree, but having a garden full of Chinese red nasturtiums.

A few close friends knew that the Gardners were planning some sort of gallery for their art collection. Not even the Gardners themselves were sure what form it would take but each had an idea—different from the other's.

By July, the Gardners were settled in the Palazzo Barbaro. The honeymoon couple Olga and Dr. Monks arrived to find the usual entourage of young men: artists and musicians making life glamorous for Mrs. Jack.

One most faithful follower was missing. Ralph Curtis, long a bachelor, had married a beautiful young widow, Mrs. Arthur Rotch. Her first husband had died only a year after their marriage, leaving her a fortune. And she had been Lisa Colt, heiress to a firearms fortune of her own.

The dark-eyed, auburn-haired Lisa had been "the recipient of much attention from Edward, Prince of Wales, in 1895" —or so it was said. She was a fine horsewoman and a "cyclist." The high-wheeled bicycle had just been superseded by a new model, widely advertised as having two twenty-six-inch wheels, and in 1896 Lisa had "created quite a sensation in London, when she first appeared there on her wheel." London papers said that "her tall and graceful figure, her long skirt that completely concealed her ankles and the swan-like movement" of her cycling gave "the impression that she moved around on casters."

The swanlike Lisa (in 1897) was not going to share Ralph Curtis with Mrs. Gardner. They would soon build "Villa Sylvia" on the Riviera and plan to ask Sargent to paint a mural for them on their dining-room wall. They would also have a little daughter Sylvia—Mrs. Jack Gardner being her godmother.

Joseph Lindon Smith arrived in Venice in September— more than compensating for the loss of Ralph Curtis. "Zo-Zo Smith," some of his friends called him—Zo-Zo being the name of a French clown. Joe loved to do a little clowning when the mood was upon him but he was never clownish unintentionally. He could set Mrs. Gardner's guests to laughing, or he could write and produce a pageant so beautiful it brought tears to their eyes.

Venice was hot that September and John L. Gardner suffered from the heat. Mrs. Jack suffered from restlessness. Suddenly she decided she must go to Sicily and there was no dissuading her, so her husband asked Joe Smith if he would go along as their traveling companion. Jack Gardner felt he could not endure the all-night cafés with Sicilian music, the open air concerts and the local operas which his wife had heard about and was determined to attend. He could go to bed early and Joe was perfectly willing to take on the job of escort for Mrs. Jack.

In addition, Mr. Gardner hired a courier. It developed, however, that too many couriers had already worked for Mr. Gardner's difficult lady, whose temper had been growing shorter still as she passed her fifty-seventh birthday. She had fired couriers one after the other lately. Finally, a competent-looking man agreed to take the job.

The express with its *wagons-lits* was standing in the station, a compartment marked *reservé* for Mrs. Gardner, another for John L. and Joe and space for Mrs. Gardner's maid. A good many young men were standing around on the railroad platform and Joe Smith, who had a way with people, found out that they were apprentice couriers in training under the man who had accepted the post with the Gardner party. He was going to show them how to get along with a difficult client.

Mrs. Gardner arrived minutes before the train left. She discovered that her new courier had brought an armload of pillows and placed them strategically in her compartment. Mrs. Jack hated pillows. "Never do anything I don't tell you to," she screamed—and began throwing the pillows out the window as the train started. She scored a bull's-eye on one or two of the grinning young men on the platform, and she accompanied her shots with colorful Italian curses.

As the journey progressed, Joe Smith noticed that their courier was met, from time to time, by someone who gave him money. Joe tactfully inquired the reason. Bets had been laid that the Gardners' courier would remain in his present employment but a short time. As a day passed, a week, and so on, the amounts bet against him rose. The courier won all wagers, because, as time went by, he found he liked Mrs. Gardner—temper and all.

Joseph Lindon Smith seemed to be one of Mrs. Gardner's

bachelors destined never to marry. He was almost the sole support of his parents, who lived with him in a big studio apartment in the Ludlow in Boston, and at the time of his only brother's death by accident, he had promised his mother never to leave her.

After the Gardners returned to Boston, Mrs. Jack asked Joe to dinner. "May I bring a girl?" he asked. She said he could.

The girl was Corinna Putnam, daughter of George Haven Putnam, publisher. Since her mother's death, she had been her father's traveling companion, accustomed to the company of literary élite in Europe and America—with members of the nobility thrown in. Corinna walked like a·princess; her dark eyes flashed with humor, and they could flash with temper, too. It would be unwise to overlook the fact that she had an exceedingly strong chin.

"Joe never asked to bring a girl before," Mrs. Gardner said to her. "Are you two engaged?"

"I don't know," Corinna said. "I would like to be." The fact of the matter was that Joe was in love with her but his mother had decided that Joe must give Corinna up. Apparently the senior Mrs. Smith had failed to observe the strength beneath Corinna's beauty.

Scenting frustrated romance, Mrs. Jack instantly took up the gage for Joe's girl. There was a look of proud courage about her that appealed to Mrs. Jack tremendously—they were "Corinna" and "Isabella" almost from the start, their friendship lasting the rest of Mrs. Gardner's life.[9]

Corinna Putnam never forgot her first dinner party at 152 Beacon Street. The subject of building a gallery for the Gardner collection of paintings and objects of art came up. The Gardners began to argue about it.

Mrs. Jack wanted to build an addition to the back of the Beacon Street house. "You'll cut off all your neighbor's light," her husband told her. She said she didn't care if she did. "You won't have any light of your own," Jack Gardner remarked. "Oh, I have a plan to fix that," Isabella said with a characteristic little toss of her head to indicate that this settled the question. Corinna could see that nothing at all had been settled.

Jack Gardner wanted to buy a piece of land on the Fenway, beyond their Beacon Street house. Filling was going on, land being made there as it had been when they built on Beacon Street.

The Fenway was impossible, Mrs. Gardner declared. It was too far away from the center of things.

As early as September, 1896, Mrs. Gardner had met Willard T. Sears, the architect, on the train going to a wedding. She asked him to see if there were any restrictions on her Beacon Street house lots that would keep her from building a museum there. He told her he didn't know of any and he wrote in his record book, "Mrs. Gardner asked me to make plans for her, showing a museum with living quarters over. She wanted me to keep the matter secret." [10]

NINETEEN

An End and a Beginning

THE YEAR 1898 began with a minor disaster and ended with a great loss. On February 7, Mrs. Gardner "slipped on the last step" of a staircase "at a friend's house, and falling, broke the fibula of one of her legs just above the ankle." This was T. R. Sullivan's version of the accident.

Someone sent a dispatch to the New York *Tribune* six days later; "Boston Society Leader Breaks Leg but Won't Tell How," was the headline. Her "physicians have been pledged to silence," and "Mrs. Gardner positively refuses to say a word."

Finally, on February 24, *Town Topics* thought they had the story. Although at first they had announced that Mrs. Gardner had "fallen on the ice as she left her carriage," they now said that she had been "descending the polished staircase in Mrs. Rollins Morse's house after a dinner dance." This time, they were probably right.

F. Marion Crawford was in Louisville, Kentucky, when he heard the news. "It seems outrageous that you, of all people, with your grace and love of movement, should have such an accident and be laid on the shelf like a plaster cast of the Venus of Medici."

Henry James wrote pleasantly: "My imagination shoved rose leaves, as it were, under the spine of a lady for whom lying fractured was but an occasion the more to foregather with Titian. Seriously, I hope you weren't very bad—that it was nothing more than the 'Europa' could bandage up with a piece of that purple of which you gave me so memorable an account." [1] Once more, he mentioned Mrs. Gardner's invariable good fortune—her few "miseries."

Everyone, including T. R. Sullivan, assumed that Mrs. Gardner would be on the shelf for a long time. "This severe accident means for her, practical seclusion from the world for many weeks," Sullivan wrote. "But she accepts this in the same high spirits which always characterize her and is already holding state receptions in bed like a French *grande dame.*"

Mrs. Jack was not going to stay in bed after the fun of playing the part of a French aristocrat had worn off. By February 24, *Town Topics* said that "Mrs. Jack Gardner is doing the high rolling act in her wheel chair . . . Except for unusual pallor, the plucky woman is looking as well as ever."

"All the papers," said she would be "a noncombatant in the social arena for weeks to come" and "those who don't love this unique personality promptly uttered sighs of relief . . . But they were too precipitate. A broken leg, forsooth, is a very small thing to stand in the way of anything Mrs. Jack has made up her mind to do."

Walter Damrosch brought *Lohengrin* to Boston and Mrs. Gardner had her wheel chair rolled on to the stage—out of sight of the audience, Damrosch must have hoped. If this was opening night, his nerves had received one jolt already. Harvard students acted as supers and paid the stage manager "from 50 cents upward" (although the manager was supposed to pay *them* a quarter). Damrosch looked up from his "conductor's stand" to see "a college boy, dressed in the armor and cloak of one of King Henry's knights, calmly standing at the foot of the throne, large spectacles on his nose, busily following the action of the libretto which he held in his hand, close to his eyes." [2]

Mrs. Gardner, enjoying herself immensely, saw Siegfried start to pull the sword from the anvil. Lightning was supposed to flash but some stagehand missed his cue. Mrs. Jack heard Siegfried continue his aria, but not in the words from the script. "Where the Hell is the *fire!*" he sang, several times —until at last stage lightning flashed. [3]

By the end of March, Mrs. Gardner was able to walk into the theater, "leaning heavily on the arm of her cavalier, George Proctor, the piano-player." Her costume was "scintillating jet" with a "watermelon pink toque." She and Proctor were preceded by "a stately and somber footman in the Gardner liveries," carrying a "capacious cushion." [4] (George had returned from Europe in 1897.)

In the spring, when the Green Hill flowers were at their height, Mrs. Gardner gave the use of her grounds for "an out-of-door concert" by the Symphony Orchestra "for the benefit of the Carney Hospital." The Sunday papers described "the graceful appearance of Max Zach as he waved his baton"—but *Town Topics* said that Zach wasn't there! "At the eleventh hour, some five members of the orchestra struck, on the plea that as all the women on the committee were rich and Mrs. Gardner herself was alleged to have untold wealth, they should have higher pay than usual." The ladies' committee settled this early labor dispute quickly. They hired the Salem Cadet Band, which "gave most appropriate and inspiring music."

Mrs. Gardner's press had been unusually favorable lately but, apropos of the Charity Concert, *Town Topics* admonished her about her hats. "She chooses the very brightest colors . . . and her hats are garden beds of richest flowers . . . The dear lady should have been in bonnets long ago!"

There was no use expecting Mrs. Gardner to wear bonnets, but she was not to enjoy her exuberant flowered hats much longer. Mrs. Francis Skinner, the former Eliza Gardner, died suddenly of a heart attack on September 22. Her brother, Jack Gardner, was cruising homeward from Portland on the *Mayflower* and could not be reached. Mrs. Gardner went into deep mourning.

Eliza Gardner Skinner was called "a leading spirit in the more conservative element of Boston's gayeties" but people said that she "never hit it off well with her eccentric, notoriety-loving and semi-bohemian sister-in-law, Mrs. Jack Gardner."

A few hours after the funeral on Saturday, Mrs. Gardner was seen in her mourning robes walking up and down the platform between her "rural protégé, George Proctor, a pianist, and Kneisel, first violin of the Symphony." [5] She had come to greet Wilhelm Gericke, arriving from Germany by way of New York, with his wife, Paula, and their little daughter, Katherine. Gericke was returning as conductor of the Boston Symphony Orchestra after an absence of nine years. Mrs. Gericke had never before left her native land and Mrs. Gardner wanted her to feel welcome in Boston.

The little family climbed into Mrs. Gardner's new and shining victoria. Katherine was astonished to hear sleigh bells —although there was no snow—and Mrs. Gardner laughed delightedly.

Her victoria was equipped with an innovation—rubber tires! That was why their ride over the cobblestones down near the railroad station was so smooth. But rubber tires were silent, pedestrians unwary, and Mrs. Gardner liked to drive at a fast pace. Since the rattle of her wheels could no longer be heard, she had ordered ten sleigh bells put around the necks of her horse to prevent accident.

The Gardners bought eight more pictures through Berenson during the year 1898, perhaps the most important being two Rembrandts: the unusual *Storm at Sea* and the handsome double portrait *Gentleman and His Wife*. The importance of her Dutch paintings nearly equaled that of her Italian masterpieces; a Dutch room in the future museum was indicated.

There was another picture that Mrs. Gardner had set her heart on. Negotiations for it had begun in the autumn of 1896 and in 1898 it continued to elude her. "So you want the Loschi Giorgione," Berenson had written.[6] "Well, you shall have it, if it is to be had . . ." Six months later, when he had lost track of the picture, "It is not the kind of thing I think of for you," he amended.

Christ Bearing the Cross, painted by Giorgione before 1510, was an extremely realistic small panel. The artist had died of the plague in Venice at an early age, leaving few examples of his work—the sort of life story which appealed to Mrs. Gardner. Perhaps at first she did not realize what a unique picture she was determined to possess.

In May, 1897, Berenson proposed bringing the Giorgione to Venice and selling it to Mrs. Gardner there because it was becoming increasingly difficult to get a *permisso* from the Italian government to export works of art. "It would be much easier for you in your vast trunks to get the picture out of Italy without risk of discovery than for me in my modest—a man's trunk is always modest—box," he suggested. Mrs. Gardner would have nothing to do with smuggling.

The Giorgione was still not in Berenson's hands in 1897, however. In June, he went to see the Zileri family in Vicenza. He wrote a dramatic story to Mrs. Gardner—painting the scene like the artist in words that he often was.

"Imagine a great stone palace, genuine Palladio, large cool halls furnished as stylishly and tastelessly as possible." This was the Palazzo Loschi, for which the picture was named. "Inhabitants thereof, a dowager countess, awfully polite, trying to treat you as an equal yet wishing you to bear in mind she is a Bourbon; smart daughters-in-law whom mourning became to perfection; three sons, one . . . handsome, alert, every inch the seigneur; another handsome but provincialized; the third squat, bourgeois-looking, before the creation of the world already destined to high office now crushing him with its burden—he is now *sindaco* [mayor] of Vicenza . . ."

The old Count Zileri had recently died—hence the mourning costumes of his daughters-in-law. He had originally willed the Giorgione to the town of Vicenza but changed his mind and left it to the family.

"Although the authorities know this, the populace of Vicenza is still in expectation of the picture. They do not understand why the transfer is delayed and that makes the family unpopular. Add to this the fact that, as Bourbons, the Zileris are ultra-clerical and therefore abhorred by the progressives . . . Every year, they commemorate at Vicenza the heroic defense of the town against the Austrians." This year the young Zileri, being mayor, persuaded the town council to give up the *festa*, with brass bands and dancing in the streets, and to have a mass for the heroic dead, with a wreath-laying ceremony on their tombs instead.

When the townspeople heard about it, "the Palazzo Loschi had for a whole hour and a half a mob before it, smashing windows, hooting and generally expressing . . . righteous indignation. Naturally, they scared the poor Zileris." They did not dare to sell the Giorgione head of Christ—but they needed money.

"After some hours" Berenson persuaded the family that a copy of the picture would do the townspeople of Vicenza just as much good as the original Giorgione—his client to pay for the copy. He agreed to take care of the *permisso*.

On December 12, 1897, "Please, please, dear Friend, do not curse at me. I have done my very best and the Giorgione is yours if you are willing to accept the conditions and willing to have me smuggle the picture out of the country, as pictures almost invariably are."

The Zileris said they were surrounded by spies and would not dare send the picture away for a year. Next, they went back on their bargain altogether and said they were going to divide the old count's estate first; that Berenson would have to deal with whichever son got the Giorgione. "I have been eating . . . a thousand times more humble pie than is good for me," Berenson wrote.

Eventually, Berenson interviewed the young Count Zileri dal Verme, to whom the Giorgione had been given. But first he made a few discreet inquiries and found that the count was so much in debt that the bank had refused him a new loan. Berenson offered the money the bank had refused, and the count took the offer, hardly bothering to bargain. Mrs. Gardner paid £6000 for the painting and around 500 francs for a copy to go to Vicenza. She agreed to return the original

Giorgione if the town of Vicenza brought suit and won the case.

On January 8, 1898, Berenson wrote, "I cabled you yesterday that the Giorgione was fairly exported. I entrusted it, swaddled like a baby in a blanket, to some friends of mine. They took it to London and delivered it to my agent, who has an order to send it, insured for £6000 to Robert's of Paris.[7] So you are now beyond question that unique creature, the owner of an unquestioned Giorgione." He said that nothing he had ever gotten for Mrs. Gardner had ever caused him so much trouble.

Christ Bearing the Cross finally reached Boston late in 1898. Mrs. Gardner cared a great deal for it—perhaps for tragic personal reasons.

On December 9, the Gardners moved back to Beacon Street from Brookline. Jack had not been feeling well. He had sent for a lawyer, whom he told to familiarize himself with Mrs. Gardner's business affairs. On the tenth of December, John L. Gardner "was stricken with apoplexy at the Exchange Club" in Boston. They brought him home and called Dr. Paul Thorndike and Dr. George B. Shattuck. Jack Gardner died at nine o'clock that night.

Mr. Gardner was sixty-one years old, but he seemed like a man "not more than fifty" and he had been in good health until the previous month or so. It was said that the usual Thanksgiving party had been given up because he was not feeling up to par. He had been putting his affairs in shape. But it was Belle Gardner who had been the delicate one—the frail girl her husband had carried in his arms to their carriage, the woman who feared heart attacks and had had several warnings. Her husband, strong and calm, had been the staff she leaned on.

Yet strangely enough, Mrs. Gardner had brought a purple pall from Italy. She had it placed on her husband's coffin and on it a great cross of violets from the greenhouse he had built for her. The Anglican Catholic funeral was elaborate for a man who had been brought up in the simplicity of Unitarian King's Chapel. But if it gave Belle Gardner comfort, it was what her husband would have wanted. She left the pall in the keeping of the Church of the Advent—until it should be used for herself, she said.

Mr. Gardner "was chairman of the board of directors of the Chicago, Burlington and Quincy Railroad, a director of the Calumet and Hecla Mining Company and of several

207

other corporations." He was "a trustee and member of the finance committee of the Suffolk Savings Bank; one of the trustees and treasurer of the Museum of Fine Arts of Boston and one of the trustees and recording secretary of the Humane Society. He was also a member of the leading clubs."

All those meetings! His wife remembered that her husband never really had time to rest—except when they went abroad.

"Mr. Gardner had no inclination for political office. His preference was for a life of quiet and helpful influence in business and social circles. With his wife, who is recognized as a society leader, he dispensed a liberal and elegant hospitality." It was Jack who made the dinner parties elegant. Sometimes, in drawing people out, Belle asked too many personal questions. "Busy Ella," he called her, teasing her a little and putting the brakes on her curiosity.[8]

When the ladies withdrew from the dinner table, the gentlemen could look forward with confidence to the best brandy, just as during the meal only the best wines had been served. "The Duke of Burgundy," the children of a business associate had called him—because Burgundy was his favorite wine. But he had sent Chianti "stravecchio" to Mrs. Bronson in Italy, knowing that this was *her* favorite wine.

"How do you manage to have such good coffee?" Maud Howe had asked, long ago.

"We are extravagant," Jack Gardner had told her with that almost imperceptible twinkle. "We use the best coffee we can buy, and we use plenty of it."

Jack's friends at the Somerset Club passed solemn "resolutions" which they presented to his widow. Other clubs, other organizations, did the same. Behind the ponderous sentences, one fact shone through like the sun. They had loved him.

It was said that Mrs. Gardner had a nervous breakdown which lasted a year after her husband's death. It is true that the shock was so severe that she could neither eat nor sleep. Her sister-in-law, Julia, was the greatest comfort at this time, because Julia's gentleness and largeness of spirit were so like Jack's. And Olga Monks came close to her Aunt Belle's heart, never to leave it.

Mrs. Gardner put a Norwegian silver cup with violets in it in front of the Giorgione *Christ Bearing the Cross*. On their first European trip, she and Jack had gone to Norway. In Rome, years later, Jack had gone out in the early mornings to buy her violets on the Piazza di Spagna.

It was not true, however, that Mrs. Gardner saw no one outside the family. She sent for the architect Willard T.

Sears, and he called on her only a little more than two weeks after her husband's death. He came by appointment, bringing with him "drawings of the new stable and alterations of the house." Mr. Sears kept a record of all transactions.[9]

Mrs. Gardner's nephew Amory was with her, Mr. Sears said. After "suggesting a few minor changes, they pronounced the drawings satisfactory and directed me to get the proposals and start work as soon as possible."

The door closed on the departing Willard T. Sears. William Amory Gardner would soon go. But even if her nephew stayed with her, Isabella was alone. It was a kind of being alone she had never experienced since her marriage, thirty-eight years ago. The servants, all clad in mourning as in John L. Gardner Senior's time, went to bed, but Isabella had never been able to sleep until late at night. The house grew silent except for the sounds on stairs or floor that all houses make in the silent hours. No one, not even Jack Gardner, knew how much Isabella loved that house on Beacon Street. Now, she had too much time to think.

Next day, Willard T. Sears "called on Mrs. John L. Gardner at 2 P.M." It was Friday, December 30, and he had the drawings with him for the museum at 152 Beacon Street. Only the evening before, she and Amory had "directed" him to "start the work as soon as possible" and he was feeling pleased because the minor changes they had suggested had been drawn up so promptly. Mr. Sears was in for the surprise of his life—but this was only the first of many.

Mrs. Gardner "informed me that she had purchased a lot of land 100 ft. by 150 ft. on the Back Bay Park to build the Museum upon.[10] That she wanted me to make new drawings & to include a small theatre with the Museum, the Museum to be one story less in height than the one drawn for her at 152 Beacon Street. She wanted the drawings as soon as possible so that they could be referred to in her will. She made no reference to the probable cost of the building."

Isabella Gardner was still alone. In a sense she always would be, no matter who might be with her. But she found a kind of consolation—she was doing exactly what her husband had wanted her to do. She had made a strange discovery. Now that she could do as she pleased, she no longer wanted her own way.

This was not a state of meek acceptance of the will of everyone else, however. Willard T. Sears would soon find this out, to his sorrow.

Book Three

MRS. GARDNER'S PALACE

TWENTY

Fenway Court

M̲RS. GARDNER MADE no mention to her architect of the probable cost of her museum, simply because she forgot about it. Jack had always attended to such things. The process of learning to live without him was going to be difficult, and Isabella was alternately over-careful of money and careless with it. She had begun by being careless.

In appointing three trustees, Jack Gardner had done his best to help his wife after he was gone. He chose George Peabody Gardner, son of his brother George; Augustus, son of his brother Joseph; and John Chipman Gray, a cousin. Later, Augustus, who was also an executor, declined to act as trustee, for no reason given; but his Aunt Belle's temperament may have had something to do with it. Gray was a lawyer with a gift for getting along with people almost as difficult as the woman he called "Aunt Belle." In point of sheer unpredictable eccentricity she probably topped his list of clients, but he was fond of her.

John L. Gardner's will left certain property which had come to him from his parents to various Gardner nephews and nieces, seven receiving bequests of $40,000 each and three the residue of this property. "The picture of my grandmother by Stuart," Mr. Gardner gave to "the oldest descendant of George Peabody Gardner," and "the letter from George Washington to my great-grandfather John Lowell" was to go to his nephew, John Lowell Gardner. To Augustus, he gave "the interest in Roque Island."

There were a number of other bequests but he left the bulk of his estate to Isabella in two trusts. One trust fund of $275,000 provided that the income would go to Mrs. Gardner but that she could not touch the principal. Thus she would have a safe but modest income, irrespective of what might happen to the rest of the property. The balance of the estate was put in a separate trust under the management of the same trustees, but giving Mrs. Gardner the right to draw on its principal as well as the income. With two minor exceptions, however, she never drew on the principal of this residual trust fund.

The will provided that the $275,000 fund would go, on Mrs. Gardner's death, to four institutions. The Boston Museum of Fine Arts and the Boston Lying-In Hospital would each receive four-elevenths, the Massachusetts General Hospital, two-elevenths, and the public library in Brookline, one-eleventh. Mrs. Gardner could dispose of the other trust fund in her own will.

John L. Gardner's estate had a gross value of $3,604,424, of which $270,000 was real estate and the remainder was cash and securities. After paying debts of $1,007,422, consisting for the most part of bank borrowings and notes due various people, and after paying taxes, miscellaneous debts and bequests, the net amount in the two trust funds at the end of 1899 was $2,303,624. During the ten years after 1900, Mrs. Gardner's income from these funds averaged $97,400 per year. Of course she also received income from funds left to her by her father.[1]

Mrs. Gardner's "seclusion" after her husband's death was no legend but a fact. For a long time, she could not bear to go out in public. Knowing how she loved music, Lena Little arranged with the newly organized "Brahms Quartette" for a concert at 152 Beacon Street—without guests. Old friends were welcome when they called but there were no dinners, even at home.

The papers found little to comment upon. Mrs. Gardner was "Boston's most interesting widow." She wore "bunches of violets as big as ever" and her veil "after the fashion of French widows" reached "nearly to the ground in front, completely hiding her features." During February, 1899, she was seen "enveloped in the heaviest crêpe from head to foot, in a Russian sleigh hung with sable robes and with coachman and footman in irreproachable mourning livery."

Although in seclusion, Mrs. Gardner was not idle. The plans which, on December 30, 1898, she had wanted delivered as soon as possible, arrived by mail toward the end of March, 1899. She studied them three days and then called at Mr. Sears's office with them. She didn't like the division of the court arches and wanted the court wider.

The heart of the museum was to be this inner court, roofed high overhead with glass. Stone fragments which Jack Gardner had bought on his last trip to Europe were now stored in a Boston warehouse awaiting the creation of this

214

garden. Among them were eight balustrades from the projecting balconies of the ornate "Cà d' Oro" in Venice, bought
while the "Cà d' Oro" was under repair. Venetians had been
glad to sell the weathered old carvings, preferring nice new
reproductions. Eight balconies, instead of extending over the
Grand Canal, were to look down on the mosaic pavement
that Jack had bought in Rome. Roman statues were to surround the pavement, the sound of water falling into a Roman
sarcophagus would recall Italian gardens where such relics
were often thus casually used, and palms and flowers would
grow all winter in snowbound Boston. What if mimosa trees
grew in Florida—Mrs. Gardner liked the scent of them and
planned to grow them in her Italian garden.

Mrs. Gardner explained to her architect that she wanted
the façade of a Venetian palace turned inward upon itself,
away from the bleak New England where such a miracle of
grace and ornament in architecture could never have occurred. When she had filled the court with flowers from her
Brookline greenhouses the sky would always seem to be blue
overhead, no matter how gray it might really be.

"Fenway Court," Mrs. Gardner named her palace. She
planned that it should be a museum only after her death and
it was not she who called it a "palace"—this was the idea of
those who were to see it and remember fairy tales. In her
own mind, Mrs. Gardner was planning a town house and, on
the top floor, a home for memories of Beacon Street.

That the way a house looks inside should affect its outside
appearance, or that one change in plan necessitates others,
were matters Mrs. Gardner was loath to accept. Looking over
the map of her plot with the house drawn upon it, she saw
that there was not room for a garden outside. The front of
the house must be narrower, she told Mr. Sears, but he was
to keep the entrance in the center. Mr. Sears explained that
in that case the entrance "would not come in the center of
the court." She said she didn't care.

"I told her I would make new sketches . . . and send them
to her as soon as possible," wrote Mr. Sears. On Monday,
thirteen days later, Mrs. Gardner brought back the plans.
"She changed the Fenway front so as to make the entrance
and the centre line of the court coincide," Mr. Sears noted a
little wearily.[2]

After Mrs. Gardner "gave her ideas as to the division of
rooms in the upper story" she knew that she needed more
material. There must be huge hooded fireplaces, for example.
They could be ornate or simple, French or Italian, Gothic or

215

Renaissance. Mrs. Gardner would know when she saw one whether it would look right or not. Whoever heard of an ancestral palace where there was no loot from other lands and where everything was of the same period? Obviously, she must go abroad again on a large-scale shopping tour.

Lena Little was invited to go along and Mrs. Gardner engaged the Palazzo Barbaro for at least the month of August. She wrote her friends in Venice that she would give no parties but that they must just come in to hear Miss Little sing. And then, when they reached Venice, a cable was waiting for Lena announcing her mother's sudden death, and she sailed for home.

Henry James had heard very late of John L. Gardner's death. He wrote from Lamb House, Rye, ". . . I haven't a memory of him that isn't delightful or mixed with delightful things. I always saw him in beautiful, beneficent conditions and places and he remains one of my images (none too numerous) of those moving in grand affairs with a temper that matched them and yet never losing its consideration for small affairs and for the people condemned to them. What a change in your life!—that is all I dare say to you . . ." [3]

James received word through Mrs. Daniel Curtis that Mrs. Gardner was cutting down on expenses after having traveled for years in royal style. "Mrs. Jack's economics are wonderful indeed and my mouth waters for the history of her period at the Barbaro as you collected it on your return," he wrote. And in another letter, "Nothing can stale, truly then, Mrs. Jack's infinite variety . . . in the whole circle of the sciences, nothing but economy was left to her. She has clearly exhausted everything else . . ." [4]

Hiring only one gondola instead of her usual fleet, Mrs. Gardner went to the antiquaries, this time covering dealers in almost anything no longer new—plus a few forgeries. She found a sixteenth-century marble fireplace at Settini's and at Dorigo's a Venetian fireplace that she liked even better. Dorigo had four antique columns of peach marble and a marble slab which pleased Mrs. Gardner. So she bought the columns and had him make the slab into a table top for her. Here and there, she saw bits and pieces of ancient wood carving which Italian cabinetmakers turned into furniture of her own contriving—unorthodox in design, but always interesting.

There were three friends of Mrs. Gardner's who were always on the alert to buy antiquities of all sorts for her. They were Richard Norton, Ralph Curtis and Joseph Lindon Smith—referred to by Joe as "your gnomes." Dick Norton was perhaps the most impulsive, getting into difficulties with the Italian government and committing Mrs. Gardner to considerable expense thereby. He was also the only one of the three who got her accounts mixed up from time to time. In 1899 he found a fine Mantegna for her.

Curtis's recommendation, a "Guardi" Venetian scene, was not as fortunate. It was judged to be by a "follower of Guardi," while a similar picture which Berenson bought for Mrs. Gardner was considered authentic.

Joe Smith was not in Europe this summer. He was in Dublin, New Hampshire, where his mother, having at first opposed his marriage, now composed a play in which Corinna Putnam was required to appear as the girl created for Joe.[5] They were married in September and Joe would eventually resume his services as "gnome" for Mrs. Jack.

All three "gnomes" resented Berenson and he returned the compliment. Norton called Berenson "dishonest" in so many words; but when Mrs. Gardner came loyally to Berenson's defense, "I assure you, I am greatly pleased to know your feeling for B.B.," Norton wrote. "It is no pleasure for me to think ill of any man."

Before his death, Jack Gardner's faith had been shaken. Among the Berenson letters was an undated fragment which read, "Please, dear friend, do not conceive that I feel any animosity toward Mr. Gardner. I feel none whatever. His suspicion seems to me natural." This fragment had the heading, "5 Via Camerata, San Domenico di Fiesole," where Berenson had established himself "during Christmas week, 1897," so the letter must have been written during the last year of Jack Gardner's life.

"I have said, I think, all that need be said," Berenson's letter continued, evidently referring to the passages Mrs. Gardner destroyed. "I shall always worship you as without exception the most life-enhancing, the most utterly enviable person I have ever had the good fortune to know. . . ."[6]

In November, 1898, just before her husband's death, Mrs. Gardner cabled that she would buy Masaccio's *A Young Man in Scarlet Turban*, which Berenson had been offering. "You really are the most lovable person on earth, sunshine become flesh and blood, I do not know how to describe you; but a miracle certainly, a goddess, I—your prophet," Berenson wrote, the day after he received the cable. By the time the letter reached Mrs. Gardner, or almost immediately afterward, she was no longer the most utterly enviable person on earth, nor was she feeling like sunshine become flesh and blood. Jack Gardner was dead.

Berenson had stayed with the Gardners at the Palazzo Barbaro during their last trip abroad together. He and Mrs. Gardner shopped for textiles and furnishings for his new home and he wrote of his room all decorated in green, the "rich and beautiful portières we bought at San Giorgio's hung on the walls." At this time he told Mrs. Gardner "all about Mrs. Costelloe," who was to share this home. Mrs. Jack was sympathetic and understanding.

There was no doubt that Mrs. Gardner was fond of "B.B.," as he now signed himself. She wanted to believe in him, but now that she no longer had her husband to advise her, she was from time to time unsure—of him and of almost everyone else. Her dealings with others distressed him and when she bought her Mantegna through Norton she refused to tell him how she got it. Even worse, from Berenson's point of view, was her habit of deciding for herself that she wanted a certain picture and then directing him to get it for her, just as he was trying to sell her something else.

"Remember that Raphael is not a great painter in the sense that Titian or Veronese or Velazquez or Reubens are," Berenson admonished. He had no Raphael he could act as agent to sell. Mrs. Gardner persisted in wanting Raphaels, and eventually he found two for her: the strongly characterized portrait *Count Tommaso Inghirami* and the delicate *Pietà*, part of a large altarpiece.

In May, 1899, just before going abroad with Lena Little, Mrs. Gardner had done once more the thing Berenson disliked most. "I have just received your cable, 'Chigi Botticelli to be sold Wednesday in Rome. Is it worth $30,000?'" Berenson wrote. He had cabled "No" and now explained. "I was for years the only critic who sustained that Chigi's Botticelli was genuine"; but he was sure that Prince Chigi would not sell the picture.

Of course it was Dick Norton who told Mrs. Gardner that the reputedly wealthy Chigi family was now hard up. *The Madonna and Child of the Eucharist,* their painting by Botticelli was called, when not referred to as "the Chigi"—the name of a succession of hereditary owners. It was just the sort of picture Mrs. Gardner liked best. The figures were real people, despite their halos. The Virgin, her beauty similar to that of Botticelli's *Venus,* held her child lovingly, and the child himself was a baby whose fingers seemed to fall by

218

chance into the sign of the Trinity. An attendant, sometimes referred to as an angel, offered the child wheat and grapes—symbols of the Eucharist. When Botticelli wanted to represent an angel, he painted wings, but this boy had a halo to indicate sainthood—a charming saint, certainly, beautifully dressed, his hair carefully curled. His expression as he watched the Holy Child was one of mingled amusement and affection. Mrs. Gardner bought many similar paintings, but none, since the Zubaran, had appealed more directly to her heart.

In June, Mrs. Gardner insisted that she wanted this picture. "As for the Chigi Botticelli," Berenson wrote, "the last certain news was that the German emperor and an English syndicate had run it up to £12,000. This almost tempts one to join the race for the pure fun of it."

Mrs. Gardner turned down a Titian and continued to pursue the Botticelli. In August, while she was in Venice, Berenson told her that the gossip in Rome was that "the Czar has bought it." But the Chigi Botticelli was in the hands of Colnaghi, the London dealer, and Berenson had to go to him to buy it for Mrs. Gardner. He hated to do it and suggested that she look at it again—reminding her that it was "not in very good condition" and "a very early work of Botticelli" anyway . . . "which he had always adored," he added. Mrs. Gardner looked at the picture in London and wanted it more than ever.

New laws had just been passed in an effort to stop the exportation of Italian art. Works of art were not to be sold even in Italy. All breaches of the law were to be punished by thirty months in prison plus a fine. "The Roman princes could die of hunger in their unsaleable galleries," said one of them bitterly; daughters could not marry for lack of a dowry, and the cost of princely living was increasing.

Word got out that Prince Chigi had sold his Botticelli for £20,000 and that he had been prosecuted and condemned to pay his government the whole sum he had obtained for the picture and serve the thirty-month jail sentence. According to the newspaper story,[7] the Botticelli had been smuggled out of Italy, "another picture being painted over the Virgin and Child which could easily be washed off."

Prince Chigi was a considerable personage in Rome. It seemed as if the Italian government meant to make an example of him, but his family "had given two popes and several cardinals to the church"; and he was powerful at court. The

219

jail sentence was withdrawn and a court of appeals reduced his fine to £80.

Among Mrs. Gardner's papers was a clipping which must have pleased her. "Mrs. Jack Gardner doesn't admit it but it is tolerably clear to me that she knows what has become of the much talked about Botticelli Madonna. Prince Chigi tried to convince the Italian government that he had sold it to Mr. P. A. B. Widener of Philadelphia for $63,000 but the latter has proved conclusively that he is not the joyful owner of the Botticelli which brought the prince into court . . . If Mrs. Gardner got it for $63,000 she has once more demonstrated her astuteness, for it's no dream talk to say that the Louvre or the National Gallery would have paid over twice the amount if international courtesy had permitted either of them to buy. The Metropolitan Museum in New York had what purported to be a Botticelli, once on a time, but the forgery came to light. Mrs. Gardner has added one more triumph to her already long list, and the only genuine Botticelli in the United States is pretty certain to turn up in her gallery soon or late."

Of course, Mrs. Gardner already owned a Botticelli—*The Tragedy of Lucretia,* which the author of the article hadn't heard about. The article was thus all the more gratifying.

By November 4, 1900, the news that Mrs. Gardner owned the picture had come out and *The Times* (London) told of it. "The Chigi Botticelli has acquired a certain celebrity of late years for reasons not connected with its artistic merits . . . When a beautiful woman has made a runaway match and when the law has been noisily invoked . . . the scandal attracts for the moment almost more notice than her beauty. So with this picture . . . Anyhow, the Botticelli in question is now in Pall Mall east, on its way to America, the final resting place, we regret to say, of so many of the finest works of European art. Messrs. P. and D. Colnaghi, who bought the picture, have obligingly placed it on exhibition for a few weeks before it goes to the gallery of Mrs. J. L. Gardner, the Boston lady who now possesses Lord Darnley's great Titian and many other pictures of high importance . . ." The Botticelli "belongs to his early period, the period of the famous 'Magnificat' of the Uffizi and the 'Madonna' of the Louvre . . . in the small front rank of the Master's easel pictures . . . Altogether, the Chigi picture . . . is of quite remarkable design and expression; the child's attitude is wonderful and Botticelli never painted a lovelier head than that of the young attendant . . ."

All these notices Mrs. Gardner clipped and collected. Her personal taste was corroborated and she was never one to mourn over other people's loss when she gained a prize for her collection. But her trip to Europe had not been much of a success from a personal point of view. She had been lonely and was "feeling seedy," so she went to Bournemouth before sailing home.

Bournemouth was where Alice, Henry James's sister, had gone for her health. Probably James suggested it to Mrs. Jack. It was a British winter resort with fine hotels and an abundance of doctors versed in the art of treating hypochondriacs. Mrs. Jack was soon exasperated by the sight of old people in wheel chairs. She dreaded an ocean voyage in winter, but Bournemouth was unbearable and she was glad to sail. She reached home on December 28, 1899.

It might have been at about this time that a young actress, Eleanor Robeson, was walking down Beacon Street when a maid knocked on a window in one of the houses and beckoned her to the door. Miss Robeson had made her debut two years earlier in San Francisco at the age of eighteen. Perhaps she hoped that she was already famous in Boston as she went up the steps of 152 Beacon Street. She recognized the great Mrs. Jack Gardner who stood in the doorway. But all Mrs. Gardner said was, "Walk erect, young woman." Then she closed the big door. Once more a Gardner legend was born as the future popular actress, eventually to become Mrs. August Belmont, laughed and told the tale. All sorts of people heard it and attached it to various and sundry other young ladies.[8]

Mrs. Gardner opened her Beacon Street house for the benefit of the Home for Deformed and Crippled Children in March, 1900. She had never done such a thing before but the cause was one she could not resist. Anxious about the increasing value of her objects of art as well as her paintings, she restricted the number of tickets to be sold and sent a statement to the press that "tickets will be sent on application only to those properly identified." Unfortunately she decided against talking with reporters, and it was easy for an antagonistic press to make her safety precautions sound like snobbery.

The prevailing attitude of women who had no living to earn, toward those who earned their living writing for the papers, may seem hard to understand. Mrs. Gardner was by no means the only one who appeared to resent the very word "reporter." But in her case the attitude was sometimes excusable. For example, a Boston Sunday paper published an article with broad black borders around it, as though for a sign of mourning. "Mrs. Jack may wed again," was the headline. "Rumor says that she will bestow her hand upon her gifted protégé, George Proctor." Much was made of the story that "the young man lives at her house, receives his pupils there" and, during the open house for the crippled children, "was on exhibition" when she "showed her pictures."

On the first exhibition day, Mrs. Gardner caught a young man "making an innocent sketch of one of the interiors." Her famous temper exploded and she "snatched the paper out of his hand." This tale, with variations, made copy for the "yellow press." Mrs. Gardner was certainly at fault; but it must also have been a stupid young man who could not get on her good side, simply by being young, a man—and an artist of sorts.

Word got around that Mrs. Jack was pleading poverty. She had just bought some expensive paintings, not to mention stonework and furnishings, and the totals which her three advisers had arrived at really frightened her. In April, 1900, *Town Topics* celebrated Mrs. Gardner's poverty in verse, with a suggestion that her next open house be for her own benefit.

This is the house that Jack built
This is his widow, sleek and trim
That lives in the house that was built by him
Whose Income, she saith has become quite slim
Since she lived in the house that Jack built.

This is the populace, fond of her
And willing to ante up two plunks per
To see the treasures so rare and fine
And pictures of value from near and far
With cloisonné vase and Dresden jar
That lurk in the house that Jack built.

This is the advice I freely give
To dear Mrs. Jack since a dame must live
And a couple of dollars forsooth, per head
When a number subscribe meaneth more than bread
That she collar the boodle and quickly be

In her former condition of solvency
In the wonderful house that Jack built.

Somehow, the idea that Mrs. Gardner would actually open her house for her own benefit took hold among those who disliked her!

TWENTY-ONE

Mr. Sears's Lament

O N MAY 27, 1900, Williard T. Sears, Architect, resumed his record of the building of Fenway Court. Trouble began at once. Mrs. Gardner had approved blueprints showing the iron roof construction for the glass covering of her great indoor garden but now she said she must have the roof construction made of wood with sliding sashes like those on her greenhouses out in Brookline. Lower ends of the rafters must curve on lines that she marked on drawings. She wanted the glass heavier than specifications—and the frames lighter! Mr. Sears had to let her have her way, nearly a year later, when she still insisted. Resignedly, he accepted a bid "for the court roof—price $8,000." [1]

Mrs. Jack went out to her lot on the Fenway and saw the line drawn on the foundation stones for the starting of the easterly brick wall. She asked how far away from her lot line it was and was told, one inch. An eighth of an inch would have been enough, she said, mindful of Venetian palaces awash with canal water—but to Mr. Sears's relief she did not tell Dan, the mason, to change it. She changed the front steps, however, the arrangement of the windows in the Gothic Room and the windows on the first floor "from casement to sliding sash, making the window reveals 12 inches instead of 16 inches." All through the month of June Mrs. Gardner made almost daily changes in her plans, sometimes of only an inch or two but always requiring new drawings and blueprints. On July 5, she told Mr. Sears that she was going to Beverly for the summer and the poor man may have been optimistic enough to breathe a sigh of relief. If so, it was premature.

On the twelfth of July, Mr. Sears got in touch with George Peabody Gardner to inquire about the matter of money. He was told that Henry W. Swift had been given the job of looking after Mrs. Gardner's finances. He was surprised but it was not actually surprising. George Peabody Gardner had been immensely patient with his Aunt Belle. He had helped her cope with Berenson's super-salesmanship and her own extravagant impulses. When expenses worried her, he tried to explain the intricacies of invested funds; the dates when coupons could be cut or interest would be paid. Isabella understood in theory, but in practice she forgot. She was always feeling either delightfully rich or terrifyingly poor. Conferences with her took so much time that her nephew despaired of being able to attend to the business of taking care of her money and his own. And now came the building of this fantastic palace!

Hopefully, George P. Gardner brought around Henry W. Swift, a Somerset Club bachelor of uncertain age—a lawyer, and a businessman without much business of his own on his mind. To her nephew's relief and delight, Aunt Belle took to him at their first interview. They were already acquainted, but now a friendship rapidly developed so that Swift presented Mrs. Jack with his photograph, which she added to her collection. Instead of being seated in pensive attitude like Clayton Johns or Ralph Curtis, Henry Swift was astride a handsome horse. Mrs. Jack judged the horse and rider to be blue-ribbon quality, and like a queen conferring knighthood, she called Swift "my man of business." Behind his back, however, friends called him "Hattie Swift" because of his "high voice and ladylike deportment." [2]

Mr. Sears told Swift that the cost of building Fenway Court would be about ten thousand dollars a month—for an unknown number of months. His commission would be ten per cent of the total cost of the building, but the way things were going it was anybody's guess how much that would be. He wanted five thousand right away.

It was a moot question with Sears whether it was better to have Mrs. Gardner at home on Beacon Street, making small changes in her house plans every day, or in Beverly ordering that nothing be done without her consent and then descending on Boston once a week for the Pops Concert—coming into his office beforehand or afterward as the mood decided her. On July 19, she was at his office and he told her that he could not attend to her requirements and do anything else, so he too appointed a deputy. His assistant, Edward Nichols, personable and patient, would work with Mrs. Gardner; and it was Nichols who met her out on the Fenway when she appeared with her own team of horses, dray, and Italian workmen.

Mrs. Gardner had brought a portion of a doorway but she had not found enough fragments to set it up. She thought she might find more of it at the storage warehouse and would hunt further for it when she came to Boston next Wednesday, she explained. Of course this brought the work on the wall surrounding and over the entrance to a standstill but the masons would not be idle—Mrs. Gardner had ordered the foundation wall that supported the main staircase taken down, saying it was not necessary. All this, Mr. Nichols faithfully reported and Mr. Sears set down in his record—lest later no one would believe it! He must now convince Mrs. Jack that a stone staircase needed support—and he would have to wait a week to talk to her at all.

When Wednesday came, Mr. Nichols met Mrs. Gardner at the storage warehouse and together they found additional pieces of the doorway—but not enough. Mr. Nichols realized that Mrs. Jack liked and accepted him or she would never have let him help her search through the warehouse. This approval had its penalties, however, because Mrs. Gardner decided to have Evans, the stonecutter, make a base to set under the door-frame fragments, but Nichols must make a drawing of the design for these blocks from a photograph she had. He must show her the drawing "before having it cut," although they had "been waiting for this doorway for over two weeks," as Mr. Sears wearily recorded. Finally, when Mrs. Gardner decided that Mr. Nichols had really made drawings "to harmonize with the sections of antique carving," she ordered the mason to "set the two jambs"—but he "must not set the cap till she came there next Wednesday."

Sears himself was "with Mrs. Gardner at Fenway Court while she superintended the setting of the balance of the doorway cap at the Fenway entrance." Mr. Swift had been asking questions about the probable total cost of the building; and in a thoroughly unhappy interview, Mr. Sears tried to tell Mrs. Jack that it cost money to build walls and then order them pulled down, to delay week after week for fragments of marble to come from a distant warehouse. Finally, Mrs. Gardner consented to have a shed built on her own building site. She promised that the next time she came to Boston she would supervise the selection of "two loads of marble to come to the Fenway shed."

The exasperated Mr. Sears probably thought that Mrs. Gardner could have given up a few social engagements in Beverly to attend to her building—since she insisted that nothing be done without her. He was right, of course. But some of Mrs. Jack's social activities were a sort of private revenge. Eliza Gardner Skinner, who had been so holier-than-thou when Isabella and Frank Crawford were together in Beverly, had now been dead two years and her son and only child had married "an obscure shopgirl, daughter of a tailor," [3] by the name of Sadie Carr. Eliza would never have received her and Eliza's friends were not going to let the girl into their charmed circle either—but Mrs. Jack gave all the parties to honor the bride that any girl could wish. The time had come when the younger generation was not going to refuse invitations from Mrs. Jack Gardner, dowagers notwithstanding.

Of course *Town Topics* took up the matter and said that "young Skinner's friends and classmates are wondering whether Mrs. Gardner, as representing the Skinner family, will take up the former Sarah Carr." They very shortly ceased wondering and came up with a quotation which may actually have been more or less what Mrs. Gardner said.

"Mrs. Jack says her nephew's humbly-born wife is a thoroughly charming woman who could tell half the enameled and padded dames and scraggly damsels in the Back Bay district how to win a husband and how to hold him, and Mrs. Jack further avers that she doesn't intend to be influenced in her attitude toward the young Mrs. Skinner by the mendacious prattle of some braggart cads—the Boston clubs are full of them—and envious, scandal-mongering old cats who can't forgive a tailor's daughter for her good fortune." The sentiments were Mrs. Gardner's if not the words. Mrs. Jack never hesitated to befriend a girl of modest background who had married into a family of wealth and distinction.

But as soon as she got back to Boston after a luncheon for Sadie Carr Skinner, labor trouble began at the Fenway building site. John Evans, the stonecutter, returned drawings prepared at the Sears office. He said he would have nothing further to do with "Mrs. Gardner's palace, owing to her having pitched into his men" while they were trying to set the cap on that Fenway front door. Evans said "he would not be bothered by her any further." When Mr. Sears broke this news to his client, he supposed she knew that good stonecutters were scarce. But Mrs. Gardner hadn't liked Evans anyway and she "said she was glad of it" when he quit.

Another stonecutter, "Mr. Sullivan," was found. But within a few weeks Mr. Nichols in desperation summoned the head of the firm. Mrs. Gardner "would have nothing further to do with Mr. Sullivan and would not use the stone he was cutting . . ."

Up to this point, it appears that Willard T. Sears had been

somewhat in awe of his difficult client. He now told Mrs. Jack that this would not do, that Sullivan was the best man to do the work that he could get. Mrs. Gardner listened to reason but Sullivan had his Irish up. The lady "had called him a liar" and he wouldn't work for her.

"After a while I prevailed on him to keep on," Mr. Sears wrote when the battle ended.

Peace, or at least an armistice, was arranged and the masons commenced setting the columns around the court, Mrs. Gardner superintending the removal of every column from the shed and directing the setting of each column, according to her architect's record. There were too many columns to set in one day, however, and Mrs. Gardner said she would not be back until the following Friday and that no columns must be set while she was away. Mr. Sears "asked her to mark the columns and allow us to keep on setting them while she was away." But the Lady Isabella had been defeated once, in the matter of Sullivan, and she was not going to haul down her flag again. "She would not consent, saying she wanted to personally supervise the setting of every column."

"The putting up of the floor timbers and the building of the walls . . . have been delayed by the delay of setting the columns," Mr. Sears noted, but he kept his masons busy "skimming off the inside courses of bricks of a portion of the corridors . . ." because Mrs. Gardner said the bricks were the wrong color and he must begin "replacing them with other bricks."

As the summer wore on, Willard T. Sears probably wished that he had never met Mrs. Jack Gardner and had never attempted to build Fenway Court. Then, on October 30, "Mrs. Gardner called and asked me to be a trustee of the Isabella Stewart Gardner Museum now being erected on the Fenway. Visited her home in the afternoon," he wrote. And the next day: "Visited Mrs. Gardner's house in the afternoon." Suddenly they were friends for life! Of course Mr. Sears was flattered to be included in the distinguished list of trustees, but it was more than that. Isabella Gardner had made him see her dream, the reason behind her seemingly senseless insistence on her idea of perfection. He found that he really wanted to help her achieve something entirely out of the ordinary.

Of course Mr. Sears's troubles were not over. Mrs. Gardner now determined that her museum project must be kept secret until the day of its completion. With her instinct for the dramatic, she visualized the scene—the suspense, the mystery and then the glorious revelation as she received her friends at a reception! An "at home, with music" she would call it, for the fun of deluding people into thinking it would be a small affair.

However, a large construction project in the still undeveloped Fenway could hardly escape attention. Newspaper reporters came around. Mrs. Gardner was mysterious and completely uncommunicative, but they knew what to do. They went to the Boston Building Department office and asked to see the building permit. It would be sure to supply some information upon which they could build a few columns of print. Then it was discovered that no building permit was on file!

Mr. Sears was still in the process of trying to get the inspector's approval for certain peculiarities of construction that Mrs. Gardner was insisting upon. Yet meanwhile, the new walls rose high, her doors were blocked to visitors. Here was a fine subject for discussion by the press and the gleeful reporters threatened to make the most of it. Mr. Sears got a letter from the Building Department office that sent him hurrying around there. Captain Damrell was in charge but his son was on duty.

Prudently, Mr. Sears set down his account of the interview with Damrell the younger. "I told him that Fitzsimmons would not sign a permit as the floor-bearing walls were over 30 feet apart . . ." This regulation had been adopted after the great Boston fire and the underling inspector would have liked to force Mrs. Gardner to cut up all her great palace-sized rooms into small ones. But Captain Damrell ordered Fitzsimmons to sign the permit and "had given me permission to go ahead with the building," Mr. Sears said.

Mr. Sears was anxious, however, and had gone around to tell Mrs. Gardner that he might be forced to put in iron columns at intervals, to support the upper floors of the palace. "She replied that she would not have them and she did not care what they said."

Mrs. Gardner had already given her consent to a "second story iron column under truss" which she thought she could "cover with silk" so that the anachronism would not be so offensive. Now she "stopped the men from setting it." With patience, and with a new understanding of Mrs. Gardner's vision, Mr. Sears argued and won. Four days later she told him he "might use the iron column, to be covered with wood . . ." and he got it up just in time.

Fitzsimmons with "a detail of men from the building department" arrived at 9:30 next morning, "to inspect the construction of the building" again. Tipped off during the previous evening by a "Mr. Mahoney of the building department," Sears was out at the Fenway site to take them around. They "expressed themselves as very much pleased," but Willard T. Sears was not. He "stopped in at Captain Damrell's office" that afternoon and "asked him why he sent three inspectors to examine the building."

Captain Damrell seems to have been very polite. "There had been no complaint," he assured the architect and on November 22 he gave the Boston *Post* an interview in which he said that "the palace is being constructed better than any building in Boston . . ." It was true that he had given no written permit but he had "granted a tacit one."

The front wall of the building, overlooking the Fenway, was still incomplete in November. It had been kept waiting for a marble plaque, designed by Sarah Whitman, artist in stained glass and a friend of Mrs. Gardner's. "The Isabella Stewart Gardner Museum in the Fenway MDCCCC" the inscription read, and on December 23, 1900, Mrs. Gardner "overlooked the setting of the tablet." This time, there were no repercussions among the stonemasons—not because Mrs. Gardner had become easier to please—but because a certain remarkable Italian was on the job.

Theobaldo Travi was big, handsome—an ex-gondolier from Venice, according to some reports. He was always called "Bolgi." [4] He had rounded up some of his friends to work for Mrs. Jack who may or may not have been stonemasons by trade, but were Italian and had an instinct for handling stone—whether in terraces for a vineyard or in arches over a city gate. Allowing for the differences between the speech of a signora and that of a workman, Mrs. Gardner spoke their language and they loved it. She liked to issue commands such as no Welsh Evans nor Irish Sullivan would tolerate; but the Italians understood and did as they pleased—*politely!* Mrs. Gardner put Bolgi in charge, giving orders that no piece of antique marble should be moved without him. This also pleased his friends who worked under him. If a piece of marble were broken, Bolgi could explain with eloquence that the accident must have occurred in Europe a hundred years earlier and that no mason on the job could possibly be to blame.

Bolgi could also play the cornet. Now that summer was over and Mrs. Gardner was once more living on Beacon Street, she spent days at a time at her Fenway building site

230

She and Bolgi devised a system whereby he could summon workmen to her side—"one toot for a mason, two for the steam-fitter, three for the plumber, four for the carpenter, five for the plasterer, six for the painter." [5] She took her lunch just as the workmen did and contributed ten cents for oatmeal to be put in the drinking water—presumably to settle some of the mud in it!

Happy working relations between Mrs. Gardner and her labor ought now to have been established as she joined them with her dinner pail. Such, however, was not the case. In June, 1901, all the carpenters went out on strike. Of course Mrs. Gardner said she didn't care—she hadn't liked them, anyway. They calmed down, and an armistice was declared which lasted until the following October, when Mrs. Gardner ordered the "floor-layers discharged for mimicking her when she spoke to them for not working!"

On December 5, 1900, Mrs. Gardner called with the incorporation papers for the Isabella Stewart Gardner Museum, for Sears to sign as a trustee. Among other signatures were her own, those of John Chipman Gray, Henry W. Swift and her nephews Harold Jefferson Coolidge and William Amory Gardner. A charter was issued on December 19 with capital stock listed as $50,000.

There were no more entries in Willard T. Sears's diary until March, 1901. At this time Mr. Sears wrote concerning a small theater to be part of the Museum on the Fenway. The Music Room was what Mrs. Gardner called it and she had asked the advice of Henry L. Higginson as to proportions "acoustically perfect." Higginson said that the Leipzig Music Hall was his ideal and lent her photographs which she turned over to Mr. Sears. His next job was to show her how the proportions of the Leipzig Music Hall, which he had never heard of, compared with her proposed Music Room.

Acoustics were little studied at this time, a successful concert room being more a matter of luck than of science. Mr. Sears succeeded in convincing Mrs. Gardner that the proportions he had drawn on the plan were good. He next proposed wood paneling for the walls, bringing to bear the opinion of various musical friends. There could be an echo from wood, Mrs. Gardner said—the walls must be plastered. She had learned that Mendelssohn Hall in New York was to be plastered in a sculptural effect simulating draped wall hangings. There was nothing for Mr. Sears to do but let Mrs. Gardner carry Nichols off to New York for a look at Mendelssohn Hall.

Mrs. Jack Gardner and her architect's assistant arrived at the scene of construction and Mr. Nichols began measuring and sketching. A foreman appeared and wanted to know what went on. Mrs. Gardner explained and was told that she must get the architect's permission to copy his design and an authorization to enter the premises. She was now past mistress at arguing with foremen, so while she prolonged the discussion the embarrassed and unhappy Mr. Nichols continued to measure and sketch—not daring to stop. He had finished when Mrs. Jack allowed herself to be "shown out." There was just time to catch the express for Boston, and if the Sears firm wanted to get in touch with any New York architects about a pirated design that was their affair.

Back at Fenway Court, elderly Italian plasterers had been hired, who in their youth had decorated ceilings with heavy ornament in high relief. They understood neither Mr. Nichols's sketches nor Mrs. Gardner's explanation. So Mr. Nichols laid off the wall in rectangles; Mrs. Gardner brought a huge bed sheet which she draped against a panel exactly as she wanted it. Then she told the plasterers to copy the folds. Copying was what Italian workmen knew best—as American sculptors in Rome and Florence had long since discovered. Mrs. Gardner's music room walls soon appeared to be lined with linen, delicately draped. The room was two stories high, this decoration covering the lower section of the wall. It was bordered at the top by a band of classic ornament which Mrs. Gardner's plasterers knew how to achieve without help. Between the sections of plaster drapery stood statues on high pedestals—Pan playing on his pipes and other gods and goddesses in archaic Greek style, similarly occupied.

There were no windows at the ground floor level of the music room, but at the second floor level, high arched windows reached nearly to the third floor. A double staircase opposite the stage led upward from each side of the room to merge in a single balcony at the second floor. Gracefully curved balconies swung outward under the high windows. If she wished, Mrs. Gardner could enter her music room from above, within the palace, while her guests filed in below from the Fenway entrance.

Drawings for the balcony railings were not approved by Mrs. Gardner until June, 1902. But two months earlier, when Mr. Sears met Mrs. Gardner in the music room "to make some experiments . . . with lighting . . . with Holophane lamps," he was dismayed to find that she had ordered all the scaffolding down from the freshly painted pure white walls.

She was "hasty," he said. But, as usual, Isabella had reasons. She said she wanted "to have the Symphony Orchestra men try the room" and this was the last week before they "finished for the summer."

Of course there would be no use in testing acoustics without an audience. And yet no one—with the exception of a very few friends—must see the palace before it was finished. Mrs. Gardner had the solution, however. She invited the blind children from Perkins Institution to come to hear the music.[6] It was said that the children from Perkins were brought from South Boston by horse-drawn omnibus. They were led into the "North Corridor"—as Mr. Sears called the "Cloister"—where they took off their rubbers, the day being rainy. They placed them in pairs along the wall where they would know, by touch, how to find them again. But some over-zealous person gathered all the little rubbers up into one pile, so that chaos resulted after the concert. Mrs. Gardner helped sort out and re-mate the strayed galoshes. Acoustics had proved perfect. Mr. Sears would not be required to redesign the Music Room!

It was a relief to find Mrs. Gardner "instructing the Italian plasterers as to the plaster finish of the Court and rooms," Mr. Sears wrote on March 31, 1901. Plastering had been held up because she had written to Berenson for "a sample of Bardini's blue" and he had forgotten the errand. Berenson had been "mildly scolded," and had gone at once to see the Florentine Bardini, who solemnly assured him that the sample would be sent, and with it the recipe for preparing it. This beautiful, intense shade of blue paint was now going on some of the walls, probably fresco, or while the plaster was fresh and still wet.

But the color for the walls of the inner court simply would not come out right. They must be pink—but not really pink —and yellow, but not really yellow; done carefully but not smoothly. Mrs. Gardner's Italian, which had been standing her in good stead, failed her at this point, and so did her English. There was a ladder leaning against the courtyard wall, with a painter's shelf projecting from it filled with assorted cans of color. Nimbly, Mrs. Gardner mounted and splashed pale terra-cotta pink—some yellow, a dash of white. Miraculously, she achieved the effect of old Venetian walls under an Italian sky. Things were brought her as she called for them—a big brush, a sponge, some water. Looking on, the workmen nodded and smiled. They could do it like that —of course they could.

This story became an oft-told tale. Mrs. Gardner would be sixty-one in one month, almost to the day, and it seemed incredible to women of her generation that she could climb a ladder! In consideration of the kind of clothes she must have been wearing, perhaps they had a point. But no one seemed to have noticed that she was an artist—if only in wall paint.

TWENTY-TWO

Nine o'Clock Punctually

IN NOVEMBER, 1901, Mrs. Gardner told her architect that she wanted her servants to move into the palace. There were as yet no floors in the corridors, no treads on the stairs, but Mr. Sears said he would see what he could do.[1]

On November 18, Mrs. Gardner herself spent the night at Fenway Court. Mr. Sears had advised her to sell her Beacon Street house, just as it stood, and apply the proceeds to the building of the palace, but he had reckoned without his client's streak of sentimentality. She loved 152 Beacon Street and she resolved to take as much of it as possible with her. The handsomely carved over-mantle from the front hall, she had installed in the living room on the top floor of the palace. Overstuffed Civil War period furniture which she and Jack had bought together cluttered these private apartments. Their bed was set up in the new bedroom in the space Mr. Nichols "measured" for it. Beacon Street was now untenable—Fenway Court scarcely more comfortable.

The paintings, the Renaissance furniture and objects of art were brought to Fenway Court long before the palace was finished, and Mr. Sears began to worry about fire and theft. Swift authorized $50,000 of fire insurance but Mrs. Gardner was horrified by the cost and theft insurance was not taken out. She grew suspicious, however—and caused the electrician who was installing her elevator to leave in a rage. Mrs. Gardner had called him a thief, he said.

Now that the owner was a resident in her palace, the scene was right out of Lewis Carroll most of the time with Mrs. Gardner taking the part of the Red Queen and shouting "Off with their heads" to all and sundry. But as in *Wonderland*, the condemned returned, more often than not, their heads still upon their shoulders. Gradually, she gathered about her people who not only managed to put up with her, but even liked her, temper tantrums and all.

Mrs. Jack elevated the stonemason Bolgi to the high rank of major-domo. For the rest of her life, he guarded her as he would have guarded a Venetian duchess. Joseph Lindon Smith designed a dress uniform for him—green knee breeches, crimson coat covered with gold braid, epaulets and Napoleonic hat of shining black. For this, he would have died for her, if he had not already committed his whole heart to her service.[2] At the beginning of the twentieth century, Italian palaces, French châteaux and German castles were being built all over the United States as men with new millions looked for romantic ways to spend their money. Their wives dragged them abroad in search of culture and they bought whatever the dealers offered, provided the price were high enough. They hired architects to build replicas which were, in the end, nothing but monstrous fakes.

Mrs. Gardner had been among the first to collect old masters. She had Berenson's advice before the craze was on and she and her husband bought to satisfy their own taste, rather than to eclipse a rival. The Gardner collection was to remain unique.

Sometimes Mr. Sears must have envied other architects, free to commit crimes in multicolored marble. Sometimes he must have suspected that fellow architects laughed at him when Mrs. Gardner broke all the rules and he had to let her have her way. She turned capitals upside down and placed them under, instead of over columns at a doorway in the Dutch Room, for example. She ordered outer-wall windows turned inward to overlook her court. When a peach marble column, about which he had warned her, actually broke, she had it replaced in concrete, to her architect's amazement. She said no one would ever notice—and she was right. But Mr. Sears could never foretell what she would do.

Sears turned down an offer to build an apartment house. It would have been an easy job but he could not bring his mind to bear on anything so ordinary. Somehow, as weeks and months went by, he and the most unreasonable client he had ever met were turning out a work of art. Fenway Court was no echo of an earlier age. It had style, defiant of time, an originality seldom encountered—a life of its own.

As soon as the ever-watchful press discovered that Mrs. Gardner was actually living at Fenway Court, announcements appeared of a housewarming which reporters assumed would be a "crush." Also, the plaque on the Fenway Court wall had been observed and read, and reporters used their imagination, visualizing a daily shuffling-through of the curious public, staring without seeing, fingering everything not under glass.

Mrs. Gardner paid no attention to false announcements of

her housewarming but the notion that her home was at once to become a public museum alarmed her. On August 4, 1902, Mr. Nichols met her "at the Fenway house this morning with new drawings for the shield tablet to be placed over the Isabella Stewart Gardner tablet on the exterior of the house." The drawings were approved, the new piece of marble was laid over the inscription and fastened into place. But no one seemed to notice that what had seemed a public invitation had been withdrawn.

Day after day, Mrs. Gardner worked over the arranging of her rooms. As an afterthought, she had told Sears to build partitions on the ground floor—there would be a "custodian's room" and guest rooms. There were bathrooms, but when Mr. Sears pointed out that unless she put in a larger water heater there would not be enough hot water for the custodian's bath she said it didn't matter. What Venetian duchess ever worried about a custodian's bath! Mrs. Gardner had other matters on her mind.

The Raphael Room and the Dutch Room were the glories of the second floor. From the Beacon Street parlor came red brocade to cover at least part of the Raphael Room walls. There was more to match or harmonize in boxes sent home from Europe. Around the doors, along walls at chair-rail height, up corners and at the ceiling line ran a delicate white meander pattern—a vine cut from wood. It had adorned the Beacon Street parlor and Mrs. Gardner loved it. Any decorator would have told her that it was impossible to combine antique Italian brocade with this French-inspired modern trimming. But any unprejudiced observer would have to admit that the effect was good! [3]

The most beautiful of Mrs. Jack's green brocades went on the wall of the Dutch Room, where it made a background that was perfect for her Rembrandts and equally successful for her new picture, bought through Berenson in 1901. This was *Mary Tudor, Queen of England,* by Moro. "Moro at his best . . . has more grandeur of style, much more poetry of color" than Holbein, Berenson had written.

Even the great Baroque pearl, worn by the queen in her portrait, had a story. It was said to have been brought home from the Pacific in 1513 by Balboa and presented to Isabella of Spain. This and further histories of "La Pelegrina," as the pearl was called, pleased Isabella of Boston. [4] On the fireplace wall in the Dutch Room, Bloody Mary gazed upon the American scene with ferocious concentration—an encouragement to Isabella Gardner in all her endeavors. If Isabella ever wavered, that face must have firmed her intention to have her way at all points.

On the third floor, the Titian Room was dominated by Mrs. Gardner's *Europa*. Visitors stopped and stared at the sight of it as they came through the opposite door—much to Mrs. Jack's delight. The walls of this room were covered with red brocade with more of the little white vine cutout around the panels, but below the Titian was a section of sea-green silk, brocaded in a slightly darker shade—the pattern, a tassel drop-repeated. This silk was "contemporary French" but no decorator's shop had supplied it. Mrs. Gardner took it out of one of her trunks upstairs and it had been part of an evening dress she had worn on Beacon Street. Pictures had been taken of the party in the old music room, Jack Gardner, looking solemn, Mrs. Jack with diamonds in her hair.

On Christmas Eve, 1901, Mrs. Gardner's private chapel at the end of the Long Gallery was consecrated by the Rev. Dr. William B. Frisbie, Rector of the Church of the Advent. A service on Christmas Eve became a yearly occasion to which only members of the family and a few close friends were invited. The chapel itself, which the New York *Tribune* described as "hung in the richest tapestry" was never shown to visitors during Mrs. Gardner's lifetime. The *Tribune* thought the "oratory . . . opened out of" Mrs. Gardner's bedroom—which it did not. If she saw the item she was pleased because the more misinformation there was, the more certain it became that her secrets were well kept.

As Fenway Court neared completion, Mrs. Gardner saw where she could use more paintings and more statuary. She bought eight old masters, five of them, including the *Mary Tudor* through Berenson, one from a New York dealer and two through Richard Norton in Rome. But Norton's chief interest these days was centered around excavations with their discoveries of what he hoped were Roman and Greek sculptures. Norton cabled, then wrote to Mrs. Gardner in May, 1901, about a headless statue. "It was dug up just a few days ago in Sallust's garden near where your kneeling man came from," he told her. "It will make those who know Greek sculpture jump for joy. I had to be very spry to get it and it must stay in hiding for a few weeks." The Copenhagen and Berlin museums, "and most of all, Warren" (Chairman of the Board of Trustees of the Boston Museum of Fine Arts) "were crazy at having lost it."

Eight months went by before Norton arranged with the Minister of Public Instruction in Rome for permission to ship the statue to Boston—on receipt of cash. Mrs. Gardner sent him about $12,000. Norton paid the money to the Sisters of St. Giuseppi, owners of the statue. And then "some of the Warren faction stirred things up," according to Norton. An attack began in the papers—exportation papers were refused —then granted—then refused again when the Italian Ministry fell. Sister Constanza, treasurer of the convent, was hauled into court! This was going too far, however, and Sister Constanza, although sentenced for selling a national treasure, was "absolved" and the statue "liberated"—not to Mrs. Gardner, but to the court in Rome. Mrs. Gardner, who was impatient to complete her inner courtyard, could hardly bear to open a letter from Dick Norton. However, he did send her a Roman marble throne, a small altar and a sarcophagus, which she put in the Court. Summoning Mr. Sears to come at once, she showed him the sarcophagus, just uncrated. Poor man—he thought some disaster had struck; but he had to admit that the carving was beautiful.

As for the "Headless Maiden"—it arrived at Fenway Court thirty-four years late, but there it stands today. Mrs. Gardner saw it in Rome but she never saw it at her palace.

The collecting of antiquities was an exciting game and Mrs. Jack loved to play it. But she played to win and defeats like this one told on her nerves. There were other tribulations in store for an amateur owner of a private museum, as she was soon to discover. A fifteenth-century *Annunciation*, painted on a heavy wood panel, was scarcely hung in the Raphael Room before the paint began to peel off. Mrs. Gardner had not been feeling very friendly toward people at the Boston Museum of Fine Arts—whose new building was soon to be her neighbor in the Fenway. They may or may not have had a hand in her difficulties over the headless statue but they were often her rivals in the old-master market. However, she knew when she needed them and she went around to see John Briggs Potter, Keeper of Paintings.

With what seemed miraculous skill, Potter transferred Mrs. Gardner's painting to a new panel. It occurred to her that she needed a conservationist and for a while John Briggs Potter lived in one of the three rooms on the ground floor at Fenway Court, taking care of the collection in his spare time. He was the first of the museum boys she acquired and grew fond of—a new group of young men to surround her, as others had done.

In 1903, John Briggs Potter went abroad and Mrs. Gardner asked him to look at some paintings Berenson was recommending to her. Potter was also to size up Berenson and report. He was "friendlily impressed," he wrote, and thought Berenson "more liable to be deceived than to wilfully practice deception . . ." The only thing which bothered Potter was "the delicate flattery" which Berenson "applied, but that is with so many people only a childish habit," he wrote.

It always pleased Mrs. Gardner to have her faith in Berenson restored, although this faith often wavered. In 1902 she bought only two pictures through his agency, in 1903, none, her most important purchase that year being a fourteenth-century Giuliano da Rimini, found for her by Joseph Lindon Smith and costing $1500. Glorious in color, signed and one of the prizes of her collection, Mrs. Gardner loved it enough to place it in the Long Gallery close to her private chapel. Fine pictures were still to come. If it was frustrating not to have the "Headless Maiden" for the Court garden, it was exciting to look forward to the discovery of still more treasures as yet unknown. At the end of the year, Fenway Court was ready for the much-longed-for opening—although not completely finished nor even fixed in its final form.

According to the Boston *Transcript*'s list more than 150 engraved invitations were issued for the evening of January 1, 1903. These went only to Mrs. Gardner's older friends—younger people having been promised a party at the palace later on. So notable was the occasion that many of the invitations and programs were kept among cherished personal papers. Sara Norton carefully pasted hers into her Memory Book.

> *Mrs. John Lowell Gardner*
> *requests the pleasure of*
> *Professor and Miss Norton's*
> *Company on Thursday evening*
> *January 1st   at nine o'clock*
> *Punctually.   R.S.V.P.*

Everyone tried to be punctual, heavy traffic resulting. The palace was cold because a long and bitter railroad strike had cut off Boston's coal supply. But the Music Room had a special furnace in which Mrs. Gardner burned wood because she hated the smell of coal—as she had already told Mr. Sears.

On the stroke of nine, Mrs. Jack stepped out on the landing at the head of her double staircase. Her guests began to climb the stairs; many of whom, when she came to Boston as a bride, had tried to make her feel that *they* were the ones standing on an eminence she could never reach. There were those, also, who had resolved no longer to recognize her because of Frank Crawford. If Mrs. Jack smiled in triumph, who could blame her!

But there was room on the stair landing for a husband and wife to stand together. Isabella stood alone. She had carried out her husband's wishes in building this palace on the Fens —and had spared no pains to make it perfect. People had come to do her honor, or to gratify their curiosity—their motives hardly mattered now. Those who really loved her had come and she knew which ones they were. Tonight, however, she did not join her guests. One of the golden armchairs Jack had bought on their last journey together was brought out to the stair landing and all through the concert Isabella sat alone.

The music had been the subject of long discussion between Mrs. Gardner and Gericke. There was no Wagner—Jack had not liked it. A Bach chorale came first, with Lena Little among the nine singers from the Cecilia Society.[5] Then came Mozart's overture to *The Magic Flute*—Chausson's symphonic poem *Viviane*, while Schubert's *Overture, Scherzo and Finale*, Opus 59, ended the concert. Among the guests was William F. Apthorp, who wrote his impressions for the Boston *Transcript*.

"There were 50 musicians from the Boston Symphony . . . Gericke conducting. The acoustics turned out to be about as perfect as the soul of musical man could desire," he wrote. "It reminded one of the old hall of the Conservatoire in Paris, the model and paragon of all music halls . . ."

Mr. Apthorp's definition of the ideal music hall was one having "the greatest amount of resonance compatible with an absence of echo . . . Listening to music in such a hall, you feel as if you were inside of some musical instrument, indeed, such a hall is a musical instrument in itself. The sound of the orchestra and voices is as elastic, as buoyant as a soap-bubble, it has a ring to it almost like a fine Chinese gong . . . The tone of the violins cuts like a knife, yet the trumpets are not too loud . . ."

Mr. Apthorp described Mrs. Gardner's music room as having "a sightliness quite its own." Accustomed to ornate, heavily gilded concert halls, he had never seen anything "so perfectly simple . . . so pure, ungarnished white, save the light wood floor and the light, straw-bottomed chairs . . ." He knew "of nothing at once more inspiring and more restful. It encourages music without interfering with it."

The concert was over at 10:15, when doors at the side of the Music Room were thrown open and the guests saw the flower-filled palace court for the first time. There was an audible gasp of delight—then awed silence. Candlelight flickered from the palace windows overlooking the Court. Iron *torchères* really had torches in them. There was the scent of flowers and sound of water—romantic sights and sounds enough to make middle-aged Bostonian couples feel like Romeo and Juliet!

"The guests had the range of the beautiful rooms, finding much to please them," said the Boston *Transcript*, putting it mildly. People instinctively "spoke in hushed tones at first," there was so much beauty, so overwhelming in effect, all seen by candlelight.

It must be admitted that guests tended to gather around the huge fireplace in each room, where big logs were burning brightly. Professor Edward Sylvester Morse, authority on early Chinese ceramics, retrieved his greatcoat from the coat rack and wore it—departing early, even so. Some said that Mrs. Jack never forgave him but this was not true. He lived in the Orient—she understood—and later he often helped her as she added items of Oriental art to her collection.

But it was cold at Fenway Court that night and to Mrs. Charles Pickering Bowditch went the credit for the witticism to the effect that Mrs. Gardner had "added a freeze of Best Boston" to her sculpture collection.[6]

Most appropriately, there was champagne at the party after the concert was over. Legends, springing up almost on the spot, differed as to what else there was, but a man who was there declared that Mrs. Gardner served her "two favorites, doughnuts and champagne," and nothing else!

A private car, chartered from the New Haven Railroad, brought New York guests to Boston, Edith Wharton being among them. A "supper was served at small tables in the Dutch Room" and Mrs. Wharton, according to a report, said in French that the refreshments were about what you would get in a railroad restaurant in provincial France. She had known Mrs. Gardner in Paris, had written a book on interior decorating full of rules Mrs. Gardner had just broken. The two ladies, similar in some respects, were not fond of each other, so that, in bidding Mrs. Wharton goodbye, Mrs. Jack told her sweetly that it was nice she could come, but she needn't expect another invitation to eat in this railroad restaurant. Mrs. Wharton had apparently assumed that Mrs.

Gardner's French was not good enough to understand her comments.[7]

People wrote to Mrs. Gardner to tell her how much they had enjoyed the concert, how overwhelmed they had been by the beauty of her palace. Berenson quoted Sara Norton as saying that Fenway Court was "an expression of genius." This was especially gratifying, as Miss Norton had not always been among Mrs. Gardner's admirers.

Professor Charles Eliot Norton kept Mrs. Gardner's reply to his own letter—for she was one of his pupils always in her own mind at least. Dated January 3, 1903, Mrs. Gardner wrote, "My head is completely turned by your praise and my heart by your kindness."

TWENTY-THREE

At the Palace

ISABELLA GARDNER BUILT her old-world palace in the Fenway at a time when a new world was taking shape around her. She installed that astonishing invention the telephone, but refused to answer it. What right had that impertinent jingling bell to interrupt thoughts and distract her attention! Mr. Sears, however, said he would see about getting her a direct line to the police station in case of intruders at the palace.

The Boston *Transcript* described the opening of Fenway Court and in the same issue quoted Professor Alexander Graham Bell's opinion that "an aeroplane kite could carry the weight of a motor and a man." Mrs. Gardner was to see "aeroplane kites" flying over her palace and to go to an aviation meet, but for the present she contented herself with looking at advertisements of automobiles—literally horseless carriages, high and narrow with big wheels. Eventually, she wrote Berenson that she had bought an auto and could drive it herself—which was considered a remarkable feat for a woman.

For the present, Mr. Sears had built a carriage house alongside the palace and Mrs. Jack remained faithful to her fast-trotting black horses. Bolgi remembered a certain night when she had gone out in the sleigh. On the way home, her coachman took the new road along the Fenway and as soon as they were free of traffic he touched up the horses as she liked to have him do. They sped along through the dark, sleigh bells jingling. When they pulled up at Fenway Court, Bolgi came out to assist his lady to alight. The sleigh was empty!

Now the coachman remembered going over a bump in the new road. Turning and whipping up his horses again, the coachman and Bolgi found Mrs. Gardner sitting in a snowbank cursing in several languages. She was also laughing, they said.[1]

A small boy who was shoveling snow remembered seeing

244

Mrs. Gardner's sleigh tip over one day. Coachman, footman in fur caps—and the great lady all went in a snowdrift. Mrs. Jack was unhurt, her language unforgettable.[2]

After the first concert on opening night at Fenway Court, word got around that the musicians had been treated like servants and ordered out a side door by an officious flunkey. Members of the famous Cecilia Society were supposed to be particularly insulted because they got no glimpse of the palace and no chance to partake of doughnuts and champagne. For years, Mrs. Gardner had gone out of her way to give musicians social standing, so probably the glory of Bolgi's new uniform and his position as major-domo went to his head and he exceeded his authority.

Mrs. Gardner gave three successive concerts, with two hundred guests invited to each. The first was on April 13, the night before her birthday, which she loved to celebrate. Musicians were especially honored; they walked about the palace, meeting John Singer Sargent, whose second talent after painting was the piano and who played informally for them. Charles Martin Loeffler's new composition, *L'Archet* was heard at each concert, and Mrs. Gardner had invited a music publisher whom she hoped to interest in his work. Those who said that the members of the Cecilia Society were on strike now said that the strike was over.[3]

There were various musical experiments at the palace. One evening a Gregorian chant sounded far above a group of listeners gathered in the cloisters "around the darkened garden with its flowers." Among unusual performances, perhaps the most notable was that of Loeffler's *Pagan Poem*. He had composed it in 1901—discussing the title with Mrs. Gardner. In 1903, he arranged it especially for the palace. This time, the audience sat in the Music Room as usual, and there were two pianos on stage. Then suddenly came the clear notes of trumpets—far off! Three trumpeters had been stationed at the high windows overlooking the flower-filled court, their parts especially written into the original score—the effect electrifying.

In 1895, the Gardners had bought a Stradivarius in Paris. Mrs. Gardner lent it to Loeffler. "The instrument sounded most beautifully, the quality and brilliancy of tone being praised by everybody," he wrote her, after playing his own composition *Divertimento in A Minor* with the Boston Symphony Orchestra.

Tymoteusz Adamowski, Mrs. Gardner's earlier favorite

among violinists, had approached Loeffler "with a curiously unfriendly gleam in his eyes" and reminded him that he had "Mrs. Gardner's violin only for the year coming"; but Adamowski, when it was his turn, did not take good care of the instrument. The Stradivarius went back into Loeffler's keeping and in 1918 Mrs. Gardner gave it to him.

Loeffler gave Mrs. Gardner a viola d'amore in 1903, a practically obsolete instrument, a part for which he had introduced into one of his compositions.

In 1904, Mrs. Gardner asked Loeffler to give a concert at Fenway Court and to be sure to play the viola d'amore. He agreed, and then discovered that Kneisel, leader of the famous quartet in which Loeffler once played, was to be in the audience.

"Mr. Kneisel cannot be amused by a viola d'amore solo and as a distinguished connoisseur which he is, I respect him enough not to spoil his joy of being with you," Loeffler wrote Mrs. Gardner, refusing to play the composition she asked for.

"I loathe the silly old tune of 'Plaisir d'amore'—more, more—more than any musician in the world," Loeffler further said. And yet he could not bear to be harsh with Mrs. Gardner: ". . . for you alone I would do it once more and then forever swear to never do it again! but before brother musicians—No!"

Mrs. Jack always loved best the men who stood up to her and dared to say no. Her reply to Loeffler's long, fiery letter must have been typical of her at her most understanding best for he replied, "Of course. With greatest pleasure. Is 4 P.M. Sunday too late? or 5? One word from you will settle the matter. There is, of course, not much written for the viola d'amore but I will bring 2 things." [4]

"You don't owe me anything at all and you must accept my playing as a homage to you and Mr. Sargent," Loeffler had previously written to Mrs. Gardner, in February or March of 1903. John Singer Sargent was back in Boston in February of that year, painting portraits and adding to his murals in the Boston Public Library.

"May I come to see you this morning between 11 and 12?" Sargent wrote immediately upon arrival. "My first thought is to report myself to you. If I mustn't come, will you telephone me at the library?"

Sargent said he had arranged a sitting with Loeffler, whose portrait he was to paint for Mrs. Gardner. She hung it in her Yellow Room, on the ground floor of the palace, along with a watercolor sketch which Sargent painted this same year, called *Mrs. Gardner in the Courtyard at Fenway Court.*[5] In one of the Yellow Room cases she placed the viola d'amore, gift of Charles Martin Loeffler.

Sargent had a commission to paint President Theodore Roosevelt. "I still need sittings of the President's portrait, and every day it gets more difficult for him to give me any," he wrote to Mrs. Gardner, in regard to her invitation to him to use the Gothic Room as his studio. "I shall soon be back in Boston," he told her. "Hadn't I better first spend my promised few days with the Sears & have that off my mind, before taking up my delightful quarters at the Palazzo?"

On March 4, Sargent had arrived in Boston and soon began the portrait of young Mrs. William Crowninshield Endicott, Jr. "Auntie Belle turned up on Thursday, evidently to find out whether the portrait had really been begun," Louise Endicott's husband wrote. Sargent was at work at 163 Marlborough Street, and William Endicott announced that he "had left the artist free to paint Louise any size he wanted not to exceed three-quarters. So I am ruined, but one does not have a Sargent painted every day and when a woman has a nice figure it is a shame not to have more than a head and shoulders." [6]

What "Auntie Belle" (by virtue of a kinship on her husband's side) really wanted to know was when to expect her guest. Not dating his note, but heading it 12 Arlington Street (the Sears address), "This is to break it gently to you that I am arriving before lunch time this morning, preceded by trains of baggage," he finally wrote.

Sargent's big easel was set up in the Gothic Room and he selected a carved Italian armchair in which he placed his next sitter, Mrs. Fiske Warren. Her little daughter stood beside the chair, leaning her head against her mother. There was much pinning up and taking down of textiles as Sargent blocked out the light from first one window and then another, until he achieved the right effect. In the end, a stained-glass window, not appearing in the portrait, was left uncovered. Some of the clear glass windows gave the right amount of north light.

The portrait was nearly finished when Mrs. Jack's nephew J. Templeman Coolidge appeared with his camera. He took pictures of Mrs. Warren, looking her age and tired besides; her little girl looking cross—and he showed at the same time an alert, gay Mrs. Warren on canvas with an affectionate, contemplative little girl beside her. In one of several photographs, Mrs. Gardner appeared in a long, black street dress

247

turning her back to the camera as she often insisted on doing.

Sargent's beard was full and black—especially in one of the photographs showing him holding a paintbrush between his teeth.[7] His figure was still somewhat portly but Mrs. Jack no longer felt like challenging him to a foot-race, although she was still proud of her own slim figure and the fact that she was still fast on her feet. She was now much interested in Sargent's love life—if any—as she was where all her men friends were concerned. He asked her if he might bring Mrs. Hunter and Miss Ethel Smyth to see the palace and Mrs. Gardner promptly invited both ladies to lunch.

For some time, Mrs. Jack suspected that Sargent's interest in Mrs. Charles Hunter, a British beauty whom he had painted in 1898, was more than platonic. She was now a widow whom Sargent had "followed" to various European resorts and who, Mrs. Gardner suspected, had now followed him to America. Occasionally, Mrs. Gardner inquired about this supposed romance in her letters to Berenson. "Mrs. Tallyho" was the nickname they gave the lady and Berenson seems to have agreed that a hunt was on, Sargent the quarry. He escaped, however. Some years later, Mrs. Gardner was asked if Sargent had ever been "secretly married."

"I always thought so," she said. Her own friendship with Sargent progressed calmly and pleasantly, but for this one source of frustration: she never could find out anything about his private life.

Apparently Mrs. Gardner missed the beginning of Loeffler's romance with Elise Fay,[8] but she knew a good deal about what seemed to be the end of it and tried to help Elise. As early as 1886, Miss Fay, an amateur violinist, was writing "dear sweet Loeffler, as long as you love me I shall be happy . . . oh Loeffler, if I were only younger! Why was I born so soon!" Miss Fay was a wealthy girl but she felt that her age was "more an obstacle to our marriage than that of money." She arranged for Loeffler to stay with her at her family's summer place "to defray expenses" because he had recently lost money. "As to your work on the violin, it is understood that I shall be always with you and you shall work 2 or 3 hours regularly."

Elise built a house in Medfield, after her parents' death—because Loeffler liked Medfield, where he and Bunker had once gone, he to compose, Bunker to paint. But years went by and Elise had to be content with being told that she was Loeffler's best friend. Then suddenly, in 1904, Loeffler went abroad for an indefinite stay. He told Elise that he was tired of having her manage all his affairs. Meekly, she wrote him, after he had gone, "I claim nothing from you—you are free, absolutely free—and if accidentally a word slips from me which makes you feel I am claiming old rights or counting on old conditions, forgive me, dearest Martin."

In Belgium, Loeffler heard a young violinist by the name of Ysaye and wrote Mrs. Gardner asking her to befriend Ysaye when he came to America. Mrs. Gardner promptly asked Miss Fay to appoint a time and then called on her to talk over the Ysaye question. This was the beginning of a close friendship between Mrs. Jack and Elise Fay. Mrs. Gardner seems not to have known Elise previously but now was determined that she should not be lonely. How much she knew about the broken romance, no one mentioned, but it seems safe to say that she found out all she could.

Loeffler returned to the United States during the summer of 1905—his stay abroad much shorter than he expected. He married Elise Fay in 1910—doubtless in spite of Mrs. Gardner's best efforts to promote the match, rather than because of them. Meanwhile, Elise wrote constantly to Loeffler. Her letters were full of Mrs. Jack.

Thomas Russell Sullivan had married in 1899, his journal apparently given up in 1903 and all mention of Mrs. Gardner either given up or deleted after 1898. He must have been a loss to her circle, just as his observations are a loss to her story. But in 1904, Elise Fay took up the tale.

Mrs. Gardner and Elise went to Ysaye's first and, as it proved, his only recital the day after Christmas, 1904. Symphony Hall "was not well filled—which probably irritated him . . . He was furious all the time and pouted like a spoiled child and behind the scenes was like a wild animal— storming away because he had to play with a piano—his contract calling for an orchestra on every occasion." Elise said she didn't believe this, "for no manager would agree to such an expense in this country." There was to have been a second concert. Mrs. Gardner had arranged a large luncheon for Ysaye and his wife—but he canceled his next concert. He left for New York, telling Mrs. Gardner that he "couldn't stand hotel life" and leaving her to explain to her friends about what happened to the guest of honor.

Elise was sorry that Ysaye didn't see Mrs. Gardner's house. "It was wonderfully beautiful the other night, the whole house lighted by candles, hundreds and hundreds of them, on the occasion of a ball which she gave for a niece. Two car-loads of people came on from New York to attend and everyone was amazed at the beauty of the place. Miss Morgan told me that nothing they could do in New York could approach the interest which these surroundings gave to Mrs. Gardner's evening. She was quite overcome and could hardly speak as she went from room to room and would look out into the Court."

The niece was Catherine Gardner, granddaughter of Mrs. Gardner's brother-in-law, George Augustus. She was just nineteen and a very pretty girl with a beautiful figure. For Catherine's coming-out party, Mrs. Gardner wore white spangled net, white orchids in her hair and she also carried white orchids.

Discreet inquiries were made in behalf of Alice Roosevelt —now being called "Princess Alice"—who would have liked to come to Catherine Gardner's debutante party at Fenway Court. But Mrs. Gardner made it clear that no invitation would be forthcoming. Princess Alice would steal the limelight and Mrs. Jack wanted to be sure that on Catherine's party-night, no one shared the center of the stage.

There were to be a series of six dances at Fenway Court for Catherine and Mrs. Gardner found a way of adding to her guest list of young men. After an evening performance at the theater, she would go backstage, compliment everyone on a fine performance—and carry off all the young men in the cast to give them a supper. They were always hungry. Then she took them to whatever dancing party might be going on —so that there would be no dearth of partners for Catherine.

In March, 1905, Elise Fay wrote that Mrs. Gardner's "musicale last Thursday evening was a brilliant affair and the music an entire surprise to everyone." Nellie Melba, now at the height of her great career, was in Boston and she and her entire company gave the concert. "Melba was in superb voice and the best of spirits and sang a long programme."

Whenever Nellie Melba returned to Boston, she saw Mrs. Jack and sang for her. They had long talks together and when Melba wrote to Mrs. Gardner, she gave news of the son whom she adored. There had been an early, unhappy marriage when the nineteen-year-old girl from Australia had married Captain Charles Nesbit Armstrong, son of an Irish baronet. He left her to fend for herself and her child, finally divorcing her in 1901. It was a story Mrs. Gardner's sympathetic questioning could bring out without difficulty. Nellie Porter Mitchell took the name of "Melba" from Melbourne, Australia, and finally made her debut as Gilda in *Rigoletto* at the age of twenty-eight, doubtless being told that she was too old to begin an operatic career. But she was one of the great sopranos of all time—forty-five when Mrs. Gardner first knew her intimately, her voice at its height of power and range.

Melba wrote of Mrs. Gardner: "She was in the middle of this vast enterprise"—the building of Fenway Court—"when I first met her and she was naturally full of excitement. Every stone of the place had to be numbered and checked. Every precious piece of carving had to be packed in shavings and preserved from careless hands. Even the Italian plants in their original pots filled with Italian earth, made that perilous journey across the Atlantic and arrived by some miracle to flower under a foreign sun.

"Of course I was longing to see 'it' as she always described her palace, but 'it' was sternly guarded from all prying eyes until it was finished. Nobody, not even the President of the United States, would have been allowed to enter. Everything, inside and out had to be perfect before Mrs. Gardner would share her treasures. Meanwhile we had to be content with rumors . . . of which one was that a certain Italian prince was lingering in prison for allowing one of his pictures to be smuggled out of Italy . . ." This, of course, was Prince Chigi, who did not actually go to prison because of Mrs. Gardner's Botticelli Madonna.

Nellie Melba did not mention the date but remembered that "one day the summons came. Mrs. Gardner rang me up on the telephone. 'It's finished,' she said, a note of triumph in her voice. 'And you're going to be one of the first people to see it. May I call for you in my brougham this afternoon?' " [9]

Mrs. Gardner gave Melba the yellow diamond which the king of Cambodia had commented upon and doubtless coveted. But of this, Melba said nothing in her autobiography. She was anxious and worried about herself in 1905. A doctor had told her that her right lung was attacked and that her singing career might be at an end. She was the sole support of "the boy," as she called her son, now twenty-six, and she wondered what would become of him. A year later, he married the daughter of a London millionaire and his mother gave him a castle in Ireland and an annuity. Melba recovered her health and her voice was unimpaired.

Not dating her letter, Nellie Melba wrote to Mrs. Gardner. "I wear your beautiful yellow diamond very often and everyone admires it. You dear, kind friend to have given it to me. I shall never forget that evening."

"All Friday, I was at Fenway Court helping Mrs. Gardner at the Bazaar," Elise Fay wrote to Loeffler in May, 1905. "She telephoned for me early in the morning as though my coming was of great importance and when I got there I saw she did not need me a bit. Mrs. Adamowski told me she just wanted me around!" Mrs. Gardner had turned her Music Room into a "Japanese village" and had herself carried around "in a genuine jinrikisha" and Joseph Lindon Smith, now back in Boston with his wife, the beautiful Corinna, had written a Japanese play to be performed at repeated intervals on the stage of the Music Room.

Mrs. Gardner's "jinrikisha man was a real Japanese," *Town Topics* wrote. "All about were little pagoda-like booths with Japanese fittings and ornaments and . . . on the stage was a Japanese grove with a temple at one side and a Buddhist shrine nestled in the trees opposite. Japanese men and women wandered to and fro as villagers, some gazing at the booths as if seeking the most favorable chance to trade, while others were tradesmen themselves, saddled with trays of all kinds of attractive novelties of Japanese handcraft."

In the opinion of *Town Topics*, Joseph Lindon Smith's production was "a curious stage show." They seemed more interested in "an exhibition of jujitsu under the direction of Prof. Uchimura, who has been teaching at Harvard." The Fair was given in aid of the Sharon Sanitarium and the reason why it was "Japanese" was that Mrs. Gardner and many of her friends were deep in a Japanese phase, their interest stimulated by the Russo-Japanese War in 1904-1905.

Yamanaka, opening a successful importing shop in Boston, advertised that he had saved Oriental works of art from theft or destruction by foreign soldiers and he offered these for sale to Americans. Mrs. Gardner bought shrine doors and painted panels. From Bunkio Matsuki, a young Japanese student brought to Salem, Massachusetts, by Professor Edward Sylvester Morse, she bought gold paper screens painted with flowers—with which to mask the hot-air furnace pipes that her architect had insisted upon.

In 1904, Okakura-Kakuzo,[10] a young Japanese scholar, was appointed to the staff of the Boston Museum of Fine Arts. Mrs. Gardner promptly added him to her entourage. He flattered her, as all too many of her friends did—but he was not one of the salesmen who constantly cultivated her, and his flattery was subtle, with what was probably genuine affection behind it.

In 1905, Okakura wrote "The Stairway of Jade" for Mrs.

Gardner, a highly symbolic poem in appreciation of the beauty of Fenway Court and the genius of its mistress. He referred to Mrs. Gardner as "The Presence," and in this he was prophetic, because Fenway Court was so personal an achievement that Mrs. Jack's presence would always be felt there. But literal-minded Americans sometimes misunderstood Okakura's symbolism and asked to see Mrs. Gardner's "jade staircase"—feeling tricked and disappointed when they learned that her staircases were mere marble, or stone with marble balustrade.

Mrs. Jack was also interested in Chinese art and gave a Chinese luncheon at a Chinatown restaurant. She and Okakura graced the head of the table, there were twenty-four guests including Japanese art students and Caucasian painters. Mrs. Gardner wore a large hat with an ostrich feather that drooped over the rim. "Around her neck was a heavy gold chain, supporting a pendant of jade stone valued at $1500. Without the least sign of awkwardness, she manipulated a pair of chopsticks of ivory," observers said.

"Oh, our Mother in Boston, how we want to see you again," wrote one of the students, thanking Mrs. Gardner for the party.

Except for the years immediately following the death of her husband, Mrs. Gardner was always spoken of as surrounded by young men. She had little time for them while she was surrounded by workmen during the building of the palace. Now she appeared with a new group—the majority of them experts from the Museum of Fine Arts.

Since 1876, the Museum had occupied a building covering most of the south side of Copley Square, with Trinity Church for its neighbor to the east. It was a huge affair of red brick, with colonnades and arches picked out in yellow in the best American railroad-station Gothic, reminiscent of the Hotel Boylston, Jack Gardner's first home. In 1899, the Museum trustees bought twelve acres of land on Huntington Avenue through to the Fenway. The land was close to Mrs. Gardner's and she was to have a huge gray-granite neighbor, but in spite of the trouble she gave her architect she finished her place first, before the Museum was begun in 1907.[11]

Matthew Stewart Prichard, an Englishman, became secretary to the director of the Boston Museum of Fine Arts in 1902 and joined Mrs. Gardner's inner circle of friends almost immediately. He was exceedingly handsome, thirty-seven years old to Mrs. Gardner's sixty-two—and she was struck by his middle name. Was he a royal Stewart like herself? Indeed he was, he said.

On August 14, 1902, Samuel D. Warren, President of the Board of Trustees wrote to Mrs. Gardner, "Mr. Prichard leads me to hope that the Museum Building Committee can obtain the benefit of your views as to the best mode of procedure . . . I assure you the Committee will be very glad to give careful consideration to any suggestion you may be willing to make . . ." No women were appointed to the board of trustees, although there was usually a Mr. Gardner among the men. Willard T. Sears was not the architect (it was McKim, Mead and White), and Mr. Sears might have warned the building committee against letting Mrs. Jack have so much as an anonymous finger in their pie, lest all the stonemasons quit.

At least at first, Mrs. Jack was discreet with her suggestions. She thought that John Singer Sargent should be asked to decorate some of the walls of the new museum building, since that past master at portraying his contemporaries had decided that he wanted nothing so much as to be a muralist. And in due course, Sargent produced processions of Greek maidens in pale colors who looked like nice Boston girls being pure-minded but self-conscious about their classic drapery.

A controversy developed, however, concerning a large collection of plaster casts housed in the old museum. When the cast collection was made, it was the pride of Boston. People brought up on it felt as though it were old home week when they actually visited the Vatican Museum, the Louvre or the British Museum. They recognized joyfully the already familiar Laocoön group, the Venus de Milo and the Parthenon Frieze and only a few noticed any difference between plaster and marble! Casts were educational, the public said. They were hideous, said Matthew Stewart Prichard—and Mrs. Jack sided with him, although her own Beacon Street casts were now set below and over the stage in her new Music Room.

In 1904, Edward Robinson, Director and Curator of Antiquities, was given a leave of absence to travel among the islands of Greece. Prichard became acting director, and he proceeded to act. He installed a new cataloguing system which was much needed, and wrote a dissertation on how a museum ought to be run, which was actually none of his business. He also provoked an open fight on the tender subject of plaster casts. Robinson, on his return, sized up the situation as a house hopelessly divided and accepted the position of director of the Metropolitan Museum of Art in New York City, much to the consternation of many. The matter of storing or displaying casts came to a vote and casts lost by a narrow margin. Prichard had won, but he had also lost, for he was not appointed director as he had hoped. Ill-equipped to work under others, he resigned, became an art teacher at Simmons College temporarily, and then went abroad.

"Dear, honest, straight-forward and mis-represented Matt," one of Prichard's friends called him. He was "lovable but cantankerous." Mrs. Gardner preserved the letters Prichard wrote to her—all 285 of them. She sent him money when he was down on his luck, and Red Cross packages when he was interned in Germany during World War I.

It was typical of Mrs. Gardner to begin by asking Prichard to take her around the Boston Museum to "instruct" her. "You impose too great a burden on me," he replied. "There is much I can learn from you, little in which I can instruct you . . ." but he promised to meet her "at the Museum at 11 o'clock, with impatience." [12]

During the summer of 1902, while Mrs. Gardner was in Brookline, Prichard lived in the unfinished palace in a small apartment on the ground floor—the present Macknight Room with its bath in short supply of hot water. He was there until October 27, when he wrote, "Please not to forget tomorrow to give your photograph to me, not that it is necessary for me to possess any memorial of you. Your kindness is especially before me today, now that all my little property has been removed to Arlington Street 3. It will be pleasant to break my rule against property in this particularly attractive direction."

Minnie Bourget had referred to the group of young men surrounding Mrs. Gardner in 1893 as the "Isabella Club." After Fenway Court was built, the new Isabella Club was larger and had more artists in its roster. Some of them were young only in comparison with the lady "Ysabella" as she now often signed herself. Dodge Macknight, for example, was forty-one when Mrs. Gardner first knew him personally. He was born in Providence, Rhode Island, studied painting in Paris, and had lived for some time in Arles, in southern France, the intimate friend of Van Gogh. Arles was famous not only for its antiquities but for beautiful women and Macknight married an *Arlesienne* (according to the papers), bringing her back to the United States to live at East Sandwich, Massachusetts, on Cape Cod.

Mrs. Gardner rarely missed an exhibit at Doll and Richards—that Boston art gallery where she had bought one of her first pictures, the Manet landscape. She now caught sight of something much more gay—Macknight's watercolors painted in the "luminist school." He was fond of purple, and so was she.

Macknight's first letter to Mrs. Gardner was dated January 17, 1901. He thanked her for letting him see Fenway Court —while the palace was being built. A year later he thanked Mrs. Jack for buying one of his pictures.

Modest to a degree, Macknight made fun of himself and wrote letters that must have delighted Mrs. Gardner. He was a fairly frequent guest at Fenway Court by 1903 and wrote, "If I could get you to stand before the staircase [at Doll and Richards] and receive people as you did in your Music Room when the Thursday Evening Club was there—(no wonder they were jealous of you, you make them all look like thirty cents)—if I could get you, I say, to receive people, I should have a tremendous artistic and financial success and incidentally they would jam in and smash Doll and Richards to pieces.

"And this, by antithesis, brings me round to what I wanted to say in the first place—will you *please* come incognito or incognita, some time Thursday afternoon and see my pictures as I am hanging them?"

It would almost seem that Mrs. Gardner, just for fun, took this very nice man at his word and "received" for him at his show, because Macknight soon became so popular that eventually Doll and Richards had to put up a velvet rope to keep purchasers at bay—then letting it down so that people could scramble for the watercolors they had decided to buy.

In March, 1904, Macknight wrote another humorous letter which had a result he never dreamed of. ". . . The only glimpse I have had of you this winter," he began, "was at the opening night of the Whistler exhibition when people all about me were madly scrambling on benches and up each other's backs to get a peep at you.

"Can't I see you at a little closer range? Won't you do me the honor to run into Doll and Richards this week Thursday afternoon? You don't know me very well, but I hope it is well enough to be aware that I am not trying to drag you in there to buy my pictures by the bushel to start a Macknight Room at Fenway Court. I know your interests are centered in other things and you may be sure that I shall not be saying to myself as you go out—'stingy woman etc. etc.'"

Mrs. Gardner actually bought ten watercolors by Dodge

Macknight and completely flabbergasted this pleasant person by hanging them in a room on the street floor of the palace —which she called the Macknight Room.

Mrs. Gardner had John Briggs Potter, Keeper of Paintings at the Museum, sketch a portrait of Prichard which she hung in the Macknight Room. Then the handsome John Briggs Potter himself was painted by Denman Ross, an artist who had inherited wealth and who was a Museum trustee and art lecturer at Harvard. It would seem as though Mrs. Gardner's artist friends all sat around painting each other's portraits during the first years at Fenway Court.

It must have amused Mrs. Gardner to have Mrs. William C. Endicott write to ask for some young men to come to a party at her summer place. Mrs. Gardner replied politely to "dear Louise"—"Proctor has taken his mother to Province-town and so many of the art museum people are away that the others have more than double work. So I fear all these young men will have to live below their privileges . . ." Meanwhile, of course, Mrs. Gardner's Brookline gardens were always dotted over with young men painting flowers. Her Green Hill music room was rarely silent of an evening and if any niece of hers needed an escort, she had but to come by and pick one out.

Mrs. Gardner finally sold her Beacon Street house to Eben Draper, who pulled down what was left of it and built a new house on the site. She had stipulated that no one should have her old address—152 Beacon Street so Mr. Draper had agreed to think of another number.

With the completion of Fenway Court, Mrs. Jack seemed to enter upon an era of success. She had surrounded herself with new friends and had become accustomed to life without her husband. There were troubles in store, however, and the rumblings of a storm—if anyone had realized it.

TWENTY-FOUR

Public Praise and Blame

MRS. GARDNER HAD been looking forward to showing her palace to the public. Her architect had warned her that she could admit only two hundred people at a time because of building regulations so she had tickets printed to be given out, two hundred a day, during open days. How often she would open her house to the public remained undecided, but she was inclined to be generous.

"Cousin Belle is flitting about, eager to see how it all affects people and chatting with those she knows and ready to explain everything to enquiring people," Louise Endicott observed. "She has become a public character and the papers are full of her doing. I do not think it is exaggerated to say that the building with its wonderful Italian atmosphere she has created is a work of genius." [1]

Although she loved to identify herself with royal Stuarts, Mrs. Jack was inclined to an idealistic view of the American public. She visualized happy citizens walking reverently through her palace, absorbing culture and thanking her for giving them this opportunity. She learned almost immediately that even when the public is made up of a majority of people of good will, there are always vandals.

Someone chipped the marbles. Loathing the cold suspicion of glass cases, Mrs. Gardner had few if any, when she first opened Fenway Court. Small objects disappeared. She saw a woman turning over the corner of a tapestry as if to study the weave. Thinking that here, perhaps, was an ardent needlewoman, Mrs. Gardner went over to explain some of the subtleties of Gobelin versus Aubusson. But the visitor had a pair of scissors in her hand and was just about to snip off a souvenir. "Tapestries slashed" was a headline in the papers.

Something would have to be done and Mrs. Gardner conceived the idea of making her blocks of two hundred tickets available to selected groups. She charged a dollar admission to help defray the expense of guards—and further to discourage irresponsible curiosity-seekers. Harvard students would behave themselves, Mrs. Jack felt sure. Those most likely to benefit from a visit to Fenway Court would be enrolled in some history of art course so she handed over her tickets to Professor von Mach of the Harvard art department. No tickets were given to the press.

A newspaperman from the *Record and Advertiser* went to the professor and "had the impudence to ask for a ticket," the professor told Mrs. Gardner. Another reporter tried to crash the gate at Fenway Court on the grounds that he had lost his ticket, but alleged classmates failed to recognize him. It was all good copy, although such poor press relations as to be almost incredible. It was great fun for the papers to imply that violence was used and reporters "ejected"; that even genuine Harvard students went sadly away for lack of a dollar.

Professor von Mach, apparently unaware of the part he played while dealing with the impudence of a reporter, wrote to thank Mrs. Gardner and to tell her not to mind "the foolish notices in the paper . . ."

Tickets were offered to teachers of art in public and private schools, but Mrs. Gardner decided that no sketches could be made and no notes taken. Corinna Putnam Smith "served as guardian-usher . . . the hours being from ten in the morning till three in the afternoon" and Mrs. Gardner was on hand— no longer friendly but suspicious and by afternoon a bundle of nerves, Corinna said.

"I entered the Titian Room, where a young woman, timid-looking, almost pathetic, was gazing" at the *Europa,* Joe Smith's wife, Corinna, recalled. "On observing that" this young woman "was about to jot down something in a minute notebook, I was about to inform her kindly that this was against regulations, when Mrs. Gardner pounced upon her like a fury, shouting, 'Don't you know you are breaking a rule?'"

The girl burst into tears and fled from the room. However, Mrs. David Kimball, a friend of Mrs. Gardner's and also a guardian-usher that day, had seen the whole thing. It was she who had given the girl, a teacher from a Worcester high school, the ticket to Fenway Court. She promptly called Mrs. Gardner to task and Isabella, already sorry for her burst of temper, wrote to invite the teacher to spend a day entirely alone at Fenway Court, with luncheon served. She could take all the notes she wished. Mrs. Gardner greeted her guest on her arrival from Worcester by an early morning train and took her back to the train at night, as she had done for many a famous personage.[2]

Mrs. Gardner's cruelty was talked about but few people said a word about her efforts to make amends. Disappointed sightseers, unable to get a ticket to see Fenway Court, began to say that the Isabella Stewart Gardner Museum ought to be open all the time, like the Museum of Fine Arts.

A man, signing himself as "A Western Visitor" wrote a long letter that was published in the New York *Tribune*'s "Illustrated Sunday Supplement." The Western visitor had heard that Mrs. Gardner's palace was "a real piece of Venice, filled with art treasures from all Europe." He said he had come East to see it and after looking over Boston Common he asked a policeman where the palace was. The officer didn't know. A theater ticket broker had an office over on Tremont Street, so the visitor went over there to ask for tickets to Mrs. Gardner's palace. "There are no tickets," said the young woman in charge. "The last open day was a week ago and all the tickets were taken a month in advance" and she didn't think there would be any more. Why the visitor thought he would find tickets to a museum at the office of a theater ticket broker, he didn't say.

The visitor professed to be surprised and shocked because the tickets cost a dollar. He thought it was a public museum, he wrote. Told that he could at least see the outside of the building, he got directions to the Back Bay district of Boston and, on arriving at Fenway Court, recorded further unhappy impressions.

"There stood the Venetian palace, quite alone in the center of a barren marsh . . . the surroundings are—well they are striking. For background, there are the tall, smoking chimneys of a group of breweries and distilleries and the odor of hops in the air. The foreground is one of the dumping-places of Boston garbage and a picturesque group of half-clad Italians was sorting a living out of the refuse . . ."

The anonymous visitor saw a sign over the door of Fenway Court "which said that the public entrance was on the street around the corner. 'It really is a public museum then,' " he told himself. " 'Those people at the theater agency are slandering this woman.' " He "made haste to ring the bell and an attendant in overalls and a jumper answered.

" 'Museum closed,' he muttered.

" 'For repairs?'

" 'Repairs, nothing,' he growled. 'It's closed for the season.'

" 'And when will it open again?'

" 'She knows,' the man said, jerking a thumb presumably in the direction of his mistress, 'and she ain't telling!' "

"When walking away," the Western visitor "met a solemn-faced individual sitting on a barrel which some scavenger had dumped upon the Fen. His long hair, careless clothes and flowing tie bespoke the artist.

" 'So you, too are shut out!' he said sadly. 'I have tried for three weeks to gain admission and they always refuse. Think what it would mean to me. Why, some of the best names are on her paintings.' "

The artist reeled off some "best names" he said he had gotten from a catalogue "a woman tossed into the roadway the other day as she was driving away from a private view . . ."

The visitor next went over to Cambridge and interviewed a Harvard man whose remarks he claimed to quote verbatim. "When the time came for tickets to be given out," the students had been "lined up worse than a band of women at a bargain sale . . . Then out came von Mach announcing that the tickets cost $1 per and about 250 of the boys turned away in disappointment . . ."

After testifying to the low ebb of Harvard student finances, the visitor said he found "a clever little woman who lives in the suburbs" and who had gotten a ticket "through an intimate friend of an intimate friend." She said the ticket was " 'good for as many looks as you can take in an hour, no overtime allowed. The attendants rush you along following the route set down in the little catalogue for which you pay a quarter . . .' "

The papers began enlarging on the theme that Mrs. Gardner had been allowed to bring objects of art through customs in Boston and had not paid duty because Fenway Court was an educational institution. Unless Fenway Court were open free at all times, with every room on view, it was not an educational institution at all, the papers argued. It was just a private home.

Perhaps it was Mr. Swift, Mrs. Gardner's man of business, or one of her nephews, who foresaw trouble and suggested that it would be a good idea to invite Collector of Customs Lyman to meet the press at Fenway Court for an interview. Unfortunately, Mr. Lyman couldn't be bothered; but instead, he spoke patronizingly to reporters. "I don't expect to receive a complaint," he said. The Isabella Stewart Gardner Museum was incorporated and acting entirely within its legal rights. He "hadn't heard anything about a question of legality except through the newspapers." And this source he dismissed with contempt.

As to the fee charged, "The Art Museum and the Natural

History Museum charge admission fees occasionally to defray expenses . . . Why shouldn't Mrs. Gardner?"

"You don't think the cases differ?" a reporter asked.

"No."

"But what—"

"But there is nothing more to say. Everything is open and above-board, so far as I know, and until I am satisfied of something different I shall let the matter rest." So ended the interview as told by an angry press.

The "Western visitor" had decided that Mrs. Gardner was "as grim as the Gothic lions outside her gate," but a woman writer named Priscilla Leonard got past the gates and wrote an article for *Harper's Bazaar* for July, 1903 which was full of praise.

Miss Leonard was sure that the first-century marble throne in the courtyard had once been occupied by Cleopatra herself. This must have pleased Mrs. Jack. The present Early Italian Room was the Chinese Room in 1903 and Miss Leonard rejoiced over two large vases of yellow orchids which stood on the table covered by a dull green cloth. Mrs. Gardner's portrait by Zorn was in this room and the color of her dress of brilliant yellow was picked up by the orchids.

It took "ten uniformed policemen and nearly as many trim maids besides to do the honors of the public exhibition days." Many visitors came in carriages so there was a traffic problem outside and wraps to dispose of within, but everything was arranged for the comfort of visitors, according to *Harper's Bazaar*. Pinkerton's men were the detectives spoken of as on the spot but actually, Mrs. Gardner had a much better idea. She relied on Harvard men.

A corps of Harvard students was organized to be on hand at Fenway Court each public day. Not only were they carefully selected as to integrity, family background and appreciation of art—but they also had to have high marks! This was because Mrs. Gardner chose to open her palace on a day just preceding a vacation. Only students on the Dean's List were allowed to cut classes at such a time. This was carefully explained to Mrs. Gardner in a letter.

One of the Harvard students remembered all his life how proud he was to be among those invited to go over to Fenway Court.[3] He remembered Mrs. Gardner, a tiny woman with flashing blue eyes. She lined him up with the rest and then produced red ribbons, one of which she personally tied to each man's arm. Looking up at him as she tied his ribbon, she thanked him for coming and made him feel like a knight-errant in the service of his queen.

Radcliffe girls also helped Mrs. Gardner on these occasions, but their memories of them were less romantic. One of them said that Mrs. Jack wore an outrageous yellow wig, had powder and rouge on her face—and watched everyone, including the watchers.

All seemed to be going well but on January 11, 1904, just a little over a year after the palace opened, the papers had a story they played up with gusto. The government officials had ruled that "where a 'museum' was open only four days a month for three months, allowing only 2,100 as the maximum number of visitors for $1 each, it could not properly be called a public museum."

"It was announced at the Treasury Department today that Mrs. Jack Gardner of Boston has just paid $200,000 in duties when threatened with legal proceedings for violation of the customs laws in connection with the importation of statuary and works of art in 1898 . . ." the New York *Times* said—and the story was all too true.

With reason, the press wondered about "the future of Mrs. Gardner's museum, now that she has just paid the duties . . ." Henry W. Swift replied briefly and with bitterness: "It is not improbable that the museum will be closed for all time, to the public."

"People seem to hate me! Why?" [4] Mrs. Gardner wrote Berenson nearly two years later. But she herself had not given up her dream of creating a supremely beautiful place, to be shown to the public after her death. "At any rate, I shall always go straight to my goal," she said.

"So this lady of the Fens knows after all *why she is hated*," Berenson replied. "Everybody is—in the measure that he goes straight for his own goals, because he is sure to spoil the fun of other people, also amiably engaged in making for their goals . . . Your enemies are one of the things that attract me to you. They make me think of mine—curse them."

Rallying from blows both to her pride and her purse, Mrs. Gardner resolved to buy nothing expensive for a long time to come. However, she had always loved Charles Eliot Norton, the man who had awakened her mind to Dante and opened her eyes to Italian art. He was over seventy now and wrote to her about his "motives" which made him "desire to dispose of some of" his pictures, rare books and mediaeval manuscripts. Put briefly, the motive was money. He had unmarried daughters accustomed to a life of leisure with no resources except culture, of which they may have had too much.

Professor Norton made out a list of items he proposed to sell, beginning with his *Marriage Feast at Cana,* by Tintoretto. He loved it. Taking it down from his study wall, the bare space hurt him but he wanted Mrs. Gardner to have it and she hung it close to the entrance to that holy of holies, her private chapel. Mr. Norton placed values, carefully verified through dealers, on each item and his total came to $13,500.

Mrs. Gardner sent him a check for $15,000 and succeeded with tact and affection in making him believe she had much the best of the bargain. So discreet was she, knowing how hurt his pride would be if anyone guessed that he was selling his belongings, that the secret never came out and one of the Norton children accused Mrs. Gardner later of accepting valuable gifts which she failed to acknowledge because of her "egocentricity."

By 1906, Mrs. Gardner's bank account had recovered to the point where she thought she would like to go abroad again. "Colli-Joe" Smith had been in Spain—sending her fine early Spanish stone carvings. He urged her to return to this little-visited country, although bandits still roamed the hills, descending on unwary travelers as in the days when Mrs. Jack was in Spain with her husband.

A dangerous adventure still intrigued Isabella. She engaged a courier—perhaps the one who in Sicily had won all bets by being able to put up with her temper. She further fortified herself with lessons in jujitsu, having become fascinated by the art at the time of the exhibitions at her Japanese festival. Thus equipped, she set out for Spain, acquiring there among other things, the stone effigy of a knight in armor. She disturbed his sleep to have him shipped to Boston, where he would eventually find repose again in her "Spanish Chapel," still to be created at Fenway Court.

Back in 1903, Joseph Lindon Smith had written at length to Isabella about a fifteenth-century artist named Piero della Francesca. Piero's strong drawing and the simplicity of his frescoes attracted Colli Smith. Mrs. Gardner liked the life-story of the painter—son of a shoemaker, apprenticed to Florentine masters, then making his way from city to city, working for a time for Lionello d'Este.

Any member of the d'Este family interested Mrs. Jack. "I want you to get and read at once Julia Cartwright's *Isabella d'Este,*" Berenson told her. "Change the time and the circumstances and the Mrs. Isabella Gardner that I know is singularly like the Isabella d'Este of whom I read . . ."

Mrs. Gardner undoubtedly bought the book. She read, among other matters, Isabella d'Este's letter to an artist employed to work on rooms in Mantua. "You can paint whatever you like inside the cupboards, so long as it is not ugly, because if it is, you will have to paint it all over at your own expense and be sent to pass the winter in the dungeon . . ." This sounded like the building of Fenway Court. [5]

Isabella of Boston promised to send Joseph Lindon Smith $40,000 to buy *Hercules* by Piero della Francesca partly because the painter had worked for a d'Este. Then came the laws against the exportation of Italian art and the *Hercules* was on the list of masterpieces not to leave the country. It had been simple enough for Colnaghi's agents to paint over the Chigi Botticelli and smuggle the canvas out of Italy disguised as a modern picture. Piero's *Hercules* was a fresco, painted directly on plaster before it was dry. A large chunk of thick plaster would have to go with the picture. Besides, both Mrs. Gardner and Joe Smith had gone on record against smuggling.

Now, in 1906, Colli Smith was abroad when Mrs. Gardner proposed that he travel by auto through Italy with her. He accepted with pleasure.

Colli wanted to show Isabella "the dear little Umbrian town of Borgo San Sepulchro" where Piero della Francesca had painted the *Hercules*. Mrs. Gardner wanted still more to see the painting she now owned but could not possess. The *Hercules* was in Florence, it developed, at the house of a dealer who thought he might get a "permission to export, after all."

Hercules was very properly muscular, rather low of forehead, with an innocent, bewildered expression on his face which was somewhat less than heroic. Mrs. Gardner was pleased with him, however. Permission was granted and the fresco was sent to Robert in Paris, to await her further orders. [6] She would have various and sundry fees plus crating and shipping expenses, not included in her plans for an economical trip abroad.

As usual, Berenson's summer travel plans did not coincide with Mrs. Gardner's, so he wrote to her about a portrait of Pope Innocent X by Velázquez, which Roger Fry of the Metropolitan Museum in New York "will move heaven and earth to get." He said that "Mrs. Potter Palmer [of Chicago] only awaits my approval of the picture to purchase" it. So, if "Dear Isabella" (they had arrived at first-name terms) could raise

$100,000, she must let him know. Perhaps she would rather "step aside."

At the end of one of the letters concerning the portrait, "Of course, I may conclude that the picture, though wonderful, is not Velázquez," Berenson wrote.

Mrs. Gardner did not step aside, and the picture was not by Velázquez.

Part of Mrs. Gardner's time, while she was in Europe in 1906, was spent in looking at objects of art which belonged to her but which, for various reasons, she could not bring home. In Rome, Richard Norton took her to see her Graeco-Roman statue. She knew just where it should go in the courtyard at home, and she probably advanced more money to help Norton in his efforts to have it sent to her. Then at the Palazzo Barberini were six tapestries, part of a series of ten which Mrs. Gardner had contracted to buy in 1903. Mrs. Gardner went to see them and was especially pleased with the two panels from the "Archduke Albert and Archduchess Isabella" series. Consent of the Italian government was already on file, so they could have been shipped to Boston. But Isabella worried about the American import duty and still hoped the law would be changed in a year or two—so she had the tapestries sent to Robert in Paris. This would protect them in case the Italian government decided to repudiate their agreement (made in 1899) as had happened in connection with the statue.

The tapestries had been part of the great Barberini collection, sold to Mrs. Charles Mather Ffoulke.[7] In 1899, the Ffoulkes were living in Florence. Mr. Ffoulke had made a fortune in the wool business but was crippled by rheumatism. Once a man of commanding stature he became pitiably dwarfed; but he had married Sarah Cushing of New York, an artist, and together they studied languages, paintings—and tapestries. Experience in the textile business was a good foundation and Charles Ffoulke became the leading collector and expert on tapestries in his time. The Barberini tapestries—most of which had been carefully stored for years—were in mint condition and the Ffoulkes wanted them all. It takes more than an ordinary fortune to become a great collector, however. In statements made to Mr. Swift in 1903 on Mrs. Gardner's behalf, Charles Ffoulke told the story.

"My fortune was not large enough to permit me to buy alone all of the Barberini tapestries, consisting of 135 pieces, and so my wife mortgaged her home, 2011 Massachusetts Avenue, Washington, D.C. to join me in the purchase." Evidently Sarah Ffoulke, as an artist, could no more resist the tapestries than could her husband as a collector. Mrs. Ffoulke "has been sole owner of part of the collection from the beginning and all of the 'Abraham and Rebecca' series . . . have belonged to her since they were originally bought." She brought one piece of the "Abraham and Rebecca" series home with her but the rest were still in Italy, labeled with her name.

"When I brought part of the 'Archduke Albert and Archduchess Isabella' series to this country in 1890 and 1891, I presented [these and other pieces], to my wife for the decoration of her house—our home in Washington, D.C.," Mr. Ffoulke went on. Two pieces of the "Archduke Albert and Archduchess Isabella" series were still in Italy, but Mr. Ffoulke guaranteed his wife's legal possession of them. He urged Mr. Swift to take care of his letter "inasmuch as I may not be living when the tapestries are called for and delivered," he said. Mrs. Gardner agreed to take the tapestries by 1908, paying $33,750 for the "Abraham and Rebecca" series; $7500 for a tapestry called the "Museum Piece" and $45,000 for the "Archduke" series.

Of course, Isabella of Boston loved the "Archduke Albert and Archduchess Isabella" series best. The set of five panels, each nearly fourteen by sixteen feet, told a sort of continued story supposed to show the Archduchess Isabella as heroine; the quest for her hand in marriage as the subject. There were fairy-tale castles in the background and in the foreground, people seemingly almost as large as life wore magnificent robes, plumed hats and jewels. Richly caparisoned horses pranced; a little dog, not unlike Mrs. Gardner's favorites, wore a jeweled collar. Borders of fruit and flowers were a botanist's delight.

Later, experts more learned than Charles Ffoulke pointed out that the tapestries were woven in Brussels in the second quarter of the sixteenth century—before the time of Archduke Albert, who was governor of the Low Countries in the seventeenth century. The subject was really the life of Cyrus the Great. But if anybody told this to Isabella of Boston, she disregarded it, listing the tapestries in her own catalogue with Archduchess Isabella still the heroine.

Mrs. Gardner went once more to Venice. She visited her old friends, the antiquarians—determined not to spend much money this time. But like many a woman who enters a shop just looking, she acquired bargains.

An embittered Ariana Curtis complained that nice people never came to Venice any more and that she had refused to rent her Palazzo Barbaro to the fast crowd of newly-rich.

The last report of Mrs. Katherine de Kay Bronson was that she disguised herself by wearing a red wig, when she went around Venice helping the poor. Everybody recognized her but the tactful Italians pretended not to know the Donna Incognita. She had left Venice, however, and died in Florence in 1901.[8] Mrs. Gardner's former young men were now middle-aged, while she was not, and never would be, willing to admit that she was growing old. Some, like Tirindelli, had migrated to America, and others, like Ralph Curtis, had married and were pretty much under wifely surveillance. Isabella still loved Venice but she left without much regret.

In Paris, Mrs. Gardner visited more of her own out-of-reach belongings, stored with Robert. She saw for the first time Joseph Lindon Smith's discovery, *Santa Engracia,* and could not help but be charmed with it. Robert's bill for storage was anything but a pleasant surprise, however. She could not help thinking how much better she could spend the money. Mrs. Jack resisted the temptations of Paris couturiers except for a beautifully cut, daringly décolleté evening dress, a dinner gown of black velvet with Venetian lace and perhaps another gown or two—all in black.

Reaching London, feeling poor but unrepentant, she wore old clothes and summoned Henry James to renew the old friendship. Dating his letter January 3, 1907, Henry James told Ariana Curtis all about it.

"I saw Mrs. Gardner (went up to see her) in town and was divided between finding her battered, depleted, disfigured, and finding how fond one is of her, always, for the perfect terms one is on with her, her admirable ease, temper and *facilité à vivre*. She struck me as what she literally was and now is—a little ancient, rusty 'caretaker' or doorkeeper taking a holiday on money carefully saved up!" [9]

It sounds as though the ever histrionic Isabella must have been enjoying her role as a bankrupt; but she was well aware that new clothes could be brought through the American customs as used if she wore them, so she was doubtless dressed differently when she met Mrs. Emily Chadbourne in London. Mrs. Chadbourne was living in a large London town house which she had leased for several years and in which she entertained international Society. Her father had been R. T. Crane of Crane Plumbing fame; her divorced husband was Thomas Lincoln Chadbourne, a Chicago lawyer of Washington, D.C. They had been among the "fabulously rich people" whom Berenson referred to in "the City of Dirt," as he described Chicago.

Mrs. Gardner met Mrs. Chadbourne for the first time in London, however. Looking around the bare walls and sparsely furnished rooms, Isabella concluded that the London landlord had provided only minimum furnishings. There was room and to spare for all those pictures, tapestries and furnishings which, because they cost much to store in Paris, she had ordered sent to London. But London warehouse costs might be just as high.

The two ladies came to an agreement which apparently it never occurred to either of them to write down. Mrs. Chadbourne would love to have all this furniture and the art objects to decorate her London home. What a saving in storage fees! Isabella Gardner set sail for America, happily conscious of a job well done.

In August, 1908, the blow fell! Mrs. Chadbourne suddenly decided to break up her London establishment and come home. She had lived abroad for more than two years and was entitled to bring home household effects free of duty. The hoped-for-remission of duty on antique objects of art had not gone into effect and she thought she might just as well bring along Mrs. Gardner's belongings and claim exemption for them. She would be doing Mrs. Gardner such a favor!

TWENTY-FIVE

The Customs Affair

*I*SABELLA remained comparatively inconspicuous between the months after her return from Europe in 1906 and the breaking of the notorious customs affair in August, 1908. She was observed by *Town Topics*—first decorously attending lectures on the "Art of Poetry" during Lent in 1907; then judging the dancing at the "All Fool's Day Festival" at the Women's Athletic Club for the benefit of the George Junior Republic. In December, she was in her box at the San Carlo Opera on opening night, the Bellamy Storers being her guests.

A new young man, Henry Davis Sleeper,[1] wrote that Mrs. Gardner asked him to tea with the San Carlo Opera Company. The cast were "somewhat less interesting than cattle," he said. "They didn't sing"—the only music being provided by Clayton Johns and Proctor, who "tried the piano." A lady from the opera company looked at her watch.

"I have an hour and three quarters yet," she said, "and I wish to have *all* these pictures *explained* to me." Sleeper was asked to show her around—an assignment which rather floored him, although he had just embarked upon a career of interior decorator, his own Gloucester home to be the future "Beauport," a museum.

The Bellamy Storers of Washington had decided to spend the winter in an apartment on the Fenway—a fine new building overlooking what was beginning to be a park with a charming waterway, instead of a city dump in marshland. They invited Mrs. Gardner to a dinner party in honor of William Henry O'Connell, Roman Catholic Bishop of Boston and future cardinal. Mrs. Charles S. Hamlin, also a guest, remembered the scene.[2]

"Mrs. Storer wrote me to say how glad they were that we could come and she hoped I would not mind wearing either a high neck dress or covering my neck with a shawl, as the Cardinal [as Mrs. Hamlin called him] did not approve of low necks . . ."

Mrs. Hamlin decided on her "white satin with a white lace

270

shawl." She was standing in front of a mirror at the Storer's, having trouble with the shawl when "Mrs. John L. Gardner swept in—she looked at me smilingly and said, 'Evidently Mrs. Storer wrote you that the Cardinal did not approve of low necks. I crossed the ocean with him and we sat at the same dining table and I know what he likes.' She threw off her wrap and revealed herself in the lowest of low necks in her usual beautifully-cut black dress and with her famous back in full view.

"In those days our evening dresses had small puffs for sleeves but not so Mrs. Gardner's. Her sleeves were simple bands of black ribbon—over the shoulder. In fact most of her dress was on the floor. She whirled around and went into the drawing room while we humbly followed but in time to see her sweep a low curtsy to the Cardinal and kiss his ring."

In accordance with her economy program, Isabella seems to have given up her auto. She no longer went to the rambling summer home in Beverly. Instead, she made a series of summer visits to friends and became past mistress of the art of wangling rides in other people's cars.

"Fancy, dear Mr. Andrew, I have this moment got your letter," Isabella wrote in 1908. She had been making a round of visits and her mail had been delayed. "Does your delightful invitation still hold out? If so, I can go to you for the night, on Tuesday 10th or on Wednesday 11th. And may I send my maid and small portmanteau down by some train and will you motor me down?" If Brookline were "too far" for "the motor" which would have to take her all the way to Eastern Point, just beyond Gloucester, she could meet Mr. Andrew at Fenway Court.

A. Piatt Andrew was not a new friend, for he and Mrs. Gardner had met in 1903. The close friendship between them, however, was just now to develop. On April 15, 1903, Andrew had written to his parents: "Today has been a gala day for me! Today the Board of Overseers confirmed the votes of President and Fellows and I was made assistant professor of economics for five years. I think I am about the youngest professor in the University! . . ." The university was Harvard. Andrew was thirty.

"Today I had another delightful experience. Through Miss Beaux's ingenious machinations, I was invited by Mrs. Jack Gardner to visit her new Fenway Court with Miss Beaux and Miss Irwin (Dean of Radcliffe) and Harry Drinker"—who was Miss Beaux's nephew. "We drove out there and were received at the entrance by Mrs. Gardner herself who showed us the wonderful place from top to bottom."

A. Piatt Andrew said he had "never seen any house in the world as beautiful . . . from the dreamlike courtyard with its fountains and ancient statues, and its palms and orchids and exotic plants, to the shrine . . . with its magnificent old choir stalls and altar where Mrs. Gardner in royal manner, has services on Christmas and other holy days . . .

"We saw Sargent there also—as he is living with Mrs. Gardner and painting portraits in one of her palatial rooms. He is a very business-like, unaesthetic-looking person—very large and burly—and with a florid face."

Five years had gone by before Andrew invited Mrs. Gardner to visit his summer home, "Red Roof"—a most unusual house which he had built for himself at Eastern Point, overlooking Gloucester Harbor.[3] Mrs. Gardner had a great curiosity about Eastern Point—a rocky peninsula covered with cat-brier, blueberries and a few wild cherry trees. The place had recently been taken over by young or youngish maiden ladies, all suitably chaperoned by one or more parents—and by bachelors similarly chaperoned. Cecelia Beaux had been the first comer, building a cottage and then a studio. Her handsome, meticulously finished portraits were in great demand.

Next to Miss Beaux lived Miss Joanna Davidge, who, during the winter, directed a select school for young ladies in Richmond, Virginia. Miss Davidge was artistic to the extent of having a plaster cast of a Raphael bas-relief Madonna set into the wall over her fireplace and sundry wood-carvings, trophies of foreign travel, made into cupboard doors and a headboard for her bed. She adored cat-brier, which seemed to represent unspoiled natural beauty to her, thorns and all, so she refused to have it rooted out, except to make a narrow path to her door. Joanna, closely guarded by her widowed mother, was the most maidenly of the ladies—yet not without hope of matrimony.

A. Piatt Andrew lived next door to Miss Davidge under his "Red Roof"—nearer the mainland than Miss Davidge and Miss Beaux, and with one more maiden lady beyond him. She was Miss Caroline Sinkler, whose fiancé had been killed in a carriage accident on the eve of their marriage. He had already signed the papers, leaving her his money, and hers was the most impressive house on the point, so far. Among her servants was a small, uniformed boy, a "Buttons." She entertained with formality, wearing a hat in her own home when she gave a ladies' luncheon; her hats fuchsia, violet or purple —fantastic and famous.

Harry Sleeper, whom Mrs. Gardner already knew fairly well, lived just beyond. He had decorated Miss Sinkler's house; her dining room with a real trellis covered with artificial roses on the wall; her drawing room painted pale pink, deepening to rose with a red carpet. Harry was sweet, gentle, affectionate. He was devoted to his mother, who protected him from the ladies when he feared they had designs on his celibacy. Still more was he the devoted slave to Piatt.

Intensely sensitive to the atmosphere of a place, Isabella Gardner could not help but be depressed by Red Roof when the all-too-frequent fog came rolling in over Gloucester harbor. Her room, always afterward so called, was up a narrow staircase and connected with a room for Ella, her maid. Dark red walls, a large crucifix hanging over the bed and small windows, fogbound, were not conducive to gaiety.

A. Piatt Andrew had an organ installed in the passage between the living room and a recently added study. Here, Isabella sat on the couch (with a bearskin and two leopard skins on it) to listen to his music. She was probably unaware of a hidden space above the books—too low to stand up in but equipped with mattress and covers where some of Andrew's guests could listen in still greater comfort. She had seen the Brittany bed in the living room but that there was a small hole over it, perhaps no one had told her. The sound of organ music could be heard the better through the hole—and was it just a coincidence that a person in the hidden alcove above could look down through it? Gossip had it that often all the guests were men, their pastimes peculiar. Yet all the ladies on Eastern Point were fascinated by Piatt and one especially keen observer thought that Miss Beaux was "sweet on him."

When the fog lifted and the sun came out, the whole atmosphere at Red Roof changed. Gloucester harbor sparkled bright and blue. Isabella's spirits lifted, macabre impressions vanished, and Isabella went out on a stone seat to be photographed with Piatt—or "A," as she liked to call him, referring to herself as "Y," amused to find herself at the opposite end of the alphabet.

Isabella wore a linen suit with leg o' mutton sleeves, long coat and wide gored skirt. She had on a toque with a black dotted veil over her face. Beside her, A. Piatt sat—head turned toward her, his handsome profile toward the camera.

A. Piatt Andrew had been chosen by President Eliot to

work in Senator Aldrich's monetary commission and he planned to go to Europe during the summer of 1908 to make preliminary studies. Mrs. Gardner told him to be sure to get in touch with Matthew Stewart Prichard—late of the Boston Art Museum. This Andrew did, Prichard showing him beautiful Greek and Roman coins which gave him ideas for new designs for American currency.

There was time for Isabella to visit A. Piatt Andrew before he went abroad and he offered her the use of his house during August, while he was away. Just before he left, his Eastern Point neighbors gave him "a week of farewell dinners [which] touched [his] heart and nearly ruined [his] digestion."

Mrs. Gardner came down for the festivities and Andrew gave her a dinner. Contrary to local report, there was little drinking but much gay talk, spontaneous play-acting, and laughter at Red Roof. Perhaps it was at this time or later that Miss Elizabeth Marbury, author and New York literary agent (with F. Marion Crawford among her clients), was there. She was quite stout and well satisfied with her state of single blessedness, but she went along with the game when each of the young men present "proposed" to her—amid howls of laughter—and she "accepted" the boy who made the best job of it.

On the following night "occurred the great fête at Miss Beaux's studio. Everyone came in elaborate costume—there were eighteen guests at dinner." "Abe," as Andrew signed himself to his parents, "was made to wear a robe of a Roman emperor, with jewelled filet." He "sat at dinner on a kind of throne of red velvet.

"Mrs. Gardner sat opposite . . . on a less imposing throne of purple with a large 'Y' in gold. The air of the studio was heavy with incense and tuberoses; the table was gorgeous with old rose damask and wreathes of fruit . . ."

Abe evidently felt that it was time for him to explain Isabella to his parents. He had to break it to them that they could not come on from Indiana to stay at Red Roof because he had promised it to Mrs. Gardner for August. "She has become a very good friend and I care a great deal about her," he wrote. As time went on, this statement proved true. A. Piatt Andrew, whatever his faults, was one of the best friends Mrs. Gardner had during her later years.

Piatt laid it upon Harry Sleeper to look after Mrs. Gardner and this Harry did, reporting in long letters sent to Piatt while he was in Europe.

On August 9, 1908, "Mrs. Gardner arrived about 5 P.M. in

Mr. Frick's auto." She had her man of business, Henry Swift, with her and "a lady from Rome." They had been to Prides Crossing, where Mrs. Gardner showed them Mr. Frick's pictures—and commandeered his auto, evidently.

She told Harry to "get her some lobsters and have the front porch looking right," because she had "invited the archbishop to supper."

Henry did not refer to the archbishop by name but said that the prelate had "refused to come in an auto, preferring his own ponderous carriage," so he arrived an hour late. He stopped at Miss Sinkler's house to ask the way to Red Roof and Miss Sinkler's Protestant maid told her mistress that there was "some kind of a priest at the door asking for a lost gardener."

Red Roof was set back from the road and close to the harbor, so that the archbishop passed it without seeing it and appeared next at Miss Davidge's door. Of course Miss Beaux heard about it and declared that Mrs. Gardner must have misdirected the archbishop in order to impress the neighbors.

Next day, Mrs. Gardner lunched at Miss Beaux's and during the afternoon "a wild man from the museum" came to spend Sunday. Unfortunately, Harry Sleeper did not get his name.

"It was a peerless moonlit night and the harbor filled with phantom-like schooners, their sails hanging limp in the air." Harry was "telephoned for and asked to play three songs on the victrola, outside," which he "ran over and did for Mrs. Gardner."

Miss Beaux had an exceedingly handsome houseman—who sometimes posed for her—by the name of Vitali. He was an ex-gondolier from Venice, and Mrs. Gardner liked to speak to him in Italian and admire his biceps. Miss Beaux was sure that Mrs. Gardner was trying to hire Vitali away from her.

While at Red Roof on one of her brief but frequent visits, Mrs. Gardner felt called upon to attend a funeral but had no suitable attire with her. She therefore "borrowed a long, black garment" from Miss Davidge's mother. Harry Sleeper said that Andrew really should have seen her in it! When she returned the dress with thanks she remarked that she had been "the success of the funeral!" Mother Davidge was "quite shocked!" Harry wrote.

"Ysabella" enjoyed watching Piatt Andrew's more or less tame bears that lived in a cage just below her bedroom window. But when a mouse ran over her face in the night, she sent for Harry Sleeper and told him to set traps.

These excursions to Eastern Point made a varied and entertaining month of August for Isabella Gardner. She needed the good times because misfortune was upon her that same August of 1908. This came through the friend in London who meant to do her a favor. Mrs. Emily Chadbourne was now in the United States but apparently the first that Mrs. Gardner heard of it was when a telegram was received at her summer home in Brookline. It was from Mrs. Chadbourne—to the effect that there was a lot of trouble with customs house people and that she was on her way to Boston to explain.

The Chadbourne household effects had been sent in bond to a Chicago warehouse, reaching there June 30, 1908. The American consul in London had told Mrs. Chadbourne that because the goods she sent were duty free it didn't much matter what value she set on them but that she should put on some sort of valuation. It would be all right to call it eight thousand dollars. Feeling happy over the pleasure she would give Mrs. Gardner, Mrs. Chadbourne included among her effects the tapestries, furniture and works of art she had borrowed. Mrs. Chadbourne was anxious, also, about the safety of effects not her own, so she insured them through American Express for sixty thousand dollars.

The goods were handled in a routine manner and placed in the warehouse pending Mrs. Chadbourne's return to America to claim them. The *Hercules* by Piero della Francesca was so big, however, that it occurred to a customs man to have a look inside the crate. Hercules was so well-known a figure among those whose business it is to appraise art that the stolid-looking fellow was recognized!

Only a few inquiries were needed to uncover the sixty-thousand-dollar insurance policy; to compare it with the eight-thousand-dollar valuation—and the fat was in the fire! All the crates were opened and an outside art expert was summoned. A value of $82,411 was placed on art objects other than household effects by W. M. French, director of the Art Institute of Chicago. Customs collectors, United States appraisers and assessors met and officially determined that "duties would be $29,203.68; penalties 50 per cent of appraised value, total $70,409.18." [4]

Before Mrs. Chadbourne could get to Boston, a special agent from the Treasury Department called on Mrs. Gardner. He asked her if she was the owner of *Hercules* and certain tapestries. She said she was. Her astonishment on being told that these and more of her belongings were now in Chicago must have convinced the Treasury agent that there was no collusion between the two ladies. The Treasury man was pleasant, Mrs. Gardner was "pleased with his manner," she said—and he with hers, it would seem.

A few days later, a man called on Mrs. Gardner, out at Green Hill in Brookline, "representing that he was a customs man, but who was really some kind of newspaper man," said Mr. Swift. This must have been the man that Joseph Lindon Smith remembered.

"Joe was spending a few leisure summer days with Mrs. Gardner in Brookline," as his wife, Corinna, told the story. "One afternoon their privacy was interrupted by an uncouth individual with an aggressive manner, appearing unannounced. He told Mrs. Gardner that she would land in jail." [5] Mrs. Jack's temper flashed. She was no longer the courteous lady who had talked to the Treasury representative but what she said, Corinna did not write down—if Joe told her.

Mrs. Gardner herself afterward declared that "nothing printed in the papers *yet* was at all like" what she said "to this man." Evidently, her remarks were unprintable!

Mrs. Chadbourne, when she arrived, offered to pay the entire cost of her disastrous effort to help a friend. Isabella of Boston could not consider accepting such a favor from anyone. Before she gained possession of her property, Mrs. Gardner had paid out $150,000.

At first, the general public was against Mrs. Jack. She appeared to be too rich, she seemed too immune from the troubles besetting ordinary humanity to rate any sympathy.

Even Henry Sleeper, who knew her well and liked her—arrogant though she was at times—hurried out to Brookline "agog to hear about the smuggling."

"At luncheon, 'Y' told" him that she "had intended letting Mrs. Chadbourne keep the goods another year, hoping for tariff revision." Sleeper could see that this was true and that the arrival of the goods was a complete surprise.

" 'Oh *now* we shall hear the truth,' " Miss Beaux had said to Sleeper when he told her he was on his way to Brookline.

" 'Poor *dear* Mrs. Gardner, I am so sorry for her,' " Miss Davidge had said. " 'Mr. Sleeper, the thing has a *very* ugly look about it, don't you think? Mamma says,' etc. etc." Henry wrote it all to A. Piatt Andrew, but if he had been able, on his return to Eastern Point, to make the ladies share his revised opinion, he did not say so.

Joseph Lindon Smith and Corinna could be depended on in adversity. "Count always on our loyalty, our pride in you,

277

and our love for you, dear Isabella," Joe wrote, speaking for himself and his wife. "Along with the affection and love of many others, let ours help to keep your courage up and spirits steadfast against all unfriendliness and unfairness shown you."

A. Piatt Andrew, writing from Berlin, Germany, said that he "should like to shoot somebody" for Ysabella.

From St. Moritz, Switzerland, Berenson wrote, "The irony of it—that you should be persecuted and mercilessly mulcted because you are, at the greatest self-sacrifice, storing up art treasures for a more appreciative generation of our countrymen."

Mrs. Henry L. Higginson remembered the days of her girlhood when she was Ida Agassiz in Italy with Belle Stewart. The coolness resulting from the Civil War, the occasional shock, the result of Belle Gardner's flirtations when she was called a "married belle"—all were forgotten and Ida wrote an affectionate letter, recalling happy memories. Henry L. Higginson himself went to friends and collected letters of appreciation of Mrs. Gardner's work in creating the future Isabella Stewart Gardner Museum. He had the letters handsomely bound and presented the volume as a surprise at a big birthday party Mrs. Gardner's friends arranged for her. This succeeded in surprising her almost to tears!

Then the press suddenly came out in Mrs. Gardner's favor. The *Evening Transcript* interviewed Henry W. Swift and wrote a fine report of the whole customs affair.

The *Transcript* followed this with an editorial, written in behalf of those who imported masterpieces—which in itself was a masterpiece of writing. "Mrs. Gardner's Mistake," it was headed!

"When duties of $150,000 on the old masters, valued at $80,000, have been paid, it may perhaps dawn on Mrs. J. L. Gardner how grievously she has offended against this great and glorious republic, in trying to import works of art. The law of this republic is very strict with all misguided persons who dare to bring to this land paintings or statuary, or valuable works of research. What these persons should do, if they wish to be favorably regarded by the law, is import dogs.

"A snarling, blear-eyed bulldog of uncertain walk and disagreeable temper, valued at $10,000 can be imported free of duty. A yelping, howling, snapping poodle of no earthly good to himself or humanity but valued at $8,000 can be imported duty free . . . But any millionaire who tries to import works of Titian, Rubens or Turner is lucky if he escapes jail . . ."

The effect of the import duty and the fines for failure to declare the works of art almost put an end to Mrs. Gardner's further collecting. Her preoccupation now was to make certain that she could leave enough money in trust to carry on Fenway Court, paying upkeep and salaries of employees after her death. She had no very clear conception of how much capital would produce the required income, so she entered upon a phase of stringent personal economy which was all that many people remembered about her.

New legends arose. Shopkeepers out on Huntington Avenue said that Mrs. Gardner would send Bolgi out to buy two oranges at a time—never a whole dozen. Ladies invited to lunch declared that they each were served only three stalks of asparagus on toast.

Many years later, Berenson was in Venice "in the company of an American correspondent he had invited to go along." The correspondent reported Berenson's fascinating conversation as they strolled about and Berenson "circled to that later Isabella, Mrs. Jack Gardner, whose vivacity and charm, he said, were unforgettable."

"But you know that after her husband died—he was the dearest fellow in the world—Mrs. Jack made a great discovery . . . She discovered that things cost money. Mrs. Leland Stanford made the same discovery after her husband died, and then she lived like a starveling. Mrs. Jack, when she came to Europe in later years and returned to the hotels where she had lavishly stayed as the Dollar Princess, asked for the cheapest rooms.

"On one visit to America"—Berenson thought it was "thirty years ago" but more time than that had slipped by—"My wife and I were her guests and at dinner the first night there was scarcely enough to eat. We thought, well, we are going to the theatre and when we get back there will be supper. There was no supper. After we'd gone upstairs to our rooms, Mary and I felt hunger pangs. We couldn't get to sleep and we stole downstairs to the kitchen to forage in the icebox. In that immense repository we found two dog biscuits." [6]

The Berensons were actually guests at Fenway Court in 1904, after Mrs. Gardner had paid the first bill presented to her by the government—this time, for $200,000 because "the public couldn't get into her museum." After the second series of duties and punitive fines, legends of her parsimony grew —all the economies she ever practiced were rolled into one. What Berenson knew but of course did not mention was that Mrs. Gardner had almost ceased to buy pictures through him. From 1904 through 1916 she bought sixteen and after that, none until 1921, when she bought a *Madonna and Child,* by Bellini, costing $50,000.

Mrs. Gardner economized in the matter of dress—even one of her young men observing that she wore a skirt all tattered and torn. Laughingly, she explained that her overaffectionate dogs had ripped it. Sometimes she appeared at dinner in a gown not too skillfully made from a discarded brocade couch-cover.

Yet she always contrived a grand effect when she pleased. William Philips, a young third assistant to the Secretary of State, was asked to escort the British and the French ambassadors to Fenway Court during their visit to Boston. "And so, with an ambassador on either hand, I arrived at the Palace and was shown into a vast room on the second floor, lighted only by firelight," he wrote. "Mrs. Gardner was seated at one end of a long table in front of the fire . . . She was dressed, as I remember, in black velvet with an immense string of pearls as her only ornament. Certainly she was no beauty but there was something compelling and indeed fascinating about her, and I recollect that my ambassadors were equally impressed." [7]

TWENTY-SIX

"Old Times and New"

IT WAS SPRING AGAIN, the time of year when the Green Hill gardens were at their best. Soon the window washers would come, Mrs. Gardner would put dust covers over the furniture and close Fenway Court. She received a letter, however, which postponed all this. "21 East 11th Street," it was headed, and the date was May 6, 1907. "My dear Lady" was the salutation and "Marion Crawford" the signature.

"I am in America for a very short time and shall be in Boston two days in the course of this month to see my aunt. It would be a great pleasure to have a sight of you, if you are to be in Boston. Will you let me know if I may?"

On May 17, Crawford wrote to his aunt, Julia Ward Howe: "Please ask no one to dinner. I come to see you and to have a good chat about old times and new . . . On Tuesday afternoon, early, I am going to see Mrs. Gardner's collection at the Fenway—wherever that may be."

"Marion Crawford arrived soon after 3 P.M. for a little visit," his Aunt Julia said. "He looks greatly improved in health since I last saw him—he must have passed through some crisis and come out conqueror—he has all his old charm." During May, a teacher from Perkins Institution had been coming to Beacon Street at intervals to "set down" the music Mrs. Howe had composed during past years but had never written. She hoped that Marion would sing some of her songs, but "Marion declares he cannot sing a note. His trouble in recent years was of the lungs." [1]

Each winter and early spring it was Mrs. Howe's custom to have one of her daughter Laura's girls from Gardiner, Maine, to visit on Beacon Street, to help as hostess and to enjoy a little Boston gaiety. In March, it had been the beautiful Rosalind's turn. "Rosalind's beau, Mr. Amory Gardner was here for lunch," Mrs. Howe said. ". . . I wish she would marry him but I fear she will not marry at all." Now it was Rosalind's sister Betty's turn to visit.

"Cousin Marion" was "enchanting, aristocratic, like quicksilver," Betty thought, "but looked fragile, sunken, like a person with lung disease." He would be fifty-three in August.

Mrs. Gardner must have set the time for Crawford to see the palace when the sun would fill the court, and when her pictures would have the best light. He wrote to her as soon as he got back to his aunt's house on Beacon Street. ". . . I can only say after one visit that I had a wonderful impression, quite indescribable because wholly new and unexpected and all good.

"What I cared for more, and shall remember with different feelings, is to have seen you happy in your very own surroundings, and not displeased to let an old ghost like me wander through them beside you. If you ever haunt the Palazzo Isabella in a future age, I shall be much honored if I am asked to haunt with you now and then!"

Isabella was not pleased with this reaction although twenty years or so earlier she would have been. In June, writing from "Hever Castle, Hever, Kent," Crawford tried to please her better. ". . . About your Palazzo di Venezia—well, I was first preoccupied with yourself, after the long silence for which I am at a loss to account. Never mind that—we have met again and it looks as if we should write to each other often. I hope so. And I saw you in your very ownest surroundings, in a place you have made for yourself after your own heart—and in which I shall probably always think of you now." [2]

It would seem that Crawford was loath to forget the Beacon Street boudoir. Isabella, however, had outgrown it, literally tearing it apart to keep only what was artistically valuable, like the little portraits in the Gothic Room. Crawford had probably neither noticed nor remembered them, for he was a novelist, interested in situation and plot, not an artist with an eye for color—although he was a craftsman, handy with tools.

Trying hard to appreciate Fenway Court sufficiently: "It is a good place, well dreamed and well realized after dreaming —so well, indeed, that I could not notice half of what I saw, for the simple reason that I knew it was there and could be taken for granted as safely as if the palace were really in Venice and had wooden roots in the canal and a damp ground floor—happily not included amongst the thing realized at Fenway!"

In October, 1907, Crawford wrote, ". . . So you are going to enlarge the Monk's Garden! I wish I could be of use. I have just built a XIIIth Century wellhead over the reservoir in my garden, from one of the drawings in Viollet-le-Duc, and it is a great success—it has three stone arches that meet to support the wheel and chain. . . . If you want any real 'antiquities' made of perfectly sound and *new* material, apply to me! . . ." This witticism and similar ones that followed may not have amused Mrs. Gardner overmuch.

Although nearly "broken down with fatigue" because of his heavy writing schedule, Crawford wrote on October 4, 1908, "It seems a long time to look ahead but it is my intention to be in Boston at the end of May . . . I shall go about April 1, and probably sail for Europe early in June. If you would let me stay with you a day or two it would be a rare pleasure.

"I burn your letters at once—I don't know why, for no one cares—but I daresay you do the same for mine," Crawford added.

But Isabella continued to keep Crawford's letters—with the exception, of course, of certain pages already destroyed. She kept one dated January 21, 1909.

"I believe that a play of mine is to be brought out in about three weeks. It is called the 'White Sister' and it really is mine and not the concoction of a 'professional dramatist' . . ." Crawford hoped that Mrs. Gardner would go to see the play and his own plans for coming to America in April had not changed, except that "if the play succeeds, which is more than doubtful . . . my wife and youngest daughter would also" come to New York. But they would be "staying with friends and my own movements would not be hampered at all and I mean to be in Boston for my aunt's 90th birthday if she reaches it, as we all hope she may." Then—"With many good greetings and wishes to you, dear, your affectionate M," Crawford signed himself. On this page Isabella wrote in pencil, "His last letter. Died April 8, 1909."

In January, 1910, Henry Adams "passed an hour with Mrs. Gardner . . ." and described her as "Mrs. Gardner with a wig, more neo-Platonic than ever was grown in Alexandria . . . as good or better than ever, but not precisely new." When Adams wrote to Mrs. Gardner back in 1906, he had addressed her as "Wonderful Woman," and later, in an undated letter evidently in reply to birthday greetings: "I envy you, who always, even at your worst, loved the game, whatever it might be, and delighted in playing it. How we others must bore you—old mummies like Henry James and me—who can see nothing in the game and only lunacy in the players . . ." Henry Adams reflected that "There are two thousand million people in the world since Carlyle's time, but now *all* fools, naturally including myself and Theodore Roosevelt . . ." [3]

Mrs. Gardner, however, was not worried very much about the game, either of life or politics. She was literally interested in *games*. In February, 1910, she organized a supper in the Dutch Room for the victorious Harvard football team. They had scored four to nothing over Yale!

When the festive evening came, Mrs. Gardner walked the entire length of the Dutch Room—her small figure erect, her jewels flashing—to receive the Harvard football captain. She had given strict orders that he was not to come to her and the blushing young man knew that the great Mrs. Gardner was conferring an honor she had refused to foreign dignitaries.

Mrs. Jack thought about sports even during a concert—or right after it. Charles Martin Loeffler, now at last married to the wealthy Miss Fay and no longer needing to give violin lessons, took great pleasure in training the boys' choir at the church in Medfield. He brought his boys to Fenway Court to sing for Mrs. Gardner, who was thrilled by the music and impressed by the faultless performance. But she proceeded to make friends with the boys afterwards and discovered that they wanted uniforms for their baseball team. She told Loeffler to get some and send her the bill.

Loeffler's letter to Mrs. Gardner describes his difficulties. He went to a "regular clothier," not knowing any better. They scornfully directed him to "the Iver Johnson Sporting Goods Company and Wright and Ditson"—establishments of which he had never heard. It was all "a matter in which I am inexperienced," he wrote plaintively. Then came the bewildering question of assorted sizes for little boys. Iver Johnson agreed to take back suits that didn't fit. At last "the B.B. suits" finally arrived. The boys were delighted and "expected to play the Dedhamites." Then it rained!

Loeffler wrote that he was going to give his choirboys "a good, sound rehearsal of the 'Dies Irae,' " since they could not go out and play ball.

Mrs. Jack had become a passionate baseball fan by 1912. In December of that year, she appeared at Symphony Hall "with a white band bound round her head and on it the words, 'Oh you Red Sox' in red letters."

In 1912, the Boston Red Sox won the World's Series, the losing team being the New York Giants. "It looks as if the woman had gone crazy," said *Town Topics*. "With this band bound like a fillet around her auburn hair, she appeared in her conspicuous seat at a recent Saturday night Symphony Concert, almost causing a panic among those in the audience who discovered the ornamentation, and even for a moment upsetting Dr. Muck's men so that their startled eyes wandered from their music stands."

There was a new generation among her husband's nephews and Mrs. Gardner's favorite was George Peabody Gardner, one of Harvard's most brilliant athletes. At first, when he was a young boy at Fay School and St. Mark's, his Aunt Belle's intense pride in him was embarrassing. Mrs. Gardner would sometimes take her friend, Corinna Smith to see him at practice, calling out "Yoo-hoo—where are you?" It was Corinna's opinion that he hid! [4] But later he grew to take pride in the sight of the small, excited figure of his Great-aunt Belle, cheering wildly on the side lines at every game his team played. He remembered her fortitude as she sat, wrapped in furs, on an upended packing case to watch him skate with his hockey team.

George Peabody Gardner graduated *cum laude* from Harvard, but that his Great-aunt Belle accepted as no more than to be expected. He was a member of the varsity track, hockey and tennis teams for three years and the varsity baseball team one year—doubtless the year when his aunt became a baseball fan. He won "eight major and two minor H's in all," [5] and his countless trophies pleased her as much or more than as though she had won them herself.

In 1912, George Peabody Gardner became engaged to Rose Grosvenor. Mrs. Gardner gave parties and she laughed when she heard that the matrons were going to allow only waltzes at the assemblies that year. She remembered well the men who had said her waltzing was graceful and the women who called it scandalous. Now she would be one of those who "allowed rebellious couples to practice the Turkey Trot."

In October, 1912, Henry Adams called to see Belle Gardner again. She was still at Green Hill, and he "drove to Brookline . . . She and I are the same age, and she is wonderfully old, and wrinkled far beyond me, but in movement and energy she knocks me silly. Of all our old set—Henry Higginson, Brother Charles and the rest—she is far the youngest and spryest but a wrinkled old fairy all the same. We had nothing much to say to each other and especially because we are all tired of Theodore and politics. The betting is three to one on Wilson . . ." [6]

In 1912, Joseph Lindon Smith and Corinna, his wife, were living in Boston, much to Mrs. Gardner's pleasure. Joe was the only one of Mrs. Jack's once-young men whose wife she really liked. It had become her custom to appoint herself "godmother" to the children of all her former admirers and Joe could not help noticing that some of them expected gifts and even bequests for their offspring. The Smiths' first child was born abroad and when Isabella cabled that she would be godmother, Joe replied, "No you don't." The second child was also born abroad. Isabella cabled as before, and Joe answered, "Wrong again." It seemed like hardness of heart, but Isabella understood and liked it.

The Smiths' third daughter was born in Boston. She had just been put into her mother's arms when a maid came to the door to exclaim, "There's a lady downstairs who says she's the baby's godmother!"

Up the stairs, right on the heels of the maid, came Isabella, bearing gifts. Corinna was "weary but happy," she remembered. "All right, you win, Isabella," she said.[7]

Isabella often took Corinna to Symphony with her. Symphony Hall, opened in 1900, was out on Huntington Avenue in Mrs. Gardner's part of town; and Corinna remembered two notable occasions. "There was sleighing in Boston" and Mrs. Gardner was "lawless about traffic." When they reached the door of the hall, she "always had her driver cut out of line and draw up at the steps. It brought everything back on its haunches but the police were used to it and let her do it."

Corinna looked back at the long line of sleighs, everybody else awaiting a turn. "Isabella, I'm a law-abiding person," she exclaimed. Mrs. Gardner gave her "a funny look."

The following week, Isabella privately told her driver to stay in line. As they approached the hall the policeman signaled grandly. Nothing happened. "Madame's orders," muttered the driver, very red in the face, when they finally reached the door. Traffic had been snarled and unsnarled several times. Symphony was half an hour late because of course the concert could not start until Mrs. Jack was in her place. An unfair practice had become correct procedure and once more Corinna Putnam Smith had to say, "You win, Isabella." [8]

The Smiths had seats in Mrs. Gardner's box at the opera or the theater. Afterwards they would go home with her, choose a room among the many in the palace to sit in and enjoy, while they talked over the evening's performance. One night (probably in 1908) Paderewski was again in Boston.

He was staying at the Tavern Club and called up Joe to say that he'd like to come out to the Smiths' for supper. They were going to Mrs. Gardner's, Joe explained, but he would see about taking Paderewski along.

"Isabella was delighted," Corinna recalled. "There was little to eat, as usual, but afterwards, instead of staying in one room, we roamed all over Fenway Court. After a while, Paderewski was so thrilled that he exclaimed, 'I must play—where is the piano?' He was led to the concert grand and played for the three of us till after midnight."

The Boston *Advertiser* revived the story that Paderewski had once played for Mrs. Gardner alone. The tale had become a legend so that the actual fee of a thousand dollars was now "three thousand." Paderewski still wore his hair long, still wondered why the American press commented on it and cartooned it. The *Advertiser* declared that Paderewski now "rode in Mrs. Gardner's carriage, round and round the Fenway, his red hair blowing in the wind."

Early one spring, Joe Smith went to Dublin, New Hampshire, to his and his parents' cottage on the lake. The house had been added to until it seemed to grow of its own accord. When Joe and Corinna were married, Sturgis Bigelow had promised them a huge Della Robbia fireplace, complete with caryatids in faience which he had brought home from Italy —if Joe could find it. Bigelow had stored it in some warehouse. Joe found it, all right, and had built a new living room, large in proportion to it, in which to set it up. Now he had promised Corinna he would install a furnace.

But Joe got interested in building a big screen-walled summer dining room ornamented with Oriental carvings. A Japanese garden would be the right thing to go outside, so Joe designed and planted that—forgetting all about the furnace. He set up a "moon gate" and wrote a pageant which required that Mrs. Gardner come up to Dublin to take the part of the moon goddess.

Isabella had herself driven by auto to Dublin by one of her young men. Later, in appropriate gauzy veils, she looked young and almost beautiful as she came through the moon gate which Joe, dressed as a magician, turned from square to round. Joe's magic always warmed her heart.

Dublin, New Hampshire, was at first the haunt of artists —a beautiful, unpretentious place they could afford to live in. The wealthy discovered Dublin and followed, as so often happens, and before long French or Italian villas overlooked the New England lake. Mrs. Gardner was first and always the friend of the artists and paid no attention to the newcomers, but they were well aware of her. One night she reluctantly accepted a dinner invitation while staying at the Smiths'.

Joe's parents were just sitting down to a supper of baked beans and brown bread as Mrs. Gardner prepared to leave for the party, high on the hill. "That smells delicious!" she exclaimed. Then she pulled out a chair at the Smiths' table. "I'll have some," she said. She arrived late on the hill—unaccountably not hungry.

When Nancy, daughter of George deForest Brush, married one of her father's most promising pupils, Mrs. Gardner was not asked to the wedding. She went anyway—and brought the bride a present of a ring set with small stones. They spelled the word "dear"—diamond, emerald, amethyst, ruby. It was a device favored by novelists which appealed to the romantic in Isabella.[9]

Abbott Thayer, Dublin artist, counted Mrs. Gardner among his friends, as indeed she proved to be. "Charity, [his] masterpiece [was] up the noble stairs" at the new Museum of Fine Arts in Boston but the fashion for large symbolic paintings showing very American-looking girls in classic robes had begun to wane, when Thayer lost more money than he could afford by cosigning a friend's note. He appealed to Mrs. Gardner, offering to sell her some pictures of his children he had intended to keep. She refused to take the pictures but sent him the money he needed, tactfully telling him that she was buying "peace of mind" which he would need in order to complete the picture he was working on—his greatest masterpiece, she felt sure. No one knew of this, of course. It was only one of many occasions when Mrs. Jack had helped an artist, never telling, but keeping grateful letters which had pleased her.

Dublin was a happy place where Mrs. Gardner spent a few days out of every summer, especially after she gave up her own "Alhambra" at Beverly. She would not have been true to form, however, if she had always been the serene patroness of artists, the perfect guest. There was, for example, the time when she brought George Proctor with her from Boston.

It occurred to Isabella that if the wealthy Dublin summer visitors heard Proctor play, they might make arrangements for a series of winter concerts in New York or Chicago. She still hoped he might become a second Paderewski.

But George went out on Dublin Lake with girls from the summer colony, singing and strumming a guitar. He practiced the piano not at all and at the exhibition concert, he played badly. Isabella was furious and lashed out at everybody—the Smiths included. Corinna talked back. It was this frankness of hers that saved their friendship many a time.

When George was twenty years old, Mrs. Gardner had told him that she "hoped a great big love affair would come along some day to knock everything to pieces for" his own "sake and art's." George was now about thirty-eight, quite a ladies' man, but great love had yet to make him a musician. On March 20, 1911, however, the Boston *Traveler* carried a story with a photograph of Fenway Court and a picture of a bride.

"Beneath a canopy of flowers in the renaissance chapel in Mrs. John L. Gardner's Venetian palace in the Fenway this afternoon, Miss Margaret L. Burtt, librarian of the New England Conservatory of Music, became the wife of George W. Proctor, a teacher in the same institution, a pianist of celebrity and a protégé of Mrs. Gardner." Margaret Burtt had been nineteen when she first became a piano pupil of Proctor's. She was now twenty-five.

If it took Margaret six years to sweep George off his feet in a great love affair, it took her less than one year to realize that she had made a mistake. On January 19, 1912, the Boston *Telegraph* had it that Mrs. Proctor, "after visiting the cottage given them by Mrs. Gardner," had "packed up her personal effects and wedding presents and left." She sued for divorce in 1916, alleging, among other things, that "when Mrs. Gardner did not send over food they had nothing to eat" and that "once when her husband and Mrs. Gardner quarreled, they had no food for three days . . ."

The truth was that Proctor liked music but hated hard work. Mrs. Jack, with all her surplus energy, could never inject him with ambition—but neither could she stop trying.

Mrs. Gardner offered an annual prize of a grand piano to the best student performer in open competition. Impartial judges were chosen but, among themselves, music students said that a Proctor pupil was sure to win. Mrs. Gardner went to all the competitions, enjoying them with much the same enthusiasm as she felt for baseball.

"You won't win this year," Proctor told Naomi Bevard,[10] who had been studying with him for two years. "But I want you to play in the competition just for the experience and next year you will have a chance."

Naomi was an earnest little girl who worked hard. Her technique was flawless, she forgot to be scared, and she won. Astonished and overcome, she rushed from the stage in tears

289

to find herself gathered into Mrs. Gardner's arms to be kissed and comforted! This frightened her still more but she was asked to play at Fenway Court, and came to realize that the great Mrs. Jack was really a warmhearted human being.

Another contest did not go quite so well. This time, Mrs. Gardner disagreed with the judges' choice, so she calmly awarded another piano to the student in second place. The judges were insulted, of course, and remonstrated with her, but she couldn't see what business it was of theirs. If she was willing to pay for two pianos and give them away, that was *her* affair.

Proctor was happy as a piano teacher. If his girl students were pretty enough, he took them tea-dancing at the Copley Plaza. Mrs. Gardner, while never admitting that she had given Proctor up, began to hope to discover genius in some pupil of his.

In May, 1911, Henry James again visited the United States, this time because of his brother William's death in Cambridge. He called on Mrs. Gardner and, as was his custom, passed judgment upon her in a letter to Ariana Curtis.

James was sorry for himself, living way out in Cambridge with "neither a carriage nor a motor nor a gondola." But he found "our old friend Isabella" to be his "principal ally" on the otherwise displeasing American scene. She had been "rather ominously ill" in April, James said, "with a sudden attack of frequent fainting and heart weakness, which has condemned her to complete inaction or immobility for the time, although the doctors don't commit themselves to the formulations of danger. Only it's the only ailment she has ever had, I believe, that she hasn't quickly thrown off; and she has now a long history of tension and effort and passionate activity behind her—together with an appearance of age to which she hasn't hitherto consented . . ."

James called at Fenway Court on the afternoon of May 7, 1911. He found Mrs. Gardner "reclining on a sort of pretty dreary loggia in the open air under an awning, with nothing but the ugly, scrubby, ragged Fenway view to look at, and the sad appearance of forlorn loneliness, so true is it that she has few personal friends and among them almost no women whom she has never done anything to attract to her—quite the contrary." James thought that "even the 'palace' looks thankless." [11]

But of course James wrote nothing of this sort to Mrs. Gardner, herself. About a month later, she was well enough to take him out to Eastern Point to have lunch with Cecelia Beaux. He wrote her in October, recalling "those evenings at your board and in your box, those tea-times in your pictured halls which flush again in my mind's eye as real lifesaving stations. It was even much of a reprieve from death to go with you that summer's day to lunch with the all-but deadly Cecelia; under the mere ghostly echo of the *enervement* of whose tongue I kind of wriggle and thresh about still—till rescued by the bounty of the dear young man, the Newfoundland dog, the great St. Bernard nosing-in-the-snow neighbor, of whose conveyance of me to his miraculous house, inanimate even though exasperated, I retain, please tell him, the liveliest, literally the fondest, appreciation." [12] Mrs. Gardner, being by now an expert in James's letter-writing style, doubtless understood perfectly.

In May, 1913, Mrs. Gardner was still copy for *Town Topics*. "Boston awaits with bated breath Mrs. Jack Gardner riding an elephant . . ." they wrote. The whole thing was Joseph Lindon Smith's idea. He had designed a "Persian Pageant" for the "charity fête" to take place at the Larz Andersons' estate in Brookline. Isabella was going to wear an "Eastern costume" with veils over her face which would cover the wrinkles Henry Adams had been so ungallant as to notice. Her own jewels were fine enough to satisfy a Persian princess and she would wear them all with bazaar baubles as well—just for fun. Isabella could hardly wait for the day. She hadn't ridden an elephant since Cambodia, but only because there had been no elephants at hand. Then the elephant balked! Not a step would it take in the parade, not even when the circus people who had loaned it provided another elephant to keep it company!

Mrs. Jack was never one to be cast down when she could not move an elephant. She had a wonderful time being a Persian princess at the fête anyway and it was only Joe who was depressed. It was not his custom to disappoint Isabella.

In 1914, Mrs. Gardner "destroyed the Music Room," which had been such a delight to her. She needed room for the ten great tapestries, some of which she had paid so dearly for in import duties and penalties. She was thinking more and more in terms of Fenway Court as a museum and as such, the Music Room was a waste of space. Alice Neilson, American-born opera singer, came from New York to give one of the last concerts. The Vincent Club girls gave a charity ball —"all roads leading to Fenway Court." It was "a crush" at which there was "ragtime dancing"—and then it was time to send for Mr. Willard T. Sears.

The floor for the great tapestry room was set over the upper half of the music room. Fenway Court was not to be without music—the concert grand piano went to the tapestry room as did the little chairs, once furnishing the Beacon Street room. Concerts would now be more intimate, guests fewer. At the floor level of the former Music Room, Mrs. Gardner built the Spanish Chapel and the Spanish Cloister. In the building of the Spanish Cloister, Isabella brought to bear several of her talents and first, her talent for getting her own way by hook or by crook. She had always wanted Sargent's painting of a Spanish dancer, the picture called *El Jaleo* which, since 1882 had been the property of Thomas Jefferson Coolidge. He had promised to leave it to her in his will and since it was a big picture, seven by seven and a half feet, he lent it to her while he closed his house during the summer. She designed the Spanish Cloister to display it.

Never had Mrs. Gardner given a picture a more dramatic setting. She stage-lighted it so that visitors on stepping through the inner door beyond the Fenway entrance saw a dancer, footlights upon her, Spanish musicians with guitars against the wall. It was realism, but there was nothing photographic about it. When Mr. Coolidge saw it in 1915, everything happened just as his connection by marriage knew it would. He gave Isabella the picture, then and there.[13]

Mrs. Gardner satisfied her craving for artistic expression, not only in the setting of the picture, but by sitting on the floor and sorting antique tile which had been bought for her in Mexico by Dodge Macknight. She arranged a pattern, blending antique tiles with modern to make a perfect design for the wall between the Spanish Cloister and the Court.

The Spanish Chapel was a very personal creation. Over an ancient altar went the Zubarán *Madonna and Child*—always hitherto in Mrs. Gardner's bedroom. One of the first pictures she and her husband bought together, it represented a past with the tragic loss of their child (and their hope of children) never to be forgotten—but it represented past happiness as well.

Mr. Sears might have hoped that a much-mellowed Mrs. Gardner would collaborate serenely with him on the alterations for the palace. Unfortunately, such was not the case. A harassed Mr. Sears in desperation sent over his grandson to see Mrs. Gardner, relying on her well-known fondness for young men. It didn't work. "You go right back to the office, young man," she said, "and tell your grandfather to send me somebody who *knows* something!" [14]

TWENTY-SEVEN

Twentieth-century Isabella

OUT IN BROOKLINE, Massachusetts, Mrs. Jack Gardner read captions under press artists' drawings, such as "The Day of St. Vitus, Sarajevo, Serbia, June 28, 1914." Pictures showed a procession of carriages and men on horseback. But in the midst of them was an open touring car, symbol of a new age and center of a tragic scene. A handsome woman, hatted and veiled, recoiled in horror from the revolver pointed at the man by her side. Crown Prince Ferdinand of Austria-Hungary seemed to spring toward the assassin's bullet. It all seemed as unreal as the melodramatic drawings themselves and Mrs. Gardner, although remembering happy hours listening to music in Vienna, must have seen no connection with present violence and a future war involving her own nation.

Events in Europe came closer, however, when Clayton Johns got back to Boston and told Mrs. Jack of his adventures during the summer. He had been in church on Sunday, August 2, in Eisenach, Germany. The "singing of the chorale and the solemnity of the congregation" had impressed him, and afterwards he had wondered why the town was so crowded with "young and charming-looking officers." Most of all, he wondered why everyone "seemed full of gloom." Finally, someone told him. "Germany had declared war on Russia the day before."

Johns was "one of thousands of stranded Americans." Trains were filled with soldiers but he finally made his way back to Berlin, where he foregathered with sundry Bostonians, also stranded. He was hurt when he and his friends were "hissed by guests and servants" in a restaurant—but it was only because people took them for Britishers. England had declared war on Germany, Johns discovered. Still living in his world of music, Johns said that the bands never sounded better in German beer gardens. But paper money was unacceptable and "Otto Mendelssohn-Bartholdy, the grandson of Felix Mendelssohn" lent Clayton Johns gold currency with which to pay his bills and buy steamship passage home.

The Holland-American line stowed passengers everywhere, even "below steerage," but Johns was glad to be aboard ship at last. "Leaving Rotterdam, we heard the cannonading in Belgium," he said.[1]

Mrs. Jack was glad to see Clayton Johns, safe and sound, but she worried about her friends who were German musicians. Gericke, for example, had just gone back to Vienna to live, visualizing a life of retirement where the enjoyment of music would not be a luxury but well within his means. Not even Mrs. Gardner in her anxiety could have imagined the hardships in store for him and his little family.

The war in Europe, although it seemed to spread like a forest fire, was still remote from the American scene, however. Karl Muck, in America by gracious permission of Kaiser Wilhelm, was conductor of the Boston Symphony Orchestra and socially popular in 1914. In March of that year he had "announced that he was tired of paying rents and had bought a house on the Fenway, within the far shadow of Mrs. Jack Gardner's so-called Venetian Palace." He said he had three years more to direct the Boston Symphony.

In June, 1915, it still had not occurred to the public to ban German music, although all hearts were with France and Belgium. Over 23,000 people sat in the cold in the Harvard Stadium from 7:30 to 11:30 at a performance of *Siegfried*—a New York production. The weather was New England's treacherous worst and "the Metropolitan Orchestra, trying to keep warm, looked for all the world like . . . refugees." They wore all sorts of headgear from skull to polo and knitted woolen caps and blankets and shawls over their overcoats. Mrs. Gardner was there, of course; and *Town Topics* thought that "there was no funnier picture in the boxes" than Mrs. Jack, "who suggested nothing so much as an Esquimeau in her all enveloping wrapping of fur."

In November, Mrs. Gardner was on hand for opening night at the opera, "her coiffure of a golden shade" and her "famous chinchilla attracting attention." Although seventy-five years old, "the still agile lady was all aglitter" in what people were surprised to note was a new dress. Mrs. Jack was not economizing quite as much as usual it would seem. She wore a gown of "silver splashed plentifully over black satin." Her box "held a large party, mostly young men." [2]

Mrs. Gardner, in her enthusiasm for good music, was heard to praise German musicians when their performance

295

pleased her. Somehow, the word reached the Berensons in Italy that she was "pro-Boche." Mary Berenson undertook to warn Isabella: "Your vibrant, tumultous soul, they doubtless lead astray with music . . ." Of course Mrs. Jack was in no need of Mary's advice but she had sufficient patience with an old friend to set her straight on the subject. Mary was glad that there was "no truth in the foul and loathsome report."

Then, on April 2, 1917, President Wilson asked Congress to declare war. George Peabody Gardner, Mrs. Jack's much-loved grand-nephew, went on active service as an ensign in the United States Naval Reserve Force—on transports whose hazardous duty it was to dodge German submarines and keep the supply lines open. His Aunt Belle was proud but anxious.

Augustus Peabody Gardner, one of the nephews she thought of as being her own boy, gave up a fine career as congressman to go back into the army. His career during the Spanish-American War had been distinguished. He now requested that his status be changed from staff colonel to line major, in order to serve with the troops, and was assigned command of a battalion in the One Hundred and Twenty-First Georgia Infantry. On January 14, 1918, he died of pneumonia.[3] "The venerable Mrs. Jack Gardner, who seldom leaves her home, went to Washington to the funeral of Major Gardner," the papers said.

It probably annoyed Mrs. Gardner to be called "venerable" but the notices were all intended to be friendly. Within a few months there would be nothing but unfriendly comment concerning Mrs. Jack in the press.

Isabella Gardner was almost universally condemned, at the time it happened, for one of the most courageous things she ever did. She refused to join the hue and cry when Karl Muck, conductor of the Boston Symphony Orchestra, was suspected of being a German spy. Henry L. Higginson was almost the only other friend Muck had.

Public sentiment had been building up against the musician like the low thunder-growl of an approaching storm. Muck's refusal to play "The Star-Spangled Banner" at the beginning of every symphony concert, on the ground that it was "musically inappropriate," caused these clouds to gather. Mrs. Gardner said that an orchestra leader had a right to choose his programs without interference.

Mrs. Jack's stand was not done nobly, or with intent to be heroic. She defended her personal friendship for the musician gaily and with humor—at least as long as humor was possible. "Muck signals to German submarines from his house on the Fenway," went one of the stories. Hadn't Mrs. Gardner seen his lights blink on and off—from the top floor at Fenway Court? "Oh yes," she replied sarcastically. "He winks at me and I wink right back at him."

Before long, the situation was far from funny. Newspaper headlines, beginning in mid-March, told a story of increasing bitterness, as "opposition grows to Dr. Muck's directing concerts." The Boston Symphony went to New York to be greeted by the headline "Muck and his enemy aliens here tonight." [4]

Henry Lee Higginson tried his best to help Muck, calling him into his office for an interview. "Will you play the Star-Spangled Banner at the beginning of our concert today and always?" Higginson inquired.

"What will they say of me at home?" Muck asked.

Higginson replied, "I do not know, but let me say this: when I am in a Catholic country and the Host is carried by, or a procession of churchmen comes along, I take off my hat . . . out of respect for the customs of the nation. It seems to me only friendly and reasonable."

Dr. Muck said, " 'Very well, I will play the Star-Spangled Banner.' " But he also said he would like to resign at the end of the current season.

"Before the concert began on Friday afternoon, I went on stage," Higginson told. "I stated that Dr. Muck had resigned; that I had asked him to play the Star-Spangled Banner at the beginning of all our concerts and that he would do so—and he always did."

Mrs. Gardner walked out of the concert, believing that Dr. Muck had been cruelly coerced into an action against his musical conscience. The papers said she had turned her back on her country, which was entirely untrue.

Higginson was attacked "as a man who employs Germans" —and in 1918 he was forced to decide that this was the last year he would underwrite the Boston Symphony. He had not yielded to public opinion, however, but to mere mathematics. The previous year, he had absorbed a loss of $52,000. "This year it will be more than that," he said, and he simply no longer had the money.

Karl Muck asked for help in getting a permit to return to Europe, and "as a final act of courtesy Mr. Higginson applied to Washington—going on record concerning his faith in Karl Muck."

Mr. and Mrs. Muck "do not intend to come back. Also they wish to keep their going a secret until the time comes . . . I am satisfied with the fact that he has done nothing disloyal or injurious in any way to our country," Higginson said.[5]

The departure was a well-kept secret, but it seems more than likely that Mrs. Gardner knew that the Mucks were leaving. Anita Muck gave her a photograph of herself about this time—showing a really beautiful though no longer young woman who looked unutterably sad.

Before leaving, Karl Muck determined to create a lasting memory of great music. He was preparing the second of a series of "choral concerts" in which a large group of Boston musicians, both amateur and professional, took part. He had been working as he had never worked before and it was the last rehearsal of "Bach's Passion Music." During this final rehearsal, on March 25, 1918, "some United States officers came to the hall and proposed to take Dr. Muck off the stage and lock him up." They were persuaded to wait until the rehearsal was over. But they would not wait to let him conduct the concert next day.

Dr. Muck "was put in a police station cell. The next morning he was taken to Cambridge and after a few days there, was sent to Fort Oglethorpe in Georgia and interned . . ."

Town Topics had a field day. Dated April 4, 1918, their article read: "Mrs. Jack Gardner's inordinate craze for posing in the limelight is again shown since Dr. Muck's arrest. Mrs. Gardner has championed the German musical director and was the first unofficial person to arrive at the jail after his incarceration, but she was unable to get any farther than a half-open door, which permitted only a friendly wave of her hand in silent sympathy. Later, after pulling every possible wire, Mrs. Jack, loaded down with delicacies of all kinds, gained admittance to his cell and endeavored to cheer the Doctor up a bit. Her activities in thus rendering 'comfort and aid to the enemy' have turned her most loyal friends, as well as the public, much against the lady."

Dr. Muck was never tried for espionage, nor were charges of espionage or the spreading of enemy propaganda ever proven against him. He was interned for eighteen months and was finally allowed to return to Europe, where eventually he resumed his musical career.

From his "War Prison Barracks" at Fort Oglethorpe, Georgia, Muck wrote to Mrs. Gardner on August 9, 1919. The rules were that he could "write only two letters and four postal cards a month." He "had to use them all for communications with Anita"; but his wife was now with him and "the first letter" he "could spare" belonged to Mrs. Gardner.

"First of all, let me thank you from the bottom of my heart for your friendship which you have shown Anita during these last sad sixteen months. You can never know and never will I be able to express to you in words what it means to me to realize that of all our many friends in Boston, at least one has stood by my poor haunted wife. And that it was you, who so openly demonstrated your feeling toward us has made me proud and happy as well. Courage and independence always seemed to me to be an integrate part of you; but how much of both you had to have just at this time, the way you did! It was your wonderful loyalty which helped Anita over the bitterness of many a hard hour . . ." [6]

The "bitterness" for Mrs. Karl Muck did not lie entirely in her husband's having been accused of espionage. Mrs. Gardner may have guessed at another cause. But it was not until late in 1919 that the papers, in their zeal to make the most of sensational news, uncovered a private and personal story. It must have shocked the usually unshockable Mrs. Jack.

Mrs. Gardner had long since stopped attending all rehearsals of the Boston Symphony, but she was once called a "rehearsal girl"—and rehearsal girls of a younger generation, still developed admiration for a musician of their choice. They were a bit older than a coming generation of teen-agers who were to swoon over crooners and their manners were somewhat better even if their judgment was not.

The Boston *Post* printed "a very small story" about a girl who carried her admiration for Karl Muck too far. "The young woman," said the *Post*, "lived in the Back Bay section of Boston" and "was but 20 years old when she fell under the spell of Dr. Muck." She was "rich, with an assured social position" and "a fine musician."

The "small story" was greatly expanded when the *Post* was accused of telling lies. The scandal had been uncovered by government agents, the girl forced to hand over letters from Muck. "Her relations with Dr. Muck were not suspected by her family" and to protect the girl and her family, the *Post* suppressed her name.

But the *Post* quoted letters which were utterly damning to Muck. "I am on my way to the concert hall to entertain the crowds of dogs and swine who think that because they pay the entrance fee they have the right to dictate to me my selections. I hate to play for this rabble!"

Muck promised that in a "very short time our gracious Kaiser will smile upon my request and recall me to Berlin. Once there, . . . our Kaiser will be prevailed upon to see the benefit to the Fatherland of my obtaining a divorce and making you my own . . ." And in another letter, "It will perhaps surprise you," Karl Muck wrote, "that to a certain extent Mrs. Muck knows of our relation. She has a noble heart and her mind is broad beyond the comprehension of the swinelike people among whom we must live a little longer."

"Think of your poor Karl," he advised her. "God bless you my darling until I hold you again in my arms and cover you with kisses . . ." [7]

These letters were published and vouched for as coming from the files of the Attorney General at the end of November, 1919. Anita Muck's face, in the photograph she gave Mrs. Gardner, had overtones of sadness now explained. Two years went by and then Mrs. Gardner received a letter from Karl Muck.

"During my whole life I have been a tenacious, energetic man who could hardly be affected by anything. Now I know it was all Anita's work . . . With Anita, I have lost the best and most devoted wife, the noblest friend, the bravest companion. All that made life worth living died with her . . ." Karl Muck remembered Mrs. Gardner as Anita's "sincere, unchangeable friend." [8]

The United States went into the World War I crusade with banners flying, young hearts high, idealism untouched by doubt of being able to attain the goal of perpetual peace. Mrs. Gardner was no longer young, no matter how hard she might try to cheat the passing years. "These are sad times," she wrote toward the end of 1918. "We have chosen to go to war, therefore we must abide by that and do our best." Taxes worried her. She had "just managed to pay two taxes—and now comes the War Tax!" She was going to "live in one room" at Fenway Court and save every cent she could toward the endowment fund for her museum.

But when A. Piatt Andrew went overseas with the Red Cross she gave him an ambulance. The "Y," he named it, because "Y" meant Isabella.

In March, 1919, Mrs. Gardner wrote to Joseph Lindon Smith. He and Corinna had sailed for France during the autumn of 1917, "the care of French children uppermost" in their minds. They had both been at the front, in "exposed positions under frequent bombardment." Corinna said she "didn't know what morale meant"; but she soon found out as homesick soldiers crowded around her, just to look at "the lady from home," after the United States entered the war.

300

Then Joe's wonderful gift as an entertainer was discovered. Four months after the armistice, Joe was still working for the A.E.F. in veterans' hospitals in France.[9]

Mrs. Gardner wrote to him: "It is so long since I have heard from you, and only indirectly do I know where you are. I have longed for your love and affection. It has been a hard year—a turning point with me . . . I have thought much of an idea so long cherished by me that you would be here to look after and take care of F[enway] C[ourt]—but it has come to me that I cannot clip your wings and tie you down. It was cruel to you to think of it and now I must put the load on other shoulders. Carter was to be, after you, the choice of man to be in charge here—and now I am obliged to turn to him to help me . . . Carter has resigned from the [Boston] Museum [of Fine Arts] and will come here June 1st . . . Carter does not know, and I have told no one except Dr. Ross that you had been the hope I had." [10]

"Joe Colli," as he signed himself, wrote from Cannes, March 22, 1919. ". . . I was proud and always shall be that I was your choice," he told "dear Isabella," but "the realization of your plans meant my coming for service when the light and spirit of the wonderful treasure house had gone out of it . . .

"It makes me very happy to think that Carter will so soon be established there to help you. He is the ideal man for the position and I think you are both to be congratulated . . ."

Morris Carter graduated first in his class at Harvard in 1898, taking an A.M. degree in 1899. He concentrated on languages and from 1899 to 1902 was a teacher at Roberts College, Constantinople. Apparently as an afterthought while at Harvard, he had taken a fine arts course under Professor Charles Eliot Norton, who "would lean back somewhat in a trance, and discuss anything from Greek architecture to the Milan Cathedral," he said. Norton's influence made Carter curious to see "the things described" but Carter said of himself, that he "never did know much about art"—and his "first visit to the Boston Museum of Fine Arts was when [he] went there to work." [11]

Carter's position at the Museum of Fine Arts was that of librarian. He immediately became one of Mrs. Gardner's Museum boys and a friend of Matthew Stewart Prichard, who said in a letter to Mrs. Gardner, "I believe in Carter, who is hard-headed, sincere and thorough." In 1906, while Mrs. Gardner was abroad, Prichard wrote, "Carter has been made to succeed me and has been given positions I never at-

tained. He is Registrar as well as Secretary to the Director"
of the Boston Museum.

Carter wrote to Mrs. Gardner in 1908, signing himself
"one more lame duck." A few months later, he addressed her
as "Dear Dea." This was September and she had asked him
to come to live at Fenway Court, in the "little suite on the
ground floor" with its bath and facilities for cooking. "If I
make my dwelling place Fenway Court, shan't I, like every
poor person, be extravagant with other people's money?" he
asked. "Could you endure having a daily milkman, a weekly
tailor wait on me? Should you turn me out if I asked an entirely respectable gentleman to spend an evening with me? I
feel that your friendliness is much more important than that
very comfortable suite. What should I do without my dea ex
machina!"

Carter finally yielded to persuasion and sent his trunk to
Fenway Court on a Saturday. During the day, Mrs. Gardner
telephoned him at the Museum of Fine Arts to tell him to
have his trunk taken out at once. She had changed her mind,
probably because she wanted the rooms for someone else. It
was almost impossible to get an expressman to move the
trunk on Saturday afternoon but somehow Carter managed
it, realizing all the while that he had understood his Dea well
and that he had been right in refusing her invitation in the
first place.

As the years went by, Morris Carter obeyed an increasingly difficult woman, even if he frequently failed to please
her. Perhaps regretting that she had turned him out of Fenway Court, Mrs. Gardner made Carter a present of a piece
of land she owned in Brookline. He was pleased and proud
for a while, planning to build a small house for himself. It
soon developed, however, that Mrs. Gardner was going to
give him items from the Beacon Street house and would expect to design his house herself to fit these fragments. The
carved staircase, which she had hitherto been unable to part
with, was now bestowed upon Carter—he to pay the cost of
installing it. "Now, or rather when you see me, tell me if I
am to go on blind faith to build a house although I haven't a
cent of money," Carter wrote anxiously during the summer
of 1909—"or have you a vision of the future too dazzling for
my eyes?" Later, anxiety mounted to panic as he had to bor-
row money from his friend George Lathrop's father who was
a banker. It was all because Carter would not strike a hard
bargain with his workmen, Mrs. Gardner thought, and she
tried in vain to infuse sternness of spirit into him. Eventually,

Carter came to resent even the gift of land which he said Mrs. Gardner had parted with only to free herself of taxes on it.

Mrs. Gardner was nevertheless fortunate in discovering Morris Carter—a man who would be faithfully committed to her service for the rest of her life and for most of his own. In 1919, when she needed him to carry out her plans for her museum, he was still at her side. The "dazzling future" that she designed for him was that he should be Director of the Isabella Stewart Gardner Museum after her death. She laid down some astonishing rules, to be sure—but his appointment was for life. On December 24, 1919, Mrs. Gardner was taken seriously ill, during the night. She had suffered a fairly severe embolism, with some resulting paralysis on her right side. Carter was now indispensable to her as she dictated letters, gave him orders concerning the servants and continued to formulate her museum rules and regulations.

Impaired activity was humiliating to Isabella and she fought for recovery with considerable success. She gave it out that she "had the flu," which was easily believed because the "Spanish influenza" had been epidemic the previous year and was still going the rounds, although in milder form.

John Singer Sargent was in the United States. He had brought his sister Emily with him and they stayed at the Copley Plaza in Boston. Emily went to Professor Copeland's lectures and wrote to Mrs. Gardner on January 16, 1920: "Mr. Copeland spoke to me to say he hoped you were not ill, he had missed you. He was grieved and shocked to hear you had been laid up since the day before Christmas."

Sargent himself brought violets to Mrs. Gardner, remembering how much she loved them. He was surprised and puzzled at not being allowed to see her. Surely the "flu" could not last so long, nor still be considered contagious. It was not until February 24, however, that he and his sister were finally told they might call. "Excepting that your lovely voice was a little weak, you seemed as well as ever," Emily wrote. But she was stretching the truth.

Difficulty with walking remained and Isabella had herself carried about the palace in a "gondola chair" such as aging Venetians used in order to maintain dignity when no longer able to step in and out of their gondolas. Mrs. Jack gave it out that she had "a lame knee" and people wrote to sympathize and describe their own arthritis.

"I am selling Brookline—tell no one," Mrs. Gardner had written to Joseph Lindon Smith in 1919. As a matter of fact, she had turned Green Hill over to her nephew George Peabody Gardner, now returned from his sea duty during World War I and in need of a home. The terms were essentially those John L. Gardner had proposed in his will in case he survived his wife. Isabella was sorry to part with a place she dearly loved but it couldn't be in better hands, she felt sure. Moving a few items such as a large Italian fireplace and her portrait by Bunker, she now made Fenway Court her summer as well as winter home.

During the summer of 1920 the papers had it that she traveled by motor to the Berkshires. This was untrue, but Isabella hated to admit that she was not able to do anything of the sort. Piatt Andrew read the newspaper story and immediately invited Isabella to take a trip with him. She was forced to prevaricate. "The doctor won't let me go on our enchanting trip on the Potomac and the James . . . He says the bad kind of grippe I have had takes time and long care to get back real strength . . ."

The matter of Sargent's murals, which he had come to Boston to paint for the Boston Museum, was a little hard to handle. Sargent invited Isabella to come to see them and "make suggestions." There was nothing she wanted to do more, but how could she get up the granite steps outside the building and then climb the stone stair within to look at what Sargent referred to as the "half-baked dome"? Mrs. Gardner was now "as famous as Bunker Hill" and she was not going to let people see how hard it was for her to walk.

Pretending to know nothing of her impaired movement, Sargent suggested a back way to get into the Museum of Fine Arts. There was a huge lift he always used, he said, and a bath chair carried up in it was a "good way to save fatigue on arrival." Sargent seemed to be speaking for himself and his own distaste for exercise.

In January, 1921, *Town Topics,* whose pages had so often been enlivened by tales of Mrs. Jack, wrote of her at considerable length. "Doubtless in all Boston no one person or personality, to describe her truthfully, is more missed from her accustomed haunts than Mrs. Jack Gardner. Her name has been, above all others, one to conjure with, not only by those to whom she is personally unknown, who have watched her movements from a respectful, almost worshipful distance and read her name in the society columns with awe, but also the wide circle of friends, extending through the professional ranks, ofttimes. . . . Hers has been a most extraordinary life.

Coming from New York an almost unknown bride—for few knew of her comparatively quiet Isabella Stewart days—to enter, through her husband's position, into Boston's most exclusive and aristocratic atmosphere, was an ordeal to daunt the bravest, but in her case met with most surprising and unqualified success. Her keen wit and ready repartee, her high spirits, keen appreciation of all the finest in art, music and drama, with a signal brilliancy and charm, all moved on with the years."

The trouble was that it sounded altogether too much like an obituary. Moreover, *Town Topics* used the words, "since her stroke some months back." The secret was out.

In some ways, however, it was easier not to have to talk about grippe, the "flu" or a lame knee any more. It had taken *Town Topics* two years to discover the secret, which was, in itself, a triumph.

TWENTY-EIGHT

Suggestions for a Museum

$\mathcal{M}$RS. GARDNER HAD been writing out suggestions for running the museum at intervals for the last ten years. "There shall be two women to live in the house on board wages to do the cleaning and to be constantly on hand . . ." The "night and day watchmen—one for each time" must also "attend to the furnace." Under the heading "Important," Mrs. Gardner urged that her museum guards of the future must be "young men whose business is ushering."

Every time she rewrote her suggestions, Isabella added further restrictions and stipulations until she realized that she needed a lawyer to put all her rules into some form that no one could change. John Chipman Gray, her husband's cousin, would be just the man. He had worked with "Cousin Belle" for a good many years now. She told him to make her suggestions eternally binding by putting them into her last will and testament, so this he did in seven long articles. In the seventh article, he really surpassed himself and delighted his client.[1]

"If at any time the Trustees . . . shall place for exhibition in the Museum established under this will any pictures or works of art other than such as I . . . own or have contracted for at my death, or if they shall at any time change the general disposition or arrangement of any articles which shall have been placed in the first, second or third stories of said Museum at my death, except in the kitchen and adjoining bedrooms on the first floor, then I give the said land, Museum, pictures, statuary, works of art and bric-a-brac, furniture, books and papers and the said trust fund, to the President and Fellows of Harvard College in trust to sell . . . and to procure the dissolution of the . . . Museum."

The "said trust fund" was stated in the will to be $1,-200,000, which was to remain invested, the income going to "the increase of salaries of professors of "said college, or in sustaining scholarships" in case the rules should be broken causing a "dissolution" of the Gardner Museum.

But even if someone added a picture or moved a chair, Harvard would not get the Isabella Stewart Gardner collection. "I direct them to sell the same in Paris, France," she had Cousin John Chipman Gray write down for her. Then, as time went by, and she had herself carried about in a gondola chair, she ordered changes in various and sundry objects and pictures—a gleam in her eye as she reflected that no one else could move so much as a candlestick.[2]

Cousin John Gray attended to the legal language concerning Carter's dazzling future. "I direct that Morris Carter shall be director of the Museum. He shall have the power to make suitable rules for the conduct of the employees and visitors . . . He shall have the sole power of appointing and dismissing . . . subordinate officers and employees . . ." The trustees could increase his salary and they could employ and dismiss all future directors but "not the said Carter unless he be incapacitated from acting as said director." Isabella could not quite leave Morris Carter free, however. There must not be more than two servants employed "for the use of said Carter" and although he could have "a vacation of one month in every year," with the trustees empowered to make it two months if they wanted to, Carter must live "on the top floor and attic" of Fenway Court—these rooms to be arranged as the director pleased.

Isabella ordained that on her birthday, "the fourteenth of April in every year, the Trustees shall have a Memorial Service conducted by the Society of St. John the Evangelist, otherwise known as the Cowley Fathers, in the chapel at the end of the Long Gallery in the building occupied by the Museum established under this will . . ." As a rule, only saints, martyrs and royalty have prayers in perpetuity—but was not Isabella queen in her own palace forever![3]

Of course there were personal bequests in Isabella's will, one going to Maud Howe Elliott, who had been a friend in a time of grief and trouble. To Pablo Casals, noted cellist and composer, "I give my violoncello, now in his possession," Mrs. Gardner wrote. Loeffler had long since been given her Stradivarius.

Like all collectors worthy of the name, Isabella Gardner had been passionately acquisitive all her life. But she was giving to the public her much-loved art collection—with plenty of restrictions, to be sure. During her earlier married years she had bought, and her husband had given her, jewels which added up to another remarkable collection. She now set about giving them away—personally, rather than by last will

307

and testament, for the most part—and without any restrictions at all.

Mary Berenson was probably the first friend after Nellie Melba, to receive a rare jewel. The Berensons were again in the United States in 1920. Mrs. Gardner sent "splendid carnations" and "narcissi, promise [of] the New Year" to their hotel in Boston, in December. But she had not been able to confess to them that she was partially paralyzed, so she spoke of "headaches" in case she was having a bad day when they came to call. "We shall come to greet you at 11:30 in your bedroom—and then, if we may, come at 2 and be with you as long as we may. Please don't have a headache. We are so devoted to you," Mary wrote.

Whether or not the Berensons actually made a visit, after seeing Mrs. Gardner's condition, is not clear, but Mary tried to conceal her surprise and sadness by overdoing the cheerful attitude—"seeing you again, with eternal youth in your eyes and voice," she put it.

Certainly Mary and Isabella had long talks both now and later. Some of Mrs. Gardner's friends had been all too anxious to retail gossip about Berenson, as in 1911, for example, when Isabella had felt it her duty to warn Mary! "I am grateful to you for your offer of a stick wherewith to beat the silliness out of poor old 'Ramus—but I fear it will take more than that," Mary Berenson had replied. Berenson's nickname " 'Ramus" was of Mrs. Gardner's "contriving," Mary said, and she always used it in her letters.

The 1911 affair was with ". . . a nice creature, full of energy and good will, a thoroughly good sort." Mary wanted to "protect" the girl "from any inconvenient scandal by being her friend." She "really hoped that a little happiness" would be good for Berenson—but she was not going to step aside because if he married the girl, who loved "an exciting, semi-rowdy life, with endless cocktails and cigarettes and champagne suppers and practical jokes," Berenson's life would be made miserable. So Berenson was "really quite ill," owing to this "psychological shock, as his doctor calls it." Mary was "really fond" of him and hoped she had been "guided aright."

"The thing has got about pretty generally owing to some silly imprudences," Mary wrote. She thought Isabella was sure to hear who the girl was—but did not tell her name. Isabella could not but admire Mary Berenson.

From this time on, Mary's letters were apt to refer affectionately to Berenson's susceptibility. In December, 1920, writing from New York, "There are also certain lovely young

308

things into whose flames that old moth 'Ramus, precipitates himself . . . Well, well! Dearest Isabella, we shall see you soon." Perhaps it was at this time of their return to Boston that Isabella asked for her jewel box and selected a gift for Mary.

Mary wrote from New York on January 11, 1921. "Duveen advised me to have the ruby reset at Cartier's as he says they make a specialty of showing off the brilliancy of precious stone, and he said he had never seen a finer 'Pigeon's Blood.' I like not the name for all its glory, but I do love the glowing jewel!" [4]

On April 23, 1921, Mary Berenson was at Villa Sylvia, Ralph Curtis's home on the Riviera. "You can imagine the eager inquiries there have been for you, the affection expressed by us all and the heartfelt wishes for your return to health. Everyone, everywhere, loves to hear how triumphantly you have dominated Fate, how unchanged . . . you are, how you never speak of being ill and make everybody forget it. And then my magical ring that glows as if a lamp were in it, is passed around." Eventually, Ralph Curtis's daughter Sylvia was the recipient of one of Mrs. Gardner's rubies, set in a ring.

Summoning her favorite niece, Olga Gardner Monks, Isabella, who was still in bed after her first embolism, held up a long string of pearls. She counted them carefully and then snipped the string with scissors at the point where she wanted the pearls divided. Then she gave Olga her share.

Small subsequent embolisms, referred to as "shocks" but never mentioned at all in Mrs. Gardner's presence, deprived her of the use of her hands. She had her maid drape scarfs and shawls about her to conceal this, and Agnes was particularly skillful in arranging "a filmy veil" over head and shoulders—always white. Isabella liked the effect, praised Agnes, and defied the time-worn custom of wearing black when age overtook her.

As soon as she was able to drive out again, Isabella had herself taken to the house on the corner of Beacon and Berkeley Streets where the former Edith Lawrence, now the wife of a Gardner nephew, Harold T. Coolidge, lived. "Aunt Belle asked me to come out and get into the motor with her," Edith recalled.

"Will you unfasten my necklace?" Aunt Belle said. Edith thought that the pearls must be somehow uncomfortable and did as she was told.

"Now put the necklace on," her Aunt Belle commanded. "I brought it for you."

"Of course I was flabbergasted," Edith Coolidge remembered, "and wore the necklace from then on." Nothing pleased Isabella more than to see people flabbergasted.[5]

To Olga Gardner Monks, Mrs. Gardner gave the huge diamonds, the "Rajah" and the "Light of India," which had so often flashed at the opera, making Mrs. Gardner's box the real center of the stage despite many an operatic prima donna's best efforts. To Olga also, Isabella brought a small but cherished object—the child's purse with the gold pieces given her by her father. "My only treasure as a child," she wrote in the note accompanying it.

Not all of Mrs. Gardner's gifts went to members of the family or even to godchildren, each of whom received tokens, large and small. There was, for example, Professor Charles T. Copeland, whose lectures at Harvard she had attended constantly until she was overtaken by illness.

James Putnam, one of "Ysabella's" most attractive young men, remembered driving Mrs. Gardner, in A. Piatt Andrew's car, from Gloucester to Cambridge in a sleet storm—to attend a Copeland lecture. The road was hazardous to a degree, the narrow wheels of the early-vintage vehicle were without chains and the car with its high carriage top and isinglass side windows threatened to skid into the ditch at every curve. But "Faster—faster!" Mrs. Gardner cried. "I shall be late—and Copey will ask me to withdraw!" [6]

She was the great Mrs. Gardner by this time but always the shy pupil sitting before her favorite professor. She was thrilled when Sargent's sister Emily, attending Copeland's lectures, brought word that Copeland had missed her when she was kept at home by illness. She now had Carter write him to ask what gift she might give him, proposing certain items. Dating his letter 31 March, 1920, Professor Copeland replied, ". . . the table but not the statuette because it would surely get broken. Mayn't I have instead some little old book you care for? I thank you heartily and pray for your recovery."

On April 9, the gifts had arrived. "I never meant a rare book . . ." Copeland exclaimed. He was "delighted with the table—the only trouble is it makes my dusky parlor look a 'tenement.'" Mrs. Gardner had asked for advice about books to have read aloud to her. "They sh'd read you from Lord Fisher's volume, *Memories—Records* is much less alive," Copeland suggested. He promised to come to see her "when lectures" stop and he later made an appointment for "Friday

the fourth [of June] I hope, at three-thirty for half an hour"
—being anxious not to tire his eighty-year-old pupil.

Mary Berenson, in one of her letters, spoke with less than her usual tact of Isabella as "improved" by her illness. As she went about bestowing her jewels and favorite keepsakes upon those she loved, this might seem to be true. But she was the same fiery Isabella when occasion called for it. She was still penny wise and pound foolish. When she discovered that the water to run her hydraulic elevator in the palace was costing five cents a ride, she had a tank installed, so that the water could be used over again. This cost more than the water company would have charged for years to come.

The days when Mrs. Gardner stood watching the public shuffle unseeingly through her museum had left their mark on her. "Don't touch," she had cried out angrily at intervals —whether anyone were touching anything or not.[7]

The fact that Mrs. Gardner had a collection of rare books as well as paintings was known only to her friends. She realized that the books ought to be catalogued, so she sent for Miss Mary Rollins, a free-lance cataloguer who had done special collections at the Boston Public Library. After they had come to an agreement as to hours and the rate of pay, Mrs. Gardner laid books out on a table in the middle of the Macknight Room, seated herself at one side, the librarian at the other. Miss Rollins reached for a volume. "Don't touch," cried Mrs. Gardner, almost automatically.

"But how am I to catalogue them then?" Miss Rollins asked.

"I'll handle the books on this side of the table—you do the cataloguing on *that* side," said Mrs. Gardner.

"I can't catalogue that way," Miss Rollins tried to explain. "It would ruin my reputation as a serious librarian."

"Then I'll have to do it myself," said Mrs. Gardner to the departing expert. Miss Rollins later said that Mrs. Gardner produced a remarkably good catalogue—"for an amateur." [8]

Beginning in 1920, when Mrs. Gardner lived at Fenway Court both summer and winter, Morris Carter kept a sort of day book for her. He put down expenses, brief notations of guests and activites—and a record of Isabella's orders, so that when she changed her mind he would have proof. Using an old notebook to save the cost of a new one, the record told of Isabella running true to form at the age of eighty: by turns parsimonious or generous, arbitrary or reasonable, as the mood took her.

"Aug. 17. Gas bill $6.29," Carter wrote.

"Aug. 27. Mrs. Gardner said she wanted the coal range now in the laundry work room, put in Margaret's kitchen, and the gas range now in Margaret's kitchen put into the laundry room."

"Sept. 6. New cook came."

"Sept. 18. Gas bill $7.02."

"Sept. 23. New cook came this afternoon."

Bolgi, still Mrs. Gardner's faithful major-domo, put a new grate in the old stove and a plumber came to install a new "water front" in it to the tune of $21.53. But now the gas bill was $8.10. So the new gas stove was never taken back to the kitchen, though cooks might come and cooks might go—their wages all of fifteen dollars a week.

Musicians, old friends of Mrs. Gardner's, were still in Europe, suffering now from food shortages. Mrs. Gardner sent supplies, in their case not bothering to count the cost. She sent money in generous amounts—worries over the palace gas bill all forgotten.

In September, 1922, John Singer Sargent called on Mrs. Gardner. She sat erect, swathed in white, her veil "a fleecy cloud from Heaven" according to Agnes, her maid, who had arranged it. Strangely, almost miraculously it seemed, the wrinkles had disappeared from her face and repose had come into it. Sargent commenced a conversation.

There was just one woman in Boston whose portrait he would like to paint, he said. But he was afraid to ask permission for fear she would refuse.

The old fire gleamed in Isabella's eyes as she commanded John not to be ridiculous. "There isn't a woman on earth who would refuse to let you paint her portrait," she declared.

"I'm glad to hear that," Sargent remarked. "You see, you are the one."

On September 14, 1922, he painted a portrait in watercolor of Isabella Stewart Gardner. There she sat, her veil not "fleecy" but austere like the stylized folds of the headdress of a sculptured Roman priestess. There was no hint of effect or striving in the pose. Her eyes looked straight forward into the future and somehow, Sargent managed to suggest with only a line or two, that the future was eternity; that Isabella knew it but was not afraid.

To be a master in watercolor takes practice, precision and genius because no brush-stroke once put in can well be changed. To paint white in all its variations, where most people see only absence of color, takes a keen eye. Sargent's watercolors were the equal of his oils and sometimes surpassed them, as Mrs. Gardner well knew, for she had bought many. His last portrait of her is one of the best things he ever did.

Isabella set it up on top of a bookcase where she could see it from her couch in the Macknight Room. There it stands, for she never took it down. It is often overlooked or underestimated by people whose eyes do not see—or discovered with delight by those who look long and carefully. This would suit Isabella. Sargent told so much about her that she would not want to have the portrait studied by anyone unwilling to be her friend.

Music, amateur theatricals, dancers, all came to Fenway Court, making it Boston's center of the performing arts, now that Isabella no longer went to her accustomed box seats. During the autumn of 1922, Loeffler came to play some of his recent compositions. The Braggiottis, who were rehearsing their act at the Keith Theater, came to dance in the Tapestry Room. Mrs. Gardner gave Berthe Braggiotti a Chinese amber necklace because she danced so beautifully.

Leslie Buswell, who had been one of Isabella's favorite young men ever since he appeared as juvenile lead with Cyril Maude in *Grumpy,* came with an amateur group to give plays in the Court. Often, he just came to call and, like Sargent, was impressed by a look of serenity in Isabella's face during those days of old age. "There was not a wrinkle. Her face was like porcelain. I held her hand," he said.

There must have been a gleam of mischief in Isabella's eyes, just the same. Leslie Buswell had criticized the two cloisonné vases she had on her mantel in her private apartment—so she left them to him in her will! [9]

She would not have been Isabella, had not a new young man attracted her. He was Edward Weeks, future famous editor of the *Atlantic Monthly.* Isabella was lying on a couch in the Macknight Room, a great brazier beside her glowing with coals, when he met her. She was tearing up letters and burning the fragments. There were pieces of heavy-quality stationery, pieces of blue or gray—different handwritings. Young Mr. Weeks looked at them as much as he dared. Were they love-letters? The romantic young man liked to think they were. [10]

Many letters reached Mrs. Gardner during her last years which were not destroyed. Count Hans Coudenhove, whom Mrs. Gardner met in Venice in 1890, now wrote her from Africa. His letters, which told of his life among Africans, his love of animals, were so interesting that she suggested that he write articles for the *Atlantic.*

Ellery Sedgwick wrote Mrs. Gardner, August 23, 1921. "Wonderful in many ways, you are most wonderful I think in your limitless interests . . ." He was in Nyasaland when he got a contribution from Coudenhove and he supposed he was "the first American to know him but nothing is hidden from the starry telescope of Fenway Court. But it is odd, isn't it, that the very mail which brought me your note brought me a second letter from Mr. Coudenhove . . . Mr. Coudenhove's second paper will appear in the October issue . . ."

"Since you had the great kindness to write so nicely about me to Mr. Sedgwick, I always have the feeling when I write for his Review, that I write chiefly for you," Coudenhove told Mrs. Gardner. She dictated replies for Morris Carter to write, telling of her life at the palace, of "the birds, the linnet and the finches" she kept in the Court.

Previously, his mental picture of her, Coudenhove said, "suggested rather the person of an Empress of Byzantium, bedecked with priceless jewels and living in a palace of marble lace." Her recent letters to him had changed all that and he much preferred the new Mrs. Jack having "palavers with coal merchants and police superintendents." This "calls for my sympathy," he suggested, "although I rather gather that you enjoy them."

"Your letter . . . pleased me awfully on account of the human touch in it, derived from your admission that you smoke," Coudenhove wrote, and he hoped that her tiny little parakeet was well and that she was still enjoying strawberries and pretzels.

He thought Mrs. Gardner should have a big dog, but she was devoted to her fox terriers, so much so in fact, that she provided in her will a gift to the Animal Rescue League of Boston "in memory of the dogs, Foxy and Rowley." And the Society for the Prevention of Cruelty to Animals was left a legacy on condition they "expended each year the sum of seventy-five dollars . . . for a free stall" in memory of three of her horses, Dolly, Pluto and Lady Betty.

John Gunn was another friend who wrote to Mrs. Gardner. He had been her courier—perhaps the one who collected all the bets when he put up with her temper-tantrums in Sicily. He had come to the United States, probably in 1904, and now, seventeen years later, recalled how she had entertained him at Green Hill. "You had had poppies planted that year on the upper side of the walk by the brick wall . . . We spoke of the height of the poppies and to measure a big one you pulled it over against my head and gave my head just the faintest graze with your hand. It was one of the thrills of my whole life. 'Are you six feet tall?' you asked in your calm, lovely voice.

" 'Yes, nearly six feet one' I said,—and that was all there was to that. We walked out of the garden and back up the winding path under the lindens and out into the moonlight again and to the home and my wonderful little scene was over . . . How many times have I dreamed of that garden and walking with you there! Sometimes I have said I must ask you to go again with me there and we would reconstruct that scene—you would do that much for me—but I never quite dared." Some of the letters Mrs. Gardner burned were doubtless more pretentious than this one from John Gunn— still a courier after many years. None could have touched her heart more than his, which she kept.

In June, 1923, *Town Topics* wrote of Mrs. Gardner's "critical illness . . . she is closely guarded by nurses and physicians," they said, "and is forbidden to greet even relatives and close friends." Five months later, on November 8, 1923, they wrote: "Still energetic, Mrs. Jack Gardner of Fenway Court timed her annual public opening of her art museum in her big mansion, to catch the trump card, John Sargent . . . The noted artist was in years past first man on Mrs. Jack's choicest visiting list . . . It's worth going to the Fenway Palace if only to see that yearly crowd of sightseers of all classes for whom the chatelaine, now full of years, fills the eye much more than her wonderful collection of art treasures. With Sargent by her side, the picture background was complete and one woman in the big throng told . . . the doorman . . . that she didn't care for the stuff but only wanted to have a good look at the lady who picked it up."

One of the throng was an art instructor at Connecticut College who remembered her student days at the Museum School when she had seen Mrs. Gardner standing in the middle of a ballroom floor "and swarming around her and trailing behind were ten or a dozen of the leading male members of Boston Society, just like flies around honey . . ." The teacher looked at Isabella Gardner now, some twenty years later. "She was seated on a little dais in one of the first floor rooms" of the palace "dressed in a lovely fabric and with an ermine robe over her knees. She was ghastly white and I was so surprised and really shocked to see her there, I just naturally spoke—and believe it or not she was friendly and gracious." Mrs. Jack was still not entirely reconciled to the

315

throng who came merely to stare, but as always, she recognized a kindred spirit at sight. [11]

There was now a very young generation of nephews and nieces for Mrs. Gardner to appraise and approve—or disapprove. One was a little boy, J. Randolph Coolidge,[12] whose mother went to call on Aunt Belle—letting him come along for the ride, although not dressed for tea. He stayed outside in the car but Aunt Belle asked about him, ferreted it out that he was outside and sent Bolgi to bring him in. Barefooted, somewhat soiled and very scared, the boy pattered along the cloister to find a lady, pale of face, seated on a marble throne in a flower-filled courtyard. The sight was not at all reassuring but immediately the lady sent Bolgi for something. It proved to be a papier-mâché tiger which Isabella Stewart Gardner presented to the youngest John Randolph Coolidge. The tiger's head was designed to be pulled off, revealing candies inside! There was but one conclusion to come to—Aunt Belle was all right.

The family had been anxious from time to time about Mrs. Gardner's health but on April 14, 1924, she celebrated her eighty-fourth birthday in fine style. She seemed so well that in July her niece Olga Monks "went down to Monument Beach, feeling perfectly safe." Morris Carter was invited by Mrs. Gordon Dexter to take her car and chauffeur and go on a vacation with his wife. The Carters had reached Pittsburgh by July 7 when a telephone call summoned them back to Boston.

The seventh of July had been a hot day. Isabella went out that morning in the now ancient Pierce-Arrow, and again in the afternoon, because the Elks were having a convention and the crowded, decorated streets entertained her. When she got home, an old friend saw her before she got out of the automobile and said she was never gayer but the exertion had been too great. Soon after she got into the house she had a severe angina attack. The doctor came and gave opiates which, at first, "did not overcome the pain." [13]

There was relief by evening, however. Isabella enjoyed the cool quiet of the palace she had built and which was now her only home. She could listen to the birds in the courtyard and hear the gentle falling of water into the marble sarcophagus at the foot of the double stairs. She knew people but could not speak. Her dear Olga came and promised to carry out the "Directions for my Funeral" that Isabella had written eleven years previously and given to her. On July 14, at 10:40 in the evening death "came peacefully."

"Next morning, as she directed," Isabella Gardner's coffin was "placed beside the Spanish Chapel and covered with her purple pall." It was the one she had used for her husband's funeral and then once more when she had begged Mrs. Thomas Bailey Aldrich to use it at the time of her husband's death because "nothing black should shroud his airy spirit in its flight." Isabella had asked that violets be placed on the coffin, "if in season"—and white roses and heather if there were no violets, the cross to be the entire length and width of the coffin. Her flowers were white roses.

"Candles were lighted at the head and feet," according to an account written at the time. There was a mirrored door at the foot of the coffin which was covered with a linen sheet against which a black crucifix was hung. "Father Burton came and read the prayers for the dead, and all the time, two sisters, either from the Order of St. Anne or of St. Margaret, remained in supplication until the body was taken to the church for the funeral.

"Saturday morning Father Burton said a mass attended only by the family and the household, Mrs. John Chipman Gray and Leslie Buswell.

"Monday morning, Father Powell said a mass which was attended by the family and intimate friends.

"The funeral was at the Church of the Advent at 12 o'clock Monday, July 21, 1924, burial in the Gardner tomb at Mt. Auburn."

"Carry my coffin high—on the shoulders of the bearers," read the "Directions for my Funeral" Isabella Stewart Gardner had written. "They will have to be told exactly how to do it." So, in accordance with her last commands, they carried her high—as for the funeral of a queen.[14]

Acknowledgments

First of all, I want to express my gratitude to Mr. George Peabody Gardner, Chairman of the Board of Trustees of the Isabella Stewart Gardner Museum. I shall not soon forget his graciousness in meeting me at the Museum to discuss my project. The kind invitation of Mr. and Mrs. Gardner to call at Green Hill gave me a most valuable opportunity to increase my understanding of a complicated subject.

Mr. George L. Stout, Director of the Museum, gave me invaluable cooperation and Mr. William N. Mason, Assistant Director while I was at work upon research, expended time and infinite patience in my behalf, answering numberless questions and finding for me the most difficult-of-access items, such as Gardner journals. Miss Evelyn Burr was unfailingly kind, no matter how often I interrupted her work or invaded her office to search files for elusive references. All the other members of the office staff deserve thanks for their cheerful cooperation.

Mr. Joseph Pratt took infinite pains with photographs made especially for this book. I would like to thank Mr. Dennis Mahoney for material brought me from his own collection having reference to Mrs. Gardner; Mr. Leslie, Guard in the Macknight Room where my questions would try the patience of a saint; Mr. Deering and other guards whose personal recollections of Mrs. Gardner I greatly enjoyed. These are gentlemen accustomed to ushering in every sense of the words Mrs. Gardner used to describe them. I wish I could mention all the other employees by name; they were unfailingly courteous and helpful and play an important part in keeping the Gardner Palace unique among museums.

All the members and connections of the Gardner family that I was able to locate were wonderfully helpful. The first among these whom I met was Mr. John Randolph Coolidge of New York. Mr. and Mrs. Coolidge invited me to call at their home when I was on the threshold of my studies. They gave me my first glimpse of Isabella as a fascinating woman of real genius and their enthusiasm for my project was the greatest help.

Mrs. Constantin Pertzoff, her husband and family went out of their way to be kind and helpful, to show me family heirlooms and to talk of Mrs. Gardner. Dr. Richard W. Dwight who took my husband and me out to the Pertzoff's home, cleared up for me in conversation many a puzzling point of family ramifications.

I recall with pleasure and gratitude my call on Mrs. Julian Lowell Coolidge, who talked of Julia Gardner Coolidge, sister-in-law of Mrs. Jack Gardner. I was privileged to meet her son, Mr. John Phillips Coolidge, Director of the William Hayes Fogg Art Museum, Harvard University, whose store of Gardner information proved both entertaining and useful.

I cannot possibly forget Marjorie Mills and her delight in my subject, her rallying to my aid. She realized that it would not be easy to find first-hand information concerning Mrs. Gardner, but when she opens her "Marge" column in the *Boston Herald* with "Dear Everybody," she means exactly that. Her friends did not fail her. I am grateful to her and to the people who wrote to her, whose names I have included in *Notes,* wherever possible.

Mrs. Thomas Howard, who knew Mrs. Gardner through her great aunt, Maud Howe Elliott, has been unfailingly kind, especially in interesting her friends in my behalf. Mrs. L. Mortimer Pratt, Jr. arranged for me to talk with her mother, Mrs. Stuart, a delightful lady who told about penances at the Church of the Advent and the sin of flirting, of which girls repented in her day. Mrs. James Craig commended me to Mrs. M. M. Osborne, an author whose work I admire and who was also able to speak the right word for me on Beacon Hill. In this connection I wish to thank Mrs. Harvey H. Bundy for the use, with the permission of Mr. George Peabody Gardner, of startling Lowell letters.

Mrs. Frederick S. Bacon opened a new chapter in Mrs. Gardner's life by inviting me to her summer home on Eastern Point, Gloucester, where she assembled neighbors, many of whom had important information; as for example, Mrs. Henry M. Newell, Mrs. Samuel Barlow and Mrs. Henry S. Drinker, Jr. It is with deep regret that I learn of the death of Mr. Leslie Buswell, one of the most helpful and delightful members of this group.

Corinna Lindon Smith, author of *Interesting People* and other books, holds a unique place among those who have contributed material. Although much younger than Mrs. Gardner, Mrs. Smith knew her well and I have kept her recollections in her own words as much as possible. Mrs. Harold Bowditch is another who knew Mrs. Gardner and, as an artist, could give me an artist's impressions.

I recall with gratitude the encouragement given me by the late Dr. Harold Bowditch. Our friendship began with his generous help to me in 1942 and has continued through the years. I carried a list of Mrs. Gardner's contemporaries to him and he gave me facts concerning them which included a description and appraisal of Mrs. Gardner's physician.

Among those who knew Mrs. Gardner, I wish to thank Edward Weeks, one of the youngest of her last group of young men, and James Putnam, in whose private affairs she took plenty of interest.

Professor Leon Edel, the Henry James authority, has been most helpful, as also Professor Robert Gale, Thomas Crawford biographer, and I much appreciate the kindness of Professor John Pilkington, Jr., biographer of Francis Marion Crawford, and Professor Edward Wagenknecht.

To meet Miss Katherine M. Gericke was like having the people in Mrs. Gardner's musical circle come to life. Although the daughter of the great Wilhelm Gericke, Boston Symphony conductor, Katherine Gericke is first of all an artist and has assisted in conservation work at Fenway Court.

Mrs. John Gray took me to see her great-aunt, Mrs. Henry D. Tudor, who remembered Mrs. Gardner well and showed me the book of photographs kept at 176 Beacon Street when the Gardners and Tudors were neighbors.

As always, libraries and librarians have been my allies, to whom I am most grateful. I would like to thank Miss Caroline Jakeman, Houghton Library, Harvard; Mr. Timothy Beard, Genealogy Room, New York Public Library; Mr. Arthur Carlson, Map Room, and Miss Geraldine Beard, Librarian, New York Historical Society; Mr. Stephen T. Riley, Massachusetts Historical Society; the staffs in the Music Rooms, Boston Public Library and New York Public Library; Miss Carol Walden, New England Conservatory of Music library; the staffs, Boston Museum of Fine Arts library, American Antiquarian Society and Sterling Library, Yale; and Miss Elizabeth Sherrard, Rare Books Librarian, Baker Library, Dartmouth.

Mr. Walter Muir Whitehill, Librarian, Boston Athenæum, encouraged me from the beginning of my project. Mr. David McKibbin, head of the Art Department at the Athenæum and authority on Sargent, was extremely helpful. He also supplied many a delightful item concerning Boston personalities.

I am grateful, as many times before, to Julia Ward Stickley, Archivist, for help at the Library of Congress and the Federal Archives. Miss Mildred Henman, formerly of the Music Copyright Department, now retired, described George Proctor and his pupils.

I could not have finished my book without the help of Miss Nancy Hoyt, Reference Librarian, and Miss Grace Walmsley of the Ferguson Library in Stamford, and Miss Bernice Merritt and staff of the Darien Free Library.

Mrs. Gardner's multiple interests led me to some unusual sources. Among these are specialists in yachting, horse racing and the collecting of jewels. I appreciate especially the help given me by Tiffany and Company, The Country Club (of Brookline), the Jockey Club, the *Morning Telegraph*, the New York Yacht Club and the Chicago, Burlington and Quincy Railroad. Also, the staff at the courthouses of Kings, Queens and New York Counties of New York and Suffolk County, Massachusetts.

Many other people have helped me in gathering Gardner legends and in sorting out facts from fancy. I wish I could name them all.

Chapter Notes

1: MRS. JACK GARDNER

1. The weather on opening night was reported in the Boston *Transcript*, together with the progress of the coal strike—and Mrs. Gardner's reception.

2. One of the engraved invitations is in a letter book; Norton Papers, Houghton Library, Harvard University.

3. Diary of Willard T. Sears, Mrs. Gardner's architect. A copy of this record is in the archives of the Isabella Stewart Gardner Museum, hereinafter called Museum archives.

4. *Town Topics*. This remarkable magazine is the source of much lively comment concerning Mrs. Gardner. It was started by W. R. Andrews in Cincinnati in 1874 and was called *Andrews' Bazaar*. Four years later, Andrews took his journal to New York where he also sold dressmaking patterns known as "Andrews' Printed Paper Patterns." In 1879, he founded *Andrews' American Queen;* and in 1885, E. D. Mann bought the paper, changed the name to *Town Topics* and started the column called "Saunterings," where most of the witty comments are to be found. Paul Meredith Potter (later a playwright) was drama critic; Alfred Trumble, a bright young journalist, became an editor untroubled by scruples, and *Town Topics* was noted for social gossip. There were those who said that "Col. Mann's reputation was somewhat lower than a horse thief in New York." Mann was acquitted in a libel suit brought against him, however, and according to Ludwig Lewisohn in *Expression in America, Town Topics* was "a school for critics and short story writers and the columns should one day be sedulously analyzed for the brilliant light that would thus be thrown upon our cultural history during certain years." See *A History of American Magazines*, by Luther Mott, vol. 4, Harvard University Press.

5. Doggett's *New York Directory*, 1840–1841.

6. Marriage announcement, New York *Evening Post*, May 1, 1839: "St. Johns Church Brooklyn, Tuesday morning 30th ult. by Rev. E. M. Johnson, David Stewart of this city to Adelia Smith, daughter of the late Selah Smith of the former place."

7. David Stewart Importer . . . President: See *New York City Directory; Longworth Directory* and *Trow's Directory*. Address was No. 10 University Place, according to Doggett's *New York Directory*. It was Number 20, according to *Isabella Stewart Gardner and Fenway Court*, by Morris Carter, 1925, Isabella Stewart Gardner Museum, Inc.; hereinafter referred to as Carter.

8. Selah Smith Administration papers, granted to Ann Smith, his widow, Nov. 2, 1818, "he having died intestate." King's County, N.Y., Courthouse.

9. See article entitled "Smithtown," Patchogue *Advance*, Apr. 9, 1959.

This legend is "shattered" in *The Town of Smithtown*, vol. I, Chap. X, ed. by Paul Bailey, Lewis Historical Publishing Co., 1949. This book says that Lion Gardiner was granted 100 square miles by Wyandach, Sachem of the Montauk Indians and bequeathed this land to Richard Smith "in return for various favors."

10. *Antiquities of the Parish Church, Jamaica, including Newtown and Flushing,* by Henry Onderdonk, Jamaica, N.Y., 1880.
11. New York State Bulletin No. 4: "Slavery in New York," A. J. Northrup, 1900.
12. Carter.
13. *Ibid.*
14. Probate records, Queens County, N.Y., Courthouse.
15. *A Small Boy and Others,* by Henry James, Scribner, N.Y., 1913.
16. This note was written to Mrs. Gardner's niece, Olga Gardner Monks, and was given by her to her daughter, Olga Monks Pertzoff, with whose kind permission I quote.

2: GARDNER–STEWART

1. *A Practical System of Modern Geography* . . . by J. Olney, 1830, Hartford.
2. *The School-girl in France* was published annonymously in Philadelphia in 1850.
3. I am indebted to the late Dr. Harold Bowditch for this story.
4. *The Gardner Memorial, a Biographical and Genealogical Record of the Descendants of Thomas Gardner, Planter* . . . , compiled by Frank Augustus Gardner, M.D., and privately printed in Salem, Massachusetts, 1933, was presented to me by George Peabody Gardner, Chairman of the Board of Trustees of the Isabelle Stewart Gardner Museum. I am most grateful for this book which has proved indispensable. Hereinafter referred to as *Gardner Memorial.*
5. *A Century of Banking in New York, 1822–1922,* by Henry Wysham Lanier, the Gilless Press, New York City, 1922. Hereinafter called Lanier.
6. Lewis Cass, Jr., was appointed chargé d'affaires to the Papal States in 1849 and promoted to U.S. Minister in Residence in Italy, serving from 1854 to 1858. His father was secretary of state under Buchanan. Appleton's *Cyclopedia of American Biography*, 1888.
7. Ida Agassiz Higginson to Mrs. Gardner: Museum Archives. Also told by Mrs. Gardner to Ellery Sedgwick: *The Happy Profession,* 1946, Little, Brown.
8. Lanier.
9. Photograph, Map Room, New-York Historical Society, New York City.
10. Carter. Letters written by Isabelle Stewart to Julia Gardner are quoted in part in Carter. They must have been returned, perhaps to some member of the Coolidge family, for they are not in the Museum archives. But diligent inquiry has failed to locate them, if they still exist.
11. *Memories of Fifty Years in the Last Century,* by Caroline Gardner Curtis and Emma Forbes, privately printed, Boston, 1947. (Presented to me by the late Charles P. Curtis.)
12. *Boston, A Topographical History,* by Walter Muir Whitehill, 1959. The Belknap Press of Harvard University. Hereinafter called Whitehill. The Somerset Club bought the Benjamin W. Crowninshield house on the corner of Beacon and Somerset Streets in 1851 and occupied it until 1872.

13. *Ibid.*
14. *Ibid.*
15. Carter.
16. *The Diary of George Templeton Strong,* ed. Allan Nevins and Milton Halsey Thomas, 1952, Macmillan.
17. *Ibid.*
18. The Hotel Boylston was owned by Charles Francis Adams. Rents were "from $400 to $3,000 and higher"—King's *Dictionary of Boston,* by Edwin M. Bacon.
19. The Boston *Transcript* and the Boston *Advertiser* for Oct. 18 and 19, 1860.

3: "TOO YOUNG TO REMEMBER"

1. *Gardner Memorial.*
2. *The Autobiography of T. Jefferson Coolidge, 1831–1920,* 1923, Boston, Houghton Mifflin; hereinafter called Coolidge.
3. *Ibid.*
4. *Ibid.*
5. *Gardner Memorial.*
6. *The Memorial History of Boston,* ed. by Justin Winsor and James R. Osgood, vol. III, 1885, Boston.
7. *Coolidge.*
8. *Memories Grave and Gay,* by Florence Howe Hall, 1918, New York, Harper; hereinafter called *Memories.*
9. Description of sewing circle: *An American Politician,* by F. Marion Crawford, 1885, Boston, Houghton Mifflin.
10. Fireworks: Boston *Daily Advertiser,* July 6, 1863.
11. *Coolidge.*
12. Draft: Boston *Daily Advertiser,* July 9, 10, 14, 1863.
13. *Ibid.*
14. *Coolidge.*

4: JACKIE

1. *Gardner Memorial.*
2. Carter.
3. *Gardner Memorial.*
4. Copy of letter of Mrs. John Amory Lowell to her son Augustus, sent me by Mrs. Harvey H. Bundy and quoted with the kind consent of Mr. George Peabody Gardner.
5. Description of characterization of Dr. Bigelow was supplied by the late Dr. Harold Bowditch.

5: PARIS AND PEARLS

1. Museum archives.
2. Material on Paris and the Exposition is from *In the Courts of Memory,* by L. de Hegermann-Lindencrone, 1912, New York, Harper.
3. *XIXe Siecle en France,* by John Grand-Carteret, Paris, 1893; *The Age of Worth, Couturier to the Empress Eugénie,* by Edith Saunders, 1955, Indiana University Press.
4. *Memories.*
5. Bigelow to Mrs. Gardner, Museum archives. This undated letter speaks humorously of the reduced price of Jacqueminot roses, thus dating it to some extent. The Jacqueminot rose was named for a

French general who died in 1867. Society notices concerning New York free spenders mention lavish use of Jacqueminots, forerunner of the American Beauty.

6. Boston *Transcript,* October, 1867.
7. Oliver Wendell Holmes to John Lothrop Motley, Nov. 16, 1872; *Life and Letters of Oliver Wendell Holmes,* by John T. Morse, Jr., vol. II, 1896, Boston, Houghton Mifflin.
8. *Memorial History of Boston.*
9. Museum archives.
10. *Ibid.*

6: BELLE GARDNER, DIARIST

1. Museum archives. Discovery of Mrs. Gardner's journals was one of the exciting moments during my days of research as guest of the Gardner Museum.
2. Long and careful study of the many small volumes of John L. Gardner's diaries at the Museum proved both useful and entertaining.

7: THE INTELLECTUAL MRS. GARDNER

1. *John Jay Chapman and His Letters,* ed. by M. A. DeWolfe Howe, 1937, Boston, Houghton Mifflin. Hereinafter called Chapman.
2. *Gardner Memorial.*
3. William Amory Gardner to Morris Carter, Museum archives.
4. *Three Generations,* by Maud Howe Elliott, 1923, Boston, Little, Brown.
5. Kindness of the late Leslie Buswell, who told me of "reading" with Mrs. Gardner when she was about seventy. Ernestine Drinker Barlow told me that she heard Mrs. Gardner's voice at about this time, not knowing who was speaking—and entered the room expecting to meet a young girl.
6. *The Letters of Mrs. Henry Adams,* ed. by Ward Thoron, 1936, Boston, Little, Brown. Hereinafter called *Mrs. Henry Adams.*
7. *Ibid.*
8. Henry James to Mrs. Gardner. Museum archives. All letters of Henry James quoted in this book were taken from the files of the Gardner Museum or from the Baker Library, Dartmouth College, with permission in each case. Some of this material which appeared in *Henry James, The Middle Years,* by Leon Edel, 1964, New York, J. B. Lippincott Company (hereinafter referred to as Edel) was quoted with permission of both author and publisher. All letters of Henry James were used with the approval of John James, literary executor of Henry James. The kind cooperation of author, publisher and literary executor is greatly appreciated.
9. Museum archives.
10. *Mrs. Henry Adams.*
11. Museum archives. See also Edel.
12. *Howells, His Life and World,* by Van Wyck Brooks, 1959, New York, E. P. Dutton.
13. *Mrs. Henry Adams.*
14. Museum archives. See also Edel.
15. *Ibid.*
16. *Howells, His Life and World,* by Van Wyck Brooks.

8: "CHANDELIERING"

1. Much of the material in this chapter I collected but used only in part

in my biography, *Three Saints and a Sinner,* which was the story of Julia Ward Howe, Louisa Ward Crawford (afterwards Terry), Annie Ward Mailliard and Sam Ward.

In *My Cousin F. Marion Crawford,* by Maud Howe Elliott, 1939, New York, Macmillan, hereinafter called *My Cousin,* letters are presented out of chronological order. Many are undated. Taken together with the letters by Crawford to Mrs. Gardner in Museum archives, I feel that the picture here presented is fair to both.

Francis Marion Crawford, by John Pilkington, Jr., 1964, New York, Twayne Publishers, Inc., (hereinafter referred to as Pilkington) contains excerpts from letters which I also found at the Gardner Museum or at Houghton Library. This excellent and sympathetic biography also includes letters from Crawford to Mrs. Gardner concerning the problems of a novelist which I have omitted, but which give further information about their long friendship.

2. *My Cousin.*
3. *A Diplomat's Wife in Many Lands,* by Mrs. Hugh Fraser, 1910, New York, Dodd, Mead.
4. *My Cousin.*
5. *Ibid.*
6. *Memories.*
7. In a letter to his mother, Crawford said that Mary Perkins finally rejected him on Christmas Eve. Pilkington.
8. *My Cousin.*
9. "Difficulties of a Flowery Reform," *The Nation,* No. 918, Feb. 1, 1883.
10. *Three Generations,* Elliott.
11. *The American Politician,* Crawford.
12. *My Cousin.*
13. *Ibid.*
14. *The American Politician,* Crawford.
15. Museum archives.

9: "NO GOODBYE"

1. *My Cousin.*
2. Houghton Library. See also Pilkington.
3. *My Cousin.*
4. Museum archives.
5. *My Cousin.*
6. Pilkington.
7. *My Cousin.*
8. Museum archives.
9. *An American Politician,* F. Marion Crawford.
10. Howe papers, Houghton Library.
11. *Studi Americani,* No. 5, ed. by Robert L. Gale, 1959, Rome.
12. *My Cousin.*
13. Museum archives.
14. *Roman Spring: Memoirs,* by Mrs. Winthrop Chanler, 1934, Boston, Little, Brown.

10: CAMBODIA FOR A BROKEN HEART

1. Mrs. Gardner to Maud Howe Elliott. Typescripts of a long series of these letters are in the Museum archives. I have preferred to use Mrs. Gardner's own account in her journal, for the most part, however.
2. All Gardner family correspondence: Museum archives.

3. For an early description of Angkor Wat, see "The Forgotten Ruins of Indo-China," by Jacob E. Connor, *National Geographic Magazine*, vol. XXIII, No. 3, March, 1912. The spelling of places has been modernized in accordance with that shown in the *Rand McNally World Atlas*.

11: HEART-WHOLE RETURN

1. Museum archives.
2. All details of the journeys are from Mrs. Gardner's journal or from John L. Gardner's line-a-day record, Museum archives. For photographs and description of temples at Madura, however, see "The Marriage of the Gods," by John J. Banniga, *National Geographic Magazine,* vol. XXIV, Dec. 1913.
3. Pickman Papers, Houghton Library, Harvard University.
4. Memorandum by Henry W. Swift, Museum archives; *Memories.*
5. John L. Gardner line-a-day record.
6. Museum archives.
7. *Gardner Memorial.*
8. Museum archives. See also Edel.
9. Edel.
10. *The Country Club, 1882–1932,* by Frederic H. Curtiss and John Heard, 1932, Brookline.
11. *Town Topics.*
12. Museum archives.

12: MUSIC AND DIAMONDS

1. All details about jewels are from Museum archives. I asked Tiffany & Co. if they had any information about the two great diamonds, "The Rajah" and "The Light of India," and Mr. William T. Rusk, President, wrote, "I am afraid there is just no way that we can tell positively just which Mrs. Morgan is referred to in our bill of March 28, 1886 . . . I have however discussed the matter with my old school friend, Mr. Henry Sturgis Morgan, and he tells me that his great grandmother, Mrs. Junius Morgan, died in 1882. It is entirely possible that this is the lady in question. However, he suggests that there may have been other Morgan ladies who are distantly related to his family who may have died at around that same period . . ."
2. Clayton Johns never married. He was remembered by Olga Monks Pertzoff as a gentle old man who often visited her mother, Mrs. Gardner's niece, Olga Gardner Monks. He was born in 1857, died 1932.
3. Lena Little was born 1865 and died in New Orleans in 1920. She was a member of the Cecilia Society of Boston and appeared as a concert artist from time to time, her picture published in musical periodicals, but with very little information about her career.
4. *American Composers . . . ,* by Rupert Hughes and Arthur Elson, 1914, The Page Co.
5. "The Great Organ in the Methuen Music Hall," by Edward W. Flint, 1961, Methuen Memorial Music Hall, Methuen, Mass. Reprinted in *Yankee* magazine, November, 1963.
6. *The Boston Symphony Orchestra,* by M. A. DeWolfe Howe, 1914, Boston, Houghton, Mifflin.
7. *Ibid.*
8. Obituary: Charles Martin Loeffler, 1861–1935, N.Y. *Times,* Boston

Herald, May 21, 1935; Olin Downes, special article N.Y. *Times,* May 26, 1935.

9. Loeffler to Mrs. Gardner, Museum archives.
10. Leon C. Elson, music critic, quoted in *The Boston Symphony Orchestra.*
11. Museum archives.
12. *Cup Race History,* by H. L. Stone and William H. Taylor, 1958, Van Nostrand: *$30,000,000 Cup,* by Jerome Brooks, 1938, New York, Simon and Schuster.
13. Chapman.

13: THE SARGENT PORTRAIT

1. Henry James to Mrs. Gardner: Museum archives.
2. I am indebted not only to *Sargent's Boston,* by David McKibbin, 1956, Boston, Museum of Fine Arts, for information on John Singer Sargent, but also to talks with Mr. McKibbin. All the letters from Sargent to Mrs. Gardner are in Museum archives and Mr. McKibbin has studied and dated many of them—a tremendous help.
3. Whistler's letters to Mrs. Gardner are in Museum archives.
4. *Dennis Miller Bunker,* by R. H. Ives Gammell, 1953, Coward-McCann, contains much information. Letters are in Museum archives.
5. Hereinafter spelled "Denis," as in the Gardner Museum catalogue.
6. My cousin Edith Buffum, former teacher of art at the Moses Brown School in Providence, R.I., studied at the Cowles Art School as a young girl. She tells me that the girls all ran to the window for a look at Mrs. Gardner when she drove up to the school in her carriage. Mrs. Jack was always "all swathed in veils."
7. Pickman Papers: Houghton.
8. Howe papers: Houghton.
9. I have enjoyed and found most useful *Berenson,* by Sylvia Sprigge, 1960, Boston, Houghton Mifflin. Mrs. Gardner's correspondence with Berenson was not found by Miss Sprigge at *I Tatti,* as she points out in this biography.
10. *Ibid.*
11. All letters from Berenson to Mrs. Gardner are in Museum archives.
12. Again, David McKibbin, Director of the Art Department, Boston Athenæum, has given me information, not only about Sargent, but also about his friends.
13. *The Happy Profession,* by Ellery Sedgwick, 1946, Boston, Little, Brown.

14: LA DONNA ISABELLA

1. *Sargent's Boston,* by David McKibbin, contains a "biographical summary" giving dates of Sargent's whereabouts almost year by year from birth to death. Evidence that Sargent was not in Spain is also found in Bunker's and Sargent's letters in Museum archives.
2. Joseph Lindon Smith's first meeting with Mrs. Gardner is told in *Tombs, Temples and Ancient Art,* edited by Corinna Lindon Smith, 1956, Norman, University of Oklahoma Press.
3. *Reminiscences of a Musician,* by Clayton Johns, 1929, Cambridge, Washburn and Thomas.
4. This story comes through Marjorie Mills and her wonderful *Marge* column in the Boston *Herald.* On December 16, 1962, she said, "So into the mail comes a letter from 92-year-old David Hanson of

Wollaston in beautifully penned script." Marjorie Mills sent me a copy of the letter which says, "I saw your statement that there were only two people living who knew Mrs. Jack Gardner. She attended the Church of the Advent where I was one of the choir boys and I remember when she arrived on Sunday morning with a pail and washed the granite steps at the front door. She also took us boys out to The Country Club and I was surprised to see that one of the seams in her tight-fitting waist had split open. There were other things that I have forgotten as I am 92 years old and have been a chorister ever since I was ten years old."

5. *Town Topics.*

6. David Stewart's will, New York County Courthouse, identifies Edgar S. Hicks as Mrs. David Stewart's brother. Edgar S. Hicks is further identified as a business associate of David Stewart in Folio 820, Conveyances of Land, New York County Courthouse. The second Mrs. Stewart, after David's death, married the German-born American painter Albert Bierstadt in 1894, "a handsome man of polished bearing," according to the *Dictionary of American Biography.* It was also Mr. Bierstadt's second marriage, and according to *Town Topics,* "The brief advance intimation of this event quite took Mrs. Jack's breath away . . ." Bierstadt had been invited "to a very smart dinner given by a prominent Fifth Avenue hostess living but a few blocks from the Stewart mansion, for the very day of his marriage. He simply regretted, saying he should be detained by a very important engagement at that time." There are no paintings by Bierstadt at the Gardner Museum!

7. *Interesting People,* by Corinna Lindon Smith, 1962, Norman, University of Oklahoma Press.

8. *Town Topics.*

9. Museum archives.

10. *Ibid.*

11. Norton papers: Houghton.

15: QUEEN OF HOLY BACK BAY

1. *The Journal of Thomas Russell Sullivan, 1891–1903,* 1917, Boston, Houghton Mifflin; hereinafter called Sullivan.

2. A handwritten copy of T. R. Sullivan's journal containing passages not in the printed version is in the Massachusetts Historical Society and will be referred to as Sullivan ms.

3. *Town Topics.*

4. *Gardner Memorial.*

5. Sullivan.

6. Sullivan ms.

7. Jephson letters and photographs: Museum archives.

8. *Town Topics* dates the locomotive story, which is a favorite among those who remember Mrs. Jack.

9. Sullivan ms.

10. Inevitably, the amount of Mrs. Gardner's inheritance from her father was exaggerated. These figures are from the "Appraisal for Taxation of the Estate of David Stewart," as filed in the probate court records of New York County. A notice published by the St. Andrews Society, found in the Genealogical Room, The New York Public Library, reads as follows: "David Stewart, born Auchterarder, Perthshire, on August 7, 1810. At the time that Mr. Stewart joined the Society he was a member of the firm of Paton and Stewart, importers of up-

holstery and dry goods at 20 Cedar Street. He married Adelia, daughter of Selah Smith in 1839. In 1851 he became director of the Niagara Fire Insurance Company; 1865 director Fulton Bank; 1868 —director New York Eye and Ear Infirmary; life member St. Andrews Society . . . he died at Hotel Champlain July 17, 1891 and was buried from Grace Church . . ."

11. *Reminiscences of a Musician,* by Clayton Johns.
12. *The Paderewski Memoirs,* by Ignace Paderewski and Mary Lawton, 1938, Scribner's.
13. Again, there was exaggeration as to the fee. This amount is from John L. Gardner's cash accounts, Museum archives.
14. *Reminiscences of a Musician,* by Clayton Johns.
15. Mrs. Munro's letter, Museum archives.
16. *Reminiscences of a Musician,* by Clayton Johns.
17. Proctor correspondence, Museum archives.
18. Henry James to Mrs. Gardner, Museum archives.
19. Henry James to Ariana Curtis, Baker Library, Dartmouth College.
20. Henry James to Mrs. Gardner, Museum archives. See also Edel.
21. Stillman to Mrs. Gardner, Museum archives.
22. *The Wings of the Dove,* by Henry James, 1902.
23. Jewels: Museum archives.

16. THE GARDNERS: ART COLLECTORS

1. Coolidge.
2. This picture, now in the Gothic Room, occasionally moves one of the guards at witticism. If people stare at it too avidly, he sometimes asks them if Adam has forgotten something. Of course Adam has not forgotten his clothes because he has yet to acquire any. The guard says that Adam has forgotten to shave! And sure enough, the rather red-skinned Adam has bluish jowls!
3. The *Catalogue of the Exhibited Paintings and Drawings,* by Philip Hendy, printed for the Isabella Stewart Gardner Trustees in 1931, gives the date of Whistler's marriage as 1886. The *Dictionary of American Biography,* which I have here followed, gives August 11, 1888.
4. "Harmony in Blue and Silver" is now in the Yellow Room at Fenway Court.
5. *The Life of James McNeill Whistler,* by E. R. and J. Pennell, 1908, Lippincott.
6. Among other pictures acquired in 1892 were *A Samoan Dancer,* by John La Farge, an American painter noted for his work in stained glass, who became one of Mrs. Gardner's many friends; and *Love's Greeting,* by Rossetti, painted "prior to 1882." The Gardners arrived on the scene a little too late to be able to find many pre-Raphaelite pictures for sale. They bought four sixteenth-century tapestries for their Beacon Street house. The cost of paintings and other objects of art in the Gardner Museum is recorded in the "Museum Books," a long series of loose-leaf notebooks which consolidate all known facts about each item and show the inventory value at the time of Mrs. Gardner's death.
7. James to Mrs. Gardner, August 1, 1893, Museum archives.
8. Sullivan.
9. Bourget letters: Museum archives.
10. This description of Crawford is from the papers of my friend the late Margaret Fayerweather, who was of great help to me while I was working on *Adventurous Alliance,* my biography of Louis Agassiz

and Elizabeth Cary Agassiz. These papers are now in the Henry W. and Albert A. Berg Collection, New York Public Library.

11. Crawford correspondence with Mrs. Gardner: Museum archives.

17: ENTER BERENSON

1. Lanier.
2. *Unforgotten Years,* by Logan Pearsall Smith, 1937, Boston, Little, Brown.
3. All correspondence, Berenson to Mrs. Gardner: Museum archives.
4. A letter from Crawford and one from Minnie Bourget, both in the Museum archives, had comments on them.
5. *Reminiscences of a Musician,* Clayton Johns.
6. *Ibid.*
7. James to Mrs. Gardner: Museum archives.
8. James to Mrs. Daniel Curtis and all the other James-Curtis correspondence quoted are in the Archives Department, Baker Library, Dartmouth College. Permission to publish has been generously given. My attention to these letters was kindly directed by Mrs. Schuyler Owen, a direct descendant of Ralph Curtis, who had placed the correspondence at Dartmouth.
9. Journal, Mrs. Barrett Wendell, Houghton Library, Harvard.
10. Sullivan.
11. Information on horse racing activities came from the Jockey Club and from the *Morning Telegraph,* publisher of *Goodwin's Official Turf Guide.* The Jockey Club told me the years in which Green Hill Stable was officially registered with them, and its colors. The *Morning Telegraph* has an extensive library of turf information, and Mr. Samuel Perlman, its publisher, very kindly helped to trace down the available information about Green Hill Stable, particularly about the horse Halton.

18: ART AND LIONS

1. I have taken the liberty of paragraphing some of Berenson's longer letters. This he rarely did, doubtless mindful of the cost of transatlantic postage, but some of his closely written pages are hard to follow.
2. I was told in Boston, by a lady who said she had the story from her mother's diary, that Mrs. Gardner was fond of lying on the bearskin rug in front of the Titian and imagining herself to be Europa. In photographs of Beacon Street interiors, there is, to be sure, a bearskin rug—but it is in front of the fireplace. I asked this lady, a stranger to me, if I might see her mother's diaries. "Oh," she said, "we burned them—it was Mother's request."
3. *History of the Boston Symphony,* by M. A. DeWolfe Howe. I am aware that there are those who believe that Mrs. Gardner did not smoke. She spoke appreciatively of Turkish cigarettes, however, in the course of her world tours and a letter from Count Hans Coudenhove (Museum archives) dated July 27, 1924, spoke of "your admission that you smoke."
4. Carl Emos to Mrs. Gardner: Museum archives.
5. Again I wish to thank Marjorie Mills, columnist for the Boston *Herald,* this time the date being February 17, 1963. "Maude Ogilvie sends a nice Mrs. Jack Gardner reminiscence for Louise Hall Tharp. 'In 1889–1899,' she writes, 'the Public Library was moved from

Boylston Street and a circus moved in for the winter. We school children could go in for a dime. Several afternoons, I saw Mrs. Jack in elegant furs taking one of the lions for a walk on a leash.' "

6. *The Saga of American Society,* by Dixon Wecter, 1937, New York, Scribner's.
7. Sullivan ms.
8. *Ibid.*
9. This conversation and the story of the dinner party is from an interview with Mrs. Joseph Lindon Smith, whose help I so much appreciate.
10. Sears diary, Museum archives.

19: AN END AND A BEGINNING

1. Museum archives.
2. *My Musical Life,* by Walter Damrosch, 1930, New York, Scribner's.
3. This story of Siegfried's aria was told to me by J. R. Coolidge.
4. *Town Topics.*
5. *Ibid.*
6. Berenson letters: Museum archives.
7. Negotiations for the purchase of pictures, jewelry and objects of art were made in British pounds, Italian lire, French francs or United States dollars, depending on the kind of money that Mrs. Gardner's agent and the seller used. Sometimes her agent wrote her in terms of two or more kinds of money. Throughout this book I have used the currency mentioned in the documents. Sums in foreign currency can be converted into dollars by applying the rates then existing, that is, one British pound was equal to $4.8665 or about five dollars; one lire or one franc equaled $.193 or about one-fifth of a dollar.
8. Mrs. Joseph Lindon Smith heard Mr. Gardner call his wife "busy Ella" at dinner, the night they discussed the building of the museum on Beacon Street.
9. Sears diary.
10. The land on which Fenway Court stands was bought by Mrs. Gardner in several parcels, the first conveyance having been dated January 31, 1899. Subsequent purchases were made in April and July, 1899 and on February 26, 1900.

20: FENWAY COURT

1. Will of John L. Gardner, Suffolk County probate records.
2. Sears diary.
3. James to Mrs. Gardner, Museum archives.
4. James to Mrs. Curtis, Baker Library archives.
5. Mrs. Joseph Lindon Smith told me this.
6. All quotations from Berenson, Charles Norton and Joseph Lindon Smith are from Museum archives.
7. Newspaper clippings in Museum archives concerning the Botticelli, not identified in text, had no source or date.
8. In her Boston *Herald* column, Marjorie Mills quotes Humphrey Doulens, president of Columbia Artists, and writes that "Humphrey has known most of the greats over the years" and told her this story.

21: MR. SEARS'S LAMENT

1. All quotations directly concerning the building of Fenway Court are from the Sears diary.

2. *Town Topics.*
3. *Ibid.*
4. Bolgi, also spelled Bolgy, and so pronounced.
5. Various versions give a different number of notes for different workmen. This one is from Carter.
6. Miss Dorothy Annable wrote me of the blind children's concert, having been told the story by Miss Helen Conley, a cousin who lived at Perkins Institution for the Blind for a number of years.

22: NINE O'CLOCK PUNCTUALLY

1. The Sears diary is, as in previous chapters, the source of all direct Sears quotations and of information concerning palace-building activities.
2. A pen-and-ink sketch of Bolgi's uniform, painted in watercolor, is in Museum archives. It is not signed but is drawn in Joseph Lindon Smith's dashing style.
3. A comparison of photographs of Beacon Street interiors with Fenway Court rooms shows this little border.
4. *The General Catalogue of the Isabella Stewart Gardner Museum,* compiled by Gilbert Wendel Longstreet in 1935, refers to the portrait of Mary Stewart as "ordered in connection with her betrothal to the future Philip II of Spain" and it is argued from this that the pearl in the portrait is not La Pelegrina, because this pearl was a wedding gift. But it is highly likely that the pearl was presented well in advance and that Moro would show it in the portrait out of courtesy to Philip. On the death of Mary Tudor, the pearl was returned to Spain and was eventually taken by Joseph Bonaparte as part of the loot which he carried off when he fled as ex-king of Spain. He left it to his nephew, Prince Louis Napoleon, who sold it in London to "the father of Lord Frederic Hamilton," according to a transcript from *Here, There and Everywhere,* by Lord Frederic Hamilton, which Mrs. Gardner kept in her files. The pearl had never been pierced and was "so heavy that it was constantly falling out of its setting." Lord Hamilton's wife lost it three times—the last time at Buckingham Palace where she saw it "gleaming at her from the folds of the velvet train of the lady immediately in front of her . . ." It was finally "bored, although this impaired its value."
5. This musical organization was first called "The Cecilia." There were 100 mixed voices selected by a committee; their first regular concert being given November 19, 1874. During the first two seasons all concerts were a capella and during the first years concerts were given for subscribers only. There were about 300 of these but in 1891 "wage earner's concerts" were given and continued for 20 years, admission being 25, 35, and 50 cents, only wage earners being eligible to attend. Blocks of tickets were given to employers for distribution. The name was changed from the Cecilia Society and in 1900 the group sang Beethoven's *Missa Solemnis* at the dedication of the New Symphony Hall on Huntington Avenue—and also at the last performance in the old Music Hall that same year.
6. The late Dr. Harold Bowditch attributed this story to this lady.
7. Mr. John Phillips Coolidge remembered hearing of this passage at arms with Edith Wharton. Since the guest list for opening night included only Mrs. Gardner's older friends, I have found no eyewitness. But I am indebted to Mr. William Mason for positive authentication of the menu of doughnuts and champagne, as told to him by the late Richard Arnold Fisher, architect.

1. I am indebted to guards at the Gardner Museum for this story of Bolgi and the coachman searching for the lost Mrs. Gardner.
2. Joseph Kenny, aged eighty-one, telephoned this to the "Marge" column of the Boston *Herald*, Feb. 3, 1963.
3. The Music Room at the Boston Public Library has bound volumes containing programs and newspaper clippings concerning the Cecilia Society. The Boston *Advertiser*, April 14, 1903, contains the story of the insult to the singers, beginning with a recap of opening night. "They were not invited to break bread . . . never again would they cross the threshold of Mrs. Gardner's tenement house, they hotly declared . . . She [Mrs. Gardner] personally assured the 16 young women . . . that the New Year's incident was one she deeply regretted . . . so last night the Cecilia members declared off the 'strike' and sang C. M. Loeffler's *L'Archet* with the usual musical appreciation."
4. Loeffler correspondence: Museum archives.
5. When, as a student at the School of Fine Arts, Crafts and Decorative Design, I visited Fenway Court in 1918, this sketch was hanging against a pillar in the courtyard. Sargent had painted Mrs. Gardner with a veil over her face, which I recognized as a tour de force but which also amused me, because I had already observed that the lady was not beautiful. This sketch is now in the Yellow Room—corroborating the statement that Mrs. Gardner changed the position of various objects before her death, although they could not be changed by anyone else afterward.
6. *The Cushing-Endicott House, 163 Marlboro Street,* by Diana Whitehill Laing, reprinted from the *Proceedings* of the Bostonian Society. I am grateful to Walter Muir Whitehill for sending me this excellent monograph.
7. See series of photographs in *Sargent's Boston*, by David McKibbin, 1956, Boston, Museum of Fine Arts.
8. After the death of Charles Martin Loeffler in 1935, his widow, the former Elise Fay, gave his correspondence and music manuscripts to the Library of Congress. All letters from Miss Fay to her future husband are from this source. All letters from Loeffler to Mrs. Gardner, quoted, are in Museum archives.
9. Boston *Post;* Boston *Herald* obituaries, Feb. 24, 1931. *Melodies and Memories,* by Nellie Melba, 1926, New York, Doran.
10. Okakura Kakuzo returned to Japan where he died while still a young man. "In his memory Mrs. Gardner and a few other devoted friends performed . . . ancient Shinto rites, the story of which gave social Boston something to talk about for nine days and more," according to an unidentified clipping in Museum archives. This probably started the story that Mrs. Jack had become a Buddhist.
11. Whitehill.
12. Prichard to Mrs. Gardner, Museum archives. The Prichard letters give a good picture of the cast controversy, famous in its day.

24: PUBLIC PRAISE AND BLAME

1. *The Cushing-Endicott House,* by Diana Whitehill Laing.
2. I have heard more than one version of this story but I use the one told by Mrs. Joseph Lindon Smith in *Interesting People*.
3. Upon reading Marjorie Mills's column in the Boston *Herald*, William

R. McAllaster kindly wrote me of this personal experience. "She [Mrs. Gardner] placed me exactly in the doorway near the Titian *Europa*," he said. He wondered if "the little red ribbons were of the same type that she tied around the necks of the lion cubs . . ." I have imagined Mr. McAllaster's feeling of knighthood but I think it shines through his letter.

4. Quoted by Berenson in his reply to Mrs. Gardner's letter: Museum archives.

5. *Isabella D'Este, Marchioness of Mantua*, by Julia Cartwright, 1903, E. P. Dutton, New York.

6. *Hercules* is now in the Room of Early Italian Paintings, formerly the Chinese Room.

7. The *Dictionary of American Biography*; also the *Catalogue of the Isabella Stewart Gardner Museum*, by Philip Hendy, 1931. In the catalogue that I bought in 1918, Mrs. Gardner remained true to Isabella.

8. Drake de Kay very kindly wrote me of his great-aunt Katherine Bronson's red wig and referred me to the *Cornhill Magazine*, Feb., 1902, which contains an article entitled "Browning in Venice; being recollections of the late Katherine De Kay Bronson." A prefatory note by Henry James says that Mrs. Bronson died the previous year.

9. James to Mrs. Curtis, Dartmouth archives.

25: THE CUSTOMS AFFAIR

1. I am indebted to Mrs. Henry Newell for all Henry Davis Sleeper letters and A. Piatt Andrew letters both to and from Mrs. Gardner.

2. This story is from excerpts of letters copied from the correspondence of Mrs. Charles Sumner Hamlin to her sister-in-law, Harriet Hamlin. Typescripts were kindly sent to me by Mrs. Leighton Brewer (Mrs. Hamlin's niece) at the suggestion of my friend Professor Edward Wagenknecht. According to *Who's Who in America*, William Henry O'Connell became Bishop of Boston in August, 1907. He was not elevated to the Cardinalate until 1911, which makes it difficult to account for the reference to "the Cardinal" except that the letter must be a reminiscence, since it says, "In those days" when describing evening dresses.

3. I was the guest of Mr. and Mrs. Frederick S. Bacon at the house formerly owned by Miss Davidge. Mr. and Mrs. Henry Newell, who were friends and neighbors of the Bacons at Eastern Point, most kindly allowed me to see Red Roof. Ernesta Drinker Barlow, grand-niece of Miss Beaux, invited me to see Miss Beaux's home and studio. Mrs. Barlow, as a young girl, had been Miss Beaux's model and told of a call made by Mrs. Gardner. Standing outside the studio door, Miss Beaux's niece heard a beautiful young voice. She entered to find Mrs. Gardner, then about sixty-eight.

4. All of the old customs house records have been destroyed. Fortunately, however, an account written some years ago, based on an examination of these records, had been preserved at the office of my publishers, Little, Brown and Company, from which this story was reconstructed.

5. *Interesting People*, by Corinna Lindon Smith; also personal interview.

6. *Duveen*, by S. N. Behrman, 1951, New York, Random House.

7. "Anecdotal Sketches of Famous New Englanders," by William Phillips, unpublished manuscript, Houghton Library, Harvard University. This undated episode I have placed at this period from information on Mr. Phillips in *Who's Who in America*.

26: "OLD TIMES AND NEW"

1. Crawford to Mrs. Gardner, Museum archives; Crawford to Julia Ward Howe, from *My Cousin . . .* , by Maud Howe Elliott. Further details are from my own notes taken in connection with my Ward family biography, *Three Saints and a Sinner*.
2. Museum archives; also quoted in part, Pilkington.
3. *Letters of Henry Adams,* edited by Worthington Chauncey Ford, 1938, Houghton Mifflin; Henry Adams to Mrs. Gardner, Museum archives.
4. Interview: Mrs. Joseph Lindon Smith.
5. *Gardner Memorial*.
6. Letters of Henry Adams.
7. Interview: Mrs. Joseph Lindon Smith.
8. *Ibid*.
9. Mrs. Harold Bowditch told me of this. Her mother was not entirely pleased to have an unexpected guest. I asked Mrs. Joseph Lindon Smith if Mrs. Gardner often went where she was not invited. "Why yes, if she thought it would interest her," Mrs. Smith said.
10. Naomi Bevard lived at the Students' House in the Fenway in 1918 when I was also there. Mildred Hinman, composer and music copyright expert in Washington, D.C., was also a fellow student and she recently supplied details about Proctor. I am also indebted to Isabelle Carpenter, a student at my school who got in touch with me as a result of Marjorie Mills's column and gave me an account of the prizewinning scene.
11. James to Mrs. Curtis, Dartmouth archives.
12. James to Mrs. Gardner, Museum archives.
13. This is a tale told with variations but this version, given me by J. R. Coolidge, seems the most authentic.
14. I am indebted to William N. Mason, assistant director of the Gardner Museum while I was doing research there, for this typical scene.

27: TWENTIETH-CENTURY ISABELLA

1. *Reminiscences of a Musician,* Clayton Johns.
2. *Town Topics*.
3. *Gardner Memorial*.
4. New York *Herald,* March 14, 1918.
5. *Life and Letters of Henry Lee Higginson,* by Bliss Perry, 1921, Atlantic Monthly Press.
6. Karl Muck to Mrs. Gardner, Museum archives.
7. A file of this entire affair is in the Music Room, Boston Public Library.
8. Museum archives.
9. *Interesting People,* Corinna Lindon Smith.
10. Mrs. Gardner to Joseph Lindon Smith, Museum archives. This letter is undated but was slightly before March 22, 1919, the date of the reply.

    Denman Waldo Ross, lecturer on the theory of design at Harvard and a trustee of the Museum of Fine Arts, was born in Cincinnati in 1852 and died in Cambridge, Massachusetts, in 1935. A competent artist, he painted for pleasure, having other sources of income. He presented Mrs. Gardner with examples of his work, which are now in the Blue Room and the Macknight Room. He also purchased items for Mrs. Gardner from time to time.

11. *Harvard Alumni Bulletin*, 1954. All first-person quotations; building of the house, etc., are Carter to Mrs. Gardner, Museum archives.

28: SUGGESTIONS FOR A MUSEUM

1. A printed copy of Mrs. Gardner's will is in the Museum archives.
2. The Isabella Stewart Gardner Museum at Number 28 The Fenway, Boston, Massachusetts, is open Tuesday, Thursday and Saturday from ten o'clock to four; on Sundays, from two to five—and also on the first Thursday in every month from ten in the morning until ten at night. It is an unforgettable experience to see the palace in the evening when the ancient candelabra shed their magic light. Mrs. Gardner loved candles and used them with a reckless disregard of fire hazard. Now, comparatively few candles are lighted to flicker at a safe distance from such inflammable items as priceless tapestries, but electricity has been used with so much art that the effect is still mediaeval.

Only on national holidays and during the month of August could a present-day Western visitor have the dismal experience of finding the Gardner Museum closed. There is no longer a fee for admission.

The guards, "young men whose business is ushering," are no longer very young, but they have the good manners implied in the all-but-obsolete word "ushering." Some of them remember Mrs. Gardner, and if properly encouraged, will tell an anecdote or two—but they will neither hear nor speak a word of evil about a great lady they have loved.

Not but what a touch of humor is permitted. Upon the dark red tiles of some of the floors, marks are painted in orange to show exactly where the feet of each chair or table must go. "Every third Tuesday in the month, Mrs. Gardner comes back at two A.M. to see if everything is all right. If not, there's hell to pay in the office," one of the guards said.

3. On April 14, each year, after the bronze gong in the Cloister sounds and visitors leave, a few friends gather in the Long Gallery. Like Miss Katherine Gericke, daughter of the former great conductor of the Boston Symphony Orchestra, for example, they have been invited to come to Isabella's birthday mass. Cowley Fathers seat themselves in the sixteenth-century choir stalls. Candles have been lighted. The chanting begins.

At this season there are Easter flowers in the court. Grown in larger, more modern greenhouses, they are even handsomer than in Mrs. Gardner's time. Her touch is evident, however, where the Chinese red nasturtiums are concerned, for these climbers hang upside down, their roots in pots on high balconies, their heads almost touching the ground far below. At all times of year, plants are constantly renewed, changes taking place before the Museum opens in the morning so that petals rarely fall and the flowers seem as immortal as the art in the rooms overlooking the Court.

In the afternoon when the Museum is open, there is a concert in the Tapestry Room and an especially fine program to be heard on Sundays. Gifted young musicians still have a chance of recognition, as in Mrs. Gardner's day. Fires burn in the capacious Italian fireplaces when the weather is chilly, for she always loved the smell of woodsmoke from an open fire.

4. Mary Berenson to Mrs. Gardner, Museum archives: letter headed New York City and dated Nov. 26, 1920—"Here we are and writing

to the Copley Plaza for rooms . . ."—places the time as at the end of 1920 and in the notebook kept by Morris Carter are entries that Bernard Berenson was in Boston from December 23, 1920, until January 11, 1921. All Berenson correspondence is from Museum archives.

5. I am indebted to Edith Lawrence Miles for this firsthand story of Mrs. Gardner's gift of pearls. Olga Monks Pertzoff very kindly showed me the pearls which had been given to her mother.

6. James Putnam told me this and many another delightful story of his association with Isabella.

7. I was a member of this crowd in 1918. Miss Mary Libby, Deaconess of Emmanuel Church and head of the Students' House, where I lived, was given a block of tickets and, as an art student and the daughter of a clergyman, albeit nonconformist, I was considered worthy to receive one. I went with my friend Mildred Hinman, then a student at the New England Conservatory of Music. At the door leading from the Room of Early Italian Paintings into the Raphael Room, I saw a very small woman in black with astoundingly golden hair. Beside her was an ornate gold-leaf table with a marble top and on it was a bowl of yellow orchids, the first I had ever seen. The lady also wore yellow orchids. "Don't touch," she cried out at brief intervals in a voice like a parrot, although we were all walking along a black rubber carpet leading from entrance to exit door with no chance to touch anything. Mildred nudged me and whispered, "That's Mrs. Gardner." I looked again and saw that she knew she had been pointed out. Her eyes were like blue icicles as our glances met.

8. I am indebted to Mrs. Winthrop Coffin, who sent me this story and whose letter I quote in part.

9. My meeting with the late Mr. Leslie Buswell was one of the highlights of my visit to Eastern Point. He had a way of describing a scene with Mrs. Gardner which made me feel that I also was seeing it.

10. Mr. Edward Weeks most kindly told me of this and also said that Mrs. Gardner suffered from periods of extreme melancholy during her last years.

11. Dorothy G. Slocum, also a student at the School of Fine Arts in Boston, wrote her art instructor at Connecticut College, Miss Orrie Sherrer, in my behalf. Miss Sherrer, while at the Museum School, saw Mrs. Gardner and gave this description.

12. This story was told me by J. Randolph Coolidge himself.

13. The story of the Elks' parade, although included in the Carter daybook, must have been written by another or told to Mr. Carter upon his return to Boston.

14. Museum archives.

Index

341

345